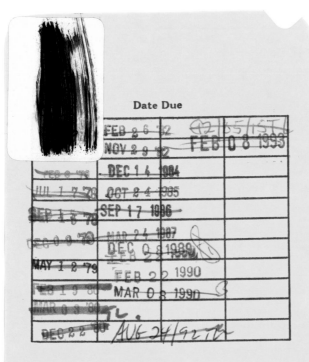

Date Due

FEB 2 6 82	92/05/15	
NOV 2 9 82	FEB 0 8 1993	
FEB 9 78	DEC 1 4 1984	
JUL 1 7 78	OCT 2 4 1985	
SEP 1 8 78	SEP 1 7 1986	
DEC 0 8 78	MAR 2 4 1987	
	DEC 0 8 1989	
MAY 1 8 79	FEB 2 2 1990	
FEB 1 9 80	MAR 0 8 1990	
MAR 0 3 80		
DEC 2 2 80	AUG 24/92	

Jan 22/93

An Introduction
to Grammar

An Introduction to Grammar:
Traditional, Structural, Transformational

Lyda E. LaPalombara

Southern Connecticut State College

Winthrop Publishers, Inc.
Cambridge, Massachusetts

Library of Congress Cataloging in Publication Data

LaPalombara, Lyda E
   An introduction to grammar.

   Bibliography: p. 385
   Includes index.
   1. English language—Grammar—1950–   2. English
language—Grammar, Generative.   I.   Title.
PE1112.L3   425   75–38579
ISBN 0-87626-019-9

Cover design by Ann Washer

To Pat Zollinger, who urged me to write this book,

and

To Rick, Dave, and Sue, who let me

© 1976 by Winthrop Publishers, Inc.
      17 Dunster Street, Cambridge, Massachusetts 02138

10 9 8 7 6 5 4 3 2 1

Contents

Preface

The development of English grammar systems has a long and continuing history. The aim of this book is to trace that history from its earliest beginnings to the current linguistics scene, and thus the scope of the book is large. I have tried to present this vast amount of material in language comprehensible to the beginning language student. The book is intended as an introductory survey both for the prospective English teacher who needs to know something about the evolution of and revolution in English language study, and for the general reader who is fascinated by language study and wants to know more about its intellectual history.

The reader should understand that the "correct" approach to grammar study and the proper philosophy about human nature and human use of language have never been and probably never will be established for all time. No one approach has remained entirely unquestioned, even in its heyday. And that is as it should be. Although prevailing attitudes at various points in our history have usually reflected the culture and intellectual climate of the moment, student and teacher alike should understand that whether or not an idea, an insight, or a whole linguistic philosophy gains recognition in its own time proves nothing about its essential value. My hope is that the acquisition of a body of general information, which this book seeks to provide, will encourage objective, nondoctrinaire attitudes about language on the part of the reader. As an added bonus, perhaps some few students will become sufficiently interested in the truly exciting recent linguistic developments to feel compelled to learn more.

This book is intended to be used as a whole. It presents three major English grammar systems in their historical, chronological order: Traditional Schoolroom Grammar, American Structural Grammar, and Transformational-Generative Grammar. Each of the book's three parts is preceded by a historical background chapter which tries to place the following grammar description in its proper historical context. Anyone who wishes may, in fact, read these three background chapters as they were written: one after the other in a kind of general running narrative which surveys the entire history of language study.

The bulk of the book consists of a presentation of each of the three English grammar systems, along with numerous exercises designed to encourage students to think about what they are reading and to formulate some ideas of their own. Because it is my belief that books which provide hard questions but no answers are needlessly frustrating— and bad pedagogy besides—I have also included an answer key at the end of the volume.

One warning: it is important that the reader understand the sense in which I use the term *grammar*. A grammar system, as here presented, is a theory which attempts to describe and/or explain the sentences of a language. Although certain usage practices and attitudes regarding usage are inevitably discussed, *this is not a usage handbook*.

This volume makes no original linguistic contributions. In fact, I could not possibly have written it without the considerable information gathered from the articles and books listed in the bibliography. Having at one time or another studied all of these sources, and having actually taught from some of them, it is unavoidable that almost all of the ideas herein contained are "borrowed" ones. I suspect that even certain expressions may well have a familiar ring. I would therefore like to acknowledge my indebtedness to these sources and to express my thanks.

My great thanks also go to Paul O'Connell, Chairman of Winthrop Publishers, for his personal faith in me and for his encouragement at all stages in the writing of the book; and to Herbert Nolan, Winthrop's skilled Production Manager, who has cheerfully seen the manuscript through to final publication.

Most particularly, I am grateful to my consulting editor, Professor John Mellon, who patiently read and criticized four or five drafts of the manuscript with great care and scrupulousness. Obviously, I assume final responsibility for whatever flaws may still exist, but Professor Mellon's advice and his linguistic expertise have been invaluable to me.

I also express my thanks to Professor William Osborne, Chairman of the Department of English at Southern Connecticut State College, where I teach, during the time when I was writing the book. I appreciate his encouragement, his understanding, and his willingness to adjust my teaching schedule so that I could have large blocks of time for the project.

Likewise, I owe thanks to my students of the past several years who, with some moans and groans but also with an abundance of good cheer, acted as the guinea pigs on whom I tested the exercises. Many of my students offered helpful criticisms and suggestions. Some of them even became enthusiastic about studying grammar!

Finally, I must thank my children, who have suffered with great good sportsmanship through a long bout of living in a manuscript-cluttered house with a mother who has too often been distracted and uncommunicative. They're good kids.

LYDA E. LAPALOMBARA

PART ONE

Traditional Grammar

1

Historical Background

ANCIENT GREECE

We know that at least as early as the fourth century B.C., Greek philosophers were intrigued by the phenomenon of language. Concerned primarily
with large questions about the nature of humans and their universe, and
working on the assumption that there *must* exist certain deep and eternal
universal truths, these philosophers turned to the study of language—
that uniquely human ability—in the hope that here they might discover
the answers to some of life's great mysteries. The earliest known motives
for language study seem, then, to have been philosophical rather than
practical.

It is impossible to assign precise dates to events so far back in history; and we can only guess about humans' speculations on their own
existence in the prehistoric period. A good deal of philosophizing must
already have taken place, however, for Greek culture was in an advanced
stage of development at the time from which, with any degree of certainty,
we can begin to trace the progress of Western intellectual history.

A prevailing belief among the earliest Greek philosophers was that
language (meaning, to them, the *Greek* language) had been given to
humans as a divine gift. Language, they reasoned, must therefore represent divine perfection. This theory of language may seem naive to those of
us living in the twentieth century. But remember, at the time when men
like Socrates and Plato were sending up these early philosophical trial
balloons, their world was very small, and very little was really known.
Although they were certainly aware of the existence of other cultures in
Europe and North Africa, they believed Greece to have been *the* original

3

civilization. Thus they had no difficulty in simply dismissing "languages" other than Greek as barbaric, degenerate babblings. Only Greek was considered worthy of serious study.

It is fascinating that similar notions were held by a great number of other isolated cultures. The Jews, the Chinese, the Eskimos, for example, all seem to have reached much the same conclusion. Unaware of or unimpressed with other civilizations, all of these cultures came to think of themselves as the original "chosen" people. Ancient Hebrew philosophers, for example, believed that God had presented to Adam, in the Garden of Eden, a fully developed perfect language (Hebrew, of course). Their explanation for the existence of other languages in the world is recounted in the Old Testament story of the Tower of Babel.

Although we have some indication that Plato may have questioned the divine-origin theory, he nevertheless appears to have been influenced by some such notion when he developed his theory of "natural logic." In speculating about words and their meanings, he concluded that a given word bears an *inherent*, *natural*, and therefore *logical* relationship to the thing or concept for which it stands. That is, he took the position that by its intrinsic, essential nature, one particular word—and only that word—*belongs* to a particular thing.

Believing as he did in the universal "rightness" of words, Plato understandably concentrated his philosophical attention on the analysis of words and their meanings. Thus he devised what is possibly the first word-classification system in the western world. His system, based on meaning, had but two word classes: *onoma* and *rhēma*. He defined words in the *onoma* class as those designating the performer of an action or that about which something is asserted; words in the *rhēma* class were ones representing the performing of the action or the asserting. You may notice that these two word classes bear a striking resemblance to traditional grammar's *noun* and *verb* classes.

Aristotle, Plato's most gifted pupil, continued with the investigation of words and their meanings in his own philosophical inquiries. Among Aristotle's important contributions to language study are these: (1) he added a third word class, *syndesmoi* (roughly equivalent to traditional grammar's *conjunction* class), which included all words that fell into neither of Plato's two classes; (2) he made note of certain structural word features, such as that nouns possess case and that verbs possess tense; (3) he provided what is probably the earliest definition of the term *word*, describing it as the smallest meaningful language unit. This definition, as you will see, is very close to the modern structuralist's definition of the "morpheme."

Aristotle's most important contribution, however, was his carefully developed system of "natural logic." Aristotelian logic was based on the concept of the syllogism, and Aristotle argued that syllogistic reasoning represented the universal system of human thinking.

After Aristotle, the next important work in language study is that of the Stoics, who made their philosophical inquiries around 300 B.C. The earliest Stoics expanded Aristotle's three word classes to four, adding *articles* to *nouns, verbs,* and *conjunctions.* Later Stoic philosophers subdivided words in the noun class into proper and common nouns. They also made detailed studies of tense and agreement in verbs and of case in nouns, concluding that nouns possess five cases: *nominative, accusative, dative, genitive,* and *vocative.*

The Stoics were also concerned with inquiring into the *nature* of language, their goal being to demonstrate that the outer forms of language reveal inner truths about human nature. Thus, the present-day linguistic interest in the outer and inner forms of language—what transformational grammarians refer to as surface structure and deep structure—may have its first faint beginnings with the work of the Stoics.

One more early Greek philosopher-grammarian, Dionysius Thrax, must be mentioned. Thrax lived in Alexandria during the last great period of the Greek empire, sometime around the first century B.C., when that city had become the center of Greek culture. In a small book entitled *Techne Grammatike,* Thrax expanded the word classes to eight, still basing his classifications largely on meaning. His eight classes were roughly equivalent to *nouns, pronouns, verbs, participles, articles, adverbs, conjunctions,* and *prepositions.* For each of these classes, he gave a detailed definition and provided many examples. This small volume was destined to become so influential that nearly two thousand years later, grammarians throughout Europe and in England were still classifying words into eight categories. To be sure, the names of the classes changed slightly from time to time, but the number remained at eight. Even more important, Thrax seems to have been influential in establishing as linguistic gospel that the best way to describe a language was to begin with a description of its words.

Dionysius Thrax was also influential in another way: it is to this same little book that we can trace the beginnings of a new attitude, one which eventually was to occasion a major break with the original purposes of the philosopher-grammarians who studied language in their search for universals. The earlier philosophers had concentrated their attention on the literary Greek which they themselves used rather than on the spoken Greek of the less well educated, but we have no indication that this was a conscious policy. Thrax, on the other hand, claimed that the *only* language worth the scholar's attention was the literary Greek of the highly educated. The spoken vernacular of the common man, he argued, had so degenerated from its original "pure" state, had been so corrupted through long years of neglect, that it was undeserving of the language scholar's serious attention.

ANCIENT ROME

Years later, when the center of Western civilization had shifted from Greece to Rome, Greek learning came to influence nearly every facet of cultured Roman life, including the study of language. We know that very large sums were often paid for the services of Greek slaves who were grammar scholars, and when Roman scholars wrote their first Latin grammars, they patterned them after the earlier Greek models. This was possible because both Greek and Latin were highly inflected languages with many grammatical similarities. We know today that such slavish imitation was bound to produce some distortions, since no language is exactly like any other in its particular grammatical manifestations. Nonetheless, with the possible exception of Varro (around the second century A.D.) we have few indications that Roman scholars questioned the procedure. Varro, one of the rare original thinkers who made any independent contributions to grammar study, argued, for example, that while Greek nouns had five cases, Latin had an additional case, the *ablative*, not found in Greek.

Varro was also interested in the old anomalist–analogist controversy which had concerned language scholars from the time of Plato's *Cratylus*. Plato, you will remember, had argued the analogist point of view: that words in particular and language in general are natural and logical. The anomalists, on the other hand, viewed word choices and language practices as arbitrary and accidental. In defense of the anomalist position, Varro pointed to the many irregularities of language. If language were completely logical, he contended, there would not be such illogical features as the absence of separate words for the male and the female of all animal species.

Quintilian, a Latin scholar whose work dates from approximately the same time as that of Varro, seems to have sided with the analogists. In a treatise on education he stressed the importance of including the study of grammar and rhetoric in the education of the cultured Roman. In his discussions of language he held that proper usage must be based on three criteria: reason, authority, and antiquity. His studies of word etymology convinced him that meaning was more significant than form in word development. He concluded that "reason" was fundamental, that word choices were made originally on the basic principles of natural logic and analogy. As for judging the correctness of current language practices, he urged the scholar to pay attention to the "authority" of current usage, which he then narrowly defined as the undisputed practices of educated men. If and when scholars were unable to agree, however, he advocated the exercise of "critical judgment," which he felt to be best served by consulting the older language practices of Greek "antiquity." In spite of his nod at the importance of current usage, then, it appears that this was a principle to which he merely gave lip service. Quintilian seems, in his own practices, to have been far more concerned with making categorical judgments about right and wrong than in becoming philosophically involved with logical principles.

The two Latin grammarians whose work has since exerted the most continuing influence were Donatus (about A.D. 350), who wrote one book on parts of speech and another, *Ars Minor*, in which he summarized the "basics" of Latin grammar; and Priscian (about A.D. 500), who wrote an eighteen-volume Latin grammar. Both of these men relied heavily on Greek scholarship, particularly on the work of Thrax. Ignoring more recent insights, such as those of Varro or even of Quintilian, they seem rather to have devoted themselves to confirming the grammatical conclusions of the older Greek scholars.

There were only a few other scattered murmurings of discontent. Caesar and Horace, for example, questioned the validity of ignoring the spoken vernacular in favor of literary Latin. But the few protests came to nothing. The prevailing practice of focusing scholarly attention exclusively on written classical Latin, and the accompanying contempt for the vernacular became the established norm.

In fact, Roman grammarians came to regard it as their sacred duty to preserve the purity of Latin from whatever decay the vernacular might impose: to correct the corrupt practices which had already taken place, and to stand guard, in general, against future language deterioration. Thus, by the end of the Roman period, "policing" language had become a major responsibility of the grammarian. It should come as no surprise, then, that this attitude influenced language study in the centuries that followed.

One more point should be made before we continue. There was an important difference between the Greek and Roman cultures: Greece had been a monolingual society, and Greek scholars had studied grammar as a part of their larger philosophical concern with the nature of humans and the universe. The educated Roman, on the other hand, studied the grammar of two languages—and for quite different, more practical reasons. As the ability to sway people with one's rhetoric came to be highly admired, Romans studied their native Latin to develop their oratorical powers. In addition to Latin, however, they also studied a foreign language—Greek— for knowledge of Greek had come to be a highly valued cultural accomplishment. As we shall see, grammar study continued to have this new, more practical role in the centuries to follow. European scholars were to study both Greek and Latin, neither of which was their own native tongue.

THE MIDDLE AGES

The Medieval period is the longest in Western Europe's history, having lasted for approximately a thousand years.* These years have traditionally been characterized by historians—from the time of the Renaissance until very recently—as ones in which scholarship suffered a severe decline and during which few new ideas were generated. In fact, Renaissance scholars referred to the Medieval Period as the Dark Ages.

To have a better understanding of developments in language study during this period, we should try to get at least a general impression of the times. The relentless invasions of the Roman armies, which took place over a span of several centuries, eventually extended the Roman Empire over a vast geographical area reaching from northern Africa to nearly all of Western Europe and England.† An inevitable result of this expansion was the widespread dissemination of Roman culture, customs, laws, religion, and of course the Latin language. Then, for a number of complex reasons—overextension, decentralization, troubles at home—the Empire began slowly to crumble. As central authority weakened, the governments of more and more outlying provinces were turned over to sympathetic barbarian kings. And when these kings in turn found themselves unable to maintain law and order or to protect their people from the multiplying bands of roaming barbarian outlaws, they ceded vast shares of their holdings to the best of their fighting chieftains. Increasingly fearful for their own safety and security, masses of peasants gave the warrior lords their property in return for their personal protection. In this way the feudal system gradually spread throughout most of Europe.

As social organization changed, so did values. In ancient Greece and Rome the powerful families had come from the wealthy, leisured, and highly educated class, but the threat to personal security during the Middle Ages gave rise to a new power structure. Nearly every man of the period

*The period is usually dated from about A.D. 400 until the late 1400s. It should be rememberd, however, that no "era" begins or ends overnight. Even in a single locality, great changes are usually gradual and are influenced by a variety of events. Since we are speaking here of most of Western Europe, it is impossible to assign precise dates.

†Most of what is said here about the Middle Ages does not apply to Spain, where for many centuries the Moors presided over a thriving culture with a high standard of living. Scholarly activity continued almost unabated in the city of Cordova, which remained a center of wealth, culture, and scholarship.

was a fighting man, the best warriors among them becoming the most powerful. In these new circumstances, scholarly learning was not in demand; in fact, many of the feudal knights and lords were crude men with little or no education.

The only Roman institution which not only survived but indeed extended its influence during the Middle Ages was the Catholic church. With its threat of excommunication, the Church represented the only power greater even than that of the feudal lords. Furthermore, what respect for Greek and Latin learning remained was preserved and nourished by the Church, principally in the monasteries scattered throughout Europe.

As for the changes which took place in the Latin language, it is important to remember that from the time of Rome's "golden era" two different levels of Latin had co-existed—the literary Latin of the classical scholars, and the common vernacular Latin of the people. Neither version of Latin emerged from the Middle Ages unchanged.

Within the Catholic church, which became the guardian of learning, Latin became the official language. Yet even Church Latin changed significantly, largely as a result of the influence of the European vernacular languages, until the Latin which is now referred to as Medieval Church Latin was a far cry from the majestic classical Latin of Caesar and Horace. The few remaining classical Latin scholars protested this "degeneration," but as was not understood then, such changes were and are inevitable.

In the meantime, these alterations in Church Latin were as nothing compared to what happened to the vernacular (or Roman Latin) of the common people. It was this common Latin that the Roman armies carried with them in the invasions, with two important consequences. First, Latin "borrowings" affected the development of many of the European vernacular languages, so that languages such as Italian, French, Spanish, Portuguese, and even English in large part, evolved as Latin-based languages. Second, the even greater impact of the local vernaculars on common Latin resulted, by the end of this long historical period, in the disappearance altogether of vernacular Latin. Latin simply ceased to exist as a spoken European language.

And what of the fate of scholarship during the Middle Ages? As has already been mentioned, beginning with the Renaissance it was long the practice of historians simply to "write off" the Middle Ages as a time when respect for learning died and when no new ideas emerged. Within the last few years, however, linguistic research has produced evidence that the situation was not nearly so bleak as had been thought. There has probably never been a time without at least a few fertile minds conceiving new ideas. Nor does it seem likely, as was long assumed, that suddenly after a thousand and more years of nothing, the exciting speculations of the seventeenth-century philosophers and language scholars could have emanated from their minds full blown and ready made.

Among the Medieval scholars whose work has recently been shown to have been familiar to those who followed was a mid-eleventh century French Benedictine abbot by the name of St. Anselm. Anselm wrote a treatise entitled *De Grammatico* in which he expressed considerable interest in grammatical distinctions such as that expressed by the concepts of the "signifier" and the "thing signified." This concern was not, of course, a new one. Scholars before him had speculated about the importance of semantic differences in word meanings. The point here is that interest in such problems did not die out during the Middle Ages.

In fact, during the last quarter of the thirteenth century, Peter of Spain (later to become Pope John XXI) was similarly intrigued with such philosophical questions as the grammatical and semantic implications of different meanings attributable to a single word or expression. Like Anselm, Peter detected an important difference between what he called the *significatio* and the *suppositio* of a word. By way of illustration—although these examples are obviously not ones provided by Peter of Spain—he recognized that a name like "Max" means two quite different things in the two sentences: "Max is the dog's name" and "Max is scratching his fleas."

We should also take note of the work of Peter Helias, a Parisian mid-twelfth century scholar, whose philosophic commentary on the Latin grammarian, Priscian, stressed that it is the philosopher rather than the grammarian who, by his analytical consideration of the "nature of things," discovers the real significance and importance of grammar study. It has been recently suggested that the genesis of scholarly philosophical grammar, which was to become so important in the seventeenth century, can quite possibly be traced to the work of Peter Helias.

The works mentioned, all of which were written in Latin, are by no means intended to represent a full accounting of the grammar studies and the reflections on language which were produced during the Middle Ages. More and more work of Medieval scholars is coming to the attention of contemporary linguists. Moreover, we are also becoming aware, after long years of neglect, of yet another important Medieval development: namely, the growing body of written grammars of the European vernacular languages. It has now been documented, for example, that written grammars of Hebrew, Arabic, Old Irish, and Old Norse existed before the middle of the twelfth century. By the end of the sixteenth century grammars had been written for nearly all of the European vernacular languages.

One of the most fascinating—and certainly one of the best—of these vernacular grammars was the *First Grammatical Treatise* (mid-twelfth

century), an Old Norse grammar written in the vernacular by a now unknown scholar who has since been called the "First Grammarian." This
work is especially interesting to modern linguists because, as has only
recently been discovered, many of his language study techniques (such as
his meticulously detailed study of the phonology of Icelandic, and his use
of "minimal pairs") were very much like those developed independently
by nineteenth and twentieth century historical and structural linguists.

The moral here is not the old cliché, "There's nothing new under the
sun," although we have long suspected this to be true. Rather, it is to
alert you to the danger of drawing absolute conclusions. All conclusions,
as any good scientist will tell you, are tentative. They are considered and
acted upon as valid only until new evidence proves them otherwise.

THE RENAISSANCE

Again, it is impossible to assign exact dates. With the understanding
that these are approximations only, we shall date the Renaissance Period
from sometime in the late 1400s up to the seventeenth century.

The term "renaissance" means "reawakening." Thus, as personal
dangers gradually became less acute, as commerce and trade once again
began to compete with agriculture in Europe's economy, and as the feudal
lords' hold over the local inhabitants consequently diminished, families
began to move from the rural communities to the cities. And as people's
fortunes improved, their attention could once more be turned to other
matters. Gradually, interest in scholarship and in things cultural was
renewed. It soon became possible for men of leisure to focus their attention once again on the work of earlier Greek and Roman scholars for
enlightenment.

Among the Renaissance scholars whose work has only recently
received the attention of twentieth century linguists was a sixteenth century Spanish classical scholar known variously by the names Francisco
Sanchez de las Brozas, Francisco Sanchez, or simply Sanctius. Sanctius
was a professor first of Greek and then of Rhetoric at Salamanca. His
book, *Minerva* (around 1587), was for many years considered the standard
work on Latin grammar. He believed that all languages, despite their
superficial differences, were simply varied developments of a single universal set of underlying principles which were common to all human language.
(There is some question whether those who, like Sanctius, pointed to the
universal "sameness" of language would have reached these conclusions
if it were not that the European languages with which they were familiar
contained a great many superficial similarities. It was not documented
until nearly two hundred years later that such surface similarities could

be accounted for simply because these languages were closely related, having descended from the same source.)

Noam Chomsky has suggested in *Language and Mind* (1968) that it was Sanctius' theory of ellipsis which most interested the seventeenth century rationalist grammarians and influenced their thinking. Chomsky believes, however, that while the rationalists were interested in ellipsis as a means of revealing the nature of human mental processes, Sanctius had devised the theory as a method for the interpretation of literary texts.

Another Renaissance scholar whose work is now thought to have been influential is the Spanish physician Huarte, who at about the same time as Sanctius arged that humans can be distinguished from animals because humans alone possess *two* powers. The first of these is rooted in the senses and thus can in no way distinguish human from beast; the second, however, is the generative or creative ability, which makes the human capable of eloquence and which is quite beyond the power of any beast.

Still other Renaissance figures are now thought to have contributed to the thinking of seventeenth century philosophers and grammarians. Peter Ramus, for example, wrote grammars of Greek, Latin, and French, and in his work *Scholae* stressed consulting the current usage of native speakers as the best guide to usage practices.

THE SEVENTEENTH CENTURY AND BEYOND

Prior to this time in Western history there had been periodic flurries of the recurrent argument between the analogists and the anomalists, philosophers of two opposing schools of thought. During the seventeenth century, this old quarrel was for a brief time revived and then ultimately supplanted by a much broader philosophical debate, that between the "rationalists" and the "empiricists."

The rationalist position was based on the philosophical writings of René Descartes, who held that certain human abilities, capacities, and ideas were innate. Although Descartes was willing to grant that everything humans learn comes *in part* from their experiences, he argued that the acquisition of knowledge is determined by certain abstract, "built-in" principles which are present in every normal person from the moment of birth. Among the most significant of unique human achievements, he felt, is the creative use of language.

The empiricists, on the other hand, whose earliest standard bearers were John Locke and David Hume, insisted that everything humans come to know—including language—is entirely explainable as sense-oriented, "learned" behavior. The empiricists were adamant in denying the existence of innate ideas or germs of ideas.

This controversy became so important that it dominated the thinking of scholars in many disciplines, including linguistics, for several decades.

Grammarians of the rationalist school returned to the almost forgotten notion of the early Greek philosophers: that the very fact of language pointed to the existence of certain eternal, *universal* truths. They followed the thinking of Descartes, who argued, as had Sanctius, that language has both an outer and an inner form. It is the inner form of language, he suggested, that ought to tell us more about the human mind. He cited language use as the particular form of human behavior most likely to reveal truths about human nature. He argued that human language is not only species-specific, it is also inevitable—it is an ability acquired by every normal person. In particular, Descartes stressed the freedom from external forces, i.e., the existence of free will, as the most significant, yet universal, characteristic of human behavior.

In support of his argument, Descartes listed these three characteristics of human behavior: its vast *scope* or diversity, its *innovative unpredictability*, and perhaps most important of all, its *appropriateness*. Such behavior, he insisted, cannot be explained simply as automatic, mechanistic responses to external events. Rather, it represents innate qualities of the human mind.

The most important work of the rationalist or Cartesian grammarians of this period was done by a group of monks at the Port Royal monastery in Port Royal, France. These scholars had become interested in the European vernacular languages, particularly in their own native French. The more they pondered, the more they became convinced that the vernacular languages were well worth the serious attention of language scholars. Intrigued by the great many similarities among languages revealed by their comparative studies, they came to believe that there must be certain basic universal language principles. They concluded that the grammarian's work ought to be focused on discovering these universals, which they were convinced would prove to be reflected in all "natural" human language.

They carried their argument even further. Convinced that French was not inherently inferior to Latin, they became part of a movement to replace Latin with French as the scholarly language in France.* They argued, moreover, that any fully developed natural vernacular language was bound to be more accurately representative of universal language principles than was Latin, which had for some time ceased to be a spoken

---

*Latin nevertheless continued to be used by European scholars until well into the eighteenth century.

vernacular language. In the years since Latin (or rather its Medieval descendant) had become the exclusive property of scholars, it had become, they felt, so "set," so rule-bound, and thus so artificial and distorted by those who had written formal Latin grammars, that it had long since ceased to be a natural language. Having evolved into a form like no living human language, Latin was not in the least representative of native language intelligence.

Believing, then, that any natural language was an outer reflection of the inner workings of human mentality, the Port Royalists urged that the only proper role of the grammarian is to describe, as accurately and objectively as possible, the actual language practices of a speaking community *as they exist*, not according to subjective prescriptive notions about what the "rules" *ought* to be, and above all not according to the rules of Latin. Such attempts to prescribe rules of correctness, they thought, were not only unrealistic and misguided, but altogether hopeless besides—exercises in futility where a living language is concerned.

Fundamental to all of these contentions, of course, was the Port Royal grammarians' basic belief in the Cartesian theory that the function of language is to convey thought. Their grammar studies were therefore aimed primarily at revealing the basic universality of human thought as reflected in all human language.* They began by analyzing human thought into three components: perception, judgment, and reasoning. Elaborating Descartes' hypothesis of the inner and outer aspects of language, they reasoned that language is *phrase*- rather than *word*-oriented; every sentence is a series of phrases, each of which represents an underlying thought or idea. Instead of the terms *outer form* and *inner form*, they spoke of *surface structures* and *deep structures*. They defined a surface structure as the observable outer grammatical form of a sentence. Underlying this surface structure, however, they posited the existence of one or more abstract basic or deep structures. The deep structure of language, although not actually expressed, represents the implicit body of abstract ideas or thought relationships which are present in the human mind and which are common to *all* human thinking. The fact that identical thought relationships are expressed by a great variety of surface forms in the particular grammars of different languages worried the Port Royalists not at all. Such surface variations were considered alternative devices for expressing the same universal thought concepts.

To illustrate this surface structure–deep structure phenomenon whereby a person on hearing a particular surface sentence proceeds auto-

---

*Probably the most famous of these works are *Grammaire générale et raisonnée*, otherwise known as the *Port Royal Grammar*, which was published by Claude Lancelot and Antoine Arnauld in 1660; and *La logique, ou l'art de penser*, which appeared two years later.

matically to analyze its deeper meaning, the Port Royalists used the now-famous sentence: "Invisible God created the visible world." The simple subject-predicate assertion, "God created the world," is all that is explicitly expressed by this surface structure. Yet, upon hearing the sentence, one immediately understands that the sentence contains not *one*, but *three* propositions or simple judgments: (1) God created the world; (2) God is invisible; (3) the world is visible. Although the speaker does not actually *say* the last two propositions, the hearer understands that they, along with the explicitly expressed third one, must be taken into account, for *all three* propositions enter into and contribute to the total deep meaning of the sentence.

The Port Royalists claimed that this sort of surface structure–deep structure relationship is basic. It is common to all languages, and thus constitutes a universal language principle.

Shortly after the publication of the Port Royal studies, Cordemoy, another Frenchman, elaborated on Descartes' "human versus beast" theme.* He argued that all forms of communication among the beasts are simply instinctive, automatic responses, and thus do not qualify as true speech. Human language, however, cannot possibly be accounted for so simplistically, for it goes beyond sense-oriented, instinctive responses to external stimuli.

This controversy between the rationalists and the empiricists eventually involved many European and English scholars from various disciplines, with vociferous advocates on both sides.

Empiricists dismissed such notions as those expressed by Descartes, the Port Royalists, and Cordemoy. They argued that humans acquire language by the simple process of listening to the language they hear spoken around them from the time of their birth, and then by imitating what they hear. Condillac, a French disciple of Locke, argued in his philosophical treatise, *Traite des sensations*, that language had necessarily evolved before thought. In fact, he contended, it is language which makes thought possible.

In defense of this position, Condillac hypothesized a situation in which, sometime after the Old Testament Deluge, an infant boy and an infant girl are alone in a desert. Condillac assumed only a kind of instinctive physical attraction and the gradual development of a desire to communicate with each other. Given this desire, they begin to notice that in certain situations involving physical responses to natural events, they involuntarily utter similar sounds. The first rudimentary "thought" evolves out of this gradual realization: that by consciously using these involuntary "signs," they can communicate. Condillac postulated that in

*Cordemoy's *Discours Physique de la Parole* was published in 1666; a second edition came out in 1677.

this way certain instinctive sounds became, by mutual agreement, the first "words." And the development of words in turn made it possible for humans to learn to think. Condillac, and other empiricists who were impressed by his theory, thus turned their attention to the etymology of words.

Another French empiricist, Jean Jacques Rousseau, who wrote prolifically in the wide areas of morality, philosophy, and education, expressed ideas which were very similar to those of Condillac. Yet, though he seems in most of his writing to be in basic agreement with Condillac's position, he did come to detect a flaw in the major premise of the boy-and-girl-alone-in-a-desert illustration. Rousseau was uncomfortable with the presumption of an a priori agreement on the desire to communicate, which it seemed to him already represented a kind of social contract; he was uncertain whether society or language had come first. The answer to this question seemed to him to be in doubt.

Arguing on the side of the rationalist or "organic" position after Descartes, the Port Royal grammarians, and Cordemoy, were such scholars as the English philosophical grammarian James Harris, who speculated in *Hermes* (1741) on the human capacity for knowledge and on human creative potential. Harris attributed these powers to freedom from the controls of instinctual drives. Yet, though he seems to have considered the possibility, he did not go so far as to claim that such powers were based, as the Cartesians argued, on innate qualities of the human mind.

So important did the controversy between the empiricists and the rationalists become, and in its wake, so much was the interest in the origin of language revived, that in 1769 the prestigious Prussian Academy offered a prize for the best scholarly essay on the subject of the origin of langauge. In his prize-winning essay, Johann Herder, a German poet and philosopher, took the position that neither language nor thought had come first. Instead, the two had evolved side by side, each influencing the other throughout the entire evolutionary process. In defense of his position, Herder argued that language is a "natural" faculty of the human mind, but he did not commit himself to the theory that language is therefore innate. Instead, he proposed that language ability had developed in the human species as the evolutionary result of weakened human instincts. Reason had had to "take over" to compensate for these weakened instincts. According to Herder, this process had inadvertently worked to human advantage.

Among the other scholars whose work seems to have been based, at least in part, on the ideas of Descartes and his followers,* was another

*For a more complete account of this philosophical school of thought and of the scholars who, beginning in the seventeenth century, made notable contributions, see Noam Chomsky's *Cartesian Linguistics*, 1966.

German, A. W. Schlegel, who argued that human language ability cannot be attributed solely to outside forces. Schlegel, however, extended the argument, for he was particularly interested in the existence of what he called the "poetic quality" of language, which he did not limit to that highly developed and comparatively rare excellence of language which can be described as true art. Although he admitted that the very possibility of poetry as an art form, however rare, was an argument in his favor, he referred rather to language as it is used by ordinary people with no particular poetic gift. Even such ordinary language, he thought, exhibits a degree of poetic eloquence which is uniquely different from the practical nature of animal communication.

Probably the last important figure in the rationalist, "universalist" stream of thought is another German, Wilhelm von Humboldt, whose large work *Über die Verschiedenheit des Menschlichen Sprachbaues* was published posthumously in 1836. The research on which the material in this book was based was done during the Romantic period, when the controversy between "organic" versus "external" origins of human nature was in full rage. Humboldt is thought by many to be the last really articulate spokesman of his time for the organic point of view, although the controversy did not go into total eclipse until sometime during the nineteenth century. Humboldt, who was largely ignored at the time, argued in favor of the proposition that there exists an organic form of language for which there are a certain limited or "fixed" number of inherent rules, the surface manifestations of which are *not*, however, predetermined. What seems to have most fascinated Humboldt was the human ability to produce an infinite and varied number of completely unpredictable surface sentences with only a limited number of rules. He pointed out, as had Schlegel, that this ability is not one possessed only by artists. Indeed, it is expressed all the time in every person's ordinary speech—even in the speech of children. It is this phenomenon which convinced Humboldt that innate language properties reside in the human mind.

Humboldt did not go on to state exactly what these innate properties might be. And he departed somewhat significantly from the strictly Cartesian notion that the same universal thought processes could be discovered in the deep structures of all languages. Humboldt, perhaps influenced by the claims of some of his contemporaries, speculated that the different surface characteristics of particular languages may very well result in cultural differences in modes of thought.

As we shall be seeing in more detail later on, a number of novel linguistic discoveries focused the interest of most nineteenth century linguists in an altogether new direction. For the time being, interest in the centuries-old debate between the rationalist philosophical grammarians and the empiricist grammarians faded. Philosophical questions about the nature of language and the mind were not to be fully revived until more than one hundred years later, when the work of the American scholar Noam Chomsky in the late 1950s rekindled linguistic interest in universal grammar.

In the meantime, a second ancient-versus-modern controversy gained prominence—one that dates back to the time of Thrax of Alexandria.

As has already been mentioned, until the early part of the eighteenth century, the great majority of European scholarly works continued to be written in Latin. Nevertheless, a few scholars had begun to write grammars of the European vernacular languages as early as the late Middle Ages. This trend continued through the period of the Renaissance. Then, during the seventeenth and eighteenth centuries, as language scholars became increasingly interested in such matters as tracing the etymologies of words, and as more and more scholars came to realize the need for paying serious attention to the fully developed European vernacular languages, interest in writing grammars of these languages became increasingly widespread. Along with this interest there developed (or redeveloped) a second major linguistic controversy: that between the descriptivist and the prescriptivist writers of particular grammars.

Among the early descriptivists were those who, like the Port Royal grammar scholars, argued that the vernacular languages were altogether respectable. The more traditional, classical language scholars, who also found it necessary to turn their serious attention to the various European languages, disagreed. Unlike the Port Royalists, who marveled at the way these vernacular languages had developed naturally without any interference from grammarians, this second group of grammarians was somewhat taken aback by the fact that these vernacular tongues had developed "behind their backs," so to speak. Realizing belatedly that the vernacular languages could no longer be ignored (since vast numbers of people were speaking them and even writing in them), they took upon themselves the "moral" duty of writing prescriptive grammars for particular languages. Fearing that it might already be too late, they made themselves responsible for writing "rules" of correct usage (Latin-based, for the most part), and for preventing abuses and misuses from further degrading language.

The descriptivists, on the other hand, who were at least as interested in usage practices as were the "law-givers," contended that a language should be described not according to a grammarian's notion about what "ought to be," but according to the language practices that actually exist among the native speakers of a language. (The descriptivists disagreed among themselves on several points. *Whose* usage was to be considered standard? Should it be the "best" or most "educated" usage, or should "general" usage as exemplified by the language practices of the majority be the guide?)*

As we turn to the development of vernacular English grammars, we will see this quarrel between the descriptivists and the prescriptivists continue.

THE DEVELOPMENT OF VERNACULAR ENGLISH GRAMMARS

English grammar study began during the late seventeenth and early eighteenth centuries. One of the earliest of these studies was a large work, written in Latin by John Wallis in 1653. Even though very few current histories of the development of English grammars mention Wallis, his dictatorial "rules" of English grammar significantly influenced the earliest English vernacular grammars, such as those written by Lowth and Johnson, who are said to have borrowed extensively from Wallis. A prescriptivist and authoritarian *par excellence*, Wallis—who was not a language scholar but a mathematician—wrote his grammar rules as though English were Latin.†

In the early sixteenth century the English language was spoken by only a small minority of the world's population. Since that time, however, great changes had taken place. English explorers and colonists had extended the influence of England's culture and language to the farthest regions of the world. Moreover, there had accumulated, by the middle of the eighteenth century, a rich body of literature in vernacular English. Yet, up until this time no one had bothered to write an English vernacular grammar.

Somewhat belatedly, then, it began to dawn on English language scholars that while they hadn't been looking, English had become a perfectly respectable, healthy, and thriving world language—one they could no longer ignore.

Once they got around to noticing what had happened, a number of language scholars became concerned about certain particularly "alarming" developments. There had recently been a substantial population shift

---

*This argument is far from resolved. Then, as now, we often witness linguists giving lip service to one principle only to follow another in their own practices.

†Among other distortions with which Wallis's grammatical pronouncements have burdened English grammars was his dogmatic assertion concerning the "proper" use of *shall* and *will*. His dictum was that *shall* is the correct form for the first person and *will* is to be used with the second and third persons in simple declarative statements. For the imperative, these forms should be reversed. So far as anyone has been able to discern, this use of *shall* and *will* has never been a usage practice in the entire history of the English language. Nevertheless, students in many English and American classrooms are cautioned, even today, to distinguish between the two.

in England, brought about by the immigration of great numbers of people from rural areas to the cities. This urbanization had in turn resulted in the rise of a new and growing merchant class. These events, combined with the earlier invention in England of the printing press, had given rise to what was in the eyes of some scholars an appalling new development: every Tom, Dick, and Harry seemed to be reading and—worse yet— writing English. Clearly it was necessary for someone to step in and do something before the influence of the lower classes, which had already had a corrupting effect on English, caused the language to degenerate completely.

Equally concerned about language, although for vastly different reasons, were the new city dwellers, who found to their distress that they desperately needed to acquire some city polish in their manners, their dress, and their speech if they were to have a hope of gaining social acceptance in urban circles.

Thus, early in the eighteenth century a few very small and rather poor grammars of English were written. It wasn't, however, until the middle of the eighteenth century that the first widely respected English dictionary and the first detailed vernacular English grammar were published, Dr. Samuel Johnson's *Dictionary of the English Language* (1755), and Bishop Robert Lowth's *A Short Introduction to English Grammar* (1762).

The men who wrote these earliest English grammars seem to have thought of themselves as both messiahs and missionaries. As saviors, they set out to rescue the English language from the abuses with which both past and present evils had threatened and still were threatening it. As evangelists, they assumed the sacred responsibility of training the "unwashed" in correct usage practices. Dr. Johnson, a predjudiced and authoritarian man, was intent on removing the "improprieties" from the language. Taking no notice whatever of current usage practices, he bent every effort to base his dictionary definitions and his rules of usage on the "best" literary practices of the past (which probably meant on Latin). Bishop Lowth, whose grammar followed on the heels of Dr. Johnson's *Dictionary*, stated that although the most reliable grammatical "authority" was reason or logic, rules of correctness must necessarily be based on the practices of the best educated among the language community. Thus, though Lowth acknowledged the importance of current usage, he clearly did not refer to the usage practices of the ordinary Englishman, for he did not hesitate to condemn "vulgar" language practices. Lowth's grammar, which was authoritarian and prescriptive, remained the most influential grammar of English for decades: some thirty years after its publication Lindley Murray published his *English Grammar*, in which he reinforced and popularized Bishop Lowth's prescriptive grammar rules. Murray's book became the first widely used school text.

It is not surprising to find that those who wrote these first English grammars were almost unavoidably influenced by the centuries of precedent. Members themselves of the privileged, educated class, they had spent years being trained in the formal rules of Latin grammar. Consequently, when they undertook to write grammars of English, it was natural that they would pattern them after the rules of Latin, with which they were familiar. The result, of course, was a number of serious distortions, but hardly anyone at the time—or for a long time to follow—seems to have noticed or to have seriously protested the procedure.

Not that there weren't a few dissident voices who cried out their objections. One such voice, widely influential for a time but in the long run not heeded, was that of Joseph Priestley, a contemporary of Bishop Lowth. Priestley, a scientist and grammarian (*Rudiments of English Grammar*, 1761), expressed dismay at such arbitrary "rules" as Lowth's assertion that the double negative was "incorrect," because two negatives in a single sentence cancel each other out. Or at John Wallis's rule about the use of *shall* and *will*, which Priestley discounted as mere "invention." Priestley and a few others, like the American lexicographer Noah Webster (*American Dictionary*, 1864), spoke out against the prescriptivists' slavish reliance on the authority of Latin. But ultimately the opinions of the pedagogical grammarians overrode the protests of these men.

It would be inaccurate to suppose, however, that the dominance of the prescriptivists eliminated the tradition of the descriptive grammarians, for linguists like Sir William Jones (1746–1794), Henry Sweet (*A New English Grammar*, 1891), and Otto Jespersen (*Language*, 1922) kept the tradition of scholarly descriptive grammar alive. Most of these investigators failed to gain wide public acclaim in their own time, but their work continued unabated. Their voices would ultimately be heard with great respect.

Meanwhile, the grammars of the prescriptivists dominated—so much so, in fact, that the term "traditional grammar" came to refer exclusively to their brand of schoolroom grammar. Reinforced by figures like the nineteenth century American schoolmaster Goold Brown—the direct authoritarian descendant of the Lowth-Murray school of grammatical thought—traditional pedagogical grammar held sway over the classrooms of England and America until very recently. For more than a century, the prescriptivist approach remained basically unquestioned.

You yourself may have been drilled in the traditional eight parts of speech, sentence parsing, sentence diagramming, and the like. If so, you probably also spent years memorizing the "thou shalts" and the "thou shalt nots" of traditional prescriptive grammar—all with the expectation on the part of your teachers if not on yours, that learning such rules and processes would help you to improve your writing. It may surprise you to

learn that many linguists today doubt whether there is a significant correlation between the two abilities.*

Why, then, you are entitled to ask, especially if no one can say with
certainty that learning the traditional grammar rules will necessarily
lead to an improvement in your English, should you even bother to study
traditional schoolroom grammar? First, because there is doubt. Second,
because it is interesting and worthwhile in and of itself to learn something
about human intellectual development. Third, because recent linguistic
developments suggest that not everything the traditional grammarians
stood for can be condemned out of hand. Increasingly, in fact, many of
the traditionalist insights are being viewed with new respect.

Last, and possibly most important, as students of the humanities
in general and as prospective English teachers in particular, it is extremely
foolish for you to try to reach an independent judgment regarding which
ideas you accept and which you reject on the basis of second- or third-
hand information—on the "say-so" of someone else. You owe it to yourself
to go straight to the study of the grammar systems in question.†

*Many contemporary linguists have claimed that a significant correlation
between the ability to score well on a traditional grammar test and the ability to
write well has not been demonstrated. According to John Mellon, a linguist and
professor of education at Botson University, however, "Everyone says this, quoting
one another, but it's not quite true. For one thing, high IQ correlates with both
abilities in question."

†Traditional rules of usage will not be presented in this book. If you wish to
examine some typical prescriptive rules you can consult almost any "school"
grammar text or handbook published before the mid-1950s. (By no means, however,
have books since then ceased to be prescriptive. Many continue to print rigid rules
of "correctness.")

2

The Grammar System: Parts of Speech

Most traditional "school" grammars begin by defining and classifying English words into part-of-speech categories, and proceed from there to more inclusive sentence components until they arrive at a discussion of the sentence itself. Because there are a great many drawbacks to this kind of approach, it is described here only with the greatest reluctance. Nevertheless, we shall do so for several reasons: (1) this was the kind of grammar taught in American schools for many years; (2) although this kind of grammar is still being taught in many schools, some readers may not have been exposed to it, and it is important to be aware of the kind of typical school grammar which the structuralists found so objectionable;* (3) it is impossible to evaluate the usefulness of a particular grammar system without first examining it carefully.

Some linguists contend that beginning with parts of speech is a great mistake because such a procedure rests on the assumption that most students are already consciously aware of the entire grammar of English sentences. Insofar as students succeed at all with the part-of-speech drills of school grammar, their success can and must be attributed to all the other things they tacitly "know" about the grammar of their language.

Plan to approach this section, as well as those that follow, with a questioning, open-minded attitude. Consider whether there might be a

---

*The many structural linguists who condemned all traditional grammar as subjective, superficial, and prescriptive were referring only to the pedagogical or "school" grammars. One can only assume that these critics who lumped together all of traditional grammar under one label were unaware of such important scholarly traditionalists as their contemporaries, Otto Jespersen, George O. Curme, Ralph Long, and others, whose work was far from being dogmatic, shallow, or subjective.

better way to begin the study of English grammar than by learning part-of-speech definitions. Do not hesitate to question a particular approach, definition, or explanation—even one that has been unquestioningly accepted for years.

Single words—and, as we shall discover later, larger constructions or word groups—can be given part-of-speech labels. Although there was some disagreement, most traditional school grammars listed eight parts of speech. The definitions that follow are typical.

Noun. A noun is a word or word group that *names* a person, a place, an idea, or a thing (object, activity, quality, condition).

A noun may be either *proper* or *common*. A noun is said to be proper if it names a particular person, place, or thing: *Jane, Detroit, Age of Reason.* It is common if it names something or someone in a more general way: *girl, city, era.*

Further, a noun may be either *concrete* or *abstract*. A noun is concrete if it names something that can be literally seen, felt, tasted, and so on: *dog, table, meat.* It is abstract if it names something which exists only as an idea or concept in the mind: *idea, loyalty, happiness, fear, mortality.*

EXAMPLES: The *pencil* was lying on the *desk.*
Driving at top *speed, Dave* won the *race.*
Tom lived in *Chicago* during the *Great Depression.*
Honesty is said to be the best *policy.*

Word groups, as we shall see shortly, may substitute for single words which name. When that happens, the entire word group is said to function as a noun (or nominal).

Pronoun. A pronoun is a word that functions as a noun substitute. Generally speaking, a pronoun may be used only when it is very clear which noun it is substituting for. When the noun for which it substitutes has not been used first, or when the noun to which a pronoun refers is ambiguous, these are cases of faulty pronoun reference. Traditional school grammars generally subclassify pronouns as follows:

Personal: forms of *I, you, he, she, it, we,* and *they*
EXAMPLES: *I* am hungry. *I* like *him. She* is with *them.*

Relative: who, whom, whose, which, that, where
EXAMPLES: He is the boy *who* met me. The place *where* he lives is Italy. The book *which* I lost was his.

Demonstrative: this, that, these, those
EXAMPLES: *This* is what I want. I like *these* better than *those.*

Note: Many traditional grammarians recognized demonstrative pronouns as "elliptical" constructions. That is, they explained the words *this, that,* *these, those* in constructions like those in the examples below as articles (like *a, an, the*) followed by "implied" (omitted) nouns.

EXAMPLES: *These* are my books. *This* is silly. I like *that.*

Interrogative: who, which, what

EXAMPLES: *Who* is coming? *What* did he tell you?

Indefinite: each, everyone, anybody, any, either, neither, some

EXAMPLES: I don't want *any. Everyone* does his own work.

Intensive: myself, yourself, himself, ourselves, themselves

EXAMPLES: He did the work *himself.* I *myself* will do it.

Reflexive: myself, yourself, himself, ourselves, themselves

EXAMPLES: He hurt *himself.* We are helping *ourselves.*

VERB. A verb is a word or word group that expresses action, condition, or state of being. The verb may be a single word or it may be preceded by one or more auxiliary words and followed by one or more particles.* Every sentence must contain a verb, for the verb is the word (or word group) that conveys what is said about the subject (a noun or nominal). The verb function is referred to as *predication.*

A verb will be either *active* or *passive.* It is active if the subject does something or merely exists: "John *threw* the ball. Mary *is* my friend." It is passive if the subject is the receiver of the action (is "acted upon"): "The ball *was thrown* by John. Her father *was fired.*"

A verb has *tense* to indicate time: present, past, future.

A verb may also indicate aspect: progressive and perfect.†

A verb is either *intransitive* (it requires no words to complete its meaning); *transitive* (it requires a *direct* object as a completer); or *linking* (it links the subject to a nominal or an adjective in the predicate).

EXAMPLES: Intransitive: The game *began.*
           She *had been crying.*
Transitive: Jay *may win* the contest.
              We *think* John handsome.
Linking: Mary *is* pretty.
              His name *is* John.

Note: Verb characteristics are mentioned here in only the most general way. Because verbs are so important, however, later sections discuss them in greater detail.

*Particle is a grammatical term for an uninflected word like *up, down, in, out, on, off, under,* which follows a verb form and significantly alters its meaning: *give up, sign on, turn off, put out,* and so on.

†Most school grammars use the term *tense* to include not only tense proper but aspect as well.

ADJECTIVE. An adjective is a word or word group that tells a characteristic or quality of a noun or pronoun. Adjectives tell such things as which? what kind of? characterized how? how many? whose?

> EXAMPLES: *Brave* men sometimes cry.
> Jane is *tall*.
> Everyone considers Jean *incompetent*.
> The *hungry, weary* men trudged on.

The adjective is said to *modify* the noun or pronoun which it characterizes or qualifies.

ADJUNCT IN A COMPOUND NOUN. Traditional school grammars generally called a word like "stone" in the expression "stone wall" an adjective. Modern grammars identify such an attributive word as an *adjunct* (in the case of "stone," a *noun adjunct*). Any word which joins with another word to form a compound word is thus an adjunct. Nouns, pronouns, verbs, and adjectives may all be used as adjuncts in compound nouns. The resulting compound word is written variously: sometimes as a hyphenated word, sometimes as a single word, sometimes as two separate words. Regardless of the written form, however, most grammarians now consider the adjunct part of the noun itself rather than a separately functioning adjective. Some examples of compound nouns (with the adjunct italicized) follow:

*base*ball	*bread* stick	*he*-man	*cry*baby
*light*house	*tennis* court	*mixing* bowl	*black*bird
*book*case	*income* tax	*driving* range	*gold* bug
*room*mate	*ice* cube	*make*-shift	*good* looks

ADVERB. An adverb is a word or word group that modifies (characterizes) a verb, an adjective, or another adverb.

Adverb as verb modifier: When the adverb functions as a verb modifier, it tells when, where, why, how, and so on. We therefore speak about adverbs of time, of place, of manner, and the like.

> EXAMPLES: He goes to the movies *often*.
> John stopped *there*.
> He drives *poorly*.

Adverb as adjective modifier: When the adverb functions as an adjective modifier, it tells how much, how little, to what extent, and so on. In other words, the adverb immediately precedes and qualifies the meaning of the adjective which it modifies.

> EXAMPLES: John is *very* happy.
> The review was *sharply* critical.
> The survivors were *barely* alive.

Adverb as adverb modifier: When the adverb functions as an adverb modifier, it qualifies the meaning of the adverb which immediately follows it.

EXAMPLES: He drives *too* fast.
            The baby cries *quite* often.
            She tires *very* quickly.

PREPOSITION. A preposition is a word or word group that functions to show a meaning relationship between its object (the nominal which normally follows the preposition) and some other word or words in the sentence. Prepositions ordinarily indicate relationships of time, space, direction, agency, or association.

EXAMPLES: *After* lunch he took a nap.
            The book is *on* the shelf.
            She gave the book *to* me.
            She signed the letter *with* a pencil.

The preposition usually initiates a word group which, together with the preposition itself, is called a *prepositional phrase.* Sometimes, however, this usual or "normal" word order is changed, so that one frequently encounters English sentences (questions, in particular) which end in prepositions. ("Which table should I put the book on?") This is the kind of sentence which used to be the bane of traditional "purists." Fettered by a belief that English grammar ought to conform to the rules of Latin grammar, they insisted that such sentences were simply not "good English." Many a school teacher, convinced that it was "bad" English to end a sentence with a preposition, worked feverishly to train pupils to "correct" such a sentence to the "proper" form: "On which table should I put the book?"

CONJUNCTION. A conjunction is a word or word group that connects two sentence components. Conjunctions can be subclassified according to the types of sentence components they connect:

Coordinating Conjunctions: A coordinating conjunction connects two grammatically equivalent constructions. The most common coordinating conjunctions are the words *and, but, or, nor, for, so, yet,* and *still.*

EXAMPLES: Mary *and* Tim are late.
            She is hard *but* fair.
            He should try harder *or* give up altogether.

Correlative Conjunctions: Like the coordinating conjunction, correlative conjunctions connect two grammatically equivalent constructions. The difference is that correlative conjunctions occur in pairs: *either . . . or, neither . . . nor, not . . . but, not only . . . but also, both . . . and,* and so on.

In an English sentence, the construction which follows the second unit of the pair should be stated in the same form as that which follows the first unit.

EXAMPLES: I lost *not* one *but* two hats.
Either you work *or* you fail.
That animal is *neither* fish *nor* fowl.
Both Jill *and* Jim are late.

Comparative Conjunctions: Because they are very similar to correlative conjunctions, comparative conjunctions are not classified separately in most traditional school grammars. As you will note from the examples, they also often occur in pairs.

EXAMPLES: Mary is *as* smart *as* Joan. (as "Joan is smart")
She is taller *than* John. (than "John is tall")

Note that in these examples, the construction which follows the last comparative conjunction is an "elliptical" sentence.

Subordinating Conjunctions: A subordinating conjunction connects two grammatically *un*equivalent constructions—specifically, an independent clause and a dependent clause.* Notice that it is the very presence of the subordinating conjunction which makes the following clause dependent (i.e., it cannot stand alone as a complete sentence).

EXAMPLES: *Until* I quit school, I worked very hard.
He slept late *because* he stayed up too late.
If she practices hard, she will probably succeed.

INTERJECTION. An interjection is a word or word group that "interrupts." According to traditional grammar, the interjection is grammatically independent of the rest of the sentence, and is not a vital sentence component; if the interjection is deleted a well-formed sentence still remains.

EXAMPLES: *Well,* I am finally finished with the test.
He was, *alas,* late again!
Heavenly days, he doesn't even know what he is doing.

That completes the list of the eight parts of speech. Many of the school grammars stop here and expect the students to do the part-of-speech drills which follow. Other texts add this very important point: one cannot possibly determine what part of speech a given word or word group is

---

*We have here an illustration of a problem referred to earlier, namely that in order to understand parts of speech, a person must already know a great deal about the grammar of a language. Our grammar has not yet defined such terms as *sentence,* *independent clause,* or *dependent clause.* Perhaps you can deduce their meanings from studying the examples.

without seeing how that construction *functions* (how it is used) in a sentence. (Any construction that functions to name something or someone will be called a noun; any construction that functions to characterize, qualify, limit, or describe something or someone will be called an adjective; and so forth.)

See how well you can do with the part-of-speech exercises that follow. Incidentally, the answers to all exercise questions are in the back of the book.

PARTS OF SPEECH   EXERCISE 1

Directions: Identify each underlined word as one of the following parts of speech:

N for Noun   ADJ for Adjective   CONJ for Conjunction
PRO for Pronoun   ADV for Adverb   INT for Interjection
V for Verb   PREP for Preposition   X for Something Else
                                              (No Category Given)

1. She spent her *mornings* at his desk.

2. *She* spent her mornings at his desk.

3. She spent her mornings *at* his desk.

4. His hair *wet* with sweat, John chopped wood.

5. He was tense before, *during*, and after the test.

6. Do not tire *yourself*.

7. I never did know why she was *so* angry.

8. I never did know why she was so *angry*.

9. How a word *functions* determines its class.

10. He came on stage *like* a veteran of the theater.

11. He worked *until* he was exhausted.

12. It is *most* likely that you are right.

13. It is most *likely* that you are right.

14. It is most likely that you are *right*.

15. She rubbed her eyes in *wonder*.

16. *That* is my favorite book.

17. The horse is so *fast* that it's sure to win.

18. Yes, I must admit it can run *fast*.

19. I am not feeling very *well* today.

20. *Heavens*, what shall we do now?

21. Everyone *but* Jim was worried.

22. *Sixteen* is an ideal age.

23. The band consists of only *four* banjos.

24. She may not worry, *but* everyone else does.

25. The band consists of *only* four banjos.

PARTS OF SPEECH   EXERCISE 2

Directions: Identify each underlined construction as one of the eight parts of speech.

1. We look upon your *leaving* as a bad idea.

2. We look upon *your* leaving as a bad idea.

3. You're *leaving*?

4. He planted the seeds while *kneeling*.

5. He planted the seeds *while* kneeling.

6. He planted the seeds *while* he was kneeling.

7. He planted the seeds while he was *kneeling*.

8. *There* are many insects in your garden.

9. That's the room I like to study *in*.

10. I *never* did know why she got so angry.

11. Father's car broke *down* on Tuesday.

12. They just built two new *tennis* courts.

13. That her wound is worse is not *surprising*.

14. *Jan's* misgivings were justifiable.

15. Jan's *misgivings* were justifiable.

16. *This* letter is not the one I lost.

17. We saw the tears *well* up in her eyes.

18. *Well*, what did you expect?

19. *However*, he is still hungry.

20. There was a snake *there*.

21. *There* was a snake there.

22. The wind blew down the *chicken* coop.

23. The wind blew *down* the chicken coop.

24. The wind blew *down* the street.

25. That boy is *charming* all the girls.

26. That boy is very *charming*.

27. *Walking* is good exercise.

28. The man is *walking*.

29. He bought a special pair of *walking* shoes.

30. She just loves *potato* chips.

PARTS OF SPEECH   EXERCISE 3

A good classification system should do three things:

1. It should be *complete*. That is, it should include *all* of whatever it is that is being classified.

2. The categories should be *mutually exclusive*. That is, definitions should be such that there is no overlapping between categories.

3. The classification system should be *consistent*. That is, it should be based on one, and only one principle of classification.

Now that you have worked Exercises 1 and 2, try to answer the following questions:

1. Is the part-of-speech classification system which is given in this book complete? Can you think of any words in typical English sentences which are not included?

2. Are the categories mutually exclusive? Are the definitions such that there is no overlapping?

3. Is the classification system based on a single consistent principle?

3

Subject and Predicate

If you had difficulty with the part-of-speech exercises, as most students do, it was probably because in order to understand how various words and word groups function in English sentences you need to have a more thorough understanding of how sentences are formed. Our purpose in this section, then, is to clarify the terms *subject* and *predicate*, the two chief components necessary to every grammatically complete English sentence. You should learn to recognize and understand each of them.

At this stage in our discussion of English grammar we shall limit ourselves to fairly elementary sentences, beginning with sentences in which the subject comes first, the predicate second—that is, sentences with "normal" word order.

The subject of a sentence names the person, the place, or the thing (condition, object, activity, abstraction, situation) which the sentence, as a whole, is talking about. The subject will thus be a noun or pronoun, or a word or word group that functions as a noun (a nominal).

The predicate of a sentence asserts or tells something about the subject. At the very least, the predicate must contain a complete verb. In addition to the verb, however, a predicate may also contain a word or words that complement and/or modify the verb.

THE SUBJECT. Let us first examine some sentences in which the subject occurs before the verb. In the following examples, the entire subject (the noun or pronoun *headword* along with all of its modifiers—called a noun phrase) is italicized. The headword (sometimes called the *simple subject*) is in boldface.

32

EXAMPLES: *The* **wind** is blowing hard.
The **girl** *in the red dress* looks unhappy.
Miss Jones has been a teacher for years.
Those two very shaggy **dogs** must be Mutt and Jeff.
Happiness is not having to take a grammar test.
Daily **walking** is good exercise.

If all English sentences were formed as simply as these we have just looked at, there would be no problem in recognizing subjects and predicates. Many English sentences, however, are a good deal more complex. Let us examine some of them.

Sentences in which words intervene between the headword and the predicate.

EXAMPLES: *The* **wind** *out of the North* is blowing hard.
Miss Jones, *who is quite old*, has been a teacher for years.
One *of the girls in the class* is feeling unhappy.
The poor **man** *mopping his brow* has a bad headache.
Brisk **walking** *at least once a day* is good exercise.

Sentences in which some other word or word group precedes the subject.

EXAMPLES: Surely *the little* **boy** will call his mother.
Before he realized it **he** had exceeded the speed limit.
(Note that the word group which precedes the main subject has its own subject: *he*)
To be sure, *the young* **man** had never seen me before.

Sentences in which the normal word order is rearranged.

EXAMPLES: On the shelf were *several* **books**.
Down the street came *a mad* **dog**.
Drinking from the stream was *a beautiful wild* **horse**.
There are *many* **spiders** in the attic.
Are *the* **women** *of the church* having a meeting?
Does *your English* **teacher** really like your composition?
When will **John** ever grow up?
(**Note:** Many students find it helpful to restate sentences like these, especially questions, in their normal word order.)

Imperative sentences in which the subject is not mentioned directly, but is implied.

EXAMPLES: Finish the work by four o'clock. (Implied *you* is subject)
Please don't slam the door. (Implied *you* is subject)

Sentences in which two or more nouns are coordinated in a compound subject.

EXAMPLES: **John** *and* **Iris** have joined the club.
Neither the **boys** *nor the* **girls** are interested.
Apples, oranges, grapes, *and* **bananas** were in the bowl.

Sentences in which the subject is not a noun phrase at all, but a phrase or clause of some other form. (This kind of noun phrase is referred to as non-headed.)

EXAMPLES: *To tell me that* is ridiculous.
Whoever broke the window ought to confess.
Washing dishes every night is a drag.
Understanding and Using English is the title of a book.

THE PREDICATE. The predicate is the part of the sentence that asserts or tells something about the subject. In the following examples, the entire predicate is italicized; the verb is in boldface. Notice that the verb may consist of a single word, or it may be preceded by as many as three auxiliary words.

EXAMPLES: The wind **is blowing** *very hard tonight.*
Miss Jones **has been** *a teacher for many years.*
The sirens **screamed** *a moment and then* **faded**. (Compound predicate)
He **must have been seeing** *a mirage.*
Is John **going** *to the fair?*
Drinking *from the stream* **was** a beautiful wild horse.
There **are** many spiders *in the attic.*
On the shelf **were sitting** some dirty dishes.
Does your teacher *really* **like** *your composition?*

Most of the example sentences in this section have been single-clause sentences. That is, they have contained only one subject-verb combination, one or both of which might have been compounded.

The **man** *and his* **wife** | **did** *the dishes and* **went** *to bed.*

(Compound subject)   (Compound predicate)

A *clause* is a word group containing a subject and a predicate. Although we shall examine different kinds of clauses in a later section, you should be made aware that English sentences often contain two or more clauses (multiclause sentences).

EXAMPLES: John is the person who is driving.

Main Clause: <u>John / is the person</u>
               subj   pred

Subordinate Clause: <u>who/is driving</u>
                  subj pred

Whoever said that is wrong.

Main Clause: <u>Whoever said that/is wrong</u>
             subj   pred

Subordinate Clause: <u>Whoever</u>/<u>said that</u>
                    subj   pred

I know that he is sorry.

Main Clause: <u>I</u>/<u>know that he is sorry</u>
          subj   pred

Subordinate Clause: that <u>he</u>/<u>is sorry</u>
                  subj pred

SUBJECTS AND VERBS   EXERCISE 4

Directions: On a piece of paper draw two columns. In Column 1, write out the subject (noun or pronoun headword only). In Column 2, write out the entire verb phrase. Do this for *all* subject-verb combinations (those which occur in main clauses and those which occur in subordinate clauses). The first ten sentences are fairly easy; the last ten are more difficult.

1. The little girl was very late.
2. Do not touch the animals.
3. Who broke the window?
4. He had been faced with a problem like this one before.
5. The leader, together with the boys themselves, worked hard.
6. The reason for the delay was evident.
7. Many problems remained unsolved.
8. Neither of her two attempts was altogether successful.
9. Many valuable books and papers were found in his room after his death.
10. He usually piled the dishes in the sink and left them there after breakfast.
11. In today's society, we take most of our conveniences for granted.
12. In front of the cheerful fire sat the old man happily smoking his pipe.
13. After the scare, she finally decided that she would give up cigarettes.
14. Soon I must give my dog a bath.
15. He made a wild guess but didn't really know the right answer.
16. Why in the world hasn't John arrived yet?
17. There in the river were some of the stolen traps.

18. What could she possibly have said?

19. To tell the truth, this is the proper time.

20. Your foolish grin makes me suspect you.

NONHEADED SUBJECTS   EXERCISE 5

> *Directions:* Identify the entire subject of the main clause in each of the following sentences. Then indicate which sentences have main-clause subjects that are nonheaded phrases or clauses. When you have finished, go back and list the subject and verb of every subordinate clause.

1. Maintaining his excellent game takes much practice.

2. She considered swimming one of his best sports.

3. What you mean is a mystery to me.

4. Going to eight o'clock classes is not for me.

5. In the middle of the street was a rusty nail.

6. To give up now is to admit failure.

7. For denting his father's car, Richard was very sorry.

8. His always being late is an annoying habit.

9. Teasing her little sister is her favorite pastime.

10. That movie you told me about sounds good.

11. What she will do now is not clear.

12. Whoever said that should confess.

13. There under the table was the lost test.

14. Her system of studying is a good one.

15. Playing with matches can lead to disaster.

16. "I don't want to" were his words.

17. The keys of my typewriter keep sticking.

18. He forgot what he meant to say.

19. *Sentence Analysis* is the name of the manual.

20. That she dislikes you is rather obvious.

4

Verbs

The Verb: Tense

Every English verb can take a number of different forms which enable the speaker to express the time concepts of past, present, and future. These different forms are referred to as verb tenses. It is important that you not confuse the terms *tense* and *time*, however, for they are not synonymous. A speaker makes use of the various forms or tenses in a number of ways to convey the idea or mental concept of time.

With the exception of the verb *be*, which—unlike other English verbs—has several alternate forms so that the order of conjugation must simply be memorized, you can learn how to conjugate any of the verbs in English (how to form all possible verb tenses) by learning the four or five principal forms ("principal parts") and how they are used.

CONJUGATION OF ENGLISH VERBS

In addition to knowing which verb forms are used to express different time concepts, a speaker of English must also learn that in certain cases the form of a verb is determined by the form of its subject. Old English verb forms, like those in most modern European languages, changed form according to the "person" (first, second, third) of the subject and also according to the subject's "number" (singular or plural). With the exception of *be*, whose forms are still largely determined by such considerations,

Principal Parts (Forms) of Verbs

FORMS	REGULAR	IRREGULAR	BE
Infinitive or Present	like	do	be, am, are
Third Person Singular*	likes	does	is
Past	liked	did	was, were
Progressive*	liking	doing	being
Perfect	liked	done	been

*The third person singular form makes use of an -*s* ending for all verbs, regular and irregular alike; similarly, the progressive form for all verbs invariably makes use of the -*ing* ending.

the only form change which has been retained is the third person singular in the present tense: (John *likes*, she *runs*, it *goes*). The rules for verb conjugation are summarized in the chart below:

Conjugation of English Verbs

TENSE	VERB FORM
Present	Present tense (infinitive) form of verb. Exception: use the special -*s* form for third person singular.
	I like; you like; he likes; we, you, they like.
Past	Past tense form of verb. Does not change according to subject's person or number.
	I liked; we liked; she wrote; they wrote
Future	Auxiliary word *shall* or *will* + present tense form of verb. Most speakers use *will* for all three persons, and in speech, particularly, they use contractions: *I'll, we'll, you'll,* and so on)
	I shall like, he will like, they will like I'll like, he'll like, they'll like

ASPECT

Present Progressive	Present tense form of BE + progressive (*-ing*) form of verb.
	I am writing; he is laughing; we are going
Past Progressive	Past tense form of BE + progressive form of verb.
	I was writing; he was laughing; we were going
Future Progressive	*Shall* or *will* + infinitive form of BE + progressive form of verb.
	I shall be writing; he will be laughing; we shall be going
Present Perfect	Present tense form of HAVE + perfect form of verb.
	I have liked; he has laughed; we have written; they have gone
Past Perfect	Past tense form of HAVE + perfect form of verb.
	I had liked; he had laughed; we had written; they had gone
Future Perfect	*Shall* or *will* + infinitive form of HAVE + perfect form of verb.
	I shall have liked; he will have laughed; we shall have written; they will have gone
Present Perfect Progressive	Present tense form of HAVE + perfect form of BE + progressive form of verb.
	I have been laughing; the has been laughing; we have been writing; they have been going
Past Perfect Progressive	Past tense form of HAVE + perfect form of BE + progressive form of verb.
	I had been laughing; he had been laughing; we had been writing; they had been going
Future Perfect Progressive	*Shall* or *will* + infinitive form of HAVE + perfect form of BE + progressive form of verb.
	I shall have been laughing; he will have been laughing; we shall have been writing; they will have been going

You may have noticed that there is considerable variation in the past and perfect forms of English verbs. Grammarians therefore say that English verbs are either regular or irregular. Regular verbs form their past tenses by adding the inflectional form *-d* or *-ed* (and in some cases, especially in England, by adding *-t*): *liked, walked, heard, bent.*

Notice also that for regular verbs like *walk, like, love,* the past tense form and the perfect form are the same. (The perfect form, remember, is the verb form which follows the auxiliary word *have.*)

Irregular verbs, on the other hand, usually form their past tenses by means of a vowel change: *write, wrote; do, did; throw, threw.* In addition, the perfect form of most irregular verbs is different from the past tense form: *wrote, written; did, done; threw, thrown.*

Compared to modern English, Old English was a highly inflected language. Yet, even Old English was a great deal less inflected a language than were the Latin tongues, for the English language was initially influenced more by the more simplified, less inflected Germanic languages than by the Latin branch of Indo-European tongues.

From the very beginning, then, down to the present day, the English language has tended toward linguistic simplification. Verbs, for example, have moved from the more numerous forms typical of irregular verbs to the fewer forms of the regular ones. If you doubt the force of this tendency, you might stop to observe that new verbs which enter the language are invariably attracted to the weak or regular verb class. Or notice the universal practice of little children, who often form the past tense of an irregular verb as though it were regular: *growed, seed* (for *saw*), *hitted.* This same tendency toward simplification can be observed in many of the English dialects: *He goed to work, He throwed the ball.* The process of simplification can also be seen in the practice, especially in some uneducated dialects, of using the same form for both perfect aspect and past tense: *He done it, I seen him coming.*

You will also notice that in all future verb tenses the uninflected auxiliary word *shall* or *will* was used. These two words, as well as a number of other words like *may, might, must, can, should, would,* and so on, are called *modal* auxiliaries. They function to indicate the mood or attitude of the speaker. Notice that the modal auxiliary always appears as the first word in the verb phrase.*

Complete conjugation charts of regular verbs, irregular verbs, and the verb *be* can be found in the Appendix. You may find it useful to refer often to these charts as verbs are discussed in more detail, in terms of traditional school grammar and the grammar systems to follow.

---

*Technically, therefore, "future" is said to be a mood or aspect rather than a tense.

The Verb: Types and Complements

When a speaker combines a subject and a verb, he makes a *predication*. A predication is an assertion, an expression, a command, or a question. The verb, depending upon the type of predication it makes in a particular subject-verb combination, can be classified as one of three basic types: *intransitive, transitive,* or *linking*. Intransitive verbs are verbs of complete predication. Verbs of incomplete predication are either transitive or linking, depending on the nature of the word or words (the *complement*) which, along with the verb itself, complete the predication.

THE INTRANSITIVE VERB: NO COMPLEMENT

The intransitive verb ordinarily requires no complement, and is therefore said to be a verb of complete predication. Lexically, the intransitive verb usually expresses some kind of action; but "action" is used here in a very broad sense to refer not only to activity of a physical nature, such as *running* or *hitting*, but also to more abstract activity like *believing, thinking, possessing,* and so on.

The following sentences all contain intransitive verbs. The entire predicate is italicized; the intransitive verb is in boldface:

1. The wind *is **blowing***.

2. The wind *is **blowing** through the trees*.

3. John ***grew***.

4. John ***grew** rapidly last summer*.

5. In this area, rain ***falls** often*.

6. The jewel ***sat** in a gold mount*.

Notice that with the exception of Sentence 6 the verb in each of these sentences is "complete"; that is, whether or not one chooses to add an adverbial verb modifier, the sentence constitutes a complete predication. To be sure, the adverbial modifier contributes something to the meaning of the sentence, but its use is optional, for the sentence would be complete without the adverbial. Sentence 6, on the other hand, is somewhat different: here the adverbial modifier affects the "meaning" of the sentence. Nevertheless, traditional grammar still classifies the verb *sat* in Sentence 6 as intransitive. Somewhat arbitrarily, perhaps, *complement* (the word or words which complete the predication) is the term reserved for a "completer" with an adjectival or a nominal function. The words "in a gold mount" have an adverbial function. To sum up, then, we can define an intransitive verb as an action verb which requires no words to complete its meaning or which requires only an obligatory adverbial.

THE TRANSITIVE VERB

Complement I: Direct Object (DO)

A transitive verb is an action verb of incomplete predication: it requires a nominal complement, called the *direct object*. The direct object is the word or word group that tells *what* or *whom* after the verb. In the following examples, the entire predicate (verb plus complement) is underlined; the transitive verb is italicized; the DO is in boldface. Notice that the direct object is a noun, a pronoun, or a noun equivalent (nominal):

1. Mr. Jones *repairs* cars.

2. My high school teacher *wrote* a good book.

3. He *called* his servant.

4. John *grew* roses in his garden.

5. He *decided* to quit school.

6. She *said* that she would leave at eight o'clock.

Notice that in Sentences 5 and 6 several words (a phrase and a clause, respectively) are required to tell *what* or *whom* after the transitive verb.

When a sentence follows the normal word order, the pattern is *subject + transitive verb + direct object*. Frequently, however, word order is rearranged in such a way that the direct object precedes the verb. Here are some examples:

Arrogant people I really *hate*. (The subject is *I*; the predicate is *really hate arrogant people*; the verb is *hate*; the direct object is *arrogant people*.)

That I *must see!* (Subject: *I*; predicate: *must see that*; verb: *must see*; direct object: *that*.)

These sentences have all been ones with a direct object complement only. There are certain sentences, however, which have other complements in addition to the direct object. Let us look at the other possibilities.

Complement II: Indirect Object + Direct Object (IO + DO)

A transitive verb may be followed by two objects: a *direct object* (DO) which is the direct "receiver" of the verb's action; and an *indirect object* (IO), which is the person or thing to whom (which) or for whom (which) the action is directed. The pattern of such a sentence is always *subject + transitive verb + IO + DO*. Note the following examples. The entire predicate is underlined; the verb is italicized; objects are in boldface:

1. She *gave* **Herb** the **test**.
              IO   DO

2. He *showed* **me** the **way** on the map.
              IO   DO

3. He *made* the **boy** a **kite**.
              IO DO

Notice that in this kind of sentence, both objects are required. Not all transitive verbs lend themselves to this pattern. Examples of transitive verbs which may be followed by an indirect plus a direct object are *give, take, show, send*, and so on.

It would be possible to state each of these sentences in another form:

1. She *gave* the **test** to Herb.

2. He *showed* the **way** on the map to me.

3. He *made* a **kite** for the boy.

In this form, the sentences follow the pattern: subject + transitive verb + DO + adverbial prepositional phrase. Thus, the IO + DO version is a sentence in which the "to" or "for" of the prepositional phrase has been deleted and the word order has been rearranged. This kind of reduction and word reordering is quite common in English. In the reduced version we call the first object an *indirect object*—because it is indirectly the object of a preposition. That is, it is the object of the implied or understood *to* or *for*. The second object is the *direct object*. The order of the complements never varies: it is always indirect object first, direct object second.

Complement III: Direct Object + Object Complement (DO + OC)

Another pattern in a sentence with a transitive verb is *subject + transitive verb + DO + Object Complement* (OC). The object complement, which always follows the DO, does two things: it refers to the direct object, either by renaming the object or by characterizing it, and it completes the "meaning" of the direct object. Thus the OC functions as either a nominal or an adjectival.

THE NOMINAL OBJECT COMPLEMENT (**OC-N**). The OC-N "renames" the direct object. It is therefore a noun or a noun equivalent (nominal):

1. The class *elected* **Mary president**.
                    DO   OC-N

2. They *called* **him** a **coward**.
             DO   OC-N

3. They *named* their **dog Max**.
                   DO OC-N

THE ADJECTIVAL OBJECT COMPLEMENT (**OC-A**). In this pattern, the direct object is immediately followed by an adjective or an adjective equivalent (adjectival) which describes or in some other way characterizes or qualifies the direct object nominal:

1. We *considered* **John babyish**.
               DO   OC-A

2. The hair style *made* **her beautiful**.
                  DO   OC-A

3. Jay *painted* his **room purple**.
               DO OC-A

THE LINKING VERB—SUBJECT COMPLEMENT

A third type of English verb, also a verb of incomplete predication, is the linking verb. At first glance, it may seem that the complement of a linking verb is a direct object because it answers *what* or *whom* after the verb. Yet if you will examine the following sentences carefully, you will notice several important differences. First, the linking verb does not express action as a transitive verb does. Second, it serves to link its subject with some word or word group in the predicate, either by renaming the subject or by characterizing it. Therefore the complement which follows a linking verb is called a subject complement.

THE NOUN OR NOMINAL AS SUBJECT COMPLEMENT (**SC-N**).* When the form of the construction which functions as a subject complement is a noun or a nominal, the linking verb serves as a kind of equal sign the lexical meaning of which is, roughly, "equals." The sentence pattern is *subject + linking verb + (noun or nominal)*. Notice that the subject does not "do" anything; it does not "act." Rather, the subject "exists"; it is "the same as" the complement, with the verb serving merely to link the two together:

1. Mary *is* **a friend**.   (*Mary = a friend*)
        SC-N

*Many school grammars use the expression "predicate noun" or "predicate nominal" for the noun subject complement.

2. Jim <u>*became* **chairman**</u>.   (*Jim = chairman*)
SC-N

3. All his life he <u>*remained* **a bully.**</u>   (*He = a bully*)
SC-N

THE ADJECTIVE AS SUBJECT COMPLEMENT (SC-A).* When the complement after a linking verb is an adjective form we call the subject complement an adjective subject complement (SC-A):

1. Mary <u>*is* **tall.**</u>
SC-A

2. After the long trip, John <u>*was* **hungry**</u>.
SC-A

3. The storms <u>*have been* **ferocious** this year.</u>
SC-A

Note that the verb *be* is frequently used as a linking verb.† Certain other verbs may also be used as linking verbs, however. A verb is said to be a linking verb when it is used to imply "state of being." Thus, a fairly good test you might make is to try substituting a form of *be* for the verb in question. If the *basic* notion of the sentence is retained with the substitution, you can be sure you are dealing with a linking verb. (No word, of course, is an exact synonym for another word, so the substitution test will result in subtle meaning change.) Some examples of verbs which may be used as linking verbs are *seem, become, remain, grow, feel, look, smell, taste, sound*:

1. The situation *seems* difficult.

2. The sky *became* cloudy.

3. She *remained* friendly.

4. He *has grown* quite pudgy.

5. John *feels* good.

6. That book *looks* interesting.

7. The meat *smells* delicious.

---

*Many school grammars call the adjective subject complement a "predicate adjective." Such school grammar terminology confuses form names and function names. *Subject complement* (SC) is a *function* term; *noun*, and *adjective* are *form* terms.

†Remember that the verb *be* may also be used as an auxiliary word in a verb phrase: *am* going, *is* saying, *were* doing, shall have *been* going.

8. The butter *tastes* rancid.

9. The music *sounds* lovely.

VERB TYPES   EXERCISE 6

Directions: Indicate whether each italicized verb is intransitive, transitive, or linking. Use these abbreviations:

I for Intransitive
T for Transitive
L for Linking

1. Three pretty girls *were sitting* on the bench.

2. The reason for his refusal *was* uncertain.

3. Some of the actors *had forgotten* their lines.

4. Listening to the noise for hours *grew* tiresome.

5. Mary Jane *grew* quite a bit last year.

6. He *grew* vegetables in a backyard garden.

7. Almost immediately he *dived* into the water.

8. They *gave* the suggestion their careful attention.

9. His reports *were* really very poor.

10. These *are* the best available tools for the job.

11. The size of the building and its beauty *awed* me.

12. In spite of our wishes, he *went* off alone.

13. After a period of doubt, she finally *became* sure.

14. He surely *must have been walking* for days.

15. They *liked* fighting with each other.

16. He *may have been* asleep.

17. She *must have had* a rich relative.

18. They *thought* Mary a great bore.

19. Angie *felt* better after the test.

20. Mary *had been having* many problems at school.

21. He certainly *should be* grateful for John's help.

22. Joe *seemed* happy with the results.

23. The new rule *made* them very angry.

24. Someone *parked* that car in the street last Monday.

25. Your answer *is* exactly what I needed to know.

VERB TYPES EXERCISE 7

> ***Directions:*** As in Exercise 6, identify each italicized verb as *I* (for intransitive), *T* (for transitive), or *L* (for linking). You may find these sentences more difficult than those in Exercise 6.

1. Only in the early spring *can* one *find* violets.

2. The excited children *burst* out of the house.

3. *Do* any of the others *have* cause for complaint?

4. Historians *feel* the real meaning was obscured.

5. Stopping for just a little rest *was* sufficient.

6. The sheep *should be* separate from the goats.

7. We *did*n't *garden* in that spot last year.

8. *Try* the drink, please, to test its sweetness.

9. *Do*n't *call* her that name!

10. The sky really *looks* ominous today.

11. I *think* the situation is hopeless.

12. His explanation *was* very far-fetched.

13. Dad *was* sick of driving.

14. In fact, he *wanted* to stop.

15. I *wonder* what the committee decided.

16. I wonder what the committee *decided*.

17. The schedule they *gave* him was one he hated.

18. The schedule they gave him *was* one he hated.

19. The ice *melted* after only five minutes.

20. *Could* he *have succeeded* in such troubled times?

COMPLEMENTS   EXERCISE 8

Directions: Indicate which words or word groups are complements of the boldfaced verbs. Then, in the order in which they occur, identify each complement as one of the following (noting that, in the case of subject and object complements, you are to further identify the form of the complement):

DO for Direct Object
IO for Indirect Object
SC-N for Subject Complement
(noun form)

SC-A for Subject Complement (adjective form)
OC-N for Object Complement (noun form)
OC-A for Object Complement (adjective form)

1. We **elected** him the boy most likely to succeed.

2. My favorite **is** the history teacher.

3. His account of the trip **was** very interesting.

4. He **decided** to quit because he was sick of studying.

5. He decided to quit because he **was** sick of studying.

6. The bird **continues** its singing.

7. It continues whether or not it **is** happy.

8. **Send** the school a transcript of your grades.

9. They **gave** him a terrible schedule.

10. She **called** him a big baby.

11. Her idea **is** good enough for me.

12. Before I **leave** you, wish me luck!

13. Before I leave you, **wish** me luck!

14. He has **given** my idea much thought.

15. We **made** Alex responsible for supplies.

16. He **labels** every attempt a failure.

17. Why **is** Martha so happy?

18. That dress **fits** her beautifully.

19. Yes, it really **becomes** her too.

20. It **is** very easy to please Tom.

COMPLEMENTS   **EXERCISE 9**

> *Directions:* List all of the complements of the boldfaced verbs. Then, in the order in which they occur, identify each complement. Use the same abbreviations as those for Exercise 8. (Notice that sometimes a complement will be a whole phrase or clause.)

1. I **think** we are lost.
2. I think we **are** lost.
3. I followed the directions he **gave** me.
4. **Will** you **give** me a lesson on the organ?
5. Perhaps you **can teach** me the new steps.
6. I **cannot guarantee** to make you a good dancer.
7. He **made** of himself a leader.
8. He **made** himself a leader.
9. She **made** herself beautiful.
10. She **made** herself a beautiful person.
11. She **made** him a good wife.
12. He **made** her a good wife.
13. She **made** him a sandwich.
14. **Isn't** language tricky?
15. She **called** him a cad.
16. She **called** him a cab.
17. She **called** him wonderful.
18. She **called** him on the telephone.
19. **Do** you **see** why foreigners become confused?
20. Do you see why foreigners **become** confused?

The Verb: Voice

The verbs in the sentence examples and in the exercises in this book have been, until now, *active voice* verbs. A verb is in the active voice when it occurs in a sentence in which the subject *acts*, or *does*, or merely *exists* (*is*). All three verb types can occur in the active voice form:

Intransitive: 1. John *walks*.
                2. He *should be leaving* soon.

Transitive: 1. He *hit* the ball.
                2. Jim *gave* me a quarter.
                3. We *thought* him foolish.

Linking: 1. Mary *is* a student.
                2. Mary *is* pretty.

Notice that when the verb in a sentence is intransitive or transitive, the subject *does* something; when the verb is linking, the subject does not *do* anything, it merely exists.

Of the three verb types, only transitive verbs can also occur in the *passive voice*. Examine the following sentences:

ACTIVE VERB	PASSIVE VERB
1. John *hit* the ball. (Subj + V + DO)	The ball *was hit* by John.
2. Tom *considers* Bill a friend. (Subj + V + DO + OC-N)	Bill *is considered* a friend by Tom.
3. Tom *thinks* Bill handsome. (Subj + V + DO + OC-A)	Bill *is thought* handsome by Tom.
4. Jim *gave* Mary a dime. (Subj + V + IO + DO)	(A) A dime *was given* Mary by Jim. or (B) Mary *was given* a dime by Jim.

Notice that all of these sentences can be made passive by the three-part process of (1) using the original direct object as the new subject; (2) changing the verb to the appropriate tense of the *be* auxiliary plus the perfect form of the verb; and (3) adding a "by" prepositional phrase whose OP (object of preposition) is the original subject. The third of these steps

50

is optional. One often sees passive sentences which do not possess a "by" prepositional phrase. Even when it is omitted, however, it is always theoretically possible to supply such a phrase.

The active voice, because it is more direct and less wordy, is usually preferable to the passive. This is not a firm rule, however, despite the fact that many traditional school grammars make it seem so. Sometimes the passive is clearly better, for sentence variety or to change word emphasis. Or there may be occasions when the speaker does not know the "doer" of the action. Not knowing who is responsible for having damaged a library book, for example, a speaker might say, in the active voice: "Someone has ruined this book." On the other hand, to emphasize effect rather than cause, a speaker might use the passive: "This book has been ruined." Because in this situation there is no particular reason to add the phrase "by someone," it is simply omitted.

One more point should be noted. If you will look again at the four active-passive sentences above you will note that there are two methods of forming the passive for sentences with complements containing both an indirect and a direct object (Sentence 4). The first method, like that for all other active sentences with transitive verbs, is to retain the IO and make the original DO the new subject. Grammarians call this complement of a passive verb a *retained indirect object*. In the second method, the original indirect object becomes the new subject, which leaves a *retained direct object* complement.

We can, then, list these three "tests" for the passive:

1. The subject of a passive sentence is not the "doer"; it does not act. Rather, it *receives* the action, it is "acted upon."

2. A passive sentence usually contains a prepositional phrase which begins with the word *by* or *with*. If the sentence does not contain such a phrase, it is always possible to supply one.

3. A passive verb always consists of at least two words, one of which *must* be a form of the *be* auxiliary. If there is more than one auxiliary word, one of them must be a form of *be*. Of course, verbs in the active voice may also contain the *be* auxiliary (*is going, was taking, have been seeing, has been loving*), so its occurrence is not in itself evidence of passive voice. What is significant is the form of the verb which immediately follows the *be* auxiliary. This form will always be the progressive (-*ing*) form when the verb is active. When it is passive, the perfect form of the verb will follow the *be* auxiliary (*is gone, was taken, have been seen, has been loved*). This last test, the verb-form test, is a far more reliable one than the first or second. The first test, in fast, which is based on the vagaries of "meaning," can be confusing simply because the notional meanings of verbs can be so varied. Consider, for example, the sentence:

The boy *had become* confused.

If "meaning" is used as the test, this sentence might be labeled passive. Notice, however, that the verb *had become* does not contain a *be* auxiliary. It is the past perfect form of the linking verb *become* (and linking verbs are always in the active voice). The word *confused* functions in this sentence as an adjective subject complement (SC-A).

ACTIVE AND PASSIVE VERBS + COMPLEMENTS　　　　**EXERCISE 10**

Directions: Decide whether the verb in each of these sentences is active or passive. Then indicate whether each is transitive, intransitive, or linking.

1. He has been feeling terrible this morning.
2. The house was painted red and green by the stupid man.
3. The coffee has been boiling furiously for several minutes.
4. A birthday card was sent his mother by Tom.
5. The stupid man painted the house red and green.
6. Tom sent his mother a birthday card.
7. The child's pulse could not be felt.
8. The baby will be named Junior.
9. That boy over there is my brother.
10. They will name the baby Junior.
11. His mother was sent a birthday card.
12. The doctor could not feel the child's pulse.
13. My brother is that boy over there.

ACTIVE AND PASSIVE VERBS　　　　**EXERCISE 11**

Directions: Find the verb in each of the following sentences. Then indicate which are active and which are passive.

1. She was flirting with the boys.
2. Mary was charming.
3. He should have been told to stop.

4. What is he saying?

5. He has finally been told the bad news.

6. They must have been asked to the party.

7. If not, they must have been sad.

8. Damage has been done to the crop.

9. Was the damage caused by freezing?

10. Her trip couldn't have been very carefully planned.

11. That young man really seems tired.

12. You will have been attending class for a month soon.

13. The reason for his failure wasn't known.

14. In better circumstances could he have succeeded?

15. The airport had been fogged in for hours.

16. The sheep should be separated from the goats.

17. He must have been exciting.

18. He must have been excited.

19. Mary was considered a terrible bore.

20. He must have been sleeping for days.

21. He should have been grateful to John.

22. The street was completely covered with mud.

23. That car has been parked there since Monday.

24. I think the situation is very nearly hopeless.

25. His behavior was frowned on.

5

Form and Function

We have found fault with the typical pedagogical word classification system because it is not based on a single consistent principle, and because school grammars, for the most part, failed to make a clear distinction between form and function. It was this failure in particular that prompted a widespread reaction against traditional grammar in the 1930s, '40s, and '50s. (The well-known pedagogical grammars were not representative of the whole of traditional grammar, but critics ignored much of the careful and respectable work of the scholarly traditionalists.) Before we proceed with our analysis, it is extremely important that we sharpen our terminology.

Single words and word groups have, on the one hand, certain formal characteristics. A noun, for instance, can be singular or plural, nominative or objective. Adjectives and adverbs can be compared. (That is, they can be positive, comparative, or superlative: *hot, hotter, hottest; bad, worse, worst; quickly, more quickly, most quickly.*) Verbs, as you have seen, may take many forms. All of these characteristics are matters of *form*, matters of which speakers are aware. They know that some words can occur in several forms, usually by the process of varying word endings. Other words, however, occur in only one form.

On the other hand, words and word groups have characteristic *uses* or *functions*. And even though form may affect function, and vice versa, it is important to understand that the *function* of a construction is something quite distinct from its *form*.

If you will turn back to the part of speech definitions you will see that at least four poorly defined concepts were used as part-of-speech classification principles: *lexical meaning, form, position,* and *function.*

54

Indeed, our objection to the classification system was just that: that first one, then another principle was adopted, and that no attempt was made to distinguish among them. Let us define these terms:

FORM. The structural characteristics of a word or a word group. Includes such characteristics as inflectional and derivational word endings in the case of single words, and word order in the case of larger linguistic elements.

LEXICAL MEANING. The lexical or dictionary meaning of a word. What a word denotes. Also, the more general "notional" meaning of a class of words ("naming" words, "action" words, and the like).

FUNCTION. The semantic and syntactic role of a linguistic element in the larger construction of which it is a part. The grammatical relationships of linguistic elements to each other, determined in English by **position**, that is, by the sentence place or slot that a linguistic unit occupies.

As you may guess from these definitions, it is not always easy to give clear-cut definitions and then to make them "stick." This is because the grammar of a language is a complicated system of semantic and syntactic devices or signals. Some of these signals are fairly distinct and separate, but more often they are interdependent and overlapping.

Keeping in mind that the task of describing the grammar of a language is a complicated one, let us list some of the important grammatical functions which words and word groups perform in English. The chart which follows, although it is by no means comprehensive, lists a number of function terms, provides a very general semantic and syntactic definition for each term, and lists the most common or "normal" sentence positions occupied by a linguistic element so functioning. Remember that many different forms (both single words and word groups) can fill most of these functional roles and positions.

Function and Position

TERM	ROLE	POSITION
SUBJECT	A nominal linguistic element which designates the "doer" of an action in an active verb construction, or the "receiver" of an action in a passive verb construction.	Usually precedes a verb or a verbal.
PREDICATE	The part of a clause which delineates the action, makes the statement or assertion, asks the question, gives the command. Consists of main verb + preceding auxiliaries + modifiers + complement(s).	In declarative sentences, usually occurs after the subject. Otherwise, position varies.

TERM	ROLE	POSITION
COMPLEMENT	A linguistic element or elements which complete the predication begun by a verb or a verbal. The various kinds of complements are listed below.	Usually follows the verb or verb phrase. May occur in a predicate phrase or a verbal phrase.
Direct Object (DO)	A nominal linguistic element which designates the receiver of the action of a transitive verb or verbal.	Usually follows a verb or a verbal.
Indirect Object (IO)	A nominal linguistic element which designates the person, place, or thing which indirectly receives or is affected by the action of the verb or verbal. Also called "indirect" because this element is "understood" to be the object of the omitted (understood) preposition *to* or *for*.	Usually occurs after a transitive verb or verbal, but before the DO.
Object Complement (OC-N)	A nominal linguistic element which completes the predication begun by a transitive verb or verbal by explaining, extending, or otherwise qualifying the DO.	Follows and is usually immediately adjacent to the DO.
Object Complement (OC-A)	An adjectival linguistic element which completes the predication begun by a transitive verb or verbal by qualifying or characterizing the DO.	Follows and is usually adjacent to the DO.
Subject Complement (SC-N)	A nominal linguistic element which completes the predication begun by a linking verb and is the equivalent of the subject.	Follows a linking verb.
Subject Complement (SC-A)	An adjectival linguistic element which completes the predication begun by a linking verb and qualifies or characterizes the subject.	Follows a linking verb.
OBJECT OF PREPOSITION (OP)	A nominal linguistic element which is governed by the preposition in a prepositional phrase.	Usually follows a preposition in a prepositional phrase.

TERM	ROLE	POSITION
MODIFIER	A non-nominal linguistic element which qualifies or characterizes another element. An adjective or adverb. See below.	See below, under Adjective and Adverb.
Adjective	A modifier which qualifies, describes, or otherwise characterizes a noun or nominal.	Position varies. May immediately precede or follow a noun or nominal, or may occur as an adjective complement in predicate (as an SC or an OC).
Adverb	A modifier which qualifies or characterizes a verb (or verbal), an adjective, or an adverb.	As a verb modifier: position flexible, but usually close to verb (or verbal). As an adjective or adverb modifier: always occurs immediately before the element which it modifies.
APPOSITIVE	A nominal linguistic element which restates or renames another nominal and which is its equivalent.	Occurs immediately after and adjacent to the nominal it renames. Is not, however, a complement.
INTERJECTION	A grammatically independent linguistic element which serves to interrupt. Is usually mildly exclamatory.	Position varies.
CONNECTIVE	A linguistic element which functions to connect and to show a meaning relationship between two linguistic constructions. Depending upon the nature of this relationship, connectives can be further classified, according to function, as subordinating conjunctions, coordinating conjunctions, or some other kind of transitional element. Conjunctions are listed below. For other transitional elements, see section on Connectives.	Position varies. (See section on Connectives which follows.)

TERM	ROLE	POSITION
Subordinating Conjunction	A linguistic element, usually a single word like *because, although, if, unless*, which functions to make a clause dependent.	Always occurs as the initial word in a dependent clause.
Coordinating Conjunction	A linguistic element (*and, but, or, nor, for, so, yet, still*) which joins two equivalent grammatical constructions.	Always occurs between the two constructions it joins.

6

Verbals

A verbal is a verb form that functions in a word group as some other part of speech. If you study the verb conjugation charts (Appendix), you will note these points:

1. The infinitive form (*to like, to do, to be*) never functions alone as a verb. ("John to score points" is not a sentence.)

2. The progressive verb form (*liking, doing, being*) never functions alone as a verb. To be part of a verb phrase, the progressive form must be preceded by a form of the *be* auxiliary (*am liking, is doing, was being*).

3. The perfect verb form (*liked, done, been*) never functions alone as a verb. To be part of a verb phrase, the perfect form must be preceded either by a *have* auxiliary for active voice (*have liked, has done, had been*); or by a *be* auxiliary for passive (*am liked, was done*). Because the past tense and the progressive form of regular verbs are spelled alike, it is easy to miss this distinction.

One of the difficulties in distinguishing verbals from verbs is that a verbal still *looks like* a verb. Moreover, verbals can still retain a number of their formal verb qualities, even when they are not used as fully inflected verbs. A verbal can be modified by an adverb, a verbal can have a complement, a verbal can even have a subject. You will observe these things when we study verbal phrases.

In this chapter, however, we shall confine our study of verbals to single words—gerunds, participles, and infinitives—which do not occur in verbal phrases. In the sentences below, the verbals are in boldface:

59

Crying is a waste of time. (Nominal function: subject)

He hates **crying**. (Nominal function: direct object)

He saw a **crying** child. (Adjectival function: modifies *child*)

The window appears **cracked**. (Adjectival function: modifies *window*)

To protest is useful. (Nominal function: subject)

He came here **to protest**. (Adverbial function: modifies *came*)

Traditional grammar classifies verbals into three types: the *gerund*, the *participle*, and the *infinitive*.

Gerund. The gerund is a verb form which functions as a nominal. You will remember that a noun (or nominal) is a word or word group that *names*. You are already familiar with most of the typical noun sentence positions (that is, sentence positions where nouns typically occur). Here is a complete list of these noun-function sentence positions:

1. *Subject* of a verb (or verbal)　　　Her **crying** made John sad.

2. *Direct Object* of a verb or verbal　　　He dislikes **studying**.

3. *Subject Complement* (SC-N)　　　His worst speech defect is **lisping**.

4. *Object Complement* (OC-N)　　　Do you call that **dancing**?

5. *Indirect Object* (IO)　　　His clumsiness gives **dancing** a bad name.

6. *Object of Preposition* (OP)　　　He devotes his time to **studying**.

7. *Appositive* (Renames, immediately after a noun or nominal)　　　His habit, **humming**, bothers his roommate.

Participle. The participle is a verb form which functions as an adjectival. Typical sentence positions in which a word or word group functions as an adjectival are illustrated below:

1. *Preceding a nominal*　　　John soon finished the **boring** job.

2. *Following a nominal*　　　The flowers, **drooping** and **faded**, desperately needed water.

3. *Adjectival Subject*	Her criticism became **devastating**.
Complement (SC-A)	
4. *Adjectival Object*	We thought the book **frightening**.
Complement (OC-A)	

INFINITIVE. The infinitive is a verb form which consists of the simple form (the *stem*) of a verb, usually preceded by the particle *to*. Sometimes the particle *to* does not actually occur, but is "understood" or implied. An infinitive may function in a sentence as a *nominal*, an *adjectival*, or an *adverbial*.

The Nominal Infinitive:

1. *Subject*	**To surrender** is cowardly.
2. *Direct Object* (DO)	He desires **to wait**.
3. *Nominal Subjective*	To quit is **to fail**.
Complement (SC-N)	

The Adjectival Infinitive:

An infinitive may function as an adjectival. When it does, it invariably follows the noun (nominal) it modifies.

1. The time **to study** is now. (Modifies the noun *time*)
2. This is a moment **to regret**. (Modifies the noun *moment*)
3. It was past the day **to register**. (Modifies the noun *day*)

The Adverbial Infinitive:

An infinitive may function to modify a verb, an adjective, or an adverb.

Infinitive as Verb or Verbal Modifier: (Adverbial of *reason* or *purpose*)

1. He practices **to improve**. (Modifies the verb *practices*)
2. He'll do anything **to win**. (Modifies the verb *will do*)
3. **To exercise**, he jogs. (Modifies the verb *jogs*)
4. Returning **to study** was hard. (Modifies the verbal *returning*)

Infinitive as Adjective or Adjectival Modifier:

1. She was too tense **to sleep**. (Modifies the adjective *tense*)
2. He was happy **to leave**. (Modifies the adjective *happy*)

Infinitive as Adverb or Adverbial Modifier:

1. He's driving too fast **to stop**. (Modifies the adverb *fast*)
2. He tries to sleep soundly **to dream**. (Modifies the adverb *soundly*; or, modifies entire predicate)
3. The rain is falling too quickly **to accumulate**. (Modifies the adverb *quickly*)

SOME QUESTIONS   EXERCISE 12

To begin to determine whether the traditional grammar system for classifying verbals is a useful one, answer the following questions:

1. What classification principle is used here?

2. Do you think the classification system includes all of what is being classified—in this case, verbals? How would you classify the verbals in these sentences:

   a) He spent most of his time **walking**.

   b) He entered the room **shouting**.

VERBALS   EXERCISE 13

Directions: Identify every verbal in the sentences which follow as a gerund, a participle, an infinitive, or a verb adjunct. Use these abbreviations:

GER for Gerund   INF for Infinitive
PART for Participle   V AD for Verb(al) Adjunct

John finds *diving* very difficult.
              1

My new *sewing* box needs *repairing*.
        2   3

Why do you want *to leave*?
                   4

He offered her his *undying* love.
                     5

She seems too *jaded to care*.
               6   7

Was the invitation *written* or *engraved*?
                    8   9

Understanding is not always an easy *undertaking*.
    10   11

The *startled* children seemed quite *shaken*.
     12   13

Upon *leaving*, the *frightened* couple saw their *wrecked* car.
      14   15   16

Going skating is very *trying*.
  17   18   19

After *failing*, Jim wished that he had tried *studying*.
      20   21

When they finished with their *swimming*, the boys went to the *bowling* alley for a few games.
                        22   23

The poor man, who was by now *exhausted* and *driven*, resigned himself to failure.
                     24   25

INFINITIVES

> *Directions:* List all infinitives in the following sentences. Then indicate whether the infinitive is used as a nominal (*N*), an adjective (*ADJ*), or an adverb (*ADV*).

1. Why do you want to leave?

2. He is doing that to help.

3. To begin is certainly not easy.

4. She seems too jaded to care.

5. He doesn't know that to cry is a sign of immaturity.

6. Will you please let me help?

7. They decided to read.

8. In fact, reading seemed a good way to relax.

9. Their only hope is to exist.

10. When life is too much for him, he drinks to forget.

11. On the other hand, drinking is not a good way to recover.

12. They refused to talk to the police.

13. She said he made her do it.

14. I don't know what to say.

15. He really likes to dance.

16. The girl cried, "Let me go!"

17. The question is to be or not to be.

7

Word Groups : Phrases

A phrase is a group of related words (1) which does not contain a subject-predicate combination and (2) which, as an entire unit, serves a part-of-speech role in the larger construction of which it is a part. Although form and function characteristics are very much interdependent and overlapping, we can classify phrase types primarily according to certain *formal* qualities.*

Phrase Forms

NOUN PHRASE. A noun phrase consists of a noun or pronoun headword plus all of its modifiers. The modifiers may occur both before and after the headword. In the examples which follow, the headword is in boldface:

the **boys**

the young **boys**

the five young **boys**

the five young **boys** in the band

the five young **boys** in the band who were late

*These classifications are not exclusively formal. The words within each phrase, for example, have functional relationships to each other.

64

Verb Phrase. A verb phrase consists of a finite verb plus all of its auxiliaries.* A verb phrase may contain two, three, or more words, the last of which is the main or "notional" verb (boldfaced in examples). All other words are auxiliaries which convey such concepts as tense, voice, mood.

must **go**   have **gone**   must have been **going**

has **gone**   had been **going**   will have **gone**

Predicate Phrase. A predicate phrase consists of a verb phrase plus modifiers and complements. The main verb, called the headword, is in boldface in the examples which follow:

must **go** quickly

had **run** swiftly toward the camp

studied her history lesson every evening for an hour

has **been** my best friend for years   (In this predicate phrase, the verb is "be"; the verb phrase is "has been"; the predicate phrase is the entire phrase: VP + complement + modifier.)

Note that a predicate phrase is an extended verb phrase. Some grammar texts do not make a distinction between the two.

Prepositional Phrase. A prepositional phrase consists of a preposition plus the element functioning as its object, usually occurring in that order. In the following examples, the preposition is in boldface:

on the floor   **toward** the house which was on fire

in the large room   **from** the moment he saw her

Verbal Phrase. A verbal phrase consists of a non-finite verb form plus its auxiliaries, complements, and modifiers. Verbal phrases can be further subclassified as gerund phrases, participial phrases, and infinitive phrases, but except for infinitive phrases, these are primarily function classifications. In the following examples the verbal plus its auxiliaries is in boldface; the last two examples are infinitive phrases:

hitting the ball   **having run** a mile every day

warped by the rain   **to admit** the truth

having broken the glass   **to finish** the work quickly

Adjective Phrase. An adjective phrase consists of an adjective plus its modifiers. The modifiers in such a phrase function to qualify or characterize the adjective; in traditional grammar, words that function to modify

*finite verb—a fully inflected verb form capable of serving as a predicate.

adjectives in this way are called adverbs. In these examples the adjective is in boldface:

> very **old**
>
> extremely **cautious**
>
> quite obviously **new**

ADVERB PHRASE. An adverb phrase consists of an adverb plus its modifiers. Again, the modifiers serve to characterize or to qualify the adverb, and such modifiers are classified as adverbs. The head adverb in these examples is in boldface:

> very **badly**
>
> extremely **often**
>
> much too **quickly**

ABSOLUTE PHRASE. An absolute phrase consists of a subject plus a participial phrase. Here are some examples of absolute phrases:

> the storm having subsided
>
> all things considered
>
> the answer having been ascertained
>
> no person being in a really invulnerable position

Phrase Functions

In addition to the internal functional relationship of the words within a phrase, the entire phrase as a unit serves a function role in the larger construction of which it is a part.

NOMINAL PHRASES. The term *nominal* applies to any linguistic element that "names." Thus, any linguistic unit can be used as a nominal: letters, figures, single words, and word groups. The kinds of phrases which are most commonly used in nominal roles are listed below:

1. *The Noun Phrase as Nominal*

   The young boys bought a dog.   (Subject)

   She bought *the young boys* a dog.   (Indirect Object)

   They encouraged *the young boys*.   (Direct Object)

   They are *the young boys*.   (Nominal Subject Complement)

   He gave a test to *the young boys*.   (Object of Preposition)

2. *The Verbal Phrase as Nominal*

   A. *Gerund Phrase*

      Hitting the ball is his specialty.   (Subject)

      He likes *running a mile every day*.   (Direct Object)

      He is famous for his specialty, *hitting the ball*.   (Appositive)

   B. *Infinitive Phrase*

      It is his duty *to study hard*.   (Delayed subject, in sentence beginning with "it" expletive)

      To yield is to obey.   (Subject)

      To yield is *to obey*.   (Subject Complement)

ADJECTIVAL PHRASES. A number of phrase forms can function as adjectivals. Here are some examples:

1. *The Adjective Phrase as an Adjectival*

   A *very old* man always sits on the park bench.

   Jones seems *extremely cautious*.

   This book is *quite obviously new*.

2. *The Noun Phrase as an Adjectival*

   She will wear her *everyday* clothes.

3. *The Verbal Phrase as an Adjectival (Participial Phrase)*

The boy *throwing the ball* is Nick.

Here is a book *warped by the rain.*

4. *The Verbal Phrase as an Adjectival (Infinitive Phrase)*

That was a moment *to remember always.*

The thing *to do now* is to quit.

5. *The Prepositional Phrase as an Adjectival*

The book *on the floor* is mine.

She finally watered the wilted plants *in her garden.*

ADVERBIAL PHRASES. Several phrase forms can function as adverbials:

1. *The Adverb Phrase as an Adverbial*

He drives his car *very badly.*

She finished the test *much too quickly.*

2. *The Noun Phrase as an Adverbial*

He jogs *every morning.*

I had a bad dream *last night.*

3. *The Verbal Phrase as an Adverbial*

She entered the room *crying bitterly.*

The group arrived *carrying a petition.*

He exercises *to lose weight.*   (Infinitive Phrase)

4. *The Prepositional Phrase as an Adverbial*

He fell *down the stairs.*

She smiled *with great affection at John.*

INDEPENDENT PHRASES. There are two categories:

1. *Absolute Phrase*

The absolute phrase is said by traditional grammar to function as a grammatically independent linguistic element:

The storm having subsided, they left the shelter.

She did a very good job, *all things considered.*

2. *Interjection Phrase*

When a linguistic unit interrupts, it functions as an interjection. Interjections are also said to be grammatically independent of the rest of a sentence:

Stop crying, *for heaven's sake*.   (Interjected prepositional phrase)

My goodness, I'm sleepy.   (Interjected noun phrase)

VERBAL PHRASES: FUNCTION   EXERCISE 15

Directions: Identify each verbal phrase in the sentences below. Then indicate the type of construction each is. Use the abbreviations shown. If the phrase is Nominal, indicate its function in parentheses after the abbreviation NOM.

PHRASE TYPES OR FORMS   FUNCTION TERMS

NOM for Nominal   SUB for Subject
ADJL for Adjectival   IO for Indirect Object
ADVL for Adverbial   DO for Direct Object
                                 OC for Object Complement
                                 SC for Subject Complement
                                 OP for Object of Preposition
                                 APPOS for Appositive

1. The task, passing the test, was one suited to a genius.

2. It's what's up front that counts.

3. Why don't you try turning off the fan before we all freeze to death?

4. The man walking in front is my friend.

5. We go there to buy fresh vegetables.

6. "Go home," she said to me for the fourth time.

7. He doesn't have a thing to worry about.

8. She liked being the center of attention.

9. The program is designed to involve parents in the teaching of students.

10. The boy carrying the books is late.

11. He came in carrying the books.

12. I hate carrying books.

13. She wrote a composition on cheating in college.

14. To quit now is very foolish.

15. The time to work hard is during your first year.

16. She marched in the parade smiling like an idiot.

17. The boy came in to tell his mother about having seen the accident.

18. The most important thing to accomplish that year was winning the trophy.

PHRASES: FORM AND FUNCTION   EXERCISE 16

Directions: For each italicized phrase, indicate the form classification and the function classification. If a phrase is nominal, indicate the specific function in parentheses.

<table>
<tr><td colspan="2">FORM TERMS</td><td colspan="2">FUNCTION TERMS</td></tr>
<tr><td colspan="2">NP for Noun Phrase</td><td colspan="2">SUB for Subject</td></tr>
<tr><td colspan="2">*VP for Verb Phrase</td><td colspan="2">IO for Indirect Object</td></tr>
<tr><td colspan="2">†PRED P for Predicate Phrase</td><td colspan="2">DO for Direct Object</td></tr>
<tr><td colspan="2">VBL P for Verbal Phrase</td><td colspan="2">OCN for Object Complement</td></tr>
<tr><td colspan="2">ADJ P for Adjective Phrase</td><td colspan="2">SCN for Subject Complement</td></tr>
<tr><td colspan="2">ADV P for Adverb Phrase</td><td colspan="2">OP for Obj of Preposition</td></tr>
<tr><td colspan="2">ABS P for Absolute Phrase</td><td colspan="2">APPOS for Appositive</td></tr>
<tr><td colspan="2">PREP P for Prepositional Phrase</td><td colspan="2">VBL for Verbal*</td></tr>
<tr><td colspan="2"></td><td colspan="2">ADJL for Adjectival</td></tr>
<tr><td colspan="2"></td><td colspan="2">ADVL for Adverbial</td></tr>
</table>

1. She put the book *on the table*.

2. He has had his job, *delivering papers*, for years.

3. The book *on the table* is mine.

4. *Mary's being rude* really bothers me.

5. It is his job *to deliver the papers*.

6. She *spent all evening grading papers*.

7. She spent all evening *grading papers*.

8. He *has been seeing* her for two months.

9. I will do the dishes *in the morning*.

10. I will do the dishes in *the morning*.

11. A pot of gold is *at the end of the rainbow*.

12. A pot *of gold* is at the end of the rainbow.

13. A pot of gold is at the end *of the rainbow*.

14. I know *the girl in the red dress*.

15. The work made her *positively weary*.

16. He *should be arriving very soon*.

*The Verb Phrase always functions in the Verbal role.

†Predicate is actually a function term, but there is no convenient name for the form of a predicate phrase.

17. He ***should be arriving*** very soon.

18. He should be arriving ***very soon***.

19. ***Things being what they are***, I quit.

20. She likes ***to think big***.

21. We found it easy ***to laugh at him***.

22. They stopped ***to listen to the record***.

23. The boy stood on ***the burning deck***.

24. The woman ***kneeling in the garden*** is planting potatoes.

25. John, ***angered by the election results***, vowed never to vote again.

8

Word Groups : Clauses

A clause is a group of related words which contains a subject and a predicate. As with phrases, the internal relationship of the words in this kind of word group are function ones, so we cannot, in the strict sense, distinguish phrases from clauses solely on the basis of the form characteristics of these word groups. Furthermore, it is somewhat doubtful that a person unfamiliar with the whole grammar of English sentences would be able to tell the difference between the independent and the nonindependent (dependent) clause, or among the various kinds of dependent clauses. Yet there are unquestionably a number of formal differences involved.

We can go so far as to claim that it is possible to distinguish between clauses and phrases on formal grounds alone, inasmuch as no phrase will ever contain a finite verb. Beyond that point, however, the lexial meaning of a clause and its function in a sentence must be the criteria of clause classification.

THE INDEPENDENT CLAUSE. An independent clause may stand alone as a complete grammatical sentence. Every sentence, therefore, consists of a minimum of one independent clause. Compound sentences contain two or more independent clauses.

Mary ran.

She ran to the store every afternoon at three o'clock.

She often runs to the store, but *she likes riding better.*

Notice that the independent clause consists of a complete subject (a noun or other nominal plus all modifiers) and a complete predicate phrase (a finite verb plus complements and modifiers).

THE SUBORDINATE CLAUSE (also called *Dependent Clause*). A subordinate clause never stands alone as a complete grammatical sentence. The subordinate clause, like the phrase, is a single unit which functions, in the larger construction of which it is a part, as a nominal, an adjective, or an adverb. Traditional grammar classifies subordinate clauses as follows:

1. *The Nominal Clause.* A nominal clause is a subordinate (dependent) clause which, as an entire unit, functions as a nominal (generally determined by its position). Such a clause is usually an important part of an independent clause: its subject, its object, or the object of a preposition. The following examples illustrate subordinate clauses in various nominal roles. The entire subordinate clause is in boldface; the subject is underlined once, the predicate twice:

That he behaves badly bothers me.   (Subject)

What he said to you sounded rude.   (Subject)

That is **what he answered**.   (Nominal Subject Complement)

We heard **what he said**.   (Direct Object)

It is true **that I am sleepy**.

(This kind of sentence is called an "it" expletive inversion. The expletive "it" makes an inversion of the "normal" word order possible. In this sentence the clause is the delayed subject of the verb.)

Her worry, **that she would be late**, was on her mind.   (Appositive)

(In this sentence, according to traditional grammar analysis, the nominal clause is considered to be grammatically independent of the rest of the sentence.)

2. *The Adjectival Clause.* An adjectival clause is a subordinate clause which, as an entire unit, functions as an adjectival modifier of a noun or nominal. This kind of clause is called a *relative clause,* and the word which introduces the clause (*which, that, who, whom*) is therefore called a relative pronoun. Sometimes the relative pronoun is omitted, but it is always "understood." In the following examples, the entire subordinate clause is in boldface; the subject is underlined once, the predicate twice:

He is the little boy **who was riding the bicycle**.

He is the person **whom I most admire**.

He is the boy **to whom I gave the book**.

He is the boy **whom I called a sissy**.

That is the house **which I lived in as a child**.

He is the boy **whose test I graded**.

He is the person **I most admire**.   (Understood **whom**)

Note: If a relative clause is to be used, a number of usage rules must be observed to insure grammaticality.

A. The relative pronoun must agree in person with its antecedent— the nominal in the main clause for which the relative pronoun substitutes. Thus, if the antecedent is a person or persons, the relative pronoun must be a form of *who* (*who, whom, whose*), or the word *that*.

B. If the antecedent is inanimate the relative pronoun must be a word other than a form of *who*, such as *which, that, where* (meaning "in which.")

C. When a form of *who* is used as the relative pronoun, the form of the word is determined by the function of the pronoun within the subordinate clause (the *case* of the pronoun). If the pronoun is nominal, *who* is the proper form. If it is objective (IO, DO, OCN, OP), the proper form is *whom*. If it is possessive, the form is *whose*.

3. *The Adverbial Clause.* An adverbial clause is a subordinate clause which, as an entire unit, functions as an adverbial modifier of the verb in the independent clause to which the subordinate clause is joined. This kind of subordinate clause has a distinctive formal characteristic: it is introduced by a subordinating conjunction. In the following examples, the entire adverbial clause is in boldface; the subject is underlined once, the predicate twice:

He showered **after he had finished the game**.

After he had finished the game, he showered.

Because he was afraid, he lied to his father.

He cried out **so that someone would come to help him**.

He said that **as if he meant it**.

4. *The Comparative Clause.* A comparative clause is a subordinate clause which, as an entire unit, functions to complete a comparison. Such a comparison is often begun in the main clause with the first of a pair of words such as *so, such, as, so much*: (so _____ that _____; such _____ that _____; as _____ as _____; so much _____ that _____). Most of the traditional texts include this kind of subordinate clause with adverbial clauses, but because it functions in a distinctly different way I prefer to list it separately.

The truck was so long **that it couldn't turn the corner**.

He was as sorry **as he could be**. (The predicate adjective *sorry* is implied here.)

Mary is a better skater **than I** (am).

SUBORDINATE CLAUSES: FUNCTION   EXERCISE 17

Directions: Identify all subordinate clauses in the following sentences. Then indicate the role in which each subordinate clause functions. Use these abbreviations:

NOM for Nominal   ADVL for Adverbial
ADJL for Adjectival   COMP for Comparative

1. The North Haven Fair, which is held every September, is a lot of fun.

2. If I argue with you now I'll be admitting that I am wrong.

3. Occurring as it does when people least expect it, his behavior is rather bizarre.

4. The test was so long that I couldn't finish it.

5. Is that the girl who complains about teachers who fail her when she does no work?

6. He told me he was very sorry.

7. What she wrote in that letter just cannot be repeated.

8. For him to act that way is a sign that he isn't very mature.

9. She is as sorry as she can be.

10. I fear that if you try to help me, you will criticize my slowness.

11. She asked me how many times they tried to call.

12. It's what's up front that counts.

13. He hasn't spoken to anyone since he came home.

14. That's the job he worked at last year.

9

The Sentence

Finally we arrive at the sentence, that grammatically separate linguistic construction so often described in traditional school grammars as "a group of words containing a subject plus a predicate and expressing a complete thought." This definition has been criticized by many modern grammarians, who point out that reliance on so vague a definition would make "Mary having washed the dishes" a complete sentence. Actually, there is nothing wrong with the definition so long as we understand the full intention of "complete thought." (Implicit in the term *predicate*, for example, is that it must consist of a finite verb or verb phrase plus complements and modifiers.)

After giving this very general definition, most school grammars go on to classify English sentences into four types, depending on the number and kind of clauses they contain.

THE SIMPLE SENTENCE. A simple sentence consists of one and only one independent clause and no subordinate clauses. The independent clause may have a single or a compounded subject, a single or compounded verb, and a single or compounded complement. In the following examples the complete subject is italicized, and the complete predicate is in boldface:

John **quit school.**

John and *Harry* **quit school at the end of the first semester.**

John and *Harry* **quit school** and **went to California.**

THE COMPOUND SENTENCE. A compound sentence consists of two or more independent clauses and no subordinate clauses. In the examples which follow, each independent clause is italicized:

76

John quit school, but *Harry continued his studies.*

John quit school; Harry continued his studies.

He came, he saw, and *he conquered.*

THE COMPLEX SENTENCE. A complex sentence consists of one and only one main clause plus one or more subordinate clauses. Notice that in this definition we use the term *main clause* instead of *independent clause.* For although *dependent clause* and *subordinate clause* are synonymous terms which can be used interchangeably, the same is not true for *main clause* and *independent* clause. Main clauses *include* subordinate clauses (as subjects, complements, or modifiers). Thus, the full complex sentence is one entire main clause. In the examples below, independent clauses are italicized, subordinate clauses are in boldface:

After he had finished one semester, *John quit school.*

In traditional grammar, the way **in which a word functions determines** *its part of speech.*

Writing the speech took more time than **I thought it would**.

He always says **what he means**.

THE COMPOUND-COMPLEX SENTENCE. A compound-complex sentence consists of two or more independent clauses, at least one of which is complex. In the examples, independent clauses are italicized, subordinate clauses are in boldface:

The pupils line up **when the bell rings**, and *someone monitors them* **while they go to their classrooms**.

Each independent clause is italicized in the examples **which follow**, and *each subordinate clause is in boldface.*

CLAUSES   **EXERCISE 18**

Directions: Identify all clauses in the sentences below in the following manner: first write out all subject/finite verb combinations that occur in independent clauses; then write out all subject/finite verb combinations that occur in subordinate clauses.

	INDEPENDENT CLAUSE	SUBORDINATE CLAUSE
EXAMPLE: Swimming is something everyone should learn, for not to know how is stupid.	1. Swimming/is 2. not to know how/is	everyone/should learn

1. After the storm stopped, we went to the beach where we had spotted a picnic place earlier.

2. When I ponder my behavior, I really don't know what makes me act as if I have never done this before.

3. A person asks her questions at the risk of betraying one's ignorance about what her driving motives are.

4. Writing the speech took a great deal more time than I had thought it would.

5. Even though he wanted the argument settled, Jay, who had no experience at that kind of thing, decided not to try.

6. He planned to give her a gift, but he was afraid she might refuse it.

7. After having worked for hours, the girls stopped and had a coke.

8. A journal writer's aim is to articulate deeply felt feelings and attitudes.

CLAUSES   **EXERCISE 19**

> *Directions:* Identify all clauses in the sentences below in the following manner: first write out all subject/finite verb combinations that occur in independent clauses; then write out all subject/finite verb combinations that occur in subordinate clauses.

1. Because he was anxious and worried, the distracted old man began calling shrilly for his dog to return.

2. Many young authors start novels about subjects they know nothing about.

3. Unless she apologizes to him, he won't go to her party.

4. Barking at a ringing doorbell is a bad habit which needs correcting in a dog that lives in an apartment.

5. In traditional grammar, how a word functions determines its part of speech.

6. Mr. Brown, who had been made unhappy by his deteriorating health, attempted suicide.

7. For years now the disabled veterans have sent people personalized name stickers which are not solicited.

8. Works which are intended for publication do not need copyrighting before they are distributed for testing.

9. I think that stopping for awhile to drink some water and stretch a bit can make one relaxed and ready to continue work.

10

Connectives

The word *connective* means "that which connects." Methods of showing connections or relationships in English vary widely. They range from such mechanical writing devices as paragraphing, hyphenation, joining words to make compound words, and so on, to such rhetorical techniques as repetition, parallelism, and subordination.

In the earlier section on parts of speech, we identified and illustrated a number of conjunctions:

1. *Coordinating Conjunctions* (*and, but, or, nor, for;* plus the more informal *still, yet, so*)

2. *Correlative Conjunctions* (*either/or; neither/nor; not only/but also*)

3. *Comparative Conjunctions* (*like, as;* and pairs of words: *as/as, more/than*)

4. *Subordinating Conjunctions* (*until, if, because*)

This process of joining or connecting is called *conjunction*.

There is another kind of conjunction (or connective) which we have not yet discussed. This is a special kind of word or expression which serves to show a "meaning" relationship between two sentences (and thus to join them). As was true for subordinating conjunctions, it is impossible to provide a complete list of such words or word groups, which traditional school grammars label variously as "conjunctive adverbs," "connective adverbs," or "transitional adverbs." Here is a partial list: *however, conversely, thus, therefore, nevertheless, consequently, likewise, accordingly, moreover, even so, as a result, additionally, in addition, in sum, in fact, then, furthermore, otherwise.*

These words and expressions are not, of course, invariably used as connective adverbs—as you can observe from these examples, where we would have to call them conjunctions:

He was first one day, *then* second the next. (Coordinating conjunction joining the grammatically equivalent sentence units, "first one day" and "second the next."

However he manages to do it, he is obligated to finish the work. (Subordinating conjunction which joins two unequivalent clauses and which serves to subordinate the clause it precedes.)

Now, however, examine the same words as they are used in these constructions:

First he acted rude to his teacher. *Then* he apologized.
or
First he acted rude to his teacher; *then* he apologized.

He reads much. *However*, he fails to remember what he reads.
or
He reads much; *however*, he fails to remember what he reads.

In these examples the words are used as connectives or transitions between two independent sentences to show some kind of relationship between the two (time, contrast). They are called *connective adverbs*. (Some books use the term "conjunctive adverb," which is misleading since such a word is not a conjunction.) Notice that because they function differently from the way coordinating and subordinating conjunctions function, we punctuate with a period or a semicolon rather than with a comma. Writers who punctuate such sentences with a comma make a punctuation error called the *comma splice* or *comma fault*.

Let us review the differences among coordinating conjunctions, subordinating conjunctions, and connective adverbs—differences important enough to justify classifying these connectives in three separate categories. Both kinds of conjunctions *occupy fixed grammatical positions*: the subordinating conjunction is always the first word (or word group) in a subordinate clause; the coordinating conjunction always occurs *between* equivalent grammatical units—or, in the case of units in a series, between the last two units. The connective adverb, on the other hand, *does not occupy a fixed grammatical position*. It may occur at the beginning, at the end, or, in some cases, in the middle of a sentence. Compare the following sets of sentences, all of which say approximately the same thing:

Coordinating Conjunction

He reads much, *but* he doesn't remember what he reads.

He was late, *so* he decided to cut his class.

Subordinating Conjunction

Although he reads much, he doesn't remember what he reads.

He doesn't remember what he reads, *although* he reads much.

Because he was late, he decided to cut his class.

He decided to cut his class *because* he was late.

Connective Adverb

He reads much. *However*, he doesn't remember what he reads.

He reads much. He doesn't, *however*, remember what he reads.

He reads much. He doesn't remember, *however*, what he reads.

He reads much. He doesn't remember what he reads, *however*.

He was late. *Therefore* he decided to cut his class.

He was late. He *therefore* decided to cut his class.

He was late. He decided, *therefore*, to cut his class.

THE PREPOSITION. Although the preposition is not a connective in the same sense as are conjunctions and connective adverbs, it *is* a word that functions to show a semantic relationship between its object and some other word or words in a sentence. In the following examples, the entire prepositional phrase is italicized, the preposition is underlined, and the OP (object of preposition) is in boldface:

She burned the book *in the* **fire**.

The dish fell *off the* **table**.

I put the lead *in the* **pencil**.

In the first sentence, the object of the preposition, *fire*, is related semantically to the word *book* by the preposition *in*. In the second sentence, the preposition *off* shows a relationship between its object, *table*, and the word *dish*. In the third sentence, the preposition *in* shows a relationship between its object, *pencil*, and the word *lead*. Notice also that in each of these sentences the entire prepositional phrase functions as a verb modifier (burned where? fell where? put where?) The entire phrase is, therefore, an adverbial.

You might have a problem seeing the difference between a preposition and a subordinating conjunction in some sentences. In fact, traditional school grammars are far from agreed on how to classify the words in sentences like these:

1. *Before* leaving, he will write a letter.

2. *After* reading the book, he was exahausted.

3. *When* practicing the piano, she uses a metronome.

Some traditional grammars call *before, after,* and *when* in these sentences prepositions, arguing that the words *leaving, reading the book,* and *practicing the piano* tell *what* after the initial word and that therefore each of these expressions is a gerund phrase functioning as the object of a preposition. This explanation seems insufficient, however, for if it is valid, how are we to explain the phrases in these sentences:

4. *When sad,* Mary goes to a movie.

5. *Although sorry,* John refused to apologize.

Clearly we cannot call *sad* or *sorry* an object of a preposition—if for no other reason than that these words are adjectives while the object of a preposition must be a noun or a nominal. A much better explanation of Sentences 1–5 seems to be that the words *before leaving, after reading the book, when practicing the piano, when sad,* and *although sorry* are reductions of the subordinate clauses *before he leaves, after he read the book, when she practices the piano, when she is sad,* and *although he was sorry.* We shall therefore call words such as *before, after, when,* and *although* in such constructions subordinating conjunctions (of elliptical subordinate clauses, as in clauses of comparison).

Another kind of construction which is difficult to analyze is illustrated in these examples:

He practices the piano *after supper.*

Before school, John mowed the lawn.

A case can be argued for either of two explanations: (1) the words *after supper* and *before school* are adverbial prepositional phrases whose OPs are *supper* and *school,* respectively; (2) these constructions are, rather, elliptical or "reduced" subordinate clauses (*after he eats supper; before he goes to school*) whose subjects and verbs are "understood."

No native speaker has difficulty understanding the meanings of such constructions. The matter of grammatical analysis is, however, quite another thing. The best solution to the dilemma posed by the problem here seems to be to consider either analysis acceptable.

CONNECTIVES   EXERCISE 20

Directions: Identify each italicized expression as one of the following:

CC for Coordinating Conjunction   CA for Connective Adverb
SC for Subordinating Conjunction   PREP for Preposition

1. He spoke often, *but* he seldom said much.

2. He spoke often; *however*, he seldom said much.

3. *Although* he spoke often, he seldom said much.

4. *As* he left the stage, he blew the audience a kiss.

5. He sank to the ground, *for* he was too tired to continue.

6. It was time *for* the game.

7. Time was short, *so* I drove fast.

8. Read the last line first; *then* study the poem.

9. I don't like him now, *nor* will I ever!

10. I drove fast *because* time was short.

11. Time was short. *Therefore* I drove fast.

12. First he gave his report; *afterwards* we asked questions.

13. I found the movie dull *inasmuch as* I had seen it before.

14. I found the movie dull, *for* I had seen it before.

15. I told him goodbye *before* I left.

16. The pay was poor, *but* I worked, for I needed the money.

17. The pay was poor, but I worked, *for* I needed the money.

18. The pay was poor. *Nevertheless*, I worked because I needed the money.

19. The pay was poor. Nevertheless, I worked *because* I needed the money.

20. The suggestion was stupid; *consequently*, we rejected it.

CONNECTIVES   **EXERCISE 21**

> **Directions:** Identify each italicized expression as one of the following:

CC for Coordinating Conjunction   CA for Connective Adverb
SC for Subordinating Conjunction   PREP for Preposition

1. *While* leaving the stage, he blew a kiss to the audience.

2. Jake was arrested *for* speeding.

3. *For* want of a nail the shoe was lost.

4. I said goodbye *before* leaving.

5. He was arrested *because* he was speeding.

6. It was a good course, *although* not the best I have taken.

7. *Although* in pain, he went on stage like a veteran.

8. Although *in* pain, he went on stage like a veteran.

9. Although in pain, he went on stage *like* a veteran.

10. We were really surprised *that* she attended the party.

11. A prepositional phrase has two important elements: a preposition *plus* an object.

12. Give the book to John, Jim, *or* me.

13. *During* intermission I'd like a large orange drink.

14. *After* pondering, he decided that he was wrong.

15. After pondering, he decided *that* he was wrong.

PARTS OF SPEECH, REVISITED   **EXERCISE 22**

> **Directions:** Now that the traditional grammar system has been
> surveyed, try a part-of-speech exercise once more. See if you now find
> parts of speech easier, and if you do, be prepared to explain why you
> think this might be so. Listed below are a number of words, each of
> which can function—in one of its forms—in more than one part-of-
> speech role. See how many functions you can illustrate with each
> word.

1. hard

2. he

3. mother

4. fast

5. hell

6. man

7. paper

8. like

9. well

10. pretty

PART TWO

Comparative Linguistics and American Structural Grammar

11

Historical Background

In the sixteenth century an Italian merchant named Sassetti wrote home in great excitement about a language called Sanskrit which he had discovered in his travels to India. Sanskrit, at that time an exclusively religious and literary language, seemed to Sassetti to contain an astounding number of words which were similar to words in his own native Italian. Moreover, Sassetti discovered from available records that Sanskrit appeared to be at least as old a language as ancient Greek and Latin.

Nothing much came of Sassetti's discoveries at the time. However, events in history have a way of accumulating until they finally demand attention. Such a point came during the late eighteenth and early nineteenth centuries in western Europe. Travel to foreign countries was by then relatively common, and as an inevitable outcome of such widening horizons, scholars began to take note of the vast number of similarities among European vernacular languages. Such "correspondences," as they came to be called, particularly the sound resemblances, struck many observers as too numerous to be merely accidental.

In the 1780s an Englishman, Sir William Jones, contributed invaluable linguistic information. Jones, a government official with the East India Company, had also become fascinated with Sanskrit. He had come across the work of an ancient Indian scholar, Panini, who had written an extremely detailed grammar of Sanskrit sometime during the fifth century B.C.

Like the earliest Greek language scholars, Panini also had devised a word classification system. But instead of classifying words according to their meanings and semantic functions, Panini had analyzed and classified words and word parts into roots, prefixes, and suffixes. As Jones examined

Panini's classifications—particularly the roots—he drew a number of conclusions. First, he became convinced that the enormous number of similarities between the roots of Sanskrit and those of Greek and Latin provided strong evidence that all three of these languages were in some way related. He decided that all three languages had branched off, sometime in the distant past, from the same source, after which each of the three had continued to develop and to change independently. He thought the available evidence suggested that the historical development of these three ancient languages had been parallel. Second, Jones hypothesized that a great many other European and Asian languages probably had histories which could be traced back to the same original parent language. Finally, Jones speculated that whatever that original source language might have been, it had been spoken so far back in history that it no longer existed.

Such speculations aroused the interest of many European language scholars, who began to conduct their own investigations. In 1816 Franz Bopp, a German language scholar who is often called the founder of historical and comparative linguistics, published *Uber das Conjugationssystem*, in which he did two things. First, he reported the results of his own comparative studies of verb inflections in Sanskrit, Greek, Latin, Persian, and several of the European Teutonic (Germanic) languages. Second, he contended that his own results, along with those of other comparative inquiries, furnished convincing support for the theory that not only had all these languages developed simultaneously, although independently, from a single parent language, but that it also was quite possible to recover enough empirical historical linguistic evidence to be able to reconstruct a fairly close approximation of that ancient Indo-European language which had been the source of them all.

Other nineteenth-century developments—ones which were not strictly linguistic—were also influencing European thought. One of the most important of these was the publication in 1859 of Charles Darwin's *On the Origin of Species by Means of Natural Selection*, followed twelve years later by a second book, *The Descent of Man*. In these volumes Darwin argued that humans had evolved, very gradually and over an enormous period of historical time, from more primitive ancestors.

Such developments encouraged scholars to question many long-held beliefs, including traditional theories of the nature and the origin of human language. It had been generally believed that far back in time, "in the beginning," humans had been divinely created and then presented with the gift of language. Although doubts about this theory had been raised periodically by some language scholars, the notion nevertheless persisted that an original, perfect language had once existed, from which, in the long years since, all of the imperfect languages of the world had arisen. Moreover, it had long been accepted that Latin, precisely because it *had* been stopped in its downward path by the conscientious efforts of the Roman grammarians, represented the least corrupted and therefore the "purest" existing language: the "ideal." Now, for the first time, there were compelling reasons for language scholars to question these assumptions. Intrigued, they went out in search of more information.

In the years between the late 1810s and the early 1870s, great numbers of archeologists, anthropologists, paleontologists, and philologists spent time in the field unearthing vast bodies of evidence which ultimately convinced most language scholars that many of the previously incomprehensible mysteries of language could be reasonably accounted for.

Among the conclusions on which comparative language scholars soon reached agreement were the following:

1. It seemed certain beyond reasonable doubt that humans had lived in civilized societies at least as early as six thousand years before the birth of Christ.

2. Enough evidence had been accumulated to convincingly support the theory of related languages, or language "families." English, most of the European languages, and a number of Asiatic languages were all now thought to have developed from a single parent language which linguists called Indo-European.

3. The development of the existing "sister" languages had taken place independently but simultaneously.

4. This development had, furthermore, taken place over a very long period of time.

5. The original Indo-European language had vanished long ago.

6. All existing vernacular languages were *still* changing and developing.

7. Language change is a continuous, open-ended process that never stops so long as a language continues to be a viable spoken tongue.

The methods developed by historical and comparative linguists in their field studies became, over the years, highly meticulous and refined. They developed a rigorously objective scientific approach. The first step, and possibly the most time-consuming one, was to gather masses of data. Once these began to accumulate they began to piece together random bits of empirical circumstantial evidence and to draw some tentative conclusions. Once such tentative conclusions were reached, more data were required to either verify or disprove a theory.

At least three different kinds of linguistic studies were carried out. The greatest number of these were diachronic language investigations: detailed studies of a particular language over a long period of time, or comparative language research over an extended period of historical time. Other scholars (although this approach was relatively rare at the time) concentrated on the careful analysis of a particular language at one specific point in historical time. These latter descriptions are referred to as syn-chronic language studies.

Linguists who concentrated their research on the diachronic study of English sought historical explanations of such language phenomena as the existence of so many regularities in word forms. Then they searched for explanations of how the exceptions or irregularities had come about. They also sought and found explanations for such things as how the English spelling system had come to be so "irrational." Historical explanations were advanced for virtually all of these language peculiarities.

At about this same time other scholars became interested in newly revived speculations about the origin of language, and numerous theories were offered. These theories ranged from the speculation that the first words had been imitations of animal sounds (the "Bow Wow Theory"); to the hypothesis that the first speakers came to imitate not only animal sounds but also other sounds of nature, like the rustling of leaves, the whistling of the wind, and so on (the "Ding Dong Theory"); to the idea that human speech had developed from the sounds humans first made to cheer one another on, once they had progressed sufficiently to engage in shared labor (the "Yo He Ho Theory"). As late as the turn of the last century, the Danish linguist Otto Jespersen suggested that language had originated with song, occasioned by the need to express such feelings as love, rather than by a need for practical communication.

These ludicrous names were not, of course, the labels originally attached to the various language-origin theories by the scholars who invented them. This happened much later, after historical evidence failed to turn up even the faintest clue, and scholars were forced to the reluctant conclusion that no one knew and furthermore that, in all prob-ability, no one ever would or could know how language had originated. It soon became frustratingly evident that human language had existed long before the first language ever acquired an even rudimentary written form. Entirely different kinds of evidence are required to retrace language development beyond the earliest written records.

In conducting their historical and comparative research, linguists found themselves relying heavily on the comparative *sounds* of languages (or at least on the apparent sounds, as could be best determined from spellings). Their methods involved the detailed study of current languages and then a study of older existing records, always working chronologically backwards. It is fascinating to read accounts of the painstaking work of these dedicated linguistic scholars. In collecting their data no material, however apparently unimportant, was ignored. Only after years of field work did they manage to accumulate enough pieces of evidence that they could begin to try putting the puzzle together. And though the picture will never be altogether complete, sometime toward the end of the nineteenth century historical linguists reached general agreement on what certain of the major characteristics of the original Indo-European language had been. Some scholars even claimed that they could pinpoint with some accuracy the central European geographic area where the original Indo-Europeans had lived.

Evidence from the kind of words in the vocabularies of the oldest forms of the language offered proof, scholars thought, that the earliest Indo-European tribes had lived settled, stationary lives. There were, for example, words for *grain*, *storage bins*, and names of domestic animals like *cow* and *pig*. Such words as those for *son, daughter, mother-in-law*, and so on, provided evidence that these people had lived in families. Later it appeared that certain groups, perhaps because the land would no longer sustain the growing tribe, had wandered off in search of new land. Scholars reached this conclusion because of the existence of a word like *salmon*, for example, when it was apparent from other words in the language that a tribe now lived in a geographic area far from where a salmon could ever have been found. Or words like *pig, cow*, and *grain* might still be a part of the vocabulary of a tribe which, from other linguistic evidence, now belonged to a nomadic culture where none of these words would any longer make sense.

Until the end of the nineteenth century European scholars devoted their efforts to this kind of linguistic detective work. Their discoveries, combined with the concomitant discoveries of the archeologists, the anthropologists, and others, served to increase enormously knowledge about the development of ancient human cultures and human languages.

In England, the work of the historical-comparative linguists culminated in the publication of the massive twelve-volume *Oxford English Dictionary*. The dictionary was first planned in 1857, but the actual writing did not begin until scholars had spent twenty years gathering data for the project. Not until 1888, thirty years after the time of its conception, was the first of four volumes published. The final volume of this major effort did not appear until 1928, seventy years after the project had begun. When it was finally completed, it represented the work of a long succession of dedicated editors and scholars, and was the supreme achievement of the English historical linguists.*

The interest of the great majority of nineteenth century linguists in England and Europe was focused on the exciting work in historical and

---

*The first supplement to the *Oxford English Dictionary* appeared in 1933. A second supplement, reproduced micrographically complete with reading glass, was published in 1971, followed by a second printing in 1972, and a third in 1973.

comparative linguistics, with the result that the contributions of philosophical grammarians such as Wilhelm von Humboldt and later Otto Jespersen were largely ignored. In the meantime, the prescriptive grammars of the pedagogues were becoming ever more firmly entrenched in English and American schools.

AMERICAN STRUCTURAL LINGUISTICS

The discoveries of the European historical-comparative linguists were influential both in shedding much light on the understanding of language development and in ridding language scholars of some of their earlier ideas about the nature of language. In addition, their newly developed empirical methods paved the way for new approaches to language study. Perhaps the most significant work which made use of these new field-study methods was that begun by a small group of American anthropologists around the turn of the century.

Having become alarmed at the rapidity with which entire American Indian cultures were vanishing, a number of anthropologists set out to record as much as they could about the still-existent but fast-disappearing primitive cultures before it was too late. When it was realized that almost without exception the languages of these Indian tribes existed in spoken form only, the project took on an added sense of urgency. Since to understand a culture it is crucial to understand its language, the first order of business was to devise means of decoding and recording particular Indian languages. While European scholars had been, for the most part, interested in diachronic language studies, scholars on the American side of the Atlantic found themselves engaged in synchronic investigations of particular languages.

For very different reasons, but driven by the same sense of urgency, another group also became involved in the formidable project of decoding Indian languages and inventing written forms for transcribing as many of them as possible. This second group was composed of missionaries who were bent on bringing Christianity to the heathen Indian tribes, and their work with Indian languages was directed toward translating the Bible into as many tribal languages as they could.

For both of these groups, the Indian tongues soon proved to be so different from any of the languages familiar to them (primarily those of the Indo-European family) that field workers found themselves utterly without guidelines. Many of the language-analysis methods which had proved to be so effective for the European linguists proved almost worthless in this new situation. Assumptions about word and phrase structure seemed simply not to apply. Moreover, it was apparent that not only were the

Indian languages in no way related or in any obvious way similar to those languages which were part of the Indo-European family; but also that most of the several hundred extant Indian tongues did not even bear significant resemblances to each other.* It was necessary, therefore, to start from scratch.

Even before they began their field work, the anthropologists had determined that they would be rigorously scientific in their methods. This meant that they would begin their work with no preconceived notions; that they would gather a large corpus of linguistic data, making every possible attempt to insure that these data were representative of the entire tribe; that they would consider no detail too insignificant or unimportant to record; and that, above all, they would refrain from making subjective judgments or reaching premature and unwarranted conclusions. As it turned out, the unanticipated difficulties presented by the Indian languages practically guaranteed that investigators must proceed with a considerable degree of objectivity. Since no Indian language fit neatly into a preconceived pattern, they were left with no other choice.

Thus, the method of analyzing the sounds of a language, which had proved so valuable as a tool for the historical linguists, became a practical necessity for the American anthropologists. Their method became one of recording hundreds and thousands of sounds, then attempting to distinguish those sound differences which were significant. Only then was it possible to devise a tentative alphabet for transcribing the important sounds of a language.

As much by accident as by design, therefore, the linguistic investigations of the American structuralists came to follow a specific order: first, they must isolate and identify the significant sounds (phonemes) of a language; next, they must determine which particular sound sequences make up the words of the language; last, the structure of the language's sentences must be analyzed and recorded.

These routines, of beginning with the most minimal level and moving up to the next, more inclusive level only after the various -emes† of the lower level had been identified and exhaustively analyzed, came to be called "discovery procedures."‡ One consequence of such procedures was the postponement, almost indefinitely in some cases, of syntactical analysis. (Indeed, it is at this third or highest "level" that structural gram-

---

*They were later found to belong to more than fifty separate language families.
†An -eme (phoneme, morpheme) is an irreducible linguistic unit.
‡It is these very methodological procedures which Chomsky attacks several decades later in his book *Syntactic Structures* (1957). Chomsky argues that by restricting language investigation to surface grammatical structures only, one cannot hope to discover the "really significant," basic, irreducible elements of language.

mar has proved to be at its weakest.) It is not surprising, then, that the most important contributions of structural linguistics were in the areas of phonology (sound structure) and morphology (word structure), particularly in the former. In fact, phonology came to be regarded as the indispensable foundation upon which all of structural grammar analysis rested.

As soon as a number of the Indian languages had been satisfactorily recorded, the structuralists made some fascinating discoveries. For example, certain Indian languages were found to be—or so it seemed—completely without a concept of verb tenses. The natives who spoke these languages must, therefore, have had entirely different concepts of time from those held by Indo-Europeans. Another revelation was the structuralists' discovery that they had been mistaken in the belief that speakers of different languages everywhere, since they were obviously viewing the same world through human eyes, would have synonyms in their languages for the same natural objects and phenomena.*

A by-product of the work of the structuralists was the development of a new understanding of dialects. On hearing two members of an Indian tribe say something differently, how were the field workers to decide which expression was "better" than the other? They were in no position to label one expression more "correct" than another. The best they could do was record their observations of who said what, and to make note of the apparent social status of each speaker.

Not only did structural linguists discover that the least socially prestigious dialects were in no sense linguistically "inferior"; they also found that every dialect in every Indian language, quite apart from the social status of those who spoke it, was a highly structured and complex system with complicated grammar "rules." Their investigations provided no support whatever for the popular belief that primitive languages must be far more simple than the languages of more "civilized" cultures.

In short, the American linguists came to realize that usage practices, while they may have psychological and sociological implications of superiority or inferiority, have no such linguistic significance.

Such discoveries modified attitudes about language usage. Prior to these developments, the prevailing (though by no means unanimous) belief had been that the terms *grammatical* and *ungrammatical* were synonymous with *correct* and *incorrect*. Latin grammar as taught in the schools of Europe, for example, had been one and the same as "correct" Latin usage. Except for a handful of grammarians (like the seventeenth-century

*For a most interesting discussion of some of these language differences, see Benjamin Lee Whorf's piece, "Science and Linguistics," in Harold Allen's reader. Whorf concludes from his field work with Indian languages (Hopi in particular) that language shapes thought rather than it being the other way around.

Port Royalists), few language scholars had stopped to consider that these two were the same for the very reason that Latin had long since ceased to be a living, changing vernacular language, and that its grammar had therefore become "fixed." The structuralists were convinced by their own research that every language and every dialect within a language has its own complex grammar rules, and that the task of the linguist is to discover what these rules are.

STRUCTURAL GRAMMARS OF ENGLISH

After they had succeeded in recording several hundred Indian languages, a number of structural linguists, greatly encouraged by their success and newly dedicated to the methods of structural analysis which they had developed and refined in their field work, turned their attention to writing a structural grammar of English.*

By this time, most of the structuralists had become extremely critical of traditional grammarians. It is hard to say whether they were unaware of the work of such scholarly traditionalists as Humboldt and their contemporary, Otto Jespersen, or whether they included these men too in their criticism. In any case, most of the structuralists expressed the utmost contempt for the methods of traditional grammarians, most of which they labelled "misguided." They attacked traditional grammar as meaning-dependent, subjective, prescriptivist, intuitive—in short, as unscientific.

Determined to make no such mistakes, their goal was to describe English grammar rigorously and objectively. They would confine their descriptions to only the *facts* of English as based on a corpus of actual utterances which could be empirically verified. Above all, they would guard against vague references to semantic meaning—a concept which they condemned as highly abstract and subjective. Rather, they would concentrate exclusively on presenting accurate descriptions of the sound, word, and sentence structure of English.†

*Although structural grammars were begun for a number of European languages as well, our discussion here will be confined to the work of the structuralists in their descriptions of English.

†How well they succeeded at this is open to question. One often concludes, on reading some of their tortuous explanations, that they fooled themselves when they claimed to reject semantics. See for example, Sledd's explanation of the substitution method for determining nominals, verbals, and adjectivals, on pp. 83–94 in his structural text. Or see Chapter 10 in H. A. Gleason's *An Introduction to Descriptive Linguistics*, which discusses synonymous replacement for determining immediate constituent (IC) cuts. Even these methods are apparently not entirely free of at least implicit reference to semantic meaning.

This is not to say that the structuralists denied the meaning-conveying property of language. They simply argued that a language conveys meaning through its sounds and its grammatical structures, and that it would therefore not be valid to show how languages convey meaning by using the very concept one is seeking to explain.*

Let us sum up some of the assumptions and methods of the structural linguists. Fundamental to their approach was the assumption that language is, first and above all, *speech*. For one thing, it was now clear from historical evidence that spoken forms of all languages had considerably predated the invention of written forms. This was dramatically reinforced by the discovery that, practically without exception, all of the American Indian languages that the structuralists had investigated were still spoken languages only. Moreover, every native speaker of a natural language acquires that language in its spoken form first. Above all—and this bears repeating here—the structuralists were determined to describe English objectively. They hoped to describe English as it is spoken, not as they thought it ought to be.

Franz Boas, and later his student Edward Sapir, were the anthropological linguists who established the basic framework. Boas was the first to formally propose that structural analysis should be conducted on three successive levels, beginning with the sound level, proceeding next to word structure analysis, and only then to the analysis of syntax or sentence structure.

Sapir further developed the system proposed by Boas. He was also probably the first to have called attention to the fact that every Indian language studied had proved to have a complicated and highly systematized set of "grammar rules."

Leonard Bloomfield is the linguistic scholar usually considered *the* major developer of twentieth-century structuralism in America, and therefore given the greatest credit for the development of structural grammar theory. First in his *Introduction to the Study of Language* (1914), and later in *Language* (1933), a revised and elaborated version of the earlier book, he presented a detailed outline of the principles of structural language analysis. He stressed particularly the importance of using empirical data only: the grammarian's task was to collect as much language data as possible, then to analyze and classify the data, and then, on the basis of objective evidence alone, to reach conclusions. No value judgments of any kind should have a place in the work of the scientific linguist, nor should anything but hard facts be used as evidence. Although most of the

*Many structuralists of the 1940s and 1950s were apparently satisfied that they had found the answer to how language conveys meaning. Interestingly, this is the very question that Chomsky was later to insist that structuralism's discovery procedures were unable to answer. Most linguists of the 1970s agree that no one can yet answer this question, and that, in fact, it may prove to be unanswerable.

structuralists had used the basic method outlined by Bloomfield, he felt that some had erred by making implicit value judgments, while others had mistakenly included an occasional reference to such ill-defined, abstract concepts as mental processes.

Beyond his role as tone setter, Bloomfield's most important contribution was probably his method of "immediate constituent" analysis. He pointed out that English sentences are expanded, from simple to very complex word sequences, on a binary principle. At any level, from simple to complex, a sentence can be divided into a pair of units (immediate consituents), each of which applies its whole grammatical or structural meaning to the other. This system of syntactical analysis became the structuralists' chief tool at the third, or sentence-structure, level of grammatical analysis.

Another important figure among the structuralists was Charles Fries. In the 1940s, Fries conducted a number of detailed studies of English which he based on actual language usage data. An early analysis was based on material collected from official United States government letters. A later, more important project made use of some 250,000 words collected from approximately fifty hours of recorded telephone conversations among a group of college-educated middle-class citizens in Ann Arbor, Michigan.

Among Fries' important contributions were these: first, he devised a word-classification system based solely on the forms or structures of isolated words.* Second, he listed five structural grammatical devices which serve, in English, to signal grammatical clues. Third, he invented a system of grammatical analysis by means of "test frames." We shall be examining all of these methods in some detail.

As his predecessors had done, Fries also assumed the three levels of structural analysis that had become the basic structural linguistic technique. Fries stressed that in working on any of these three levels, there should be no careless overlapping.

Other structuralists who made important contributions include George L. Trager and Henry Lee Smith, who constructed a phonemic alphabet for English and who were thus instrumental in making possible the structuralists' work in phonology; and many others who made their own important contributions: Nelson Francis, Mary Haas, Archibald Hill, Zellig Harris, Charles Hock, etc. These people and many others worked with great energy and enthusiasm during the forties and fifties and beyond. Many of them are still very much in the linguistic picture, continuing to make important contributions to the study of language.

*This is the structural classification system which was used by James Sledd in *A Short Introduction to English Grammar* (1959), and which is presented later in this book, with the important exception that Fries rejected such traditional terminology as *Noun, Pronoun, Verb,* and so on, in favor of *Class I, Class II, Class III,* and so on.

Some Contributions of the Structural Linguists

DIALECT STUDY. One of the most important branches of linguistics which was stimulated by structuralism is in the field of dialectology. In 1930, a group of American structuralists began work on *The Linguistic Atlas of New England*. That particular volume was published, in parts, from 1939 until its completion in 1943. At that time, four additional regional dialect surveys got underway: one for the Middle and Southern Atlantic states; one for the North Central states (Wisconsin, Michigan, the Ohio Valley); one for the Upper Midwestern states (Iowa, Nebraska, the Dakotas); and one for the Pacific Southwest (Nevada and California). Most of these have by now been completed. In addition, field work for still other regions is either already completed or underway. The ultimate goal is a complete *Linguistic Atlas of the United States*.

In collecting data for these dialect surveys, field workers armed with tape recorders collect speech samples from at least three levels of usage; they are careful to include both rural and urban variations, and in urban areas, they include the speech of minority groups as well as samples from the middle and upper-middle levels of society. All of these recorded data are subsequently analyzed, and phonetic transcriptions of the speech variations are devised.

One of the most significant benefits of this research into dialects has been a new attitude which it has engendered, especially among school teachers. While minority dialects had for years been looked down on as "inferior," the current view is that no dialect variation is linguistically better or worse than another. The simple recognition that every dialect is based on a grammar system—often a complicated one—of its own has already enabled a great many English teachers to respond more usefully to the language problems of minority students who need to learn the prestige dialect of the middle-class, educated white majority if they are to have social mobility. Enlightened English teachers no longer disparage minority dialects. Nor do they demand that students abandon their native dialects (which, after all, will ordinarily continue to be useful and vital to them). Rather, English teachers are increasingly adopting the much more sensible approach of teaching "standard English" in much the same way that one would teach a second language to a foreign student. Certainly this change in attitude is a great step forward, and we have the dedication of a great many structural linguists to thank for it.

THE TEACHING OF FOREIGN LANGUAGES. Structural linguistics has also affected the teaching of second languages. Particularly impressive were the results achieved by those structuralists who, during the period of World War II, devised effective new methods for teaching second languages to adults. Once again there was an urgent timetable—which seems to have been the trademark of structural linguistics. It became necessary to teach the languages of the occupied countries as thoroughly and efficiently as possible in the shortest possible time. Among those who achieved notable success in this area, the name of Charles Fries especially stands out, the methods of second-language teaching he developed having since been widely adopted by foreign language teachers in America's public schools and universities.

DICTIONARIES AND USAGE LABELS. Another practical consequence of the work of the structuralists was its effect on the makers of dictionaries. Arguing that it is the lexicographers' job merely to record existing usage practices as honestly and as accurately as possible rather than to act as linguistic policemen and moralists, the structuralists insisted that dictionary makers should be languages historians, not legislators. Such views were at first considered "heretical," but they eventually took hold. In 1961, the now famous (although infamous at the time of its publication) *Unab-* 1961 *ridged Webster's Third International Dictionary* was published by the Merriam Webster Company.

If you want to have some fun, go back to the year 1961 and the couple of years following and read some of the outraged reactions to the publication of Webster's Third. Protests appeared almost everywhere: in a good many professional journals, in newspaper editorials, and in magazine articles. The structuralists who had been responsible for this "outrage" were accused of advocating the kind of language anarchy that was sure to ruin the English language, of championing an indecent "anything goes" attitude toward proper English usage, of offending good taste, and even of subverting the morals of young people. How, asked the critics, could a dictionary be guilty of so irresponsible and unprincipled an act as including a word like *ain't* among its entries?

This entire commotion seems rather funny to us today.* You probably have on your desk one of the recently published collegiate dictionaries, most of which contain words a good deal more controversial than *ain't*.†

---

*A good collection of essays, editorials, and reviews, which includes both condemnations and defenses of Webster's Third International, can be found in Gorrell, Laird, and Freeman's *Modern English Reader*.

For an earlier but similar reaction, see Benjamin Franklin's letter of 1789 to Noah Webster, reprinted in Clark, Cox, and Craig's *About Language*, p. 218. Franklin urges the lexicographer to stand guard against improper language practices. Franklin's comments about the disgraceful recent deterioration of English, and especially his examples (many of which have formal status today), offer useful insights into language change.

†*The American Heritage Dictionary*, for example, contains most of the "four-letter" words currently in use. So does the most recent edition of the scholarly *Oxford English Dictionary*. In fact, many of these words have a long and interesting etymological history.

No word is excluded from today's dictionaries on the grounds that it is inappropriate, in poor taste, or even offensive at certain levels of usage. The new dictionaries do, of course, label the various usage levels of words or of some definitions of words; but the only criterion for inclusion is that a word be one which is actually used by a significant number of speakers or writers of English. Above all, lexicographers define words according to what they actually mean to their users, not according to how they might prefer that a word be used or according to what they believes its "true" meaning to be.

Structural Grammar in American Public Schools

For several decades, structural linguists wrote only professional articles and monographs addressed to other linguists. Beginning in the late 1950s and early 1960s, however, a number of somewhat watered-down structural grammars were published for use in the schools.* Very often, such books appeared as part of an elementary-through-high-school "linguistic series." Most of them are a kind of hodgepodge which contain some traditional grammar, some structural grammar, and—most recently —some transformational grammar.†

Nevertheless, structural grammar has made a sizable impact on even these traditional grammars. Most current authors of dictionaries and usage handbooks have either softened their "pronouncements" or have ceased altogether to make statements about the "rights" and "wrongs" of language. There has been a gradual but steady shift towards a more open and realistic approach to usage practices. Good English teachers today urge their students to use the kind of language which is appropriate to and suitable for the occasion at hand, recognizing that the sort of language which is right for one situation may well be unsuitable for another.

Some structuralists, carried away by their own enthusiasm, took extreme positions that they could not support. Yet, despite the equally extreme accusations of some of their critics, very few responsible structural

*Probably the historic "first" of these books was *Patterns of English* (1956), a high school text by Paul Roberts, which presented a lucid explanation of the immediate constituent approach. One of the most prolific writers of grammar textbooks in modern times, Roberts had already published *Understanding Grammar* (1954) while he was still a traditionalist. In the eleven years which followed the appearance of *Patterns* Roberts wrote at least four more major grammar books for high school and freshman college level students. He also put together one of the first linguistics series. Beginning in the early sixties, Roberts' texts incorporated much of the thinking of early transformational grammar.

†My own gness is that the majority of American schools are still using predominantly traditional grammar texts. I base this conclusion on the experience of my own three children and on that of the students in my grammar classes.

linguists ever did or ever would have suggested that it "doesn't matter" what kind of English a person uses. They simply urged language users and teachers to recognize the linguistic facts of life. Skillful use of language has always involved "good taste"—by which is meant the recognition of what is appropriate, including the deliberate use of "bad taste" when a particular effect is desired or when a particular occasion warrants it. Except for a few die-hards, the most hostile critics have either lowered their voices or faded away.

For nearly three decades, the structural linguists were in the forefront of language studies. During this same period, in fact, the methods of empirical science which had originated with the nineteenth-century comparativists extended to many other disciplines as well. Sociology, anthropology, psychology, and political science, as well as linguistics, came to be referred to by many scholars as behavioral "sciences." Many structural linguists entertained the heady hope—for some the certainty— that just around the corner was the time when they would be able to program a computer with exactly the right kind of "hard" language data that would result in a language-producing machine. They also spoke enthusiastically of programming computers to do machine translations.

To be sure, there were some dissenters. But for the most part, their voices were either unheard or ignored. The methods of the empirical behavioral sciences, along with their staunch antimentalism, dominated the American intellectual scene for almost thirty years.

12

The Grammar System

The structural description of English begins with an analysis of the sounds of the language in general, and then goes on to isolate mutually exclusive groups of sounds which have semantic significance, the phonemes. From there, the grammar description proceeds to the next highest level, the word structure (morphology) of English, which involves the isolation of the smallest meaning-bearing units, the morphemes, which make up the words of the language. Finally, structural grammar analyzes the phrase structure, or syntax, of English. At this level, the grammarian looks for the various ways in which words can be combined to produce grammatical English sentences.

One of the first things that a structural description of English revealed is that English is not a highly inflected language, as are Latin and many contemporary European languages. Indeed, many of our words do not take inflectional endings at all. It was immediately obvious to the structuralists, therefore, that the traditional method of patterning English grammars after Latin models had produced gross distortions. Such distortions showed up in two ways: (1) English grammar descriptions had frequently been based on rules which simply do not apply; and (2) many of the characteristic and grammatically significant linguistic signals of English had been ignored.

As you study the following pages, you may find it difficult to eliminate semantic considerations from your thinking. Particularly for the native speaker of a language, the "meaning" of sentences is so inextricably tied to their grammar that it is often hard to sort out which is which.

The structuralists themselves, as you will discover, had the same kind of difficulty despite their best intentions. Perhaps you will find it easier to achieve an objective, scientific attitude if you think of yourself as a Martian who is hearing spoken English for the first time, who does not have the vaguest notion what any of the words or sentences mean.

What Does the Structuralist Mean by the Term GRAMMATICAL? When the structuralist speaks of a sentence as "grammatical" or "ungrammatical," he runs the risk of being seriously misunderstood by the non-linguist. Although a good many people probably mean "correct" or "good" or "proper" English when they use the term "grammatical," and "incorrect" or "inferior" or "uneducated" when they call an expression "ungrammatical," a linguist means something quite different by these terms. For a linguist to state that an English expression is "grammatical" means only that it is the kind of English you might expect to hear from a native speaker—no matter at what social level or in which native dialect. An "ungrammatical" expression, by contrast, is one which you would never expect to hear a native speaker utter, regardless of geographical location or level of education.

In other words, there are certain characteristic structural patterns which are typical of English and others which are not. Given a list of nonsense words, for instance, native speakers will agree that, even though they have never before encountered such words, some of them *sound like* English and others do not. Consider these "words," for example. Which ones *could* be English? Which *could not*?

1. reldue	4. hedroger	7. nglot
2. barsk	5. erlude	8. htiw
3. skrote	6. csakz	9. lkagen

Some of these may actually be words in another language, but certainly none of them are English words. The point is this, however. The first five *could* be English words; the last four could not conceivably be. As a native speaker, you simply "know" that the sound combinations in these last four examples are not possible in English. This suggests that there are rules which determine the sound structure of English words. The structuralist is interested in discovering the grammar rules which determine acceptable sound combinations and in ruling out other possibilities.

Similarly, when we look beyond word structure and consider English phrase structure instead, we discover that certain word combinations *are* grammatically possible but that others *are not*. That is, quite apart from their meanings, strings of words can be judged as either grammatical or ungrammatical English structures. Considering only structure, not meaning, which of the following sentences do you reject as sentences that would never be uttered by a mature native speaker, regardless of education?

1. He took a cruise to the islands.

2. I no washed my hairs today.

3. She pocketed the cash and ducked the hell out of there.

4. It is to have sorry from that story.

5. My mommy telled me that was a no-no.

6. The boy he have encounter the sharp of the table.

7. She should've went home right off.

8. Time passed from day by day and closed to big day.

9. I'd like to see that word die out altogether.

10. Thirty days liked thirty years to me.

Except for Sentence 5, the odd-numbered sentences are all ones that might be spoken by a mature native speaker. (Sentence 5 sounds like the sentence of a little child who has not yet mastered the grammar structure of English.) The even-numbered sentences, on the other hand, are "ungrammatical" in the sense that they do not conform to the grammar rules of English syntax. Although these deviant sentences may actually communicate their meaning to you, they do not sound like sentences a native speaker would utter.* Most native English speakers are able to make sense of the even-numbered sentences only because in processing them we interpret them as the nearest well-formed sentence.

As for those sentences which qualify as "English," the structuralist would not call them "ungrammatical," for they *do* conform to the basic rules of English syntax. (The linguist would be the last to certify all of these "grammatical" English sentences as acceptable formal usage, however. He simply distinguishes between levels of usage on the one hand and grammaticality on the other.)

If, instead of a sentence like "He should've went home right off," a native speaker were to see a random string of English words, such as "For pencil a the pen a use test not," he would automatically reject the string of words as a nonsentence. There is simply no way to interpret such a string, for it doesn't even come close to resembling English syntax.

---

*Sentences 2, 4, 6, 8, and 10 are actual sentences from non-native speakers and writers. Sentences 4, 6, 8, and 10 were taken from writing samples required of all foreign-student applicants to the graduate school at Southern Connecticut State College.

This discussion of what is grammatical and what is ungrammatical may remind you of those marvelously ungrammatical directions which so often accompany products manufactured in foreign countries. Most of you are probably familiar with those little birds that bob back and forth, dipping their beaks in water with each forward bob. Here is a set of directions which came with such a bird made in Japan:

1. Firstly, set down BIRD'S head completely into the water for get wet.

2. Balance BIRD'S by inserting the cross piece in the two slots provided in the stand. The cross piece does not be adjusted or bent.

3. Water in glass must be changed once a day with cold water, and Keep glass filled every time. Body of thei BIRD'S is a precision instrument, so please carry on carefully.

4. BIRD'S is move more smoothly put the place of warm and well-ventilation, but do not set it near signs of fire. The contents is Not-Inflamable, but if the high heat is touched, then the pressure of contents are going up, so please take care of above caution.

NONSENSE SENTENCES   **EXERCISE 23**

Directions: Determine the part-of-speech function of each italicized word. (Some of them are legitimate English words, some are not.) Without access to semantic considerations, on what do you base your judgments? What grammar clues are you using?

Berkling	*at*	the	*groobles,*	the	*whutful*	*glinns*	*katingly*	*groved*
1	2		3		4	5	6	7

a	*funkel*	*and*	a	*beegled*	*hortion,*	*chomed*	an	*arat,*	and	*wabed*
	8	9		10	11	12		13		14

the	*blarb*	*in.*
	15	16

The	*boral*	*shlumps*	*takidly*	*garfed*	the	*flans,*	*and*	*then,*	*despite*
	1	2	3	4		5	6	7	8

a	*fragly*	*kation,*	the	*blick*	*in*	the	*gorb*	*froked*	*out*	*morably.*
	9	10		11	12		13	14	15	16

After the *sloopiest* *wamtokers* had *evotably* *loofed* at the *crambet,*
 1   2   3   4   5   6

the *rallopatches* *that* had been *gibbering* the *barbles* *skomed* their
         7   8   9   10   11

blibbles *up* and *scorked* *in* *over* the *groote.*
   12   13   14   15   16   17

Why do these sentences sound like English? Do you realize that a person could diagram them? It looks as if, all along, you have been using a good deal more of your knowledge of English to determine parts of speech than traditional grammar's semantic part-of-speech definition would lead you to believe, doesn't it?

ARTIFICIAL LANGUAGE*   EXERCISE 24

Directions: This is a test to determine how rapidly and accurately you can infer and assimilate the vocabulary and grammar of an artificial language.

Study the words, sentences, and pictures below. You will notice that some of the words change slightly depending on their grammatical functions within the sentences. Try to determine the meanings of the words and the syntactic meanings of the word changes.

kon rolim   na tacket   na yox

kon rolie   ka clarie

Kon rolima
gufiles na yogid.

Ka oza gufiles
na yoxid.

Kon rolima trafes
na tacketid.

Kon roliea trafes
na wobetid.

The following questions are based on the grammar and vocabulary you
have just learned. Choose the response which best fills the blank for each
expression. You are encouraged to look back at the pictures as often as
necessary.

na _____
  (A) wobet
  (B) gufiles
  (C) rolim
  (D) tacket

Ka _____ trafes na platid.
  (A) rolima
  (B) yoga
  (C) roliea
  (D) clariea

Kon roliea _____ na wobetid.
  (A) gufiles
  (B) trafes
  (C) clarie
  (D) rolim

ka _____
  (A) clariea
  (B) clarid
  (C) clarim
  (D) clarit

Kon rolima talipes na _____.
  (A) regnan
  (B) ardid
  (C) omatin
  (D) erma

Kon roliea _____ na tacketid.
  (A) protie
  (B) cadim
  (C) sones
  (D) gustid

THE SYSTEM OF LANGUAGE

How does a language do what it does? Specifically, how does a language enable people to communicate with one another? We are obviously not talking about the primitive communication animals are capable of through their grunts, cries, and various forms of physical behavior. People use such means too, as recent studies of "body language" demonstrate. But we are speaking here about the kind of human communication made possible by language—communication which is intricate and complex and involves a great deal more than merely responding to physical stimuli, which can be done through physical gestures like smiling, frowning, grimacing, or shoulder shrugging.

First of all, a language must be a system which is agreed upon by all members of a particular speech community, since everyone has to use the same set of signals. Second, a language must contain grammar rules —devices for signaling meaning and meaningful relationships.

The first language device we are likely to think of is vocabulary, since words are the carriers of meaning in every known human language. Thus, it is clearly important for speakers to learn what the words of their language "mean," in the semantic or dictionary sense of the word. But apart from vocabulary, a language must have a system for putting its words together in meaningful relationships. This is the role of a grammar, and it is what the structuralist refers to as "grammatical meaning." Here are just a few of the functions which the grammar of a language performs:

1. *Nominalization:* a method of indicating names for objects and ideas; also, a means of changing a non-naming structure to a naming one

2. *Predication:* a method of making an assertion or an affirmation

3. *Modification:* a means of associating particular qualities, limitations, or qualifications with a particular word or idea

4. *Subordination:* a method of showing the relative importance of ideas of unequal significance

5. *Coordination:* a method of showing that certain words or ideas are of equal importance

6. *Complementation:* a means of completing a construction begun by a verb

The list could go on, but the point is made. All of these functions, and many more, such as indicating a relationship between subject and verb, verb and object, are performed by the grammar of a language.

As structuralists investigated the grammar of one language after another, they concluded that every one of them makes use of a system of grammatical devices—signals which serve to alert the listener to grammatical functions. Even though much the same kinds of grammatical relationships are thought to exist in every language, the particular surface structure forms for accomplishing these functions vary widely, even among members of the same language family. Indeed, such evidence tended to verify what the structuralists had long argued: that it makes little sense to describe one language (English) according to the unique grammar system of another language (Latin). Every language makes use of its own set of signaling devices.

Another interesting discovery is that every language so far studied has a great profusion of grammatical signals. Some tongues make extensive use of word inflections, others rely primarily on tonality, and still others depend on word order. Regardless of the primary kind of signal or signals, however, every known language has been found to use many more of them than seem absolutely necessary. The linguist refers to this grammar characteristic as *redundancy.* As an example, consider this English sentence:

A man was there.

How do you know that the sentence refers to only one man? English grammar provides at least three different clues. First of all, the word *man* has the singular inflection. Second, the determiner, *a*, signals "singular." (No English speaker would say "a men.") Third, as if to insure that there be no mistake, the English grammar system adds yet another signal: the verb form is third person, singular. That is, *was* "agrees" with *man*. (Linguists call this kind of agreement between different elements *concord*.)

Here is another example.

The singers were gathered in the hall.

How do you know that the word *singers* is a *nominal* (i.e., it functions as a noun or "naming" word), and furthermore that it is *plural* and the *subject* of the sentence? There are at least five different grammatical signals that provide this information: (1) the inflectional *-s* ending signals "plural noun"; (2) the derivational *-er* ending is one that speakers of English know can be a "noun ending"; (3) the determiner *the* signals "a noun is coming"; (4) the plural verb inflection, *were*, signals "subject-verb agreement"; (5) word order signals grammatical relationships to the speaker of English, whose expectation is that the noun subject usually precedes the verb form. All of these grammatical signals, some of them redundant, are crucial to the English grammar system. And we haven't even mentioned a sixth signal, *intonation*, which is so "built in" to the grammatical understanding of English speakers that we are probably unaware of its importance. Yet, if you will just try saying several noun phrases out loud, you will discover that there is an undeniable intonation pattern: the noun or nominal headword invariably receives the strongest stress.

At first glance, it may strike you that there is an overproliferation of grammar signals, and in fact, it has been postulated that this is a "flaw" in most languages, the explanation for which is that all languages are changing continuously. During this evolutionary process, the argument goes, new signals will appear, but the old signals may or may not be dropped. When they are not dropped, the grammar of a language contains superfluous signals.

It has even been suggested that this "overabundance" of grammatical signals has to do with the psychology of change: that most people tend to resist the new, so that even when a new system is an established fact of a grammar system, there are those who continue to follow the older pattern.

Some of this reasoning may be valid. We know, for example, that certain English verb inflections, such as the third person singular form and the eight different forms of *be*, are probably "hold overs" from Old English, which was a highly inflected language. Most of the inflectional signals of Old English have been dropped, and word order (sentence position) has instead become the overridingly important grammatical signal in modern English; yet, for some reason the "unnecessary" inflectional signals have in certain cases been retained.

On the other hand, we may simply have learned English at some point in the middle of this evolutionary cycle. Certain English dialects have already gotten rid of the third person singular verb inflection, as can be seen by comparing the standard version with an English dialect version:

STANDARD ENGLISH	DIALECT
I have	I have
you have	you have
he *has*	he *have*

In the standard version, we are provided with two signals that the subject is singular. In the dialect, one signal is considered sufficient.

Still another example of overabundant signals may be illustrated in these examples:

STANDARD ENGLISH	DIALECT
I have a dog.	I have a dog.
I have *three* dog*s*.	I have *three* dog.

Two signals are given in the standard version to indicate that *dog* is plural. In the dialect version, on the other hand, the word *three* already indicates "more than one"; thus, the plural inflection on *dog* is unnecessary.

Although resistance to change may be responsible for some of this redundancy, sound experts have recently offered another explanation for this universal linguistic phenomenon. Controlled audio experiments involving both a sender and a receiver have produced evidence that when a grammatical signal is given only once—or sometimes even twice—rather than over and over again, the receiver who is in less than an ideal listening environment often misses the signal and thus either loses or misinterprets the message. In an ideal environment, a profusion of signals would not be necessary, but listening environments are seldom ideal. More often our concentration is disrupted by noises, interruptions, and other distractions. Thus, signal redundancy insures that the message will "get through." It seems that "too many" signals may serve a purpose after all.

ENGLISH GRAMMATICAL SIGNAL DEVICES. If you will now turn back to the nonsense sentences of Exercise 23, you can perhaps better understand how it was that you knew so much about the functions of meaningless words. Most native speakers of English would have no difficulty at all determining which of these words are nouns, which are verbs, which are adjectives, and so on. This is because people who have learned a language are thoroughly familiar, however unconsciously, with the grammatical rules of that language.

Structuralists have determined that English grammar makes use of five essential signaling devices:

1. *Inflectional Endings or Word Forms.* Although English has not retained many of these, those which remain enable the speaker to distinguish between *singular* and *plural*; *verb tenses*; *positive*, *comparative*, and *superlative* adjective forms; and occasionally, as is true for personal pronouns, between *subject* and *object*.

2. *Derivational Endings.* We can change the "class" of many English words by using typical noun endings, verb endings, adjective endings, and so forth. Thus, such word endings in the nonsense sentences as *-tion*, and *-er* signaled "possible nominal"; *-ful* and *-ly* signaled "possible adjective"; *-ly*, on the other hand, also signaled "possible adverb." Often, of course, derivational endings do not provide sufficient information, and must be used in combination with other grammatical signals.

3. *Structure Words.* In our relatively uninflected language, such words as *a, an,* and *the* (noun determiners); *very,* and *quite* (qualifiers which occur before adjectives and adverbs); *must, may, shall,* and so on, (auxiliary words that tell us a main verb is coming); and *of, for,* and *with* (prepositions which signal a nominal is coming) all function as important grammatical devices. Indeed, you probably found yourself depending on words like these as much as on any other signal in determining the grammatical function of words in the nonsense sentences.

4. *Intonation.* If you doubt the importance of intonation signals, try asking any native speaker to read the nonsense sentences aloud. Then, if you can find a non-native, and compare the two readings, you are probably in for a surprise.

5. *Word Order or Sentence Position.* Probably the most important signaling device in English grammar is word order. Indeed, you probably used the position of a nonsense word to verify the suspicion created by another grammar signal or to discount it. In the second example, for instance, the "words" *takidly, fragly,* and *morably* all have *-ly* endings. Though you may have suspected "adverb," it is also possible that these words might have been nouns (*bully, jelly*) or adjectives (*chilly, friendly*). Your knowledge of English word order, however, probably insured the proper classification of these words. Knowing their semantic meanings would, of course, have helped, for there is still a chance that you

might have interpreted the phrase *"The boral shlumps takidly garfed* the flans" as Determiner + adjective + noun adjunct + noun + verb, though this would be complicated by the *-s* ending on *shlumps*. With the other two words, there can be no question once you observe their positions:

a *fragly* kation (between an article and a noun)

and

froked out *morably* (proximity to a verb, plus its position *away from* a determiner, a preposition, or even a noun)

The fact is that we make use of all of these signals, and we probably need them all.

GRAMMATICAL SIGNALS   EXERCISE 25

Directions: Although every signaling device is almost always used in combination with others, one principal device is used in differentiating the following pairs. Indicate which one (or ones).

1. Bathing women are interesting.

   Bathing women is interesting.

2. My boy friend watches fences.

   My boy friend fences watches.

3. She is a lighthouse keeper.

   She is a light housekeeper.

4. Jane looked stupid.

   Jane looked stupidly.

5. She deserted the frightened people.

   She frightened the deserted people.

6. Anthony is the best student.

   Anthony is *the* best student.

7. The pretty girl is young.

   The girl is pretty young.

8. The poor man was hung.

   The poor man was hungry.

9. We consider your answer final.

   We consider your answer fine, Al.

10. We cooked the meal in a pan.

    We cooked the meal in a panic.

11. Either Mary did it, or Elsie did.

    Either Mary did it, or else he did.

12. He's always charming to the ladies.

    He's always charming the ladies.

13. He has pants.

    He has panted.

14. We ought to note his answer.

    We ought to answer his note.

15. The crew has orders to light up the turn.

    The crew has orders to turn up the light.

16. The extension cord was short.

    The extension cord was shorting.

17. His problem is age.

    His problem is aging.

18. He was unable to place the name.

    He was unable to name the place.

19. He seems to be hoarse.

    He seems to be a horse.

20. Who ate all the tuna fish?

    Who ate, all the tuna fish?

21. His job is to ticket the merchandise.

    His job is to merchandise the ticket.

22. She did a white wash.

    She did a whitewash.

23. He enjoys dancing women.

    He enjoys dancing with women.

24. Those boys love challenge.

    Those boys challenge love.

25. The photography class will film the exhibit.

    The photography class will exhibit the film.

GRAMMATICAL SIGNALS   EXERCISE 26

Directions: Sentences can be ambiguous for a number of reasons. All of the sentences in this exercise are ambiguous. In some cases, the ambiguity results from the inclusion of too few grammatical signals— a common problem with newspaper headlines, telegrams, and the like. In other cases, a sentence is ambiguous for some other reason. See if you can discover why each of these sentences is ambiguous:

1. They have written invitations.
2. Martha had frosted cakes for her party.
3. Did you see the French fry?
4. Mike Roy has a cooking thing.
5. The senator was outraged to learn that the rioting students were stoned.
6. That food is for the birds.
7. She hates frying chicken.
8. The answer called for needed study.
9. He sensed after certain words that he heard a trace of a foreign accent.
10. He printed precisely to prevent misreading.

STRUCTURAL GRAMMAR DESCRIPTION

Their work with unfamiliar Indian languages had convinced the structuralists of the primary importance of *spoken* utterances. Of course, there was no alternative in that situation, but the success they achieved made them conclude that even for a language with a well-developed written form, the only logical place to begin a language description was with the sounds of that language.

When they set out to write a structural description of English, therefore, they determined to proceed in the same way as they had with the Indian languages, by collecting a large body of actual utterances. (Such a collection is known to the linguist as a *corpus*.) Only later would these utterances be subjected to analysis.

The problem, however, is that just any corpus will not do. What is needed is an *adequate sample* which will be, among other things, typical and characteristic of the language as a whole. It is important, therefore, to have good sampling techniques. This requires that even before planning a sample, the linguist must have some idea of what constitutes a sentence and of what is considered grammatical and ungrammatical by native speakers.

Once a sound preliminary analysis has been made, the linguist can go into the field to begin collecting the sample (or, more probably, several samples as a kind of insurance against error). The entire project can break down right here, however, unless field workers are very skilled in the art of good sampling and very alert. They must constantly guard against bias and distortion, either one of which can creep in in a number of ways. First, they must be scrupulously on guard against their own prejudices, for it is crucial that field workers be as objective as possible. Next, they must be alert when working with informants. They should plan their sampling in such a way that informant bias is ruled out, and should be aware that their very presence is quite likely to affect the results and can easily lead to distortions. Distortions can also be produced by the subject about which an informant is being interviewed, so it is good practice to obtain utterances over a wide range of topics. It takes great skill and much patience on the part of the field workers to meet all of these requirements. Failure at this vital initial stage of a language investigation will produce very unscientific results.

Another problem is that of deciding how large a sample and how many different samples are required. The structuralists' aim is to collect a corpus which is truly representative of the sentences in a language. Yet, they cannot possibly collect enough sentences to cover every possible sentence pattern, for each speaker can create an infinite number of sentences, every one of which is made up of a number of smaller constructions (or parts) strung together in a variety of patterns. The linguists' concern is to be sure that their samples contain an adequate number of these smaller constructions. Otherwise, the samples will be unrepresentative and distorted. Skilled field workers can probably accumulate an adequate sample if they collect around one thousand utterances spoken by many informants at all levels of society. The number of sentences cannot be arbitrarily set at a thousand, however, because much depends on the size of a language community and on the homogeneity of its members.

In the process of data collecting, researchers must constantly double check with their informants to be sure that the sentences included in the corpus really belong there. An informant's rejection of an utterance does not necessarily mean, however, that it should be ruled out, for an informant may reject a sentence for a number of reasons. If, therefore, the researcher is told by an informant, "We don't say that" or "We wouldn't say that," these responses must be interpreted cautiously. Consider these English sentences, for example, any one of which might elicit one of the above responses from an informant:

1. People in America eat their children.

2. There is no God.

3. He took a cruise to the cleaners.

4. The vague dogwood burns ice grandly.

5. That noogle on the haspit garps my wote.

6. Jesus Christ, that bastard really screwed me!

Sentence 1 might be rejected because it isn't true; Sentence 2 because the informant does not believe there is no God. Sentences 3 and 4, on the other hand, might be rejected because they are semantically inappropriate; and sentence 5 because it is nonsensical. Sentence 6 might easily be rejected because the use of such words is taboo to a particular informant. Yet structuralists would not rule out any of these sentences, because grammaticality is different from truth value, belief structure, or notions of propriety. What they are looking for is how the grammatical sentences of a language are put together: the structural characteristics of utterances, quite apart from any of these other considerations.

As you can see, then, the anthropologists who investigated indigenous American Indian languages must have encountered many difficulties in this first phase, and interviewers had to be extremely skillful to collect valid data.

Many, though not all, of the same problems had to be dealt with once the structuralists began to apply their language description methods to the task of writing a structural description of English. Because they had the advantage of being already thoroughly familiar with the language, they could guard against certain pitfalls. But knowing the language also had its disadvantages: they had to be doubly vigilant against permitting any of their own language habits and prejudices to influence the scientific validity of their work.

Once an adequate corpus has been collected, the next step is to analyze the data properly. At every stage of the work, the conclusions are tentative, and must be tested and re-tested. Investigators must be prepared to go back to an earlier stage if new evidence turns up to suggest that more information is needed or that an earlier conclusion was wrong.

The most useful structural description of a language must analyze that language's structure at all levels: sound structure, word structure, and phrase structure. Although these three levels are interdependent when a language is considered as a whole, each is also independent of the others in the sense that it is distinguishable and can be described in its own terms.

Structural linguists came to view these levels as hierarchical. That is, they started at the lowest level, sound structure or phonology, and systematically worked their way up the hierarchy. Of course, as Gleason admits, it is not really practical or even possible to analyze each level separately. In fact, it is both convenient and sometimes necessary to look ahead to the next higher level (or levels, in the case of phonology) to reach at least a tentative conclusion. Before the analysis is completed, however, descriptive *statements* about a given level must be justified in terms of *that level only.*

Analyzing the sounds of a language is not an easy task. For one thing, as the nineteenth-century comparative linguists discovered, the spelling system of a language which has a written form cannot be relied on. (Most American Indian languages did not have a written form, of course, but in writing structural descriptions of English or other Indo-European languages, linguists needed to be aware of the vagaries of some spelling systems.) For a number of historical reasons, the spelling system of a language seldom reflects accurately its many distinct sounds. Consider the English words *though, through, rough, bough,* and *cough,* for example.

Because in most languages there are many more separate and distinct sounds than their spelling systems would indicate, comparative linguists became interested in devising a phonetic alphabet which would represent each separate speech sound with a different phonetic symbol. Ideally, such an alphabet would eventually contain symbols for every sound in every world language. (This has since proved an unrealistic goal.) The first incomplete International Phonetic Alphabet (IPA) was finished in the late nineteenth century by the English linguist, Henry Sweet.*

Despite such obvious variations as those produced by differences in human voice qualities, conversational speed, and the like, many of the sounds in a language *seem,* to the ear of the native speaker, to be similar. And this may seem true even when a sound spectrum test shows them to be different. It is this phenomenon that interests the structural linguist, and out of which developed a new linguistic concept—that of the *phoneme.* The term *phoneme,* of course, is an invented construct designed to symbolize a highly abstract phenomenon, and thus it is not easy to provide a short, accurate definition. We can begin with this: a *phoneme* is the term which labels a given *class* of mutually exclusive significant speech sounds. Every language contains its own unique set of phonemes, and these vary greatly from one language to another. A phoneme in

---

*It now appears that the International Phonetic Alphabet can never be complete. Scholars have recently discovered through sound spectrum tests made possible by modern technology that the range of human speech sounds is virtually infinite, not only among all world languages, but even within a single language. Even the same person pronounces a sound in a slightly different way each time he utters it.

isolation has no "content," in the sense of semantic "meaning." But when it is used in combination with other phonemes, it *conveys* meaning. (When we look at phonemic analysis in more detail, it will be possible to refine this rather general definition.)

The notion of the phoneme seems to have originated with a French linguist, Ferdinand de Saussure, toward the end of the nineteenth century. It was not until Henry Lee Smith, Jr., and George L. Trager formulated an American phonemic alphabet in the 1950s, however, that American structural grammarians were provided with the tool which made their important contributions to phonemic analysis possible.

Before we become involved with phonemics, however, it will be useful to reach a general understanding of the broad field of phonetics, and to learn a little about the notational terms used by phoneticists and their system of transcribing speech sounds.

Phonetics, which is the general term for the study of speech sounds, includes three branches: acoustical phonetics, auditory phonetics, and articulatory phonetics. It is the third branch, articulatory phonetics, which most interests linguists, for they are concerned primarily with (and this is a definition of articulatory phonetics) describing the processes involved in the production of human speech sounds.*

---

*Acoustic or acoustical phonetics is the study of how speech sounds are transmitted (as opposed to how they are actually produced). Architects who design auditoriums, for example, must be knowledgeable in this area. Auditory phonetics is the study of how speech sounds are received or heard. Manufacturers of hearing aids, radio receivers, and the like are vitally concerned with this branch of phonetics.

13

Articulatory Phonetics

As you look at the diagram on the next page, you will notice that the speech organs can be grouped into upper and lower. The upper organs include the *nasal cavity* (passage), the *upper lip*, the *upper teeth*, and the *roof of the mouth*. The roof of the mouth has four distinct areas, all of which we use differently in producing speech sounds. Put your tongue on the roof of your mouth just behind your upper teeth and run it back and forth a bit. Those little bumps or ridges are the speech area known as the *alveolar ridge*. The second area is the smooth, hard portion of the roof which you can feel by running your tongue back from the alveolar ridge. This area is called the *hard palate* (or sometimes just *palate*). Running your tongue still farther back, you will notice that you come to an area which, although still smooth, is soft. This is the *soft palate* (or *velum*). The fourth area is way at the back of your throat, and you cannot feel it with your tongue. If you examine your throat in a mirror, however, you can see it dangling down from the roof of your mouth—a soft, pink appendage known as the *uvula*. (Most of the scientific terminology which phoneticists use are words derived from Latin roots. *Uvula*, for instance, means "small grape" in Latin. You might find it interesting to look up the other terms in this section as well.)

The lower speech organs consist of the *lower lip*, the *lower teeth*, the *vocal cords* (which are in the voice box just behind your Adam's apple), and the *tongue*. Like the roof of the mouth, the tongue can be divided into four distinct speech areas: the *tip* (*apex*), the *front*, the *center* (*dorsum*), and the *back*.

All of these speech organs are used, selectively, for producing the human speech sounds. Let us look briefly at how they work.

122

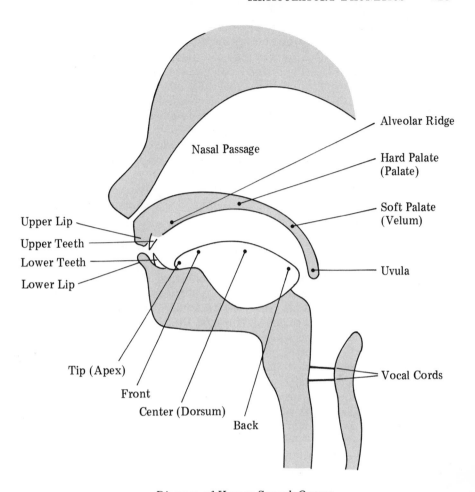

Diagram of Human Speech Organs

Phoneticists take into account *at least* four factors to describe speech sounds, sometimes more. They can be informally outlined as follows:

1. *Use of the vocal cords.* Every speech sound we make is either *unvoiced* (*voiceless*) or *voiced*. That is, either the vocal cords are involved in the sound production—in which case they vibrate and we say the sound is *voiced*; or the vocal cords are not involved—in which case there is no vibration, and we say the sound is *voiceless*. If you will try saying the beginning consonant sounds of the words *pit* and *bit* while at the same time holding your hand lightly against your throat, you will see that the *p* in *pit* is unvoiced but that the *b* in *bit* is voiced.

2. *Articulation.* Every speech sound we make is articulated with both a lower and an upper speech organ—and in a certain manner. Looking again at the diagram, try opening and closing your mouth several times. Do you see that the lower half of your mouth moves while the upper half stays relatively stationary? Now if you will try the *p* and *b* sounds again, you will notice that the lower lip (which is moveable because of the hinged-jaw action) comes up to meet the upper lip. For every sound you make, one of the lower organs (the *articulator*) will move up to make contact or near-contact with one of the upper organs. The upper organ, then, represents the place of contact (the *point of articulation*). Nearly every one of the descriptive terms for speech sounds includes information about the *articulator* and the *point of articulation*, and in that order.

In addition to these factors, there are also two different kinds of articulation: oral and nasal. You can test for yourself whether a sound is oral or nasal simply by holding your nostrils closed while pronouncing it. If, as with the *p* in *pit* and the *b* in *bit*, you hear little or no distortion, you can be sure the sound is oral. That is, the air you exhale while you are pronouncing the sound is expelled through the mouth. Now, still holding your nose, pronounce the *m* in *met*, the *n* in *net*, or the *ng* in *sing*. With these sounds, which must be pronounced while releasing the breath through the nasal passage, closing off that passage results in noticeable distortion. What actually happens when we pronounce these nasal sounds is that the uvula in the back of the throat (see the diagram) is pressed down and forward in such a way that the oral passage is closed off. Thus the air must be expelled through the nasal passage. Because English contains only three nasal sounds, they are labeled; all other speech sounds, although they are not labeled, can be presumed to be oral.

3. *Breath Release.* Because every speech sound we make in English is produced as we exhale, the diagram of speech organs, to be accurate, should also include the lungs. Some languages apparently contain speech sounds which are made while the speaker is inhaling, but you will probably find such a feat impossible.* There are two kinds of breath release in the production of English speech sounds: the *stop* (or *glottal stop*) and the *continuant*.

Stops. Again, if you will go back to our old standbys, the *p* in *pit* and the *b* in *bit*, we can illustrate the stop. Notice that before you actually pronounce the initial consonant sound in these

---

*I was once told by someone knowledgeable in the music world that the reason Frank Sinatra seems never to take a breath in some songs is that he has learned to sustain a note while he is inhaling.

words, you momentarily block off the air passage somewhere in the region of the voice box (or glottis). Then, after a little pressure builds up, you release the air. Once pronounced, the sound is finished—that is, it is not possible to hold or sustain it. This is what the phoneticist means by a *stop*. Beyond this general process, however, there are subtle differences in the manner of the air release. If you hold the back of your hand directly in front of your mouth while you say the *p* and the *b*, you will notice that with the *p* you feel a small puff of air but that with the *b* you do not. As a matter of fact, we even say the *p* sound in different ways, depending upon where it occurs and in what word. Still holding your hand in front of your mouth, try the *p* sound in these three words: *pin, spin, top*. Do you notice a difference? The manner of breath release in these three sounds are called *aspirated*, *unaspirated*, and *unreleased*, respectively. We shall have more to say about these differences a bit later.

Continuants. In making this kind of speech sound, the breath is not held back. Rather, it is allowed to flow freely and unimpeded, as in the sounds *m-m-m-m-m* or *s-s-s-s-s*. The speaker can make the sound last until he runs out of breath. Further subdivisions of continuants are these:

the *fricative*, which is further subcategorized as:
    (a) the *sibilant* (examples are the *s* of *sip* and the *f* of *fine*)
    (b) the *glottal fricative* (an example is the *h* of *hot*)

the *affricative*, which is a sound somewhere between the stop and the fricative (an example is the *j* of *jet*)

This brief explanation is sufficient for our purposes. The information given here should make our discussion of English phonemes a good deal simpler, particularly in helping you to make sense of the consonant and vowel charts in the next chapter.

14

English Phonemes
and Phonemic Analysis

Structural linguistics is a language description method concerned with both *expression* and *content*. It attempts, however, to explain content by discovering how a language's expression system (its grammar rules) conveys meaning. The goal of a structural analysis is to isolate all of the structures which a language uses, from the smallest (sounds) to the largest (sentences), and to discover how these structures are organized into the various sequences or patterns which enable the language to convey information and ideas.

The analysis begins with the collection of vast amounts of data: as many speech sounds as possible must be recorded. The International Phonetic Alphabet is a useful tool at this stage, as it provides a notation system for transcribing the various sounds. Ideally, the field workers' recorded sounds should be over- rather than underdifferentiated. That is, it is much better to have too many sound transcriptions and then be faced with the task of weeding out those that are irrelevant than it is to have too few and find that it is necessary to go back to Step One. (It might be stated parenthetically that linguistic investigators must have the patience and the willingness to admit, at any stage of their investigations, that they have gone off on a wrong track and be prepared to return to an earlier stage if corrections prove necessary. A good deal of trial and error is necessarily a part of such an investigation, even when linguists are skilled and experienced.)

Irrelevant speech sounds must be weeded out because, of the great flood of sounds used by the speakers of every known language, only a very few are significant. That is, only a limited number of sounds contribute to a language's meaning. Such sounds are what linguists refer to as a language's *phonemes*—sounds which in and of themselves contain no meaning, but which in combination with other phonemes contribute to semantic meaning. Once sufficient data has been gathered, speech sounds which are significant must be distinguished from those which are not. All through a structural language investigation, but particularly in the early stages before any clear patterns have emerged, much of the work must be viewed as tentative. If later developments do not bear out the preliminary hypotheses, corrections must be made. However—and this requirement the structuralists considered essential—each level of analysis must, in its final form, be based on empirical evidence available at only that or a lower level. At no time should conclusions be justified on evidence from a higher level. This stricture against "mixing levels" was a crucial one in the discovery procedure methods of the structural linguists.*

Work at the phonological level in the description of English was made possible largely by the contributions of Trager and Smith, who devised a method of isolating English phonemes and who developed a phonemic alphabet for American English phonemes. Their most important technique for isolating phonemes was establishment of the "minimal pair": a pair of words which differ by only one sound. If this one sound difference makes a difference in the meaning of the two words (is significant), then each of the contrasting sounds is a phoneme.

Here are some examples of minimal pairs:

*p*at/*b*at   The single contrast is between the initial *p* and *b* sounds.

ta*p*/ta*b*   Further verification that *p* and *b* are separate English phonemes.

sta*p*le/sta*b*le Still another minimal pair to substantiate that /p/ and /b/ are separate phonemes.

As you can see, the task of isolating phonemes is a painstaking procedure. The more minimal pairs that can be found as evidence, the less likely it is that a mistake has been made.

Once all of the English phonemes have been isolated, the next task is to determine that these sounds labeled as phonemes are considered significantly different by the native speaker. Sometimes, especially when

---

*In conducting a linguistic analysis at the phonological level, for example, it is doubtful that structuralists could know, without reference to the morphological and syntactic levels of English, that the difference between the *p* and *b* sounds is phonemically significant in the pair, sta*p*le and sta*b*le, but not phonemically important in the words, *p*an and s*p*an. Once they discovered these facts, however, they had to write their descriptive statements of phonemes in terms of the phonological level only; they did not permit themselves to include references to higher levels when they wrote their conclusions.

linguists are working with an unfamiliar language, they will hear distinct sound differences which the speakers of the language say do not exist. Conversely, they may fail to hear differences—perhaps because they are not phonemes in the investigators' native langauge—which the respondent says are important. To understand how this happens, consider the *p* sound, already isolated as a phoneme, in the following three words: *p*an, s*p*an, ta*p*. Although the English speaker considers all of these *p* sounds the same, a demonstrable difference can be proved to exist. Try saying each of these *p*s while holding the back of your hand directly in front of your lips. You will feel a definite puff of air with the *p* of *pan*, but not with the others (unless you exaggerate their pronunciation, as would not be done in normal speech). The /p/ in *pan* is aspirated, but the other two are unaspirated. Further careful observation will demonstrate that the /p/ of *tap* (again, think of the word as a part of a larger expression) is not quite completed, or in the vocabulary of the phoneticist, it is an unreleased sound. Clearly, then, it can be demonstrated that each of these three /p/ sounds is distinct. Yet these variations *make no difference* to speakers of English (or, more properly, to listeners). Such variations within a single phoneme class are called allophones. A phoneme can therefore be defined as a class of one or more allophones. Linguists classify all such variations as members of a single phoneme because native speakers do not consider them to be separate.*

An analogy might be useful here. Suppose that you are planning a peculiar sort of zoo in which you will house a great many different kinds of four-legged domesticated animals. You will house all animals of the same class in a different section of your zoo: you will put all the dogs in one section, all the cats in another, the horses in a third, the cows in a fourth, and so on. Each of these animal classes is roughly comparable to the phoneme.

Within each of the animal categories, there is a variety of subclasses. For example, among the dogs you may have are a German shepherd, a collie, a cocker spaniel, a golden retriever, and so on. The same thing is true for the cats, the horses, and the cows. For your purposes, however, it is not necessary to make these further distinctions. Rather than separating each' dog, cat, or whatever according to breed, it is sufficient that you merely house together each category of domesticated animal with shared attributes. Each general category is comparable to a phoneme, and individual breeds are comparable to allophones.

---

*The work of structural linguists in isolating the phonemes and allophones of individual languages has allowed for an important breakthrough in the teaching of second languages. The language student, who may not himself be able to distinguish the phonemes of an unfamiliar language, can be made aware of the significant differences by a teacher who is trained in linguistics, and particularly in phonemics.

Among linguists, there is general agreement that the English language contains about forty-five phonemes, each consisting of one or more allophones. (This number appears to be just about average among the known languages.) Generally speaking, English phonemes are of two kinds: (1) segmental phonemes, which comprise the twenty-four consonant and nine vowel sounds of the language; and (2) the suprasegmental phonemes, which include twelve significant intonation sounds: four for pitch, four for stress, and four for juncture.

Before we examine each of these phoneme classes in detail, it is important to emphasize one extremely important point. Structural linguists considered their allo-eme classification method to be their most valuable descriptive device. This same method was, to them, their most important tool at *all* levels of analysis.

English Segmental Phonemes

Consonants. There are twenty-four consonant segments in English. These include six stops, one affricative, nine fricatives, three nasals, and four semivowels. (There is disagreement whether to classify /h/ as a fricative or as a semivowel.) All of these consonant segments are listed in the following chart, *English Consonant Sounds*. You will notice that many of them occur in voiceless-voiced pairs. Because there are many consonant sounds in each of these two categories, the linguist always indicates whether a consonant is voiced or voiceless.

Vowels. English pronunciation includes only nine vowel segment phonemes, all of which are listed in the chart entitled *English Vowel Sounds*. Since all vowels are oral, all are voiced, and all are continuants, linguists do not find it necessary to indicate these factors in their notations for vowel sounds. They do, however, need to make two sets of distinctions: (1) they must describe what the tongue does when a person produces a vowel sound, i.e., whether the tongue is "humped" high, low, or in between; (2) they must indicate in what part of the mouth the sound is formed—towards the front of the mouth, in the center, or in the back. The chart shows these two features of vowel production.

Pronounce the nine different vowel sounds and at the same time pay attention to the part of your mouth you are using and to the position of the "hump" in your tongue. You may notice other things as well, such as lip position, how wide open your mouth is held, and so on. But phonemicists do not find it necessary to indicate these things in the vowel notation system, probably because they just happen automatically when the mouth and the tongue are performing "properly."

Diphthongs. We should not end our discussion of the segmental English sounds without mentioning diphthongs. Perhaps you are wondering what happened, in this classification system, to such sounds as the *e* in *we*, the *a* in *date*, and the *i* in *bite* (sounds which we have traditionally referred to as long vowel sounds). The fact is that these sounds are not phonemes at all. Rather, they are combinations of phonemes, for during the process of pronouncing them, your tongue does not remain in a fixed position. Instead, the tongue lowers from one position to another. Try pronouncing the long *a*, *e*, and *i* sounds, and you will see that this is true. (There is disagreement among linguists whether the long *o* sound in *boat* should be included among the vowel phonemes; some phoneticists argue that this sound too is a diphthong.) Phonetic transcriptions which show the two or more phonemes involved in the pronunciation of each of these sounds are given in the third chart, *English Diphthong Sounds*.

English Consonant Sounds (Trager-Smith Phonemic Alphabet)

		VOICELESS		VOICED	
Stops	bilabial	/p/	pin, tip	/b/	bin, robin
	apico-alveolar	/t/	tin, rot	/d/	din, rod
	dorso-velar	/k/	cod, rock	/g/	god, pig
Fricatives	labio-dental fricative	/f/	fine, fan	/v/	vine, van
	apico-alveolar sibilant	/s/	sip	/z/	zip
	apico-dental fricative	/θ/	thin	/ð/	then
	fronto-palatal sibilant	/š/	shoe, lotion	/ž/	azure, pleasure
	glottal*	/h/	hot		
Affricate	apico-alveolar	/č/	church, much	/ǰ/	judge, edge
Nasals	bilabial			/m/	mud, similar
	apico-alveolar			/n/	no, any, tan
	dorso-velar			/ŋ/	sing, bang
Semivowels	apico-alveolar lateral			/l/	leap, pal
	apico-alveolar {median / retroflex}**			/r/	rat, sorry
	{bilabial / labiovelar}** semivowel			/w/	won, winner
	fronto-palatal semivowel			/y/	yes, yet

*There is disagreement whether to classify /h/ as a fricative or as a semivowel.
**Disagreement exists concerning the method of producing this sound.

English Vowel Sounds (Trager-Smith Phonemic Alphabet)

Position of "Hump" in Tongue	Part of Mouth in which Sound is Produced		
	FRONT	CENTER	BACK
HIGH	/i/ s*i*t	/ɨ/ ag*e*s, j*u*st (adv.)	/u/ f*oo*t
MID	/e/ s*e*t	/ə/ m*u*d, *a*bout	/o/* h*oe*, b*oa*t
LOW	/æ/ s*a*t	/a/ f*a*ther	/ɔ/ *a*we, b*o*ss

*Some linguists claim this sound in English is a diphthong and they give its phonemic symbol as /ow/.

English Diphthong Sounds (Trager-Smith Phonemic Alphabet)

			Before /r/	
/iy/	f*ee*t		/ihr/	h*ear*
/ey/	m*a*te		/ehr/	d*are*, w*ear*
/ay/	r*i*ght		/ohr/	c*ore*, m*ore*
/ɔy/	c*oy*, *oi*l		/uhr/	t*our*, p*oor*
/uw/	n*oo*n, b*oo*t		/ahr/	b*ar*, c*ar*
/ow/*	h*oe*, b*oa*t			
/aw/	pl*ow*			
/eh/	y*eah*			

*This is the sound that some linguists call the mid-back /o/ (See Vowel Sound Chart).

SEGMENTAL PHONEMES   EXERCISE 27

Directions: Transcribe the following words into phonemic symbols. Follow the model in the example.

Example: laugh   /læf/

1. book
2. fatty
3. found
4. shine

5. phone
6. orlon
7. proved
8. midnight

9. shank   **13.** miss

10. fads   **14.** shoe box

11. limbs   **15.** dish

12. chopped   **16.** ditch

SEGMENTAL PHONEMES: CONSONANTS   EXERCISE 28

> *Directions:* Indicate with five different contrasting pairs each of the following kinds of segmental phonemes and give the phonemic transcription for each of the illustrated sounds. Follow the model in the example.

Example: /p/ *p*it : /b/ *b*it

1. Five pairs showing initial consonant phonemes

2. Five pairs showing middle consonant phonemes

3. Five pairs showing final consonant phonemes

SEGMENTAL PHONEMES: VOWELS   EXERCISE 29

> *Directions:* Indicate with contrasting pairs ten different vowel phonemes. Be sure that you give examples of words in which only one vowel sound is in contrast.

Suprasegmentals

In addition to using vowel and consonant sounds, human speech is also characterized by such voice qualities as pitch, rhythm, speed, and stress—in a word, *intonation*. Certain of these intonation qualities have been isolated as distinctive sounds and classified among the phonemes, and are called *suprasegmentals*. Again, like vowel and consonant sounds, the suprasegmentals are meaningless in isolation. That is, they function as part of the entire structural system and it is only in combination with other sounds that they convey meaning.

To see how intonation can affect meaning, pronounce the following sentences out loud:

1. This is a green house.

2. This is a greenhouse.

3. This is a green house?

4. This is a greenhouse?

5. This is a *green* house. (as opposed to some other color)

6. This is a green *house*. (as opposed to store, bank, bakery)

The way we intonate an expression obviously can make a difference in meaning. Linguists more or less agree that twelve of these suprasegmental phonemes can be distinguished in English, four each in three separate categories—*pitch, stress,* and *juncture.*

PITCH. The pitch of an expression is simply its "tune," the levels of highness or lowness with which we speak. Some linguists contend that since pitch levels are relative and can be determined only in context, it is somewhat misleading to classify them as phonemes. And while it is true that levels of pitch do not take on meaning until they appear in the context of an expression, it is also true that as individual sounds they can be distinguished from each other.

It is important for you to understand that when linguists speak of pitch levels, they are not referring to specific musical notes such as *high C* or *low C* or the *G* below *middle C.* Rather, they refer to a number of levels, from low to high, within any one speaker's normal voice range. Thus, a basso profundo can be said to speak English within the same *range* of levels as does the squeaky-voiced little child.

If you are still uncertain how pitch level can signal meaning difference, try this. Suppose that someone says to you, "I saw a good movie last night." Can you answer with the single word "What?" in such a way as to convey, with just that one-word question, these three different meanings?

"What?" (meaning "What was the name of the movie?")

"What?" (meaning "You don't mean it? I'm amazed.")

"What?" (meaning "I didn't hear you. Will you repeat what you said?)

As you can see, it is quite possible to signal significant meaning differences merely by tone of voice. Probably other intonation factors are also involved, but certainly variation in pitch level is one important way to make a distinction in these three examples.

Most linguists agree that four separate pitch levels are distinguishable in American English, and they number these levels 1, 2, 3, 4 from lowest to highest. When written out on a four-line musical scale, the three "What?" answers can be illustrated roughly as follows:

Example 1	Example 2	Example 3
What was the name of the movie?	I'm amazed!	I didn't hear you. Will you repeat what you said?

You may find it difficult to hear all four of these levels. If so, don't be dismayed. The fact is that although we all managed as babies to pick up the pitch levels that matter in our language, it was a largely uncon-scious and automatic process. Most adults have considerable difficulty hearing all four pitch levels. It is almost as if once we mastered the sig-nificant phonemes of our language we stopped hearing certain language features.

For our purposes it is sufficient to recognize that pitch levels exist, that we all make use of the same ones in our speech, and that they do have grammatical significance. Although individual differences exist, there is a range of pitch levels which is characteristic of American English. Most of us are quick to notice the different intonation patterns of those who are not native speakers of English.

Pitch pattern, then (usually in combination with other intonation sounds) can convey the following kinds of linguistic information:

1. The kind of sentence spoken. That is, we can tell from the sound of a sentence whether it is a statement, a question, or an exclama-tion. Pitch pattern is the primary signal here.

2. Something about emphasis. Although another phoneme, stress, is the primary sound that conveys emphasis, stressed words are also typically spoken at a higher than normal pitch level.

3. Something about relationship of ideas. To put this in grammatical terms, pitch patterns aid us in detecting which elements in a grammatical string are functionally related to each other, again most typically in combination with other intonation phonemes. Thus, the meaning difference between the two sentences, "This is a green house" and "This is a greenhouse" is partly signaled by differences in pitch (though probably even more importantly by stress):

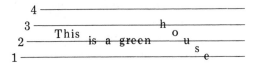

This is a green house.

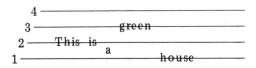

This is a green house.

To discover the characteristic pitch patterns (tunes) of declarative, interrogative, and exclamatory sentences, pretend that your mouth is taped shut and then try to hum the tune for each of the four following sentences:

1. I am coming.

2. Are you coming?

3. Yes, I'm coming.

4. I am *too* coming.

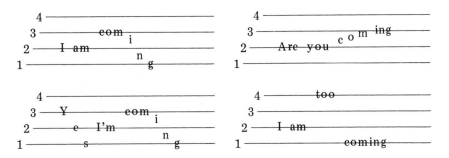

Generally speaking, an ordinary declarative statement spoken in a normal tone of voice can be said to fit a 2-3-1 pattern. The first sentence above illustrates the declarative sentence pattern. Sentence 3 also illustrates the declarative pattern, except for the word *Yes* at the beginning. But do you notice that the single word *Yes*, which could have served all by itself as a single-word comment, fits the 3-1 pattern on which the declarative sentence ends?

Some questions, though not all, fit the 2-3 pattern of the second example. Of course we have different kinds of questions. Sometimes we ask for a simple yes or no answer, as in Sentence 2 on page 135, or as in Sentences 3 and 4 on page 133. The intonation pattern for this kind of question is basically a 2-3 pattern, the last word ending at the 3 level. For the kind of question that asks for a substantive answer, however ("Where are you going?"), the pattern seems to be the same as that for the declarative sentence. The listener must rely on other grammar clues to know that this is a question.

The last example illustrates a sentence in which the voice reaches the fourth pitch level. It seems that Level 4 is reserved for words or syllables that are both higher in pitch and more strongly stressed. But remember, we already discovered that two or more phonemes are often used in combination to convey grammatical meaning. (Incidentally, Sentences 5 and 6 on page 133 both fit a 2-4-1 pattern like Sentence 4 above. Here is how they look:

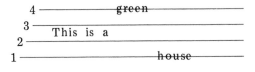

This is a *green* house.

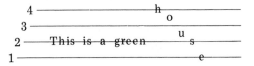

This is a green *house*.

Let us sum up. The ordinary *declarative sentence* begins on a level which linguists arbitrarily call 2. Towards the end of the statement, the pitch rises to Level 3 and then quickly fades away to the lowest pitch level in the range (Level 1). The *yes-no question* sentence ordinarily begins at Level 2 just like the declarative sentence. However, at the end of this kind of question the voice rises to Level 3 and stays there. This upward pitch at the end of a sentence thus acts as a grammatical clue: it signals a yes-no question. A single word or even an entire sentence that is a strong *exclamation* will rise to the highest pitch level of all, Level 4.

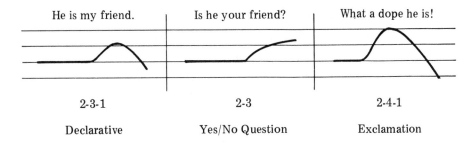

He is my friend.	Is he your friend?	What a dope he is!
2-3-1	2-3	2-4-1
Declarative	Yes/No Question	Exclamation

Of course, in all of these examples other sound factors are also at work. Probably the most important of these is stress.

STRESS. Stress simply means the degree of emphasis or accent we put on certain words (or on certain syllables within words). Although stress varies somewhat among the dialects within our language, it is reasonably safe to say that there are typical stress patterns in English (or in any language) that make it distinctive. For instance, words like *a, an, the, and, or, for, in, before,* and so on normally receive very little stress. Important words in a sentence, such as nouns and verbs, generally receive a fairly heavy stress. In a noun phrase, lexical modifiers like *black, white, pretty* receive greater stress than structure words like *a, an, the,* but less stress than the nouns they modify. On the other hand, in noun phrases in which the noun is a compound (*greenhouse*) or in which the noun consists of two words—a noun adjunct plus a noun (*White House*)—the first syllable or the noun adjunct typically receives strongest stress.

Linguists speak of four stress levels, but may people have become "stress deaf," and may not be able to hear all four of these levels. The symbols for the four stress phonemes are as follows:

SYMBOL	TERM	DESCRPITION
/ ´ /	Primary	Strongest
/ ˆ /	Secondary	Second Strongest
/ ` /	Tertiary	Third Strongest
/ ˜ /	Weak	Weakest

Here are some phrases with the stresses marked. Notice that in this book stress marks are placed directly above the vowel sound of the syllable receiving a given stress. Where the stress mark is placed will vary from one source to another. Be sure to check up on the practice of whatever text or dictionary you are using.

the prĕtty gírl   the Whíte Hoûse

the blâck and whîte dóg   the cár ôperàtor

If you have great difficulty distinguishing all four stress levels, don't let it worry you too much. In fact, most transformationalists in recent years have argued that there are only two levels, stress and no stress. For our purposes, it is certainly sufficient for you to be able to identify strongest and weakest.

JUNCTURE. A juncture is a pause. Again, linguists have identified four levels of juncture. From smallest to largest, they are as follows:

SYMBOL	TERM	DESCRIPTION
/+/	Plus Juncture	Smallest
/ | /	Single-bar Juncture	Next Largest
/ ‖ /	Double-bar Juncture	Third Largest
/#/	{Double-plus / Double-cross} Juncture	Largest

The first three of these usually occur within sentences, while the last one is most often a terminal juncture. Again, however, there is considerable disagreement among linguists in the way they analyze juncture or even whether they recognize all four listed here. Since many texts do list these four, however, they are included here.

Linguists speak of two types of transitions between sounds: *close transition* and *open transition*. In general, what they mean by close transition is the absence or near absence of a pause. Actually, of course, an infinitesimal pause occurs between every two sounds, and certainly there is a tiny pause between the syllables of a word, as for instance in the word *in·fin·i·tes·i·mal*. But linguists have devised no phonemic symbol for such pauses. Instead, *close transition* is indicated by the lack of a notation.

Open transition refers to the short but noticeable pause between words or between parts of a compound. The notation for this small juncture is /+/. Study the following pairs to see if you can hear the difference between open and close transition:

CLOSE TRANSITION		OPEN TRANSITION	
ahead	/əhed/	a head	/ə+hed/
Anapolis	/ænæpəlis/	an apple is	/æn+æpəl+iz/
already	/ɔlrediy/	all ready	/ɔl+rediy/
altogether	/ɔltuwgeðər/	all together	/ɔl+tuwgeðər/
nitrate	/naytreyt/	night rate	/nayt+reyt/

The next largest pause, called the single-bar juncture, is represented by the notation /|/. Some early structuralists claimed that this juncture exists in speech, and that therefore sentences like the following are ambiguous only when they are written (inasmuch as we have no way in our writing system to indicate single-bar juncture):

Your friends are interesting people.
(are interesting /|/ people; or are /|/ interesting people)

We need a modern language course.
(a /|/ modern language course; or a modern /|/ language course)

They asked for more pertinent documents.
(more /|/ pertinent documents; or more pertinent /|/ documents)

Mary has hand-stitched quilts.
(has /|/ hand-stitched quilts; or has hand-stitched /|/ quilts)

He passed away from the traumatic scene.
(passed /|/ away from the scene; or passed away /|/ from the scene)

This early insistence by some structuralists that single-bar juncture occurs in speech was always controversial. But no linguists any longer claim there are two audible junctures denoting a difference in meaning for sentences like the examples above when they are in contexts of normal use. In fact, *empirical* experiments conducted under controlled conditions have failed to yield evidence that the two are heard differently or that they are acoustically different.

The double-bar juncture, symbolized by the notation, /‖/, is the third largest pause. To hear what it sounds like, try saying some elements in a series: black, red, green, orange; or a, b, c, d, e. The pause between each of these elements is a double-bar juncture. The same kind of pause occurs after introductory sentence elements like the following:

At the stroke of midnight /‖/ the doorbell rang.

No /‖/ I refuse to go along with your plan.

As soon as he had finished the puzzle /‖/ he went to bed.

Indeed /‖/ she is a beautiful person.

The last of the junctures is the double-plus or double-cross juncture, symbolized with the notation, /#/. This is the longest of the pauses, the kind you hear at the ends of sentences; few people have difficulty hearing this pause.

A FINAL WORD ABOUT PHONEMES: If the twelve suprasegmentals are counted as language sounds, English contains at least forty-five different linguistically significant sound classes. Of course, every person's speech contains a great many more than forty-five distinct speech sounds or *phones*, but listeners have learned to hear only those distinctions that make a difference in meaning. This means that we have had to learn to ignore the great majority of these sounds. Furthermore, this winnowing out of all but a minimum of significant sounds is a process which all speakers of every language do automatically when they learn as children to understand their native language.

Speech is, of course, a two-way process. As speakers we produce many hundreds of sounds; as listeners, we sort out those classes of sounds that matter—the phonemes. Nearly every phoneme is a collection of many different phones (allophones) which, even though they are demonstrably different, speakers and listeners regard as identical. A phone, then, is a physical reality, while a phoneme is an abstraction. Yet speakers and listeners everywhere, regardless of their particular language, have little difficulty abstracting out of the flood of sounds that comprise human speech the twenty to sixty phonemes necessary for understanding the sentences of their language.

In addition to being able to sort out the phonemes and allophones of their language, users are further able to detect overlapping phonemic signals when, as often happens, two or more of them operate together. (An example is the combination of pitch and stress sounds so characteristic of many intonation patterns.*) The incredible capacity of the human nervous system enables every normal child to sort out the phonemes of its language by age two or three—and possibly earlier, since if is well known that understanding precedes spoken performance.

SUPRASEGMENTAL PHONEMES: PITCH   EXERCISE 30

Directions: Write out the following sentences on four-line pitch-level scales. Then indicate the intonation pattern by number.

1. He's a big sissy.

2. You *said* it!

3. Help! I've been robbed!

4. Are you hungry?

5. Yes, I'm starved.

---

*The fact that they occur together (or are in complementary distribution, to use linguistic terminology) has something to do with the ease of the task.

SUPRASEGMENTAL PHONEMES: STRESS   EXERCISE 31

Directions: Indicate where (over which syllable or which word) in each of the italicized structures you intonate with the greatest emphasis. Assume ordinary conversational tone.

1. She has *naturally* curly hair.
2. He works as a *cashier*.
3. They come from a big *family*.
4. The *entire* group was late.
5. He refuses to *participate*.
6. The *waitresses* went out on strike.
7. What is your *favorite* color?
8. The coffee pot *turns off* automatically.
9. She often *turns off* course.
10. That was his *final* instruction.
11. That was his *finale*.
12. What is this world going to *come to*?
13. When is this world going to *come to*?
14. The book's *content* is clear.
15. The book's *content* to be clear.
16. His plans have been *carried out*.
17. She is an *intimate* friend.
18. When do you expect to *graduate*?
19. The child received a kidney *transplant*.
20. The big *transport* plane took off.

SUPRASEGMENTAL PHONEMES: STRESS   EXERCISE 32

Directions: Indicate two intonation patterns for each of the following:

1. abstract
2. addict
3. conduct
4. conflict

5. contest

6. entrance

7. ferment

8. intern

9. misprint

10. proceeds

11. produce

12. progress

13. refuse

14. research

15. resume

16. a madhouse

17. a singing teacher

18. a Greek pupil

19. a cleaning woman

20. a moving truck

STRESS   EXERCISE 33

Directions: Many words such as *out, in, up, down, over, off,* can be used either as adverbial modifiers or as prepositions. Study the following pairs, and then indicate the word which receives the strongest stress, as in the preceding exercise. Does stress offer a clue about parts of speech here?

1. He *ran down* the road.

   He *ran down* a pedestrian.

2. She *ran up* the dress seam.

   She *ran up* the stairs.

3. They *ran off* the path.

   They *ran off* the copies.

4. The wind *blew down* the street.

   The wind *blew down* the tree.

5. He *passed out* from hunger.

   He *passed out* of the room.

6. He *looked over* the top.

   He *looked over* the materials.

SUPRASEGMENTALS   EXERCISE 34

Directions: Read the expressions below. Why are they ambiguous? Would they be ambiguous if they were spoken? Using the example below as your model, indicate by notations for two different intonation patterns the two possible meanings of each sentence. (Use the single-bar notation to indicate pause, and the strongest stress mark to indicate emphasis.)

Example: We watched the big chicken feast.
   a) wátched the big chicken|féast
   b) wátched|the big chícken feast

1. He is a man eating tiger.

2. Now there's a mind provoking experience.

3. That is an eyebrow raising doubt.

4. He went to the dark room.

5. Where did the victim come to?

6. I want more generous pledges.

7. He caught them both laughing and talking.

8. They signed on the cast.

9. Jones's classes have satisfied students.

10. The test we'll take soon will be over.

15

English Morphemes and Morphemic Analysis

The procedure in a structural language investigation is first to complete all analysis at a given level, and only then to move on to the next level in the hierarchy. Thus, morphology can be considered only after the study of the phonological level is complete. All analysis at the phonological level must, in its final form, make no reference to either the higher morphological or syntactical levels. This means that there is no way that a phonological analysis, regardless of how complete it may be, can reveal anything about the structure of words or of sentences.

Investigation at the morphological level is confined to word structure, and while investigators *may* make use of the methodology and conclusions of the lower phonological level, they *may not* justify any of the morphological analysis by reference to the higher, syntactical level.*

Just as the concept of the phoneme was basic to the first level of structural analysis, the concept of the morpheme is basic to the second level. The first step, therefore, is to isolate all of the word parts which seem to function as significant units in word structure. A morpheme is such a unit and can be very generally defined as a minimally significant grammatical unit which contributes to the grammatical and semantic meaning of a word. Just as morphemes will be shown to be composed of a combination of phonemes, words will be shown to consist of a combination of

---

*It is doubtful that the structuralists were really able to keep the three levels as rigidly separated as they claimed to. Furthermore, as you will see, the validity of this requirement has been seriously challenged by other linguists, the transformationalists in particular.

144

morphemes. We shall see that the meaning of a word is dependent on the morphemes which make it up and the order in which they occur.

It is virtually impossible to list all of the individual morphemes present in any given language. For this reason, linguists once again make use of the allo-eme analytical device that proved so useful at the phonemic level: "morpheme" is the term for a class of one or more allomorphs, all of which have similar grammatical and semantic meaning and all of which have the same characteristic distribution.

As it was with phonemes, the minimal pair technique is useful in isolating the morphemes of a language. (A minimal pair, remember, is a pair of elements which are identical in all respects except one.) Consider the following minimal pairs:

girl/girls	strong/strongness	contend/intend
like/liked	truth/truthful	inhale/exhale
sad/sadder	truthful/truthfulness	lit/unlit

By using hundreds and hundreds of such minimal pairs, linguists are able to isolate and identify the morphemes of English. Some of these will be constituents that are meaning-bearing in the lexical sense (*in* = in, into; *ex* = out, away from). Others will contain more of a linguistic or grammatical meaning (plural, past, comparative).

Once a list has been made of all elements thought to be morphemes, the next step is determining which are allomorphs—that is, which morphs occur together in a single morpheme class. Again, it may turn out that certain elements on the original list will have to be discarded.

The next and most vital step is to determine whether they occur in systematic distributional patterns. For example, a group of morphemes like *re-*, *un-*, *ex-*, *dis-*, and the like, although they differ markedly from one another in terms of their internal phonemic structure, might all be found to occur characteristically as initial word elements when they are analyzed according to their behavior in the larger environment of word structure. Where a given kind of morpheme may or may not occur is thus shown to be grammatically significant.

Analytical procedures reveal that English contains two very broad categories of word elements: *roots*, and *affixes*. The affixes, in turn, can be subdivided into *prefixes*, *infixes*, *suffixes*, and *superfixes*. We shall examine each of these types.

Roots. Every English word has a root (also called a base). In addition, the root *may* (but not necessarily must) have one or more affixes preceding or following it. These affixes may be added directly to the root, or to a structure consisting of a root plus one or more affixes. Any morpheme or combination of morphemes to which an affix can be added is called a *stem*. Thus, the word *calls* consists of a stem /call/, which is a root, and an affix /s/; the word *recalled* contains a stem /recall/, which is a root plus an affix, and the affix /ed/. A word or a stem which contains a combination of two or more roots is a compound: *childhood, baseball, lighthouse.**

The linguist also makes another distinction between types of roots. A root may be either a *free morpheme*, meaning that it can occur alone as a word; or it may be a *bound morpheme*, meaning that it never occurs alone but must always occur in combination with another morpheme. Each of these morpheme types is illustrated by the italicized element in the following list of words:

FREE MORPHEMES	BOUND MORPHEMES
*box*es	*morph*eme
*base*less	de*tract*
*fix*ed	in*duce*
*follow*ing	ob*tain*
*hippopotamus*es	*struct*ure

Notice several things: first, whether or not an element is a morpheme is determined by its distributional characteristics. That is, a single occurrence or even two or three similar occurrences of a word element proves nothing. The linguist must be certain that a unit always occurs in a particular form. For instance, in analyzing the word *thermometer, thermo* might appear to be a morpheme. (*Meter* certainly is, because it can occur as a word and cannot be further divided without altering its meaning.) Careful investigation of many other English words reveals, however, that in words like *isotherm, thermal, thermic, thermionics,* and so on, the *o* is missing. Thus, despite the fact that the *o* is present in many English words (*thermodynamics, thermonuclear, thermostat*), the linguist is forced to conclude that *o* is a formative, and therefore a morpheme in its own right. (It contains no semantic content, but rather it serves a grammatical function.) The appearance of the same formative in the stems of other words (phil-*o*-sophy, morph-*o*-logy, typ-*o*-graphy) offers support for this

---

*Actually, this is an example of "mixing levels." A discussion of compounds necessarily involves us on the syntactic level (Level III), even though many compounds are written as single words.

conclusion. *Thermo, philo, morpho, typo*—all of these are stems consisting of a root plus a formative.*

Another thing to note, already alluded to in the preceding paragraph, is that in addition to distributional characteristics, linguists must pay attention to meaning in their morphemic analysis. That is, a unit is said to be a morpheme only if it cannot be further divided without drastically changing its grammatical (and thus its semantic) meaning. Two criteria must be used, then, for recognizing morphemes: meaning and distribution.

A morpheme is not the same thing as a syllable, even though it often happens that a morpheme consists of a single syllable. The term syllable refers to a word unit containing a single stress. A morpheme, on the other hand, may consist of one syllable, two or more syllables, or even a part of a syllable (as with the /-s/ affix on the word *thinks*). To put this distinction somewhat differently, the term *syllable* refers to a phonemic characteristic, while the term morpheme refers to a *morphemic* characteristic, which has grammatical or structural implications. Thus, the words *box, base, follow, armadillo* all contain but a single morpheme, even though *follow* is composed of two syllables and *armadillo* contains four.

Sometimes, in combination with another morpheme, the vowel nucleus of the base undergoes a pronunciation modification. For example, the word *walked* (and many more words like it) consists of two morphemes, the root /walk/ and the suffix /-ed/. A great number of English verbs have this form. However, there are other verbs like *see, find, throw*, and the like, which, in the same syntactical environment where *walked* is found, are discovered to assume a different phonetic form: *saw, found, threw*. Structuralists vary in their methods of describing this phenomenon, though they all agree that *saw* consists of two morphemes, the root *see* plus the past tense morpheme (represented by {-ed}). The presence of the {-ed} morpheme has the effect of modifying the vowel sound of the morpheme to which it is attached. (In a sense, therefore, the past form here is an *infix allomorph* of the past tense morpheme.) *Saw* can thus be described in either of the following ways, the second of which this book will adopt:

$$saw = see + \text{ɔ} \longleftarrow (iy)$$

or

$$saw = see + \text{-ed}$$

*A formative is the element of a word which is not contained in the base, but which is necessary to give the word a suitable form.

AFFIXES

Prefixes. A prefix is an affix which precedes a stem. All English pre-fixes are bound morphemes; that is, they may never stand alone. They are morphemes because they are meaning-bearing, and because they have characteristic distributional patterns. A word may contain more than one prefix, but they must occur in a fixed order. Thus, the word *unrewarded* contains two prefixes, *un-* and *re-*, which must occur in that order, never the other way around.

Occasionally, we find a prefix, like *en-*, which has the same phonetic features as a suffix. The linguist notes, however, that their distribution or position unquestioningly distinguishes them as two different classes of morpheme:

Prefix: *en*dear, *en*rich, *en*trap

Suffix: brok*en*, writt*en*, be*en*

Suffixes. An affix which is added following a stem is known as a *suffix*. All suffixes are, like prefixes, bound morphemes; that is, they can never occur alone as words. They usually do not form stems. Here are some examples:

1. radio*s*	3. fix*ed*	5. fret*ful*	7. sign*ify*
2. box*es*	4. sing*ing*	6. sing*er*	8. warm*ness*

You will note that these suffixes are different from each other in a sig-nificant way. The suffixes on the first four words perform a different gram-matical function than do the suffixes on the last four words, and the suffixes can be subdivided into two general classes on the basis of this dif-ference in grammatical function. The first four above are *inflectional* suffixes, the last four are *derivational* suffixes.

Inflectional Suffixes. There are very few inflectional suffixes in En-glish. In fact there are so few of them (about twenty) that they can all be listed. Some words occur in a number of related forms, each of which is grammatically distinguishable from the other by the form of the suffix which follows the stem. The function of this particular kind of suffix, known as an inflectional suffix, is merely to change the form of the word. It does not, however, change the word's class, by which we mean that all the forms of that word (*walk, walks, walking, walked*) continue to occur in the same syntactic environment. Words that have this feature can be put into four large *paradigmatic classes*, by which we mean that all of the words of a particular class can assume any of the forms represented by a given paradigm or set of patterns. (Such patterns are known as inflectional series.) These four paradigmatic sets can be illustrated as follows:

CLASS 1	CLASS 2	CLASS 3	CLASS 4
boy	write	she	sad
boys	writes	her	sadder
	wrote	her, hers	saddest
man	writing		
men	written	I	good
		me	better
box	go	my, mine	best
boxes	goes		
	went		
	going		
	gone		

Thus, we can classify all words which occur in the Class 1 paradigm as *nouns*, all those which occur in Class 2 paradigmatic patterns as *verbs*, all Class 3 words as *personal pronouns*, and all Class 4 words as *adjectives*. The classification principle here is one of form. That is, only those words which can assume all or most of the forms represented by one of these four sets of patterns can be described as paradigmatic or inflectional words. All other words are of a different type and must therefore be analyzed and classified according to a different principle.

Derivational Suffixes. Although English makes use of a very limited number of inflectional suffixes, that is not true of derivational suffixes. Derivational suffixes are units like *-ful, -al, -th, -ment, -ize,* which do not occur as parts of a paradigmatic or inflectional series. As we shall see when we analyze the syntactic environments in which particular word types can occur, however, derivational suffixes also perform a grammatical function. That is, by adding a derivational suffix to a word, we can change its word class. Consider the word *sad*, which, because it can assume the three forms *sad, sadder, saddest*, can be called an inflectional adjective. Suppose, however, that the linguist finds the word *sadden*. An affix, *-en*, which is not among the suffixes listed in the ø, *-er, -est* paradigm, has been added to the word stem *sad*. (Do not permit the spelling to confuse your thinking here. Remember, the linguist is investigating spoken, not written, English.) Suddenly, the addition of this *-en* affix changes the word to one which can be called a verb, since the word now can assume all of the forms which are listed in the verb paradigm: *sadden, saddens, saddened, saddening, saddened.**

There are far too many derivational suffixes for us to be able to provide a complete list of them. Still, most native speakers of English would have little difficulty in listing a number of "typical noun endings," "typical verb endings," "typical adjective endings," and so on. The point is that derivational endings clearly contribute grammatical information. If you doubt this, go back to the nonsense sentences in Exericse 23 and note how many of these "meaningless" words you were able to classify merely on the basis of their derivational endings. This is the structural linguists' point: grammatical meaning can lead to an understanding of semantic meaning (though they would deny that the reverse is true).

Words often contain more than one suffix. You might therefore find a word with several derivational suffixes in a row, like *healthfully* (heal + *-th* + *-ful* + *-ly*). Or often you see a word which contains both derivational and inflectional suffixes: *healthier* (heal + *-th* + *-y* + *-er*). Grammarians have discovered that when a number of suffixes are attached to a word stem in this fashion they occur in a fixed sequential order. Generally speaking, only one inflectional suffix will be among these affixes, however, and the inflectional ending will occur as the last in the series.†
Interestingly, native speakers of a given language know automatically which ones go where, although they would find it difficult or impossible to explain what the system is.

Superfixes. There is one more morpheme, the *superfix*, which represents the combination of phonemes that, taken together, indicate the total intonation pattern of a word. There is, however, considerable disagreement among linguists as to whether the superfix can really be classed as a morpheme, the argument being that the pronunciation of an entire word is a syntactical rather than a morphological matter. Certainly this is true. On the other hand, a dictionary, which lists the characteristic grammatical and semantic features of isolated, out-of-context words, always indicates alternative pronunciation or intonation possibilities. Although the grammatical significance of a word's intonation features, when alternatives

---

*There is some question about whether this discovery is one that would likely be made at the morphological level. Possibly it would not be made until the syntactic level, in which case we have another example of level "mixing."

†As always, apparent exceptions leap to mind. What about words like *fixedly* and *brokenly*, for example? Perhaps some transformational process converts the *-ed* and *-en* suffixes from inflectional ones to derivational ones, perhaps not. Linguists vary in their analyses.

exist, is not always revealed until the word is analyzed in a larger context, it nevertheless seems undeniable that such patterns *can* be independently and preliminarily described. Furthermore, certain words (like *infinitesimal*, for example) will be pronounced in isolation or in context in precisely the same manner. For these reasons, despite the fact that some linguists consider a word's intonation pattern to be more syntactical than morphological, the superfix is included among the morphemes in this book. A word's superfix, therefore, is the combination of phonemes—*pitch, stress,* and *juncture*—which represent the pronunciation (or pronunciations) of a word.

MORPHEMES: ROOTS   EXERCISE 35

Directions: Write out all of the roots in each of the following structures. Indicate which constructions are compounds.

1. nominal
2. bookish
3. outstanding
4. firehouse
5. unreconstructed
6. morpheme
7. football
8. prefix
9. painful
10. handmaiden
11. antecedent
12. typewriter
13. submarine
14. terrain
15. asexual
16. scripture
17. bedbug
18. lightbulb
19. finish
20. contain

BOUND MORPHEMES   EXERCISE 36

Directions: Using the same constructions as those in Exercise 35, indicate which contain bound roots.

MORPHEMES: PREFIXES   **EXERCISE 37**

> *Directions:* Write out all of the prefixes in the following structures.
> Can you reach any tentative conclusions about prefix order? Do not
> worry about the original etymological form of a prefix, simply pick out
> the prefixes as they occur in these English words.

1. ambidexterity
2. bisect
3. demitasse
4. hyperactive
5. retrogression
6. monogamy
7. postdated
8. semicircle
9. unicorn
10. disenchanted
11. disregard
12. redistribute
13. unrelenting
14. uninspired
15. undisturbed
16. antidote
17. prefix
18. subliminal
19. procedural
20. demote
21. reincarnate
22. inactive
23. undecided
24. transpire
25. unprogrammed
26. misjudge
27. asexual
28. re-enact
29. introduce
30. syntax

MORPHEMES: DERIVATIONAL SUFFIXES   EXERCISE 38

> *Directions:* Identify the suffixes listed below as derivation noun, adjective, or verb suffixes. Supply at least one word containing each suffix to justify your answer.

1. -able (-ible)
2. -age
3. -al
4. -ance (-ence)
5. -ate
6. -dom
7. -ee
8. -eme
9. -esque
10. -ful
11. -hood
12. -ic
13. -ify
14. -ish
15. -ize
16. -less
17. -ness
18. -ous
19. -th
20. -ure

MORPHEMES

> ***Directions:*** For each of the following words, list the root(s), prefix(es), derivational suffix(es), and inflectional suffix(es).

1. players
2. leaflet
3. falls
4. signifying
5. obnoxiousness
6. manliest
7. quickly
8. hopefully
9. given
10. pacifiers
11. friendly
12. friendlier
13. misappropriated
14. golden
15. stealthy
16. truthfully
17. beheaded
18. unreconstructed
19. antedated

16

Morphology— Classifying Words By Their Morphemic Structure

The analysis and classification of words involves two criteria, their formal morphemic structure, and their syntactic behavior. The first of these can be studied at the level of morphology. The second, however, will require the third grammar level: phrase structure or syntax.

We have already said that all English words will belong to one of two broad types, depending upon whether or not they occur in a series of related forms like those illustrated by the paradigms. The morphemic structure of words can therefore aid us in beginning to classify them.

NOUNS. We shall call a word a *noun* if it has a series of forms like those in the paradigm: *boy, boys, boy's, boys'* or *man, men, man's, men's*.* Notice that this definition is *not* a lexical one. It says nothing about a noun's being a word that names a person, place, or thing. As a matter of fact, a great many nouns do contain this kind of meaning. On the other hand, some

---

*Structuralists disagree over whether the singular and plural possessive forms ought to be included in the noun paradigm. At the strictly formal morphological level, however, it seems best to include these two forms at this stage of word analysis, since they are certainly observable forms a noun can assume. When we continue word analysis at the level of syntax, we may find good reason to correct this formal definition by discarding the possessives and relying on only a two-member paradigm.

In all probability structural analysis would not reveal the exceptions (irregular word forms) until Level III (Syntax). The investigator would then have to return to Level II and justify including these forms solely on the basis of Level II criteria. This admission, of course (made by Gleason, among others), is enough to have made some linguists doubt the validity of the structuralist "discovery procedure" method, and also to doubt whether the stricture against the "mixing of levels" should, in fact, be rigidly adhered to as a valid language investigation method.

nouns, like *goodness, kindness, honesty,* mean no such thing. Considering the traditional definitions to be vague and inexact, the structural grammarians vowed to keep all semantic references out of their definitions. The word definitions in this chapter are therefore strictly *formal* statements about the internal morphemic structure of words and the series of structural patterns certain English words can enter. These formal word features can be accurately described without reference to meaning or any other features.

Our formal definition of the noun is therefore as follows: A *noun* is a word that has a maximum of four forms and a minimum of two forms which correspond to the paradigm: *boy, boys, boy's, boys';* or *man, men, man's, men's.*

PRONOUNS. The formal definition of the pronoun is necessarily much more limited than the traditional lexical definition. Words in this class will include only the personal pronouns, *I, you, he, she, it,* and the word *who.* These words must be grouped in a class separate from nouns because they occur in a paradigm which contains more members than the noun paradigm. Specifically, except for *you* and *it,* the pronoun has a separate object form; second, most pronouns have two singular and two plural possessive forms. The *pronoun* will therefore be formally defined as any word which has a maximum of eight or a minimum of three forms that correspond to the paradigm: *I, me, my, mine, we, us, our, ours.*

VERBS. The regular verbs of English have only four forms. Most irregular verbs (*do, write, fall*) have five forms, two of which (the past and the perfect) are forms in which the vowel sound of the verb stem undergoes a phonetic change. Occasionally we find a verb like *hit* or *set* which has only three forms. And then there is *be,* with eight different forms. Our formal definition must take this wide variation into account, and thus we will define a *verb* as a word which has a maximum of eight or a minimum of three forms which correspond to the paradigm: *do, does, did, doing, done.*

ADJECTIVES. The last of the English word types with a set of paradigmatic forms is the adjective. This set includes three forms, the null (ø), the comparative (*-er*), and the superlative (*-est*). The formal definition is as follows: An *adjective* is a word that has three forms which correspond to the paradigm: *sad, sadder, saddest;* or *good, better, best.*

Note that this definition excludes a word like *beautiful,* traditionally called an adjective. That is, in order to be compared, *beautiful* must be preceded by a separate word, *more* or *most.* So far as the formal structure of *beautiful* and all other words like it is concerned, we must regard it (them) as words incapable of taking inflectional forms. Further classification of all such words will have to wait, therefore, until we analyze words according to their syntactic characteristics.

Beyond these four word types which fall into paradigmatic classes, all remaining English words must, at this level of analysis, be grouped together as noninflectional words. Remember that at this stage we are analyzing words in *isolation*, that is, *out of context*.

Strictly speaking, if we are to be restricted to describing only those morphemic word features that are discoverable without access to information regarding the behavior of words in larger constructions, we would probably not be able to include the irregular words among these four major morphological classes. This book has therefore cheated a little, as most structural descriptions do, yielding to the compelling force of syntax.

Uninflected Words. All other English words are uninflected. That is, they have only one form. In general, these uninflected words fall into two broadly similar morphemic types:

Uninflected words, like **to**, **and**, **when**, **the**, **very**, *and so on, which never accept affixes*

Uninflected words, like **oral, porous, frantic, faultless,** *which take derivational suffixes but which do not accept inflectional suffixes.* Note, however, that all words with derivational endings are not necessarily uninflected words. Most derived nouns and verbs can take all of the inflectional forms in the noun and verb paradigms, respectively, and will therefore be classifiable as members of one of these large paradigmatic classes. Examples of such words follow:

NOUNS	ADJECTIVES	VERBS
kingdom	cleanly	publicize
plantation	friendly	darken
resemblance	chilly	signify

Adverbs. There is one kind of uninflected word that, although it has only one form and cannot therefore be classified on the basis of a set of related forms, does stand out as different from all the other uninflected words. These are words like *quickly, happily, sadly, poorly,* many of which occur in our corpus. All such words have the *-ly* derivational suffix, and none of them fit into a paradigmatic series. Yet were it not for the suffix each of them could be classified as an adjective. There are, of course, other derivational words which can be classified as nouns, verbs, or adjectives before the addition of the derivational suffix. But the particular words we speak of here seem to be much more common. Since their unique morphological structure makes them word forms which are easily identified, and because they do appear so frequently in sentences, we decide to label them *adverbs*.

We will call a word an *adverb*, then, if it meets all three of the following morphological conditions:

1. It must be a word with the *-ly* derivational ending.

2. Before the addition of the *-ly*, the word must have been the null form of an adjective (*quick, sad, swift*).

3. After the addition of the *-ly*, the word will not fit into any paradigmatic series. That is, it can now assume only one form.

COMPOUNDS. All of the structures we have broadly categorized as either inflectional or uninflectional words suggest that we may now write a definition for the term *word*. We shall call a word any structure which contains a root or a stem plus a theoretically unlimited number of prefixes and/or suffixes. The important thing here is that a word may have *only one root*. On the other hand, we have observed that some structures have two or more roots. Actually, English abounds in such structures. Such constructions are called *compounds*.

Many compounds are written as if they were single words: *however, classroom, lighthouse, washcloth, furthermore, outstanding, blackmail, strawberry*. Others are hyphenated: *city-state, red-letter, black-market,, blue-collar*. Probably most often, they are written as two words: *book case, chicken coop, doll house, ironing board*. Traditional school grammars quite often treated the first group of compounds as words, and the second and third as adjectives plus nouns. What these grammars failed to recognize was that they are all alike. (Jespersen did recognize this, but few traditional school texts did.) This failure can probably be attributed to the habit of describing the grammar of a language as though it were a primarily written rather than spoken form.

The structuralists, who focused on spoken English, saw immediately that all of these structures are the same. Furthermore, just as words consist of a root, with or without derivational and inflectional affixes, plus a stress pattern, the compound also has a characteristic stress pattern as part of its morphological structure: *clássroom, boók case, cíty-state*. Although this stress pattern is not invariable, it is significant in a great many cases.

Yet another observation can be made: a great many compounds are made up of two roots or stems, the last of which may be a word that fits one of the paradigm classes. For instance, a compound like *classroom* can be put through the entire noun series: *classroom, classrooms, classroom's, classrooms'*. Similarly, the last stem may take all of the forms in the verb inflectional series: *stonewall, stonewalls, stonewalled, stonewalling*; or the adjective paradigm: *slap happy, slap happier, slap happiest*.

ALLOMORPHS. You will remember from the first level of grammar analysis, phonology, that some phonemes have allophones—variations in sound which, although they can be shown to exist, do not have grammatical significance. Speakers and listeners alike learn to ignore the differences, regarding all allophones as alike. Similarly, at the morphological level linguists distinguish between morphemes and allomorphs. A morpheme might consist of a group of allomorphs, all of which occur in the same syntactic environment and convey similar grammatical meaning. That is, all of the allomorphs which can be subclassified under the same morpheme type are found to have similar characteristics of both meaning and distribution; they all have the same relationship to the structure with which they are most closely associated.

Some morphemes seem to be one of a kind, while others have numerous variations. We have already seen, for example, that *boy* is made plural by the addition of the plural inflectional morpheme, {-*s*}. Actually, the pronunciation of this morpheme is /z/. Now, paying attention to sound, notice how we make these words plural:

SINGULAR {ø}	PLURAL {-*s*}	
radio	*radios* (radio + /z/)	
cap	*caps* (cap + /s/)	
box	*boxes* (box + /ɨz/)	
house	*houses* (house + /ɨz/ with a change in the pronunciation of the final consonant in the stem)	

$$\left\{\begin{array}{l}child\\brother\\ox\end{array}\right\} \quad \left\{\begin{array}{l}children\\brethren\\oxen\end{array}\right. \quad \text{(stem + /in/ with or without a concomitant modification of the stem)}$$

$$\left\{\begin{array}{l}man\\mouse\\tooth\end{array}\right\} \quad \left\{\begin{array}{l}men\\mice\\teeth\end{array}\right. \quad \text{(stem + plural morpheme which modifies the vowel form of the stem)}$$

| *sheep* | *sheep* (stem + zero allomorph) | |

$$\left\{\begin{array}{l}criterion\\alumnus\end{array}\right\} \quad \left\{\begin{array}{l}criteria\\alumni\end{array}\right. \quad \text{(words borrowed from other languages which retain original forms)}$$

As you can see, there are quite a few variations, most of which the speaker is scarcely aware of. All of these different morphs indicating plurality are allomorphs, i.e., class members belonging to the single morpheme class {-s.} In other words, the plural morpheme does not signify sound, nor does it symbolize spelling. All it does is to carry the grammatical information: *plural*.

Some of the verb inflection morphemes also have allomorphs. In fact, the {-ing} morpheme is the only one which has only one allomorph. The third person singular inflectional morpheme, for example, can take at least three different phonetic forms; and there are a good many past and perfect aspect morphemes which produce modifications in irregular verb stems.

NULL FORM ({ø})	THIRD PERSON SINGULAR FORM ({-s})
type	*types* (stem + /s/)
run	*runs* (stem + /z/)
pass	*passes* (stem + /ɨz/)
do	*does* ⎫ (stem + allomorph which
say	*says* ⎬ causes a modification in
have	*has* ⎭ the stem)

The past tense morpheme, also, has a great many allomorphs, some of which are illustrated in the following list:

jab	*jabbed* (stem + /d/)
step	*stepped* (stem × /t/)
treat	*treated* (stem × /ɨd/)
{*hit*	*hit* (stem + zero allomorph)
{*set*	*set*
ring	*rang* ⎫
cling	*clung*
mean	*meant*
feed	*fed* all of these
write	*wrote* irregular forms are
send	*sent* said to be morpho-
think	*thought* logically conditioned
throw	*threw* allomorphs*
freeze	*froze*
grind	*ground*
take	*took* ⎭

*There is nothing phonological about their occurrence. Rather, the irregularity is a peculiarity of the morpheme in question.

Similarly, there are numerous {-en} allomorphs, most of which follow quite irregular patterns.

In the same way, irregular adjectives display a number of allomorphs:

{ø}	{-er}	{-est}
sad	*sadder*	*saddest*
good	*better*	*best*
bad	*worse*	*worst*
many	*more*	*most*

Some of these words have what are called phonologically conditioned allomorphs, which means simply that the phonetic form of the morpheme is determined by the sound of the last vowel or consonant of the stem. Others are morphologically conditioned; that is, they are "irregular" for whatever accident of a language's historical development. They simply must be learned.

The usual practice is to decide on a single notation symbol for each of the inflectional morphemes, and to represent each of the allomorphs of a particular morpheme by this same symbol.

Classification of Words by their Morphological Structure

TERM	MAXIMUM FORMS	MINIMUM FORMS	PARADIGM (INFLECTIONAL FORMS)			
			Singular {φ}	Plural {-s}	Singular Possessive {'s}	Plural Possessive {s'}
NOUN	4	2	boy man sheep* this* that*	boys men sheep these those	boy's man's sheep's	boys' men's sheep's

TERM	MAXIMUM FORMS	MINIMUM FORMS	Singular (Subject)	Singular (Object)	Plural (Subj)	Plural (Obj)	Singular Possessive	Plural Possessive
PRONOUN	8	3	I you he she it who	me you him her it whom	we you they they they who	us you them them them whom	my, mine your, yours his her, hers its whose	our, ours your, yours their, theirs their, theirs their, theirs whose

*Even though on first analysis these irregular forms will be missed, we will find that as soon as syntactic environment reveals more about characteristic noun distribution, we can come back and add them. *This* and *that* are classified as nouns solely on the basis of their morphological structure: each of these words has a plural form but no other forms.

Classification of Words by their Morphological Structure (continued)

TERM	MAXIMUM FORMS	MINIMUM FORMS	PARADIGM (INFLECTIONAL FORMS)				
			{ø}	{-s}	{-ed}	{-ing}	{-en}
VERB	8	3	like do set {be am are}	likes does sets is	liked did set {was were}	liking doing setting being	liked done set been
			Positive {ø}		Comparative {-er}		Superlative {-est}
ADJECTIVE	3	3	sad bad good much, many		sadder worse better more		saddest worst best most

FORMAL WORD CLASSES   EXERCISE 40

Directions: Classify the following words, according to their morphological structure, as one of the following:

N for noun
PRO for pronoun
V for verb

ADJ for adjective
ADV (-ly) for uninflected -*ly* adverb
UW for uninflected word other than the
    -*ly* adverb

1. tightened
2. its
3. different
4. those
5. less
6. gorgeous
7. always
8. fastening
9. theirs
10. falters
11. slowly
12. primal
13. chilly
14. reflection
15. shall
16. truism
17. slanted
18. ought
19. crept
20. went

21. wildly
22. cent
23. funny
24. going
25. foolish
26. whom
27. good
28. taken
29. during
30. the
31. more
32. insured
33. fled
34. truth
35. cook's
36. faster
37. should
38. sanctify
39. slyly
40. came

VERB FORMS   **EXERCISE 41**

Directions: Supply all inflectional forms for the following verbs.

1. love

2. earn

3. talk

4. say

5. come

6. get

7. lie*

8. lay

9. see

10. be

*This is the verb "to recline," not the verb "to tell a fib".

17

English Syntax and Syntactical Analysis

We can go no further with word classification at the strictly morphological level. Our next task is therefore to look beyond isolated word forms to determine the syntactic environments in which certain word types typically occur. The assumption, of course, is that there will be a system: some patterns of organization which contribute to grammatical meaning.

We can begin the syntactical analysis of words by first determining the characteristic distribution of words in the four major paradigmatic series. But before we begin, we need an investigative method.

METHODOLOGY: TEST FRAMES

One of the most basic methodological tools developed by the structuralists for analyzing the syntactic structural distribution of constructions is the test frame. Test frames are simply phrases or sentences with a blank space for the structure which is to be tested. They permit linguists to discover syntactic class membership, and to answer the following questions objectively.

1. Is there a systematic set of word order patterns in English?

2. If so, what kind of structures go where?

3. Are there typical sentence positions which certain structures characteristically occupy?

4. If so, is this a consistent syntactical feature of certain structures?

5. Are there particular syntactical positions which are never occupied by certain structures?

166

If word order is grammatically significant in English, then it should be possible to devise test frames for the purpose of identifying all of the word classes. And if the test frames do succeed in verifying the importance of syntactic position, linguists should be able to classify words and larger structures as well by this syntactic criterion.

Since thousands of English words fall into the patterned forms represented by the noun paradigm, this seems a good place to begin. For a noun test frame to be valid, it must make it possible to answer two important questions about noun distribution:

1. May the form being tested for (noun, at the moment) *always* occupy the blank position?

2. Are all other word forms excluded from this position?

Suppose that, putting ourselves in the place of the linguist, we start out with the test frame, "____ cry". Certainly, nouns like *boys*, *babies*, and the like can fill the blank position. But so can other words, like the verb form *do*, or the uninflected word *why*. This means that we need a better test frame.

Examining the English sentences in our corpus, we discover that nouns quite often occupy the position immediately after *a*, *an*, and *the*. Following this clue, we might try a new frame: "The ____ cry." In this new test frame, words like *do* and *why* are excluded. Nevertheless, we still do not have a valid test frame, because we find that a verb form like *disturbed* can still occupy the blank slot.

Perhaps the test frame can be sharpened if we narrow the possibilities by requiring a noun morpheme after the test word: "The ____{-s} cry." This, at last, seems to be what we want.

Of course this single test frame will not be sufficient to permit the classification of nouns according to every syntactic environment in which noun structures may occur. If, as Fries argued, a sentence is a structural pattern which is made up of "parts of speech" which can be identified *both* by their formal markers (the various paradigmatic forms) *and* by their position or positions in the pattern, then we must test for all sentence positions in which that part of speech can occur. In other words Fries, who was the first of the structuralists to classify parts of speech by both formal and syntactic position criteria, and James Sledd, who later carried this dual classification system to its ultimate stage, both recognized that "position" in a sentence pattern or patterns becomes an important classification criterion.

Consider for a moment how we can determine the adjective class according to the characteristic adjective positions. Let us suppose we have in our corpus the sentence, "The ice is cold." This is obviously an

English sentence, and obviously an adjective (as determined by its form characteristics) occurs in a post-verb position. If we try to use "The ice is _____ " as a test frame, however, we find that several other word forms besides the adjective can fill the sentence slot equally well. For example, the verb form *melting* fills the slot, as does the uninflected word form *here* or *there*, or even a pronoun form like *mine* or *his*.

One way to narrow the possibilities might be to include the word *very* immediately before the blank space in the test frame: "The ice is very _____." This frame now seems to exclude words like *melting*, *here*, and *mine*. On the other hand, only the null form of an adjective will fill the slot, which means that we must devise test frames to account for the other two adjective forms in the subjective complement position. This can be done, we discover, by the simple expedient of requiring an {-*er*} or an {-*est*} suffix on the word that is to fit the slot: "The ice is much _____{-*er*.}" The fact that the -*est* adjective form cannot be made to fill the post linking verb position suggests, however, that it is ungrammatical to do so. (We do not say "The ice is coldest." In fact, {-*est*} adjectives seem to occur immediately preceding nouns.)

Some of the most useful adjective test frames which linguists devised after much testing, rejecting, and re-testing, are ones which require that the same word form fill each of two slots in frames like these:

$$\text{The} \underline{\quad} \{\emptyset\} \text{ ice } \begin{Bmatrix} \text{is} \\ \text{seems} \end{Bmatrix} \text{very} \underline{\quad} \{\emptyset\}$$

$$\text{The} \underline{\quad} \begin{Bmatrix} \text{-er} \\ \text{-est} \end{Bmatrix} \text{ ice } \begin{Bmatrix} \text{is} \\ \text{seems} \end{Bmatrix} \underline{\quad} \begin{Bmatrix} \text{-er} \\ \text{-est} \end{Bmatrix}$$

Hundreds of test frame models similar to these provide a method for determining the fundamental sentence positions for particular word forms already identified as belonging to one of the inflectional paradigm classes, so there are now two criteria for classifying "parts of speech."

SYNTAX: TEST FRAMES   EXERCISE 42

Directions: Below are sentences representative of seven different structural patterns. They will be referred to by number for this exercise.

1. Birds fly.
2. John hit the ball.
3. John gave Mary a book.
4. They judged us happy.

5. The class thought her a loser.
6. The climate is warm.
7. Martha is a teacher.

1. Is this a good test frame for the two slots in Sentence 1: _____ _____. Explain. If it is not, what would be a better solution?

2. Is this a good test frame for the verbal slot in Sentence 2: John _____ the ball. Devise a test frame for each of the other three slots in this sentence pattern.

3. How could you provide for the possibility that the subject of Sentence 2 might be a noun phrase like "the boy"?
Or how might you provide for the possibility of filling the direct object slot with a proper noun rather than an NP?

4. Which sentence number might this be a good test frame for: The boy was _____. Explain, and if possible, provide a solution to the problem you see.

5. The following test frame fits either Sentence 4 or 5, which means it is no good: The boy thought her _____. How can you change the frame to a good one for Sentence 4? Now, how can you change the test frame for Sentence 5?

6. If you wish to devise a test frame for a sentence like Sentence 1, which adds an adverbial slot after *fly* (as in "Birds fly swiftly"), is this a good one: Birds fly _____. Can you improve it?

METHODOLOGY: IMMEDIATE CONSTITUENT ANALYSIS

Another important methodological tool for syntactic analysis, and probably structuralism's most useful one, is a method called immediate constituent analysis (IC analysis), first developed by Leonard Bloomfield. Having observed that many words seem to come in pairs, he wondered if entire sentences might not also be constructed by a system of successive layers of pairs. If sentences could be shown to consist of several layers of successively smaller constructions, each with its own pair of immediate constituents, much could be learned about syntactic relationships. Not only could pairs of words be shown to have a direct syntactical relationship to each other, but the same might be demonstrated for larger constructions as well.

Consider, for example, a sentence like this one:

The pretty girls in the car are smiling gaily at each other.

Beginning at the word level (which is the smallest sentence constituent), one intuitively senses a close relationship between several pairs of words:

Now, if we consider each of these four pairs as a single grammatical unit at the next higher level, we see that the new construction becomes a constituent which relates immediately to some other constituent:

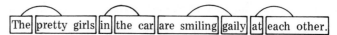

Then, at the next level, each still larger construction, becomes in turn an immediate constituent until the largest syntactical construction of all is reached, the sentence:

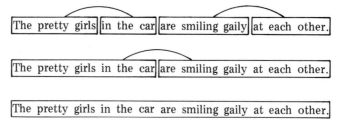

If this reasoning is correct, the process should work in the other direction as well. That is, starting with the largest unit, the sentence, it should be possible to make successive binary cuts until single words are reached. Each time a cut is made, the two constituent parts of a construction should relate completely and directly to each other: that is, they should be immediate constituents which apply their entire grammatical meaning to one another. The following diagram shows the same sentence analyzed into immediate constituents from sentence to single words (ultimate constituents):

Sentence:	The pretty girls in the car	are smiling gaily at each other.						
Level 1:	The pretty girls	in the car	are smiling gaily	at each other.				
Level 2:	The	pretty girls	in	the car	are smiling	gaily	at	each other.
Level 3:		pretty	girls		the	car	are	smiling			each	other.

So far, of course, you may object that immediate constituent analysis has relied heavily on the analyst's intuitive feelings about where the cuts should be made (including the considerable assistance of intonation patterns). No more seems to have been accomplished than was possible with traditional sentence diagrams. If, however, linguists were able to demonstrate that each construction larger than a single word could be replaced with a single word, that would be objective evidence to verify that a larger construction can function as a single grammatical unit. These replacement words need not be synonymous paraphrases. The only requirement is that they be words that function syntactically, both as a construction and as a constituent at the next higher level, in the same way that the larger construction functions. Thus, the construction *pretty girls* can be shown to perform the same grammatical function as a word like *men, women, boys, girls,* or some other plural noun does, and vice versa. *Are sitting* is replaceable with a single past or present intransitive verb, and so on. The following diagram illustrates the process:

The	college	girls	who	are	studying	in	class	speak	in	low	voices.
The	coeds		who		study		there	speak	in	whispers	
The	coeds				studying		there	speak	softly		
The	coeds				studying			whisper			
The	students							whisper			
They								whisper			

IC analysis is not, of course, infallible. In fact, there are some sentences which for various reasons do not lend themselves to this kind of analysis.* Nevertheless, it proved to be a generally useful tool which enabled the structural linguist to discover many things about grammatical syntax and which revealed much about the constructional patterns of English sentences. It also provided him with an objective method (or so he thought) for describing and identifying sentence constituents and syntactical behavior without recourse to his intuitions about lexical meaning. This latter claim has since been seriously challenged, but we will save the attacks on structural procedures until later.

---

*Not all sentences can be treated by the successive one-for-two word paraphrase replacement technique used to verify constituent boundaries. All sentences can, on the other hand, be parsed, although the IC diagrams for sentences like "It's disgusting the way he tries to curry favor" will probably become so involved that they reveal very little.

The following is an IC diagram of a fairly complex English sentence.

The girl in the room who waved her hand after the tests came back wanted my attention very badly														
The girl in the room who waved her hand after the tests came back	wanted my attention very badly
The girl in the room	who waved her hand after the tests came back	wanted my attention	very badly
The girl	in the room	who	waved her hand after the tests came back	wanted	my attention	very	badly
The	girl	in	the room		waved her hand	after the tests came back		my	attention	
		the	room		waved	her hand	after	the tests came back	
					her	hand		the tests	came back
								the	tests	came	back

As IC analysis shows, English sentences are constructed in an organized, patterned way. The smallest unit at the syntactical level of structural grammar analysis is the word, and the largest unit is the sentence. Within these lower and upper limits, the sentence is the only unit that is not a constituent and the word is the only unit that is not a construction.* All units in between are both constructions and constituents, depending upon which level of sentence analysis is being discussed.

We can therefore define a constituent as any syntactical unit which combines with another syntactical unit to form a construction. A construction can be defined as any syntactical unit containing constituents. For example, the construction *the girl in the room* is itself made up of eight constituents: one prepositional phrase, two noun phrases, and five words. Only two of these, however (*the girl* + *in the room*), are immediate constituents. Each of these constituents is itself a construction made up of its own two ICs (*the* + *girl*; *in* + *the room*), and so on.

Every constituent can be classified according to two criteria: (1) in terms of its own internal constituent makeup; and (2) in terms of its grammatical function (relation), as a unit, in the larger syntactic environment (i.e., its syntactic relationship to other constituents).

In the next chapter we shall classify all English sentence constituents into two sets of classes according to these two criteria. Before we leave this discussion of IC analysis, however, it should be observed that the structuralists found no *new* constituents. All they did was to develop

---

*A word does have constituent parts, but these are analyzed at the morphological rather than at the syntactical level of grammar.

more "objective" empirical tests for validating the intuitive parsing of the traditionalists.

SYNTAX: IMMEDIATE CONSTITUENT ANALYSIS   EXERCISE 43

Directions: For the sentence *The boy who is driving the car will park behind the house*, write out at least one syntactically different construction (two, if you can) which can replace each of the constructions listed below. The replacement need not mean exactly the same thing lexically as the structure it is replacing, but it must be a construction which functions in the same way grammatically. (For example, do not replace a subject with a predicate.) Maintain the same basic syntactical sentence pattern and the same basic grammatical relationships.

1. *the boy*

2. *is driving*

3. *who is driving the car*

4. *the boy who is driving the car*

5. *will park*

6. *behind the house*

7. *the house*

SYNTAX: IMMEDIATE CONSTITUENT ANALYSIS   EXERCISE 44

Directions: Reduce each of the following three sentences to ultimate constituents (single words) by as many levels of immediate constituent "cuts" as are required. Follow the same procedure as that used in the previous chapter. Notice that each of these three sentences makes use of exactly the same words. The only difference among them is word order. Do you see any evidence that syntactical position can make a difference in the grammatical meaning of a construction?

1. The small boy planted many tulip bulbs in the garden.

2. The boy in the garden planted many small tulip bulbs.

3. In the small garden, the boy planted many tulip bulbs.

SYNTAX: IMMEDIATE CONSTITUENT ANALYSIS   **EXERCISE 45**

Directions: Cut each of the following constructions into immediate constituents. Keep making cuts until you get down to single words.

1. on the table
2. five very pretty sorority girls
3. having hit the huge red ball
4. after the men had left the party
5. the young woman who is coming through the door
6. because he should have finished the book

18

Syntactic Classes

Up to this point we have gone only as far with classifying as the internal structure of words will permit. On the basis of their morphemic composition, all words have been divided into two broad groups: (1) inflectional words which have a number of related forms that correspond to four major paradigms; and (2) uniflectional words which take only one form. Of the second group, we have isolated the *adverb* (narrowly defined as the null form of an adjective plus *-ly*); other *derivational* words like *beautiful, porous, frantic,* and the like; and a host of word forms which never accept either a derivational or an inflectional suffix. We cannot proceed beyond this level of analysis without dealing with syntax.

Now, however, armed with the kind of information provided by test frames and IC analysis methods, we can continue the classification. When all of the words and all of the larger-than-word constructions have been put into two different classes according to their internal structure and their external behavior, there will be a total of thirty-two classes: eighteen form classes and fourteen function classes.

The chart on the next page represents the completed classification system. As we discuss structuralism's methods of arriving at these conclusions, you may find it helpful to refer back to this outline to see where we have been and where we are going. The first seven form classes (down to the broken line) are the only ones so far identified.

The linguist's goal is to identify particular syntactical positions characteristically occupied by given constructional forms and to determine the syntactic relationships which exist between and among constituents. This process begins with the distributional analysis of the word forms already identified as nouns, pronouns, verbs, adjectives, and

Classification by Form and Function

FORM CLASSES	FUNCTION CLASSES	
Words (Classified by Permitted Affixation) Noun Pronoun Verb Adjective Adverb (-ly) Other Uninflectable Words *Constructions* (Classified by Internal Structure) Compound Word Noun Phrase Predicate Phrase Verb Phrase I Verb Phrase II Adjectival Phrase Adverbial Phrase Absolute Phrase Prepositional Phrase Wh Clause, Relative Clause Subordinate Clause Sentence	*Lexical Words and Constructions* (Classified by Major Grammatical Functions)	*Structure Words* (Non-major Function Classes Occurring as Constituents of Constructions)
	Nominal	Relative (Wh Word) I Interrogative I Intensive Reflexive
	Verbal	Auxiliary
	Adjectival	Determiner Relative (Wh Word) II Interrogative II
	Adverbial	Relative (Wh Word) III Interrogative III
		Preposition Subordinator Coordinator Qualifier

adverbs. If each of these structures does occur in characteristic and exclusive positions, it will be possible to identify particular sentence slots as noun slots, or verb slots, or whatever. The terms *noun, verb, adjective,* and the like, will not be used in reference to noun or verb or adjective positions, however, for structuralists do not want their terminology to reflect more than one kind of feature. The following terms will be used instead:*

*See Sledd, *A Short Introduction to English Grammar,* in which this approach is used.

Nominal Position: any basic position which may always be occupied by a noun or a pronoun form.

Verbal Position: any basic position which may always be occupied by a verb form.

Adjectival Position: any basic position which may always be occupied by an adjective form.

Adverbial Position: any basic position which may always be occupied by an *-ly* adverb form.

In the process of establishing these positions, it becomes apparent that particular grammatical relationships exist between the construction which occupies a given slot and some other construction in a different sentence slot. It also becomes obvious, at some point in the analysis, that a given slot, a nominal slot for example, might sometimes be occupied by a structure other than a noun. When this happens, however, the replacement construction behaves exactly as the noun behaves in that position. It is then possible to see how it is that a verb form, say, which occurs in a nominal position instead of in a basic verbal position, functions grammatically in the same way that the noun in that same syntactical environment functions.

Before we examine replacements, it will be useful to list all of the major sentence positions along with the grammatical functions of structures in these positions.

NOMINAL POSITIONS AND FUNCTIONS. IC analysis permits the linguist to isolate the following seven syntactic positions which are characteristically occupied by a noun or a pronoun:

1. *Birds* fly.

He wants *John* to win.

John's winning was expected.

First $\begin{Bmatrix} \text{noun} \\ \text{pron} \end{Bmatrix}$ in a $\begin{Bmatrix} \text{noun} \\ \text{pron} \end{Bmatrix}$ + verb pattern. Structure in this slot functions as subject of a verb.

2. She is digging *worms.*

They expect to have a *party.*

The $\begin{Bmatrix} \text{noun} \\ \text{pron} \end{Bmatrix}$ following a transitive verb form. Structure in this slot functions as direct object of a verb.

3. He showed *them* the books.

She sent the *chief* a letter.

The first of two $\begin{Bmatrix} \text{nouns} \\ \text{prons} \end{Bmatrix}$ following a transitive verb form. Structure in this position functions as the indirect object of the verb.

4. We consider John a *sissy.*

{Noun / Pron} following a direct object nominal; functions as object complement (is related to direct object across an implied linking verb).*

5. Mr. Jones is the *leader.*

{Noun / Pron} following a linking verb; functions as subject complement (is related to subject across the linking verb).

6. He went to the *store.*

John came to *school.*

{Noun / Pron} following a preposition; is related, through the preposition, to another sentence constituent which typically precedes the preposition.

7. My sister, *Mary,* is young.

{Noun / Pron} following any nominal and related to that nominal across an implied linking verb.

VERBAL POSITIONS AND FUNCTIONS.

1. She *tries* too hard.

By *trying* hard, he *has succeeded.*

All verb forms of any verb phrase; when several verb forms occupy this position, the last verb is the headword of the verb phrase.

ADJECTIVAL POSITIONS AND FUNCTIONS.

1. Jane is *tall.*

Adjective following a linking verb; relates to subject across the linking verb.

2. I call that dog *muddy.*

Adjective following direct object; relates to DO across an implied linking verb.

3. a *good* boy; the *old* man

Adjective preceding a nominal; relates to the nominal.

*A pointed question can be raised here. How did the structuralist identify transitive, intransitive, and linking verbs, for example, without recourse to meaning? Yet James Sledd's formulas in *A Short Introduction* . . . make these distinctions, as does Verna Newsome in *Structural Grammar in the Classroom.*

4. God *Almighty*   Adjective immediately following a nominal. Structure in this position relates directly to the nominal.

ADVERBIAL POSITIONS AND FUNCTIONS. You will remember that in classifying words by the first syntactic criterion (according to their internal structural features) we tentatively singled out the *-ly* adverb for two reasons: (1) it is a word with a unique morphological composition; and (2) its frequency of occurrence aroused our attention. As we now try to establish whether words of this type do in fact occupy characteristic sentence positions, we see that our suspicions are justified. Most of the time, the adverb occurs in close proximity to a verb form, which suggests there is a grammatical relationship between the two. In fact, there is only one adverbial position which places the adverb at some distance from the verb (illustrated by Example 4 below). Yet intonation patterns, which have been helpful in determining where the IC cuts should be made, provide reason for believing that this initial sentence position is not characteristic. (Our observation has been that when words appear in their typical positions, no unusual pauses occur within a sentence.) Notice too that wherever the adverb occurs it always receives the strongest stress.

1. He *quickly* left.
He must have *quickly* left.   Immediately preceding the main verb.

2. He left *quickly*.
He must have left *quickly*.   Immediately following the main verb.

3. He finished the work *quickly*.   At the very end of the predicate phrase.

4. *Quickly*, he finished the work.   In the initial sentence position.

CLASSIFYING THE OTHER UNINFLECTIONAL WORDS. We have now established four major syntactic positions and have classified constructions which characteristically occupy these positions as nominals, verbals, adjectivals, or adverbials. Had structuralists not been so determined to banish semantic considerations from their grammar analyses, they would have admitted that (1) the entire IC cutting procedure probably worked as well as it did because they *were* paying some attention to meaning; and that (2) the word classes so far identified as nominal, verbal, adjectival, or adverbial are all *lexical* words.

A lexical word is a word with a vocabulary meaning. Such a word has meaning content when it stands alone. Our two systems of classification have, at this stage of our investigation, accounted for most such lexical words. Some remain, however, that have not yet been syntactically classified.

One type of lexical word overlooked in the earlier paradigmatic classifying are irregular nouns like *chaos*, *sheep*, and *trousers*, which have only one form for both singular and plural; and irregular words like the noun, *mouse*, and the verbs, *see*, *go*, *throw*, and so on, which have irregular paradigmatic forms. All of these may now be classified as both formal nouns, verbs, adjectives, and so on, and also as syntactic nominals, verbals, and so on.

The remaining kind of lexical words are those like *beautiful*, *frantic*, *porous*, *rapidly*, *hurriedly*, which never occur in related forms. We shall therefore continue to classify such words as uninflected words by our formal criterion. By the second, syntactic criterion, however, we find that we can put them in nominal, verbal, adjectival, and adverbial classes along with the other lexical words. *Beautiful*, for example, is an adjectival because it can replace a formal adjective in any characteristic adjectival sentence slot. The same thing is true of many compounds. That is, if a compound can replace a noun, it is a nominal; if it can replace a verb, it is a verbal, and so forth.

Ultimately, we find that we are able to classify all lexical words as nominals, verbals, adjectivals, or adverbials. The only words that are left are uninflected forms like *a*, *the*, *of*, *from*, *must*, *and*, *which*, *very*, and so on. These are words that, for the most part, are devoid of meaning content when they stand alone. An examination of any corpus of collected English utterances will reveal, however, that these little words, known as *structure words* or *function words*, are far from unimportant. In fact, as another glance at the nonsense sentences with which we began our discussion of structural grammar will verify, the whole of English syntax seems to rely heavily on the grammatical information which these structure words provide.

CLASSIFYING THE STRUCTURE WORDS. Although they have little or no lexical meaning, structure words, as you will see, carry a great deal of grammatical meaning. IC analysis shows that most of these words occur as constituent members of larger constructions. As we analyze and classify the uninflected, no-suffix words, therefore, we shall inevitably be involved with the larger constructions of which they are a part or with which they are intimately associated. We shall classify both the structure words and the larger constructions as we complete our syntactic analysis of English sentences.

If at any time during the course of studying the next few pages you become confused, you should turn to the outline of syntactic classes on pages 192 and 193.

1. DETERMINERS as Constituents of **NOUN PHRASES.** Determiners are words like *a, an, the, some,* which, when they occur, always occur as contituents in a larger construction called the Noun Phrase (hereafter NP). (The NP construction, in turn, becomes a constituent of a still larger construction at some higher level of the sentence building process.) The following are all examples of NPs. The noun or compound noun which heads each NP is in boldface; each determiner is italicized:

the **boy**	*the* big beautiful **pine tree**
a big **boy**	*a* shiny bright red **apple**
an **apple** in *a* dish	**boys** who hate girls
some very strong **men**	*the* young **man** in *the* shower singing at *the* top of *his* lungs
my too-friendly **dog**	*this* idiotic, overly friendly **dog** who won't stop licking me

The NP is called a "headed" construction. This means that it contains one constituent (usually a noun or a compound noun) which dominates the entire construction, a fact that can be verified by demonstrating that the head construction (headword) can grammatically substitute for the entire construction of which it is a part when the NP becomes a constituent in a larger syntactic environment, as in IC replacements.

Every NP is constructed according to an organized, systematic word order pattern. We shall save a detailed analysis until the next chapter, but for the moment please note that when a determiner occurs as one of the constituents, it always precedes the nominal head construction.

In addition to having a determiner as a possible constituent, an NP might also contain other constituents, some of which may themselves be phrases or clauses with their own set of constituent members. Consider, for example, the NP, "*an* **apple** in *a* dish." *Apple* is the noun headword, preceded by a determiner, *an,* and followed by a prepositional phrase, *in a dish,* which itself consists of a preposition plus an NP. In other words, English syntax is such that we often find layer upon layer of constructions, each nested within another. The NP can be defined as a group of grammatically related words containing a noun or nominal headword.

Now let us consider words like *a, an,* and *the,* which we have been calling determiners. The label is actually a shortened version of noun determiner, and thus describes the grammatical function performed by a word in this class. Note that although nouns and nominals can occur, even in NPs, without being preceded by a determiner, *the reverse is never true.* Whenever a determiner does occur a noun always and inevitably follows. It may follow immediately or there may be intervening constructions, but speakers of English can count on its appearance sooner or later. Thus, these little structure words perform a significant grammatical function: they signal "A noun will follow."

Some nouns require that a determiner precede them, as can be demonstrated with these test frames: (Use *a, an,* or *the* as a prototype.)

_____ boy ate. He found _____ apple. I gave it to _____ boy.

The words *a, an,* and *the,* traditionally labeled articles, always function as determiners in determiner slots like these. Other words can replace them, however, such as possessive forms of nouns or pronouns (*Mary's, John's, my, her, his*); or words like *this, that, these, those, some, many.* Any word form which functions in the determiner position is syntactically classed as a determiner. The *determiner* can therefore be defined as *any word or construction which is a constituent in an NP and which determines that a noun must follow.*

2. AUXILIARIES as Constituents of **VERB PHRASES.** As with determiners, we find that we cannot fully describe words of the auxiliary class without taking note of the verb phrase (VP) construction of which an auxiliary is often a constituent part. We shall define the *VP* as *a construction consisting of a verb headword often preceded by one or more auxiliaries.* The number of auxiliaries seems to be limited to three subclasses in the active voice, four in the passive. Three sets of examples follow. Set 1 examples illustrate two-word VPs, Set 2 illustrates three-word VPs, and Set 3 illustrates four-word VPs. These are all active voice VPs. The verb headword is in boldface and the auxiliaries are italicized:

1. *may* **leave,** *shall* **go,** *ought to* **see,** *might* **come**
   have **left,** *has* **gone,** *had* **seen**
   am **leaving,** *are* **going,** *is* **doing**
   do **leave,** *does* **go,** *did* **see**

2. *may have* **left,** *should have* **gone,** *will have* **seen**
   may be **leaving,** *should be* **going,** *ought to be* **seeing**
   have been **leaving,** *has been* **going,** *had been* **seeing**

3. *may have been* **leaving,** *must have been* **going,**
   will have been **seeing,** *ought to have been* **doing**

All of the examples just given can be used as intransitive verbs and may therefore function as the entire predicate of a sentence or a clause. However, a VP might have a transitive or a linking main verb as headword and therefore be only a constituent of an entire predicate phrase:

might have **hit**, *is* **being**, *may have been* **pleasing**

We shall call all VPs, whether their headword is transitive, intransitive, or linking, Type I VPs (or VP I) to distinguish them from a second kind of VP (VP II) which, because of missing auxiliary words or because of the fact that they all begin with an *-ing* word, an infinitive, or an *-en* verb form, can never function as part or all of the predicate in a clause or a sentence:

having **seen**, *being* **done**, *having been* **arrested**, *to have* **seen**

These are the verb phrase forms which traditional grammar called verbals rather than verbs, and subclassified further as infinitives, gerunds, or participles. We shall not use the traditional terminology here, because in structural linguistics the term *verbal* is the name of a syntactic class.

Either a VP I or a VP II may contain at least one auxiliary. For Type I VPs, the auxiliary is any constituent which fills the slot in any of the following test frames for active voice verbs:

1. He _____ go. He _____ be going. He _____ have gone.
He _____ have been going.

2. He must _____ gone. She _____ gone. He will _____ been going.

3. He must _____ going. She _____ going. He will have _____ going.

As you can see from these test frames, an auxiliary may be a member of one of three subclasses. The kind of auxiliary required in the Set 1 test frame slots is known as a *modal* (unless the sentence is emphatic, in which case a form of the verb *do* can fill the slot). The modal is an uninflected word, not a verb, according to the formal structural definition of verb. It and all other auxiliaries are, however, intimately associated with the main verb; in fact, they always precede it. Therefore, we classify all auxiliaries as subclasses of the larger verbal class. Some examples of typical modals are *shall, will, could, would, may, might, must, can*, and sometimes a two or three word form like *ought to, used to, was to*, and so on.

The slots of the Set 2 test frames must be filled by a form of the auxiliary verb *have*; and the Set 3 slots must be filled by a form of the auxiliary verb *be*.

Observe these three things (and remember, we are discussing active VPs only):

1. One, two, or three auxiliaries may precede the headword of a VP.

2. Regardless of how many auxiliaries are present, they must occur in a given order: Modal + *have* + *be*.

3. A close grammatical relationship exists between every auxiliary and the auxiliary or verb which immediately follows it:

    a) the modal imposes the null (ø) form on the verb to its immediate right;

    b) *have* imposes the *-en* form on the verb which immediately follows it;

    c) *be* imposes the *-ing* form on the verb immediately following it.

In summary, we can define the auxiliary as a ***modal, have,*** or ***be,*** *any or all of which may precede a main verb in a VP, and in that order.* Thus, although a verb may occur without an auxiliary, an auxiliary never occurs unless it is followed by a main verb in a VP. Other constituents may or may not intervene. The occurrence of an auxiliary therefore signals in English that a main verb will follow.

VPs as Constituents in **PREDICATE PHRASES.** If the main verb of a VP is an intransitive verb, it may function as the immediate constituent of the subject noun or NP. That is, it may function as the entire predicate. If, however, an adverbial or a complement occurs, the VP combines with it or them to form a larger construction called the predicate phrase (Pred P). The *predicate phrase* can be defined as *a construction made up of a verb or a VP constituent plus an adverbial or a complement or both, either one of* which may be *a single word or a larger construction.* Here are some examples of predicate phrases (the constituents are marked):

must have finished quickly verbal adverbial	(VP I + Adverb)
backed into the corner verbal adverbial	(Verb + Prepositional Phrase)

must have been losing his mind
     verbal   nominal
               (complement)
	(VP I + NP)

quietly put the test in the waste basket adver- ver- nominal adverbial bial bal	(Adv + V + NP + Prep P)
having written the major an angry letter verbal nominal nominal	(VP II + NP + NP)
being backed into a corner verbal adverbial	(VP II + Prep P)

Predicate Phrases as Constituents in Clauses or **Absolute Phrases**. Since there are several kinds of clauses, we shall examine their internal constituent structure later. It is enough to know at this point that a clause consists of at least a subject nominal plus a predicate phrase containing a fully conjugated verb. The absolute phrase, on the other hand, also contains a subject and a predicate, except that the predicate contains a VP II, a partially conjugated verb. Examples of each of these follow:

Predicate Phrase as IC of a Clause

The old man has worked hard for his money.   (NP + Pred P containing a VP II)
   nominal   verbal
   (subject)   (predicate)

John will surely succeed.   (Noun + Pred P containing a VP II)
nom-   verbal
inal

Predicate Phrase as IC of an Absolute Phrase

The storm having stopped   (NP + VP II)
  nominal   verbal

His talent being so great   (NP + Pred P containing a VP II)
  nominal   verbal

3. Qualifiers as Constituents in **Adjectival Phrases and Adverbial Phrases**. Another structure word, which *always occurs as a constituent in a larger construction, and which functions to determine that a larger head constituent* must *follow, is the qualifier.* Using the uninflected word *very* as the prototype, we can note that when *very* occurs, *either an adjectival or adverbial headword* must follow. In fact, the qualifier proved useful in test frames for these two major classes. The construction in which a qualifier is a constituent will therefore always be like one of the examples below. The qualifier is italicized, and the headword is in boldface:

ADJECTIVAL PHRASES	ADVERBIAL PHRASES
very **happy**	*very* **happily**
quite **sad**	*quite* **sadly**
rather **pretty**	*rather* **well**
extremely **beautiful**	*extremely* **poorly**
utterly **without hope**	*most* **unhappily**

Notice that certain inflectional or derivational words may function as qualifiers. Any structure which can replace *very* (or some other prototype like *quite*) in the qualifier slot functions as a qualifier.

Traditional grammar lumped qualifiers with adverbs. It is not clear whether the traditionalists made their adverb class a kind of catchall class because they just did not want to increase the number of word classes, or whether they failed to take into account the "double life" some words can lead. In the examples below, for instance, the words *greatly* and *utterly* can belong to either the adverbial class or the qualifier class, depending on the contextual syntactic environment:

ADVERBIAL	QUALIFIER
He wished *greatly* for a vacation.	He was *greatly* unhappy.
He stopped loving her *utterly*.	She was *utterly* hopeless.

4. PREPOSITIONS as Constituents in **PREPOSITIONAL PHRASES.** *The prepositional phrase is a non-headed group of grammatically related constructions among which two constituents* must *be included: an uninflected, no-suffix word called a preposition and a nominal which functions as the object of the preposition.* Ordinarily the prepositional phrase occurs intact, and in the word order given in the definition. This is not a firm grammatical rule of English, however, so that sometimes a sentence will end with a preposition. This is especially true of questions ("Whose party are you going *to*?" in which the word *party* is the object of the preposition). Please note also that a prepositional phrase *does not* contain a headword. That is, no one constituent in the construction can grammatically substitute for the entire construction. Here are some examples of prepositional phrases, with the preposition italicized:

of those words	*into* the dark, damp basement
after the fact	*for* Pete's sake
to me	*from* the lower depths

Notice that there may or may not be intervening words between the preposition and its object. Nevertheless, the preposition in this construction determines that a nominal will follow.

It would not be wise to use a word like *to* or *for* as the preposition prototype for constructing test frames, since each of these words characteristically functions in an entirely different syntactic environment as well as in the prepositional phrase. Probably a word like *of* or *from* is safe. But you should understand that for many structure words, there is nothing about their internal structure which permits us to classify them as anything but uninflected, no-suffix words. (In fact, they *have* no internal structure). We call a word a preposition only if it occurs in the preposition slot of a prepositional phrase and, as a consequence, performs a prepositional grammatical function.

That function is two-fold. First, the preposition signals that a nominal will follow. Second, the preposition establishes both a syntactic and a semantic relationship between its object and some other construction outside of the prepositional phrase itself.* Depending upon what that syntactic relationship between constructions is, the entire prepositional phrase, as a unit, functions as a nominal, an adjectival, or an adverbial.

5. Wh Words and **RELATIVES** as Constituents in Wh and **RELATIVE CLAUSES.** The relative clause and the wh clause can each be recognized as a patterned construction which contains a wh word (called a relative when it occurs in a relative clause) in the initial or near-initial position. The wh word may function as a nominal, an adjectival, or an adverbial constituent within the clause construction. Both clause types are derivations from original sentences or main clauses, one constituent of which is replaced by the wh word. This derivational process is illustrated in the examples below:

Relative Clause

Original Sentence: *The man is coming down the street.* The man is John.

Relative Clause: The man *who is coming down the street* is John. (The wh word (relative) *who* replaces the nominal *man* of the original sentence. *Who* functions within the relative clause as the subject nominal. The entire relative clause functions in the larger syntactic environment as an adjectival constituent of the NP which also contains the word *man*.)

Original Sentence: *I live in a house.* The house is on Maple Street.

Relative Clause: The house *where I live* is on Maple Street.

or

The house *which I live in* is on Maple Street.

or

The house *in which I live* is on Maple Street.

---

*Unlike most other structure words, certain prepositions (not all) convey considerable semantic meaning (*in, out, to, from, up, down,* and so on).

(In the first of these three derivations the relative *where* replaces the prepositional phrase *in a house* of the original sentence. In the second two derivations, the relative *which* replaces the noun *house*. In the first derivation, the relative functions within the clause as an adverbial; in the second two derivations, the relative functions as a nominal. In all three versions, however, the entire relative clause is an adjectival which relates to the noun which immediately precedes it. This preceding noun or nominal is called the *antecedent*.)

Wh Clause*

A wh clause differs from a relative clause only insofar as its function as an entire unit in the larger contextual environment is concerned. In isolation, it is not ordinarily possible to distinguish between the two, for their internal makeup is often exactly the same. However, the wh clause always functions in its entirety as a nominal, while the relative clause functions as an adjectival. Generally speaking, the wh clause derivation takes place when the wh word replaces an unknown nominal of the original sentence. There is never, therefore, an antecedent present before such a clause. Here are some examples:

Whoever broke that window should admit his guilt. (Subject)

Charge that to petty cash or to *whatever you call it*. (OP)

Mary doesn't know *whom to blame*. (DO)

How he knows **what he knows** is a mystery to me. (#1 = Subject;
     1   2
#2 = DO)

6. INTERROGATIVES as Constituents of **Wh QUESTION** Sentences. A wh question is a sentence which asks for a lexical rather than a yes-no response. The wh word which occurs in the initial (or near-initial) position of such questions is called an interrogative. Most of the same word forms that occur as relatives or wh words also occur as interrogatives. Their grammatical and semantic function is different, however. The interrogative signals that the sentence is a question—a quite important signal when you stop to consider that unlike the yes-no question, which ends on an upward pitch, the intonation pattern of a wh question does not differ from that of an ordinary declarative sentence.

*Traditional school grammars, so far as I can determine, did not use the term, "Wh Clause."

As constituents within the wh question, interrogatives may function as nominals, as adjectivals, or as adverbials. Here are some examples:

Interrogative as Nominal (Interrogative I):

Who is going?   To *whom* did he give the book?

What shall I do?   *Which* should he choose?

Interrogative as Adjectival (Interrogative II):

Whose picture is that?   *Which* movie did you prefer?

Interrogative as Adverbial (Interrogative III):

Where are you going?   *How* did she do that?

When will you finish?

Occasionally, we even see an interrogative functioning as a qualifier:

How well does John write?   *How* much do you love me?

7. Subordinators as Constituents of **Subordinate Clauses.** A subordinate clause is a derivation in which a no-suffix, uninflected word is added in the position immediately preceding an entire sentence or main clause. This construction is easy to identify: if it were not for the presence of the subordinator (which is what we call the added word), the clause would be an independent clause. The subordinator performs two grammatical functions: (1) it changes the grammatical form of the construction to which it is added; and (2) it relates the entire construction of which it is a part to another construction in the larger syntactical environment. This relationship is definitely a semantic and possibly a grammatical one. The entire subordinate clause may, in turn, function as an adverbial, an adjectival, or a nominal:

The Subordinate Clause as a Nominal:

That he dislikes me is obvious.

He wondered *why I disliked him.*

I really feel *that this movie will never end.*

He asked me *when it would end.*

The Subordinate Clause as an Adjectival:

Mary arrived on the day *after John left.*

The day *before they got married* was John's birthday.

The Subordinate Clause as an Adverbial:

He quit working *when he had earned fifty dollars.*

He seldom finishes a job *because he is impatient.*

Unless the train arrives soon, I shall be late.

8. INTENSIVES as Nominal Constituents in Other Constructions. The intensive will probably not be as common in our corpus as most of the other structure words. Actually, the structure which functions as an intensive is a *compound* consisting of a personal pronoun form plus *-self*: *myself, yourself, himself, itself,* or the plural form, *-selves*: *ourselves, yourselves, themselves.* The intensive may occur in one of two nominal positions:

1. as an appositive immediately following a personal noun or pronoun: I *myself* will do it; The boys *themselves* are the culprits.

2. at the end of a sentence containing the same personal noun or pronoun to which the intensive refers: I will do it *myself*; John has washed the car *himself*.

As you can see, the intensive serves the grammatical and semantic purpose of intensifying or emphasizing the personal noun or pronoun to which it refers. The sentence would be syntactically complete if the intensive were not present, but it would *mean* something different.

9. REFLEXIVES as Nominal Constituents in Other Constructions. The very same compounds as might occur in the intensive slots may also occur in another sentence position and with an altogether different function. Instead of being a kind of "extra" for the sake of emphasis, the reflexive functions as a nominal object (a DO, IO, or OP) when the personal noun or pronoun to which it refers occurs as the subject:

I hurt *myself*. (Direct Object)

John gave *himself* a haircut. (Indirect Object)

She sent a letter to *herself*. (Object of Preposition)

10. COORDINATORS as Independent Constituents. We can call the coordinator an independent constituent in the sense that it does not combine with another constituent to form a larger construction that may function as a constituent grammatical unit. Rather, coordinators perform the dual grammatical function of indicating grammatical and semantic relationships between constructions and of enabling the speaker to produce compound sentences or sentences with compound parts.

The coordinator position, which is always between the structures it joins, may be occupied by one of a limited number of uninflected, no-suffix words: *and, but, or, nor, for, so, yet, still.* The word *and* is a good prototype for frames designed to test for the coordinator position. (This is because *and* is characteristically a form that functions only in this way, whereas words like *for* or *so* may occur as other classes. For example, in the adjectival phrase construction *so good*, *so* is a qualifier; in the prepositional phrase *for his own sake*, *for* is a preposition.) As long as they are the same kind of constructions, coordinators may join any two structures from single words (the smallest of our syntactic constructions) to entire sentences (the largest construction). Here are a few examples, with the coordinator italicized:

Tim *and* Mary were late. (Two nouns)

Boys in the eighth grade *and* girls in the seventh grade are planning the dance. (Two NPs)

She washed *and* dried the dishes. (Two verbs)

She washed the dishes *and* dried them. (Two predicate phrases)

She washed the dishes *and* I put them away. (Two sentences)

Syntactic Classes

CLASS DESIGNATION	PHRASE-STRUCTURE POSITION	PROTOTYPES
NOMINAL (Nom)	Subj, DO, IO, OP, Subj Comp, Obj Comp, Appos	N, Pro, NP
Nom/{Relative / Wh word} I	Nom slot in relative or wh clause	Pro or UW
Nom/Interrog I	First slot in wh question	Pro or UW
Nom/Intensive	Appos or end of sentence	Compound Word
Nom/Reflexive	In Pred P as some kind of object	Compound Word
VERBAL (Vbl)	Main verb or VP	V, VP, Pred P
Vbl/Auxiliary	Preceding headword V in VP	Modal, *Have*, *Be*, *Do*
ADJECTIVAL (Adjtl)	Preceding or following headword N; Subj or Obj Comp	Adj
Adjtl/Determiner	Usually first slot in NP, always preceding headword	UW (*a*, *an*, *the*)
Adjt./{Relative / Wh word} II	Adjtl slot in relative or wh clause	Pro or UW
Adjtl/Interrog II	First slot in wh question	Pro or UW

Syntactic Classes (continued)

CLASS DESIGNATION	PHRASE-STRUCTURE POSITION	PROTOTYPES
ADVERBIAL	Verb or VP IC; Sentence IC	Adv (-ly)
Advl/{Relative / Wh word} III	Advl slot in relative or wh clause	Pro or UW
Advl/Interrog III	First slot in wh question	Pro or UW
PREPOSITION	First slot in prep phrase	UW (of, from)
SUBORDINATOR	First slot in subordinate clause	UW (if, because)
COORDINATOR	Between equivalent grammatical constructions	UW (and, or)
QUALIFIER	Immediately preceding an adjl or advl in an adjl phrase or an advl phrase	UW (very)

SYNTAX: CLASSIFYING LARGER-THAN-WORD CONSTRUCTIONS BY THEIR FORMAL FEATURES

EXERCISE 46

Directions: Using the abbreviations below, classify each of the following constructions solely on the basis of their internal features.

NP for Noun Phrase or Nominal Phrase
VP for Verb Phrase
Pred P for Predicate Phrase
Abs P for Absolute Phrase
Adjtl P for Adjectival Phrase

Advl P for Adverbial Phrase
Prep P for Prepositional Phrase
R Cl for Relative Clause
S Cl for Subordinate Clause

1. walk very fast
2. rather hurriedly
3. frozen custard
4. which hurt him
5. the last possible moment
6. toward the door
7. that he is sorry
8. that I meant
9. the time of the day to leave
10. before I left
11. before the judge
12. had loved in vain
13. after the festivities

14. the badly broken window
15. the work having been finished
16. may be scratching
17. by your leave
18. to whom he gave it
19. the very right time
20. was swimming in the pool
21. swimming pools
22. the wind having stopped
23. while I was shaving
24. every morning
25. at night

SYNTAX: CLASSIFYING BY FORMAL AND SYNTACTICAL CRITERIA

EXERCISE 47

Directions: Classify each italicized structure as follows: (1) formal Class of Construction, as determined by internal structural composition, and (2) syntactical Class of Constituent in the larger syntactical context. Give subclass + major class where appropriate. Use the following abbreviations:

Form Class Designations (Answer I)

N = Noun

PRO = Pronoun

V = Verb

ADJ = Adjective

ADV = Adverb (-*ly*)

UW = Other uninflectable words

CW = Compound Word

NP = Noun Phrase or Nominal Phrase

ADJTL P = Adjectival Phrase

ADVL P = Adverbial Phrase

VP = Verb Phrase

PRED P = Predicate Phrase

ABS P = Absolute Phrase

PREP P = Prepositional Phrase

REL CL = Relative Clause

WH CL = Wh Clause

SUB CL = Subordinate Clause

Function Class Designations (Answer II)

NOM = Nominal

VBL = Verbal

ADJTL = Adjectival

ADVL = Adverbial

DET = Determiner

AUX = Auxiliary

QUAL = Qualifier

PREP = Preposition

REL = Relative

WH = Wh Word

INTERR = Interrogative

SUBORD = Subordinator

COORD = Coordinator

INTS = Intensive

RFLX = Reflexive

Example:

He found the book by *himself.*

Answer:

I	II
CW	NOM/RFLX

1. *She may* have *been* leaving.
     1   2   3

2. *After* she had run *for miles*, she stopped.
       4   5

3. *Where* are you going?
      6

4. The man *who* is speaking is Al Jones.
        7

5. The man *who is speaking* is Al Jones.
              8

6. Which company are you sending it *to*?
                                         9

7. She found the book *herself*.
                        10

8. He depended on *using his notes*.
                      11

9. John paid *his and* Jim's dues.
                12   13

10. He was *rather* sorry.
                14

11. He must have told me that *a thousand times*.
                                   15

12. Some people don't study *very* hard.
                             16

13. He can run *quite fast*.
                  17

14. *What I like about him* is his verve.
        18

15. *Unless I'm wrong*, he'll be late again.
           19

16. The night *before the game*, they rested.
                     20

19

Syntactic Patterns

English sentences can range in length from one or two to a theoretically limitless number of words. Indeed, most of the sentences which most of us speak and understand are a great deal more complex than we realize. Yet we speak our native language without conscious thought about the grammar rules we use when we put our sentences together. Structural linguists believe that such language ability is a learned process, made possible by two factors: (1) humans' powers of observation and their highly evolved brain capacity, which make it possible for them to reason inductively; and (2) the structured, highly organized nature of language.

To what extent these factors explain language acquisition is open to question, but it is undeniable that language is systematically structured. Consider grammatical word order, for instance—probably the most important structural grammar signal in English. Below are four sets of scrambled words, none of which make any sense at all as they stand. See if you can arrange all of the words in each set so that every word is a constituent in a grammatical English noun phrase:

1. *ovens, fine, brick, five, all*

2. *soap, television, silly, a, operas, couple of*

3. *clay, muddy, courts, the, tennis, three*

4. *many, friends, lovely, girl, John's, French*

When you are finished, you will find the answers at the bottom of the page.*

*1. All five fine brick ovens. 2. A couple of silly television soap operas. 3. The three muddy clay tennis courts. 4. John's many lovely French girl friends.

Does it surprise you that when you compare your answers with those of other English speakers, we all come up with the same sequences? The fact that we *do* suggests that there must be a system. By taking these four sequences and lining them up with similar words in vertical columns, we find that we are able to discover what the system is:

1	2	3	4A	4B or 5	5	5	5
all		five	fine		brick		ovens
	a	couple of	silly		television	soap	operas
	the	three	muddy		clay	tennis	courts
	John's	many	lovely	French	girl		friends

First, we note that in this kind of NP the head constituent occurs as the last element in the series (5). This head constituent is sometimes a single noun and sometimes a compound, composed in these examples of two or more noun forms. All of the constituents preceding the headword are adjectivals (or modifiers, although structural linguists probably did not use the term "modifier"). As we analyze the formal features of the adjectivals, we further discover that much of the reason (perhaps most) for our having designated "like" items in separate columns has to do with our combined understanding of their formal characteristics *and* their syntactical distribution *and* their lexical meanings. In other words, it is hardly enough to describe only the syntactical positions of items by, for example, classifying them as predeterminers, determiners, immediate postdeterminers, second position postdeterminers, and so on. We find that we use all kinds of signals, including lexical ones. We are much less inclined, for example, to call the items in Column 3 uninflected words or nouns or whatever they are than to call them number words. Likewise, although the constituents in Column 4A are adjectives, most of us are likely to call them *descriptive* adjectives. Moreover, we would differentiate between descriptive adjectives like *muddy*, *silly*, and *lovely*, and a word like *French*, which seems to be more specifically attributive. In fact, we sense that *French* is so specific that it is really part of the base constituent, *French girl friends*. We would never say "John's many French lovely girl friends."

Although an NP is frequently dominated by a single headword, the head constituent in every one of these four examples is a compound: *brick ovens, television soap operas, clay tennis courts, French girl friends*. Compounds are among the most fascinating constituents in English sentences. A compound can function not only as a head constituent in a noun phrase, but also as an adjectival, an adverbial, and a verbal: *outstanding, never-to-be-forgotten*; *ear piercingly*; *to stonewall*.

Some generalizations about word order in NPs appear to be these:

1. Most frequently the first word is a determiner.

2. Sometimes, however, there is a predeterminer—a word or a phrase like *all, all of, most of, several of, some of.*

3. Number words precede descriptive adjectives.

4. Noun adjuncts come last and are by definition part of a compound head constituent.

Notice that all of these adjectivals are single word modifiers. Generally speaking, single-word modifiers precede the headword and adjectival phrases and clauses follow the headword. The following is a list of adjectival NP constituents, along with examples to illustrate the syntactic pattern of an NP which contains each type.

Adjectival Constituents Which Typically Precede the Headword:

1. Uninflected, no-suffix word (determiner)	*the* boy, *some* prunes, *a* girl
2. Noun or Pronoun Determiner Replacements	*John's* hat, *my* car, *their* books, *that* list, *these* people
3. Lexical Descriptive Adjective or Adjectival	*pretty* child, *hungry* cat, *fancy* pants, *cool* day, *fanciful* idea, *rigid* attitude, *final* exam
4. Verb Form	*rotten* meat, *faded* page, *shouting* children
5. Structure Words other than Articles	*in* group, *through* street, the *down* staircase

Noun Adjuncts should be considered adjectival rather than nominal. Semantically, they function attributively to form a new compound noun:

> *ice cube, wine glass, dog face, fruit cake,* the *headword modifier,* the *typewriter keys,* an *ocean liner,* a *piano tuner,* some *paper clips.*

Or the head constituent can be a multiple compound:

> the *Greyhound bus station,* the *railroad station ticket window,* the *United States field service.*

Adjectival Constituents Which Typically Follow the Headword:

1. Adjective or Derivational Adjectival	God *Almighty,* body *beautiful,* the worst book *imaginable*

2. Uniflected, No-Suffix Word	that boy *there*, the oldest person *around*, the problem *here*
3. Compound Word	the dog *outside*, folks *nearby*
4. Verb Form	the child *crying*, time *to quit*
5. Verb Phrase	the man *sitting on the bench*, ability *to hit the spittoon*
6. Prepositional Phrase	men *in love*, kids *at school*
7. Noun Phrase (said by some grammarians to be a reduced relative clause)	Mary, *my friend*
8. Relative Clause	Mary, *who is my friend* the tree *that fell*
9. Subordinate Clause	the day *before they arrived*
10. Reduced Relative Clause (relative omitted)	the time *we had a fight*

One more comment about the noun phrase: an NP of whatever length can always occur in *any* nominal sentence slot. When you consider how many nominal slots there are in English sentences, you begin to get a picture of just how expanded a sentence can become by this device alone. Pick up any daily paper or magazine and choose a longish sentence at random, and chances are you will discover that it contains many NPs. Here, for example, is a sentence from a *Newsweek* acount of President Nixon's last week in office:

> His Presidency ended in the narrow compass of seven days in August, but it died of what John Dean aptly called a cancer that grew and metastasized over two of the most dolorous years in the life of the American Repulic.*

I count eight noun phrases in this sentence, several of them nested within another noun phrase. And although this is a beautifully worded sentence, its pattern is not in the least unusual. You yourself speak or write sentences of this complexity every day of your life.

Adverbial Constituents in Predicate Phrases. Just as adjectival slots can be filled with many constructions other than the adjective prototype which

---

**"Seven Days in August," *Newsweek*, Special Issue, August 19, 1974, p. 22. Copyright Newsweek, Inc., 1974. Reprinted by permission.*

helped us to determine adjectival positions, so may constructions other than the *-ly* adverb fill an adverbial slot. Here are some examples:

1. An *-ly* Adverb (Prototype)   *quickly* goes, goes *quickly*, may *quickly* go

2. Uninflected Word   *always* goes, goes *now*, goes *then*, goes *there*, goes *rapidly*

3. Noun   goes *home*, works *nights*

4. Compound Noun   works *weekends*

5. Adjective   went *crazy*, sings *loud*

6. Noun Phrase   works *every morning*, sings *all the time*

7. Verb   came in *crying*, left *tired*

8. Verb Phrase   walked away *carrying a petition*, jogs *to keep fit*

9. Prepositional Phrase   ran *around the barn*, left *in the morning*

10. Wh Clause   goes *where they direct him*

11. Subordinate Clause   cries *if he feels sad*, sank *because he couldn't swim*

Not only may all of these constructions function in adjectival and adverbial slots, but a variety of constructions can also replace an entire NP in a nominal slot. Most often the process by which an NP replacement takes place is a transformational one. Linguists refer to such a conversion as a nominalization. Looking only at the surface structure result, the following kinds of constructions can be found in nominal positions:

Nominalizations:

1. Any word or construction can be the subject of *be*   *Now* is the time. *"On the table"* is a prepositional phrase. You have too many *and's* in this sentence.

2. Adjective or Derivational Adjectival as Headword (Probably there is an implied noun or nominal in these examples, which would make them reduced NPs)   The *beautiful* are often dumb. He gave money to the *poor*.

3. Verb	I hate *jogging*. *Swimming* is his favorite sport.
4. Compound Verb	He enjoys *car racing*. *Blackmailing* is a crime.
5. Verb Phrase or Predicate Phrase (Notice that these are non-headed nominals)	His ambition was *to hit a homer*. *Walking to work* is good exercise. She meant *to rewrite her notes*. (This last example might be a catenated VP; i.e., the verb headword could be *rewrite* and *meant to* could be a modal.)
6. Wh Clause	*What he is doing* bothers her.
7. Subordinate Clause	*That he will marry her* is doubtful.

Using Nonverbs as Verbs:

Substituting Nonverb Constructions for the Verb Headword

1. Noun	Don't *"John, John"* me, just tell me where the road is!
2. Pronoun (actually, a compound)	That kid is *me-tooing* his mom right out of her mind.
3. Adjective	He played in the puddle and *muddied* himself.
4. Coined derivational verb	He *guesstimated* a ten-point drop in the stock market. Jones must always *speechify*.

This list gives you a general idea of the variety of sentence patterns and substitutions possible. There are many construction replacement possibilities not mentioned here, but they would be difficult to explain without becoming involved with transformational grammar. In Part Three of this book, we shall deal with a number of these possibilities.

THE SENTENCE. A sentence differs from a phrase or a dependent clause in that it is independent. One of the best indications of that independence is the intonation pattern of the basic declarative sentence, especially the rise and final fall of the voice, which at the end of the sentence is pitched gradually lower and lower until it fades away.

Confined as they were to describing only the structure of surface utterances without reference to lexical meaning, the structural linguists were less well able than the traditionalists to distinguish between sentences like these:

Mary fed Fido biscuits.

They elected John president.

Both must be described as Noun + transitive verb + Noun + Noun.

Limited as they were in this way, it was possible to write formulas for only four elementary sentence patterns, and they had no way to satisfactorily explain transformations. The four patterns are these:

1. $\left\{\begin{matrix} N \\ Pro \end{matrix}\right\} + V\ (+Adv)$

2. $\left\{\begin{matrix} N \\ Pro \end{matrix}\right\} + V + \left\{\begin{matrix} N \\ Pro \end{matrix}\right\}\ (+Adv)$

3. $\left\{\begin{matrix} N \\ Pro \end{matrix}\right\} + V + Adj$

4. $\left\{\begin{matrix} N \\ Pro \end{matrix}\right\} + V + \left\{\begin{matrix} N \\ Pro \end{matrix}\right\} + \left\{\begin{matrix} N \\ Pro \end{matrix}\right\}\ (+Adv)$

Since an adjectival can follow a headword noun, there was no way to tell merely from their patterns that sentences like

He thought John silly.

and

He was God Almighty.

are really not alike.

It was at the level of syntax, therefore, that the structuralists had the least success. Although several structural linguists—Noam Chomsky and his professor, Zellig Harris, among them—tried to write phrase-structure rules, they achieved only minimum success. And as we shall see, his frustration soon led Chomsky to reject much of the structuralist methodology.

FORM AND SYNTAX   **EXERCISE 48**

> *Directions:* Supply an actual example to illustrate each of the following constructions functioning in the constituent syntactic position asked for. You need not use complete sentences for every illustration.

CONSTRUCTION	FUNCTION/POSITION
1. Noun	Adverbial
2. Verb	Adjectival
3. Verb	Nominal
4. Verb	Verbal/Auxiliary
5. Adjective	Qualifier
6. Noun Phrase	Adverbial
7. Noun Phrase	Adjectival
8. Verb Phrase	Adverbial
9. Verb Phrase	Nominal
10. Prep Phrase	Adjectival
11. Prep Phrase	Adverbial
12. Rel Clause	Adjectival
13. Wh Clause	Nominal
14. Sub Clause	Adjectival
15. Sub Clause	Adverbial

FORM AND SYNTAX   **EXERCISE 49**

> *Directions:* Supply an example to illustrate each of the following constructions functioning in the syntactic position asked for. You need not use complete sentences for every example.

CONSTRUCTION	FUNCTION/POSITION
1. Noun	Adjl (Adjunct)
2. Noun	Adjl/Det

CONSTRUCTION	FUNCTION/POSITION
3. Pronoun	Adjl (Adjunct)
4. Pronoun	Adjl/Det
5. Wh Word	Nom/Rel
6. Wh Word	Nom/Interrog
7. Wh Word	Adjl/Interrog
8. Wh Word	Adjl/Rel
9. UW (*through*)	Adjl (Adjunct)
10. UW (*out*)	Adjl (Adjunct)
11. Verb Phrase	Adjl
12. Sub Clause	Nom
13. Absolute Phrase	Advl (Sent. IC)
14. UW (*in*)	Adjl (Adjunct)
15. Adjective	Nom

PART THREE

Transformational-Generative Grammar

20

Historical Background

In 1957, at the height of structuralism's influence on linguistic studies, a young professor of Modern Languages at the Massachusetts Institute of Technology published a book which challenged many of the basic beliefs of the linguistic "establishment." The professor was A. Noam Chomsky, and his book, a 108 page monograph entitled *Syntactic Structures*, was soon to have a profound effect on language studies.* In this small volume, Chomsky leveled major criticisms at the structuralist approach to language study—criticisms which ranged from a general charge that the entire structuralist theory had been built upon "wrong" assumptions to the rejection of such specific structuralist methods as their taxonomic data-gathering techniques and their belief in the adequacy of "discovery procedures."

We should recognize, of course, that the very best of the structuralists had often modified the rigid requirements of structural linguistics to make use of specific insights. One linguist who did this was Zellig Harris, who recently had begun to express the hope that structural grammarians might find a way to move beyond the classification and description of utterances. He felt that linguists ought to extend their research in an effort to arrive at more farreaching theories concerning the "logic" of language regularities. In fact, during the early fifties, Harris and his student Noam

*Chomsky's book was based on his Ph.D. dissertation, written in 1955 at the University of Pennsylvania under the direction of Zellig Harris. The dissertation was based on research conducted by Chomsky while he was a Harvard Fellow (1951–55). It is said by some that the dissertation contains the seeds of everything Chomsky has done since.

Chomsky had worked together to develop a phrase-structure grammar which, although modeled along the rigorous lines set down by the structuralists, also made some use of scholarly traditional notions which the structural purists had for some time rejected.*

It seems fairly clear, then, that Harris's views played a role in encouraging (if not in actually seeding) Chomsky's doubts about the adequacy of the structuralist approach. Whatever the catalyst, Chomsky's own inquiring mind seems early on to have begun to harbor serious misgivings about the theoretical assumptions, the methods, and the future possibilities of the "Bloomfieldian" school of structural linguistics in which he had received his earliest training. It is important for us to understand that despite Chomsky's having come to his views, as is often said, "through" structuralism, his own thinking has been much more closely allied from the beginning with that of the philosophical traditional grammarians from Plato through Humboldt. He does not elaborate on his belief in the existence of a universal grammar in *Syntactic Structures*. But the concept is certainly there: one of his most compelling arguments is for the need, in developing grammars of specific languages, to be certain that these particular grammars fall within the framework of a *general* linguistic theory. This interest in the general nature of language is to be one increasingly emphasized in Chomsky's later work. Here he merely states that it is a "crucial topic."

Chomsky confines himself in *Syntactic Structures* to laying a careful foundation and to outlining the direction in which he believes linguistic study ought to proceed. His first chapter is devoted to carefully defining —and in some cases, redefining—a number of linguistic terms. Next, he states his aim: that of determing the basic underlying principles of a "successful" grammar. He then proceeds to examine a number of generative grammars and to demonstrate that no particular grammar thus far formulated meets his standards of adequacy. Last, he presents a new formulation, phrase structure rules plus transformation rules, which he believes is more accurate and more useful. In the process, Chomsky argues than an adequately formulated *grammar* of a language *is*, in fact, a *theory* of that language.

*At the time when Chomsky wrote *Syntactic Structures*, certain of his views had not yet departed radically from those of the Bloomfieldians. Nevertheless, from the very outset, he strongly criticized the structuralists' taxonomic approach.

In his "Preface," Chomsky acknowledges his considerable indebtedness to Zellig Harris for many ideas and suggestions. (Harris, for example, had already done some early work on transformational structure and had developed a number of string transformations.) Chomsky adds, however, that in this book he proceeds from a somewhat different point of view.

Chomsky believes that the first problem in developing a correct theory (grammar) is that of selecting criteria. Certainly an adequate grammar should be one that is capable of producing grammatical sentences and ruling out ungrammatical ones. But beyond this, a grammar should be able to produce (or to project) *all* of the grammatical sentences possible in a language. Thus, Chomsky argues, it is entirely proper to begin with the assumption that a grammar's adequacy can be tested against the intuitions of a mature native speaker. This is an important point. What Chomsky is saying is that utterances cannot be identified as "grammatical" solely on the basis of their having been spoken—and then collected by a linguistic field worker. An adequate grammar should be able to explain, rather, what the speaker *knows to be possible*. No grammar can be said to be adequate unless it is able to mirror the speaker's ability both to produce and to understand an unlimited number of grammatical utterances—even, and crucially, ones which he has never spoken or heard before.* Beyond everyday clichés and speech formulas, the native speaker's typical utterances are completely novel. (The possibility of their ever having occurred before or their ever occurring again is close to zero.) A grammar, then, should somehow be able to reflect this phenomenon; and this is the chief reason that Chomsky is opposed to the kind of grammar which is based on what he considers an unrealistic, high statistical probability of sentence occurrence—the inevitable outcome if one is to consider only those utterances which have been collected.

To illustrate this contention, Chomsky asks the reader to consider this now-famous pair of sentences:

1. Colorless green ideas sleep furiously.
2. Furiously sleep ideas green colorless.

Not only are both of these sentences unfamiliar (in the sense that they have never been spoken or heard before), but they are also "nonsense." Yet, despite the fact that neither sentence has "meaning," every native speaker of English can recognize that the first sentence is grammatical English, while the second is not. An adequate grammar of English should be able to account for this ability.

These examples suggest another interesting fact: a native speaker can distinguish "grammatical" and "ungrammatical" sentences even when the utterances themselves are devoid of semantic "meaning." Chomsky concludes, accordingly, that a grammar model should be based on syntax

---

*In *Syntactic Structures* Chomsky does not mention that the mature speaker's competence is not necessarily always reflected in grammatical performance. In later works, however, he discusses this "problem" at length.

rather than on semantics. Syntax is an independent component of a grammar system, and one which is primary.*

Before proceeding to the examination and evaluation of grammar models, Chomsky adds one more condition which must be met by an adequate grammar: a correct grammar must be able to account for recursiveness, a process whereby the repeated application of a small number of rules permits the generation of infinitely long sentences. It is apparently a property of all human languages.

Having thus laid the groundwork, so to speak, Chomsky next proceeds to examine and evaluate two known grammar models, and after he finds each of them lacking, to suggest a third, more powerful model. The first of these grammar models, an "elementary linguistic theory," is known mathematically as a "finite state Markov process." It is a simple, linear, left-to-right model which can be graphically represented by the following diagram:

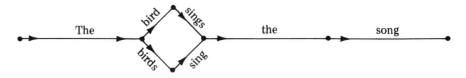

This model can be thought of as a kind of language-generating machine.† Beginning at the left and proceeding always to the right in the direction of the arrows, each node represents a state where, a choice having been made, the machine "switches" to a new state. At the final node a complete, grammatical sentence will have been generated.

The model can now be expanded by providing a lexicon (a list of words) from which, at any given point, one choice must be made. For example, in the enlarged model below, one must first choose between *a* or *the*; that choice having been made, the machine switches to the next state where one word must be chosen from among the three choices listed. Notice, however, that at the stage where the second lexical choice is made, the speaker is committed to a particular path. Thus, if *boy*, *girl*, or *bird* is chosen, the next choice has to be either *likes* or *sings*.

---

*Chomsky's early insistence on the autonomy of syntax is, no doubt, a legacy inherited from Bloomfieldian structuralism, in which he received his earliest linguistic training. As you will see, Chomsky gradually changed his views in the years that followed.

†The term "machine" is a mathematical term, not to be confused with a mechanical device that turns out products assembly-line fashion. Rather, mathematicians refer to their models as machines which give instructions for the generation of an infinite number of correct answers.

When the final choice is made, the machine switches to its final state, and a complete sentence has been generated:

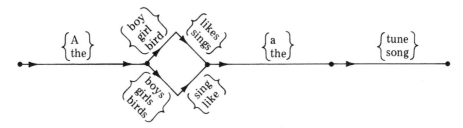

The model can be even further extended by the device of including one or more "closed loops" at various points along the path. One then has the option of going around any closed loop once, twice, or any number of times before proceeding to the next state and eventually to the final state:

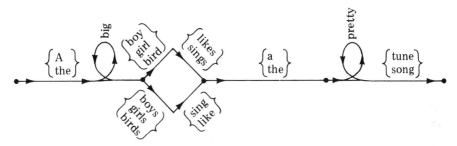

As you can see, by adding closed loops we can construct a model grammar which is able to account for recursiveness and thus to derive infinitely long sentences. Moreover, it is possible to construct similar models for all varieties of sentences in a language and to provide a huge lexicon which includes entries for all possible word choices. Theoretically, at least, it should be possible to provide enough separate models to account for an infinite number of the grammatical sentences in a language.

If we grant that the formulation of such a model is possible, complex though it would obviously have to be, we are forced to admit that it is a very powerful grammar indeed. And yet, argues Chomsky, it will not be good enough. Aside from its complexity, a Markov grammar is still not adequate, for there is no conceivable way that such a grammar can account for *all* possible sentences in a language. Precisely because each state along the prescribed left-to-right path is determined by that state immediately preceding it, there is simply no method for explaining grammatical interdependencies between nonadjacent, discontinuous elements. Yet, human languages do have this "mirror-image" characteristic.

Consider the English sentence below as an illustration:

Mary, who, *although she is pretty,* thinks herself ugly, *is pathetic.*
  a   b   *c*   b   *a*

Notice that in this sentence a is dependent on a, and b is dependent on b, for subject-verb agreement.

We must therefore reject a Markov grammar model, for it cannot explain a linguistic characteristic like subject-verb agreement when other words intervene between the subject and the verb. Yet this sort of interdependence between discontinuous elements is, as already pointed out, a characteristic common to natural languages. We therefore need a more powerful grammar—one which will fit into the framework of a general linguistic theory. Although a Markov model can explain *much* of what is true about English sentences, it ultimately leads to a dead end.

Even if it should be possible to devise some highly complex method by which a linear grammar model could overcome this difficulty, it would still be inadequate. If a model could be constructed which would generate only English sentences, such a grammar would not be able to explain all possible sentences. If, on the other hand, it were possible to construct a model that could generate all possible sentences, it would also generate a great many nonsentences.

The second grammar model which Chomsky examines is a phrase-structure grammar (also called constituent or IC grammar). For a number of years linguists, including Chomsky himself, had been attempting with only limited success to write a satisfactory model for an IC grammar. It is in *Syntactic Structures* that Chomsky shows, for the first time, that it is possible to construct a formal, mathematical phrase-structure grammar model. Having seen an analogy between mathematical and linguistic systems, he demonstrates that language, like mathematics, is a system in which a finite number of rules are able to generate an infinite number of correct results.

The "set theory" of mathematics is a particularly useful device, because it can handle syntactic relations between certain discontinuous elements in a string, a phenomenon which cannot be explained with a linear model that describes only individual phonemes, morphemes, and words. A simple arithmetic example might help to make the set theory clear to you. Consider the following two problems:

$(3 + 4) \times 10 = 70$

$3 + (4 \times 10) = 43$

Notice how the device of bracketing several separate constituents into a single set enlarges and changes an explanation.

The phrase-structure grammar which Chomsky presents in *Syntactic Structures* consists, then, of a limited number of formal rules which explain the linguistic processes involved in generating simple English sentences. Then, borrowing still another mathematical device, he shows how a derivation generated from these "rewriting" rules can be graphically represented in a branching tree diagram. (Both of these processes will be explained in the next chapter.)

By formalizing phrase-structure rules in this way, Chomsky is able to demonstrate formally what their strong points and their weaknesses are. He can prove, for example, that a phrase-structure model constructed along these lines is a far more powerful grammar than was the simpler linear model. Yet, though it is superior to the Markov model, it is still lacking, for like the earlier model, a phrase-structure rule is completely dependent upon the string immediately preceding it for its next step in a derivation.

What we need then is a still more powerful model, a model which makes use of phrase-structure rules but is then able to go beyond them. The solution, he thinks, is to add a transformational component to the grammar—a higher level which contains rules for scanning and converting entire derivations. It is this kind of grammar model which Chomsky outlines in *Syntactic Structures*. He calls his model a transformational-generative grammar theory. In the chapters that follow, we shall examine Chomsky's three-part TG grammar.

But before we continue, several things should be stressed. First, the grammar model presented in *Syntactic Structures* is admittedly incomplete. Chomsky contents himself in his first book with describing the broad outlines of his theory and in presenting arguments to prove that such a theory is better than any previous grammar systems.

It is important also that you avoid the mistake, made by many linguists at the time, of viewing Chomsky's transformational grammar as an extended structuralist theory. Although his grammar is like the grammar of the structuralists in being syntactically based, his goals have been, from the beginning, fundamentally different from those of the structuralists. Basic to Chomsky's argument is his insistence that a grammar theory, if it is to be adequate, must be able to explain a native speaker's linguistic intuitions. It is a description and explanation of mature language competence that Chomsky is after: a theory which is able to account for the grammar knowledge that every speaker has in his head.

These views were quite daring ones for a serious language scholar to voice in the 1950s. Remember, this was the period in American academics which was dominated by the behavioral scientists' empirical methodologies. It was a time when expressions like "insight," "mind," and "intuition" were considered dirty words.

21

TG Grammar, Early Form: An Overview

OVERVIEW

Since the earliest attempt to write grammars of language, investigators have found it useful to employ symbols and terminology to represent abstract linguistic concepts. These abstract mental concepts can probably best be defined as certain ideas about language or facts of grammar on the basis of which actual sentences are produced. Traditional grammarians, for example, used terminology like *subject, object, complement, singular, plural*. Structural linguists added some terminology of their own: *phoneme, morpheme,* and so on. In saying that a grammar theory should attempt to explain underlying mental concepts, therefore, Chomsky was not suggesting a new and startling procedure. He merely wanted to extend the process, to get at even deeper, more abstract linguistic "facts." His two major contributions in *Syntactic Structures* were these: (1) he introduced a precise, mathematical method of writing grammar rules; (2) he added a third level, the transformation level, to grammar theory.*

The model generative grammar proposed by Chomsky was a three-level, rule-based system:

Level I: Phrase-Structure Rules

Level II: Morphophonemic Rules

Level III: Transformational Rules

---

*Chomsky defined "linguistic level" as a set of descriptive devices (symbols), such as phonemic, morphemic, or phrase-structure rules, which are useful to the linguist for representing the construction of a grammar.

216

Level I: *Phrase-Structure Rules*

To make clear just what a phrase-structure grammar consists of, we shall begin, as Chomsky does in *Syntactic Structures*, by formulating some simple model phrase-structure rules (PS rules). The rules given here will, admittedly, generate only a small number of English sentences, but our main purpose at the moment is to illustrate what PS rules are like and to explain how such rules are supposed to be interpreted.

Let us begin by writing a set of rules which will represent the derivation of the sentence "The boy liked the dog."*

PS RULE	INTERPRETATION OF PS RULE
1. S $\longrightarrow$ NP + VP	A Sentence (S) consists of or is rewritten as ($\longrightarrow$) a Noun Phrase (NP) plus a Verb Phrase (VP).
2. NP $\longrightarrow$ D + N	A Noun Phrase consists of a Determiner (D) plus a Noun (N).
3. VP $\longrightarrow$ MV + NP	A Verb Phrase consists of a Main Verb (MV) plus a Noun Phrase.
4. MV $\longrightarrow$ T + V	A Main Verb consists of a Tense-marker Morpheme (T) plus the base form of a Verb (V).
5. T $\longrightarrow$ past	A Tense morpheme consists of *past*.
6. D $\longrightarrow$ *the*	Determiner is rewritten as the word *the*.
7. N $\longrightarrow$ {*boy, dog*}	Noun is rewritten as either the word *boy* or the word *dog*. (Braces indicate that one must be selected.)
8. V $\longrightarrow$ *like*	Verb is rewritten as *like*.
9. past $\longrightarrow$ *-ed*	Past is rewritten as the affix *-ed*.

In order to apply the PS rules, we must begin at the top with the term *Sentence* and proceed toward the bottom, applying only one rule at a time. That is, we rewrite only one element or constituent with each rule application. As we progress with a derivation, we will occasionally find it necessary to go back to a previously stated rule and apply it over and over again. Note, for example, that Rule 2 tells us to rewrite NP as D + N. Rule 3 then instructs us to rewrite VP as MV + NP, which means

---

*These rules are similar to, but not exactly the same as, the ones presented by Chomsky in *Syntactic Structures*. I have taken the liberty of making a few changes.

we once again have the symbol NP to convert to D + N by the application of Rule 2. Thus, the PS rules can be said to account for the repetitive or recursive nature of language—the linguistic fact that a noun phrase can be contained within a verb phrase, a verb phrase can be contained within a noun phrase, and so forth.

Beginning with Sentence, a PS grammar can show the entire derivation for each simple sentence in the language. Notice that there is only one element to the left of the arrow, whereas to the right of the arrow we are deriving an increasingly complex string of elements. Thus, we call the elements to the right of the arrow a *string*. In a PS grammar, every sentence is represented by a *set* of strings, unlike the left-to-right Markov model, which represented a sentence by a single string. In the derivation of the sentence "The boy liked the dog," the last string—the one which results after the application of all the PS rules—is called a *terminal string*.

The entire derivation for the sentence "The boy liked the dog" can be shown as follows:

PS RULE	RESULTING STRING
1. S $\longrightarrow$ NP + VP	NP + VP
2. NP $\longrightarrow$ D + N	D + N + VP
3. VP $\longrightarrow$ MV + NP	D + N + MV + NP
2. NP $\longrightarrow$ D $\times$ N	D + N + MV + D + N
4. MV $\longrightarrow$ T + V	D + N + T + V + D + N
5. T $\longrightarrow$ past	D + N + past + V + D + N
6. D $\longrightarrow$ *the*	The + N + past + V + D + N
7. N $\longrightarrow$ {*boy, dog*}	The + boy + past + V + D + N
8. V $\longrightarrow$ *like*	The + boy + past + like + D + N
6. D $\longrightarrow$ *the*	The + boy + past + like + the + N
7. N $\longrightarrow$ {*boy, dog*}	The + boy + past + like + the + dog
9. past $\longrightarrow$ *-ed*	The # boy # *-ed* + like # the # dog (The double plus, #, indicates word boundaries.)

Notice that we perform twelve separate operations before we arrive at the terminal string:

The # boy # -ed + like # the # dog.

The entire rule rewriting procedure can be "recovered" and graphically represented by means of a "branching tree" diagram. Each node on the tree represents one of the elements to the left of the arrow; the elements which branch off from a node represent the symbols to the right of the arrow. A node is said to wholly "dominate" the elements which immediately branch off from it. Thus, both NP and VP are dominated by S; both D and N are dominated by NP; and so on. The tree diagram gives us a complete and easily comprehended picture of the derivational process described by the phrase structure level:

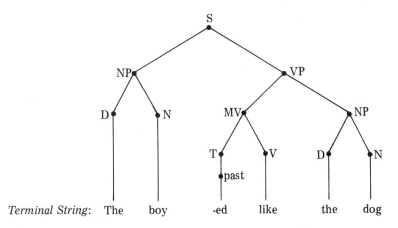

Terminal String: The   boy   -ed   like   the   dog

The tree diagram may help you to understand the reason for the insistence that only one element be rewritten at a time. This process may strike you as needlessly tedious, but as the tree illustrates, there is a good reason for the procedure. Generative grammar rules, remember, seek to explain every single operation performed by a speaker of English in constructing the sentences of the language. Each of the phrase-structure rules represents one of these linguistic operations.

The simplified phrase-structure rules presented here do not, of course, represent a complete phrase-structure grammar of English, nor are they meant to do so. The purpose of using such a simplified model is simply to explain what PS rules are and how they are applied. What these particular rules describe is a finite language—and a very limited one at that. In fact, they are capable of generating only four terminal strings:

1. *The # boy # - ed + like # the # dog* (The boy liked the dog.)
2. *The # boy # - ed + like # the # boy* (The boy liked the boy.)
3. *The # dog # - ed + like # the # boy* (The dog liked the boy.)
4. *The # dog # - ed + like # the # dog* (The dog liked the dog.)

Enlarging the PS Rules. If we hope to write the kind of grammar that will explain all and only the grammatical sentences of English (a requirement which Chomsky insists should be the aim of an adequate grammar), we shall obviously have to extend our rules. In this section, we shall see how the phrase-structure rules can, in fact, be vastly extended in order to more accurately represent the facts of real language.

Consider, for example, that the rules of our simplified grammar permit the choice of only two nouns, *boy* and *dog*, both of which are singular. Yet, every speaker of English knows that most nouns can take either a singular or a plural form. Therefore, we must modify the NP rule:

$$NP \longrightarrow \begin{Bmatrix} NP_{sing} \\ NP_{pl} \end{Bmatrix}$$

Noun Phrase is rewritten as either singular noun phrase (NP_{sing}) or plural noun phrase (NP_{pl}).

$$NP_{sing} \longrightarrow D + N + \emptyset$$

NP_{sing} is rewritten as Determiner plus Noun plus singular (null) affix.

$$NP_{pl} \longrightarrow D + N + \text{-s}$$

NP_{pl} is rewritten as Determiner plus Noun plus plural affix (symbolized by *-s*).

Another linguistic fact which our simplified rules fail to account for is that the use of a determiner is sometimes optional, especially with a plural noun (*Boys liked dogs* is just as grammatical as *The boys liked the dogs*). But that problem is easily taken care of. All we need do is put the determiner in parentheses, and then include the instruction that any parenthesized element or series of elements is to be interpreted as optional, sometimes occurring, sometimes not.

$$NP_{sing} \longrightarrow (D) + N + \emptyset$$

$$NP_{pl} \longrightarrow (D) + N + \text{-}s$$

It is a further linguistic fact of English that the speaker has far many more available noun choices than the words *boy* and *dog*, many more verb choices than *like*, many more determiner choices than *the*, and so on. As the number of entries in an English dictionary will attest, it is not practical for us to attempt to list all, or even most, of these lexical items. We can solve this problem by listing three or four representative items, followed by an ellipsis (a series of three dots) which tells us there are many more choices:

$$D \longrightarrow \{the, a, an, some, \ldots\}$$

$$N \longrightarrow \{boy, dog, man, John, ball, book, \ldots\}$$

$$V \longrightarrow \{like, take, give, run, hit, write, \ldots\}$$

One of the most serious shortcomings of our simplified phrase-structure grammar is that it permits the use of only one verb, *like*. Moreover, the VP rule provides for only one kind of verb complement, the NP. Clearly, the rules need to be expanded to include other verb types, and they need to include information which tells the different kinds of complements required by the different verb types. Consider these verb phrases, for example:

The boy *gave the child a present.* $(\text{VP} \longrightarrow \text{MV} + \text{NP} + \text{NP})$

The boy *ran.* $(\text{VP} \longrightarrow \text{MV})$

The boy *thought the girl pretty.* $(\text{VP} \longrightarrow \text{MV} + \text{NP} + \text{Adj})$

The boy *felt hungry.* $(\text{VP} \longrightarrow \text{MV} + \text{Adj})$

The boy *is here.* $(\text{VP} \longrightarrow \text{MV} + \text{Adv})$

Obviously, if our PS rules are to reflect these English sentence possibilities, we must expand the rule for rewriting the VP:

$\text{VP} \longrightarrow \text{MV} \, (+ \, \text{Comp})$ Verb Phrase is rewritten as Main Verb alone, or Main Verb plus Complement.

$\text{MV} \longrightarrow \begin{Bmatrix} V \\ be \\ have \end{Bmatrix}^{*}$ Main Verb is rewritten as Verb, *be*, or *have*.

$V \longrightarrow \begin{Bmatrix} V_i \\ V_t \\ V_l \end{Bmatrix}$ Verb is rewritten as Intransitive Verb (V_i), Transitive Verb (V_t), or Linking Verb (V_l).

$\text{Comp} \longrightarrow \begin{Bmatrix} \text{NP} \\ \text{NP} + \text{NP} \\ \text{NP} + \text{Adj} \\ \text{Adj} \\ \text{Adv} \end{Bmatrix}$ Complement is rewritten as one of the five choices listed.

These suggestions for modifying and elaborating the simplified phrase-structure rules are by no means complete. Many further variations occur in real English sentences—that the NP can be rewritten to provide for the use of a pronoun rather than a noun, or that an adverb can be optionally added to the VP. Nevertheless, enough illustrations have been given here to show the need for expanding the PS rules. PS rule expansion will be discussed in more detail in Chapter 22.

*The reason for listing *have* and *be* separately will not become clear until a bit later. The braces mean that among the choices given, one *must* be selected.

LIMITATIONS OF A PHRASE-STRUCTURE GRAMMAR. It is clear that a fully elaborated phrase-structure grammar is a more powerful grammar than the first model grammar (the left-to-right Markov model) which Chomsky analyzes in *Syntactic Structures*. Nevertheless, he argues that even a fully developed PS grammar is not good enough. There are still many English sentences which either cannot be explained at all or which, at best, can be explained only "clumsily" and in a way that is not "revealing." What is needed, then, is an even *more* powerful grammar, one which will include a transformational level. But before presenting the rules for a transformational level, Chomsky gives a number of situations which illustrate the inevitable complexity and difficulties which must result from attempting to incorporate all grammatical instructions in a phrase-structure grammar.

Conjunction. Every speaker "knows" that from Sentences 1 and 2 below, Sentence 3 can be derived:

1. Jim liked the dog.

2. Jane liked the dog.

3. Jim and Jane liked the dog.

A speaker knows that Sentence 3 can be derived from Sentences 1 and 2 by looking back beyond the most recently formed string. Sentences 1 and 2 are almost exactly alike, differing only in that the constituent *Jim* appears in Sentence 1 where *Jane* appears in Sentence 2. They are the same kind of constituent and they are stated in a similar form—which indicates that the element *Jim* and the element *Jane* derive from the same source. A comparison of the set of derivational strings for Sentence 1 would prove to be identical to the set of strings for Sentence 2 up to but except for the final noun choice.

In fact, we can state the rule for conjunction as follows:

1. If Constituent X in String 1 and Constituent Y in String 2

    a) are derived from the same source, and
    b) are stated in the same form; and

2. if all other constituents in String 1 and String 2 are identical to each other (i.e., if String 1 and String 2 differ in no other way), then

3. we can derive String 3 by substituting for Constituent X in String 1 the new string $X + and + Y$ (the double shaft arrow means "is transformed to")

$(X + like\ the\ dog) + (Y + liked\ the\ dog) \Longrightarrow$

$X + and + Y + liked\ the\ dog.$

The difficulty with this rule, however, is that we cannot include it or anything like it in our PS rules. At the PS level, remember, we are able to rewrite only one constituent at a time. That is, no more than a single element appears to the left of the arrow. Furthermore, each step in a phrase-structure grammar is wholly dependent only upon that derivation which immediately precedes it. A phrase-structure grammar, then, does not provide for the capacity to look back beyond the immediately preceding string to one or more previously derived strings. It is for this reason that we require a third set of rules (in addition to Phrase-Structure Rules and Morphophonemic Rules, the latter of which we have not yet examined).

Active and Passive. A second linguistic phenomenon which would be difficult to explain within the confines of a PS grammar, but which is quite simply explained by transformational rules, is the "relationship" which every speaker knows to exist between active and passive sentences like *Jim liked the dog* and *The dog was liked by Jim*. If we have rules which permit us to rewrite an entire string, that is transformation rules, the active-passive relationship can be quite easily explained:

$$N_1 \# \text{ past} + V_t \# D \# N_2 \Longrightarrow D \# N_2 \# \text{ past} + be \# \text{ -en} +$$
$$V_t \# by \# N_1$$

A transformation rule permits us to perform a whole series of operations on a string in order to convert it into another string.

Verb Formation—The Auxiliary Rule. Our simplified PS rules permitted only one verb form, the past tense. Yet, as every speaker of English is aware, there are many other possibilities. Consider these sentences:

1. The boy *took* a bath.

2. The boy *takes* a bath.

3. I *take* a bath.

4. The boy *may take* a bath.

5. The boy *is taking* a bath.

6. The boy *has taken* a bath.

7. The boy *may be taking* a bath.

8. The boy *may have taken* a bath.

9. The boy *may have been taking* a bath.

As shown by these examples, the verb form in an English sentence may consist of from one to four words. But even when it is only one word, we have a choice of past or present tense. This means that the simplified rule for verb tense must be modified. Moreover, as Sentences 2 and 3 above illustrate, the present tense affix may be either ø or *-s*. Again, we run into an inadequacy of a PS grammar: the speaker must know whether the subject of the present tense verb is third person singular (in which case the *-s* affix is required) or whether the subject is something else (in which case the affix must be ø). This is the kind of information which Chomsky refers to as "context sensitive." And it is obviously the kind of information which cannot be provided in a PS grammar, for it requires that we be able to look back beyond the rule for rewriting Tense. In fact, we must go all the way back to the rule for the NP in order to discover whether we are dealing with an NP_{sing} or an NP_{pl}. In other words, the rule for the present tense choice is no longer a PS rule:

$$\text{present} \Longrightarrow \begin{Bmatrix} \text{-}s \text{ (in context of } NP_{3rd,sing}) \\ \text{ø (in all other contexts)} \end{Bmatrix}$$

In addition to the problem with present tense, we need to be able to explain the behavior of auxiliary words. As we noted in Part Two, an auxiliary word can be one of three choices: a form of the verb *be*, a form of the verb *have*, or an uninflected word like *will, can, must, may*, which is called a *modal*. The behavior of auxiliary words is altogether regular and describable, but it is not possible to incorporate such information in a PS grammar, for again, what is involved here is the ability to see that the choice of a particular auxiliary will have a *delayed* effect. Whether or not one chooses to use an auxiliary word is optional. However, once a choice has been made, the auxiliary chosen imposes a condition upon the affix of the verb which immediately follows it. A *modal* imposes the null affix (ø); *have* imposes the *-en* affix; *be* imposes the *-ing* affix. (We are speaking here of active voice verb forms only, since as has been already demonstrated, the passive voice verb forms will be accounted for by a passive transformation rule.)

We need, also, to provide for one more rule of verb formation. Although it is possible to choose anywhere from no to three auxiliary words, if more than one is chosen they must appear in a given order.

What all of this means is that we must elaborate considerably upon the PS rule for the formation of the main verb (MV). Up to a point, the modified rules will be nothing more than a few more detailed PS rules. But as soon as we become involved in a "context-sensitive" situation (as, for example, in Rule 10 below), we require a transformational rule. We also have the additional difficulty that we are involved with discontinuous constituents, and discontinuous elements of the sort that occur in the auxiliary verb phrase cannot be adequately handled by a PS grammar.

MODIFIED PHRASE STRUCTURE RULES

    1. S $\longrightarrow$ NP + VP

    2. NP $\longrightarrow \begin{Bmatrix} NP_{sing} \\ NP_{pl} \end{Bmatrix}$

3. $NP_{sing} \longrightarrow (D) + N + sing$

4. $NP_{pl} \longrightarrow (D) + N + pl$

5. $sing \longrightarrow \text{ø}$

6. $pl \longrightarrow \text{-}s$

7. $VP \longrightarrow MV (+ Comp)$

8. $MV \longrightarrow Aux + V$

9. $V \longrightarrow \begin{Bmatrix} v \\ be \\ have \end{Bmatrix}$

10. $v \longrightarrow \begin{Bmatrix} v_i \\ v_t \\ v_l \end{Bmatrix}$

11. $Aux \longrightarrow T \; (M + \text{ø}) \; (have + \text{-}en) \; (be + \text{-}ing)$

12. $T \longrightarrow \begin{Bmatrix} past \\ pres \end{Bmatrix}$

13. $past \longrightarrow \text{-}ed$

14. $pres \Longrightarrow \begin{Bmatrix} \text{-}s \text{ (in context of } NP_{3rd, sing}) \\ \text{ø (in all other contexts)} \end{Bmatrix}$

15. $Comp \longrightarrow \begin{Bmatrix} NP \\ NP + NP \\ NP + Adj \\ Adj \\ Adv \end{Bmatrix}$

16. $D \longrightarrow \{the, a, an, some, \ldots\}$

17. $N \longrightarrow \{boy, dog, man, John, book, \ldots\}$

18. $v_i \longrightarrow \{walk, run, fall, \ldots\}$

19. $v_t \longrightarrow \{like, take, give, write, \ldots\}$

20. $v_l \longrightarrow \{seem, appear, feel, remain, \ldots\}$

21. $M \longrightarrow \{will, can, must, may, \ldots\}$

22. $Adj \longrightarrow \{sad, good, \ldots\}$

23. $Adv \longrightarrow \{here, there, \ldots\}$

Level II: Morphophonemic Rules

After we have applied all phrase structure rules (in our expanded model), the resulting terminal string is still not an English sentence. We will have terminal strings like these:

The # boy + ø # -s + feel # bad.

The # man + -s # -ed + like # the # book + -s.

We must therefore turn now to the second level of the generative grammar, the morphophonemic. The rules in this level are called morphophonemic rules (M rules), and what they do is provide instructions for converting strings of morphemes into strings of phonemes. Note once again that M rules are different from PS rules, inasmuch as more than a single element occurs to the left of the arrow:*

$$boy + ø \longrightarrow boy \qquad\qquad man + ø \longrightarrow man$$
$$boy + \text{-}s \longrightarrow \text{boys} \qquad\qquad man + \text{-}s \longrightarrow \text{men}$$

After we have applied all of the rules from the phrase-structure level of our grammar (PS rules) and all of the rules from the morphophonemic level (M rules), we will have strings like these:

The # boy # -s + feel # bad.

The # men # -ed + like # the # books.

These strings are still not sentences. To produce an actual sentence, we must turn to the third level of our generative grammar—the transformational level.

Level III: Transformational Rules

Before presenting a model for the third level of his transformational-generative grammar (hereafter abbreviated TG grammar), Chomsky devotes an interim chapter of *Syntactic Structures* to "the goals of a linguistic theory." A linguistic theory of a language, he repeats, *is* a grammar of a language. The linguist's chief concern ought therefore to be the

---

*These are extremely simplified M rules. The linguist, for one thing, would state the rules in phonemic symbols. Secondly, he would include instructions which would explain that the past morpheme *-ed* is pronounced /id/ in words like *fitted* and *instructed*, where the affix is voiced; but that *-ed* is pronounced /t/ in words like *walked*, where it is spoken as an unvoiced consonant.

Standard rather than phonemic spellings are used here. However, do heed this warning: Do not permit yourself to be blinded to the fact that the purpose of M rules is to show how combined morphemes are pronounced, not how they are spelled.

evaluation of a grammar once it is presented. It is extremely important that, in order to develop a good theory, the linguist decide on criteria of adequacy.

In Chomsky's view, the grammar of a particular language ought to meet two conditions if it is to be an adequate theory:

1. It will have to generate *only* sentences which are considered acceptable by the mature native speaker. He labels this goal *external conditions of adequacy.*

2. It will have to be constructed according to a *general* theory of language structure—one which defines such terms as *phoneme*, *phrase*, and so on, independently, without exclusive reference to a particular language. He calls this goal the *condition of generality.*

Moreover, there must be a relationship between the external and the general conditions.

Next, Chomsky considers what kind of proof is needed to permit the justification of a grammar theory. The strongest requirement is to be able to show that the theory, from a corpus of actual sentences, constitutes a precise but practical method for automatically yielding a grammar describing all possible sentences of a language; i.e., it must provide a *discovery procedure.* Conversely, if it can be shown that there exists a natural language situation to which the theory does not apply, then that theory is obviously inadequate.

In Chomsky's view, no theory has yet been formulated which can meet the first of these requirements. The most promising system had seemed for a time to be a more fully developed phrase-structure grammar; and, in fact, he had worked for some time to develop a formal PS grammar. But he has come to the conclusion that the task is impossible—or, at best, not worth the effort. An adequately developed PS grammar would necessarily have to be so complex that it would be hopelessly impractical. It is this conviction which has led him to develop his altogether new transformational-generative grammar theory.*

In particular, Chomsky renounces the beloved "discovery procedure" of structural linguistics. He sees no sensible reason to oppose the "mixing of levels"—one of the structuralists' favorite taboos. In fact, he thinks

---

*Chomsky's ultimate aim is to construct a truly general grammar theory—one which will define language universals: abstract principles of language which apply to the underlying structures of all natural languages and which can therefore be justified as valid explanations of what native speakers "know." This is a subject with which he became increasingly fascinated. Meanwhile, he feels that the best way to proceed in this direction is by writing a great many carefully formulated TG grammars of particular languages.

that the structuralists have been mistaken in conceiving of their *method* as their *theory*. A grammar theory should not be aimed at isolating such surface phenomena as the *-emes* in a language. Rather, it should be a *general* theory—the more general, the simpler, and thus the better.

Indeed, he goes further. He argues that the *procedure* whereby one arrives at a grammar, whether by intuition,* by trained guesswork, or by some other method, is of little significance. What *does* matter is the evaluation of a theory once it is formulated. To demand more of a grammar than that it provide an evaluation procedure is both unnecessary and unrealistic.

A second and weaker requirement of a grammar theory is that it should provide a method for determining the *best* among alternate theories; i.e., that it should provide a *decision procedure*. This requirement he also dismisses as unrealistic. The problem, as he sees it, is that at present we do not even have a theory for deciding between two contending grammars.

It is for these reasons that Chomsky favors a third, weakest requirement: that a grammar theory should seek to do no more than provide an *evaluation procedure* for determining merely which among two proposed grammars is the *better*. The linguist's proper task, accordingly, is a threefold one. First, it is necessary to state precisely what the external tests (criteria) are. Linguists must agree on what it is that an adequate grammar should describe: namely, that it should describe all possible grammatical sentences of a language. Second, it must be possible to develop explicit formulations within the general framework of these external goals for defining such linguistic structures as a sentence, a phrase, a phoneme, and so on. Last, it must be simple and practical. Of two systematic explanations, the more complex will be rejected in favor of the simpler theory. The ultimate goal is to provide a mechanical, objective, nonintuitive method for evaluating a proposed grammar and for comparing it with other proposed grammars.

To those linguists who would object that this means setting their sights too low, Chomsky argues that it is the best we can do at present. Besides, what he suggests is really no different from the method used by other sciences, like physics or chemistry. Few sciences would seriously consider trying to develop a general, practical, mechanical method for deciding the best alternative theory. There would be little point in setting such a goal without some idea of how to achieve it.

Suppose, for the sake of argument, that an adequate PS grammar is formulated (according to agreed-upon criteria as outlined above). If,

---

*By "intuition," Chomsky does not mean merely "vague feelings." He uses the term to mean unformulated but invariant linguistic behavior, or language habits.

when this PS grammar is compared with a second equally adequate grammar theory, it can be demonstrated that the second model is both simpler and more revealing than the first model, then clearly the second one is the superior theory.

It is this claim that Chomsky makes for a transformational-generative grammar theory. A careful examination of transformational rules and of their implications leads, he contends, to a totally new concept of linguistic description—a concept which is simpler, more revealing, and therefore more powerful than the description provided by any other grammar to date.

According to Chomsky's three-level TG grammar, the sentence derivation process can be generally outlined as follows:

1. Beginning with the abstract concept *Sentence*, we apply all of the PS rules to construct an extended derivation. When the PS rules are exhausted, we have a terminal string whose constituents are words and morphemes.

2. Next, we apply T rules to the terminal string of the PS component of the grammar. At this point, we *must* perform whatever obligatory transformations are called for by the constituent structure of the string. We *may* or *may not* choose to apply one or more additional optional transformations. (These terms will be defined in the following pages.)

3. Last, we apply whatever M rules are required to convert the string of morphemes into a string of phonemes.* The final result is an actual grammatical English sentence.

The innovation here, as you can see, is the addition of a third level, the transformational level, complete with its list of T rules. Unlike a phrase-structure rule, a transformational rule operates on an entire string of elements (or even on a set of strings). It has the effect of changing the original constituent structure to a wholly new constituent structure, and it can do this in one of a number of ways: it can add constituents, it can delete constituents, or it can rearrange constituents.

An investigation of the nature of transformations has led Chomsky to the conclusion that they are of two quite different types: *obligatory transformations* and *optional transformations*. An obligatory transformation he defines as one which *must* be applied to every derivation from the phrase-structure level of the grammar if the result is to be an actual English sentence. An optional transformation, on the other hand, *may* or

---

*It is probably more accurate to say that the appropriate M rules are applied as needed throughout the entire sentence derivation process. Some of these can be applied to morphemes in the terminal string of the PS part of the grammar; others must wait until the obligatory T rules put certain morphemes in the proper order.

may not be applied. We can construct actual sentences without using optional T rules. When we do use them, however, they may be applied either to terminal strings or to prior transformations.

This distinction between optional and obligatory transformations means that, depending on whether a sentence is constructed by the application of obligatory T rules only, or whether by the application of both obligatory and optional T rules, sentences are of two fundamentally different types. Thus Chomsky speaks of kernel sentences and transformed sentences (also called transforms or transformations).*

Kernel sentences can be defined as those sentences which result from the application of obligatory T rules, and obligatory T rules only, to terminal strings of the PS grammar. Transformations are all those sentences which result from the application, in addition to obligatory T rules, of one or more optional T rules either to a terminal string or to a prior transformation. The terminal strings which underlie kernel sentences can thus be said to provide the basis or kernel for all of the sentences in the language. Kernel sentences, however, are the only ones which are derived exclusively from terminal strings. We can put all of this information in a kind of formula as follows:

Kernel Sentence = One Terminal String + One or more Obligatory Transformations

Transformation = One or more Terminal Strings + One or more Obligatory Transformations + One or more Optional Transformations

At this point you are probably confused. How, you may wonder, can Chomsky claim that this new grammar is "simpler" than a linear or a phrase-structure grammar. (And he does claim, you will remember, that a transformational grammar is simpler, more revealing, and more powerful than previously formulated grammars.) Let us see if we can recapitulate his argument:

1. The addition of a transformational level makes it unnecessary to provide PS rules for sentences which are not kernel sentences. Therefore, PS rules must be provided for kernel sentences only.

2. All other sentences (i.e., all sentences which are not kernel) can then be derived, by means of optional T rules, from the terminal strings which underlie kernel sentences.

*This imprecise use of the term *transformation* is, I think, unfortunate. It has led to considerable confusion. It became common practice, especially among textbook writers, to speak of kernel sentences as *un*transformed sentences. Strictly speaking, since *no* sentence is possible without the application of at least a few obligatory T rules, every English sentence is a transformation. Nevertheless, one frequently finds the terms *kernel sentence* and *terminal string* treated as synonymous.

To illustrate what he means, consider the passive. Passive sentences, you will recall, are transforms; we therefore do not have to account for them in our phrase-structure rules. If, on the other hand, we did not have the transformational component in our grammar model, we would have to write our PS rules so that passives are provided for. This means we would have to include in our Auxiliary rule the possibility of (*be* + *-en*):

Aux $\longrightarrow$ T (*M* + ø) (*have* + *-en*) (*be* + *-ing*) (*be* + *-en*)

Then we would have to write a subrule to explain that if (*be* + *-en*) is chosen, that choice imposes the requirement that the final or notional verb be followed with a *by* phrase. We would also need to explain that (*be* + *-en*) may not be chosen unless the notional verb is a transitive verb. Chomsky's point is that we would get so bogged down with subrules that the grammar would become hopelessly complex. The whole problem is vastly simplified, however, by the addition of a transformational level to the grammar. For then all we need to do is to specify the *kind of terminal string* to which the passive transformation rule may apply: NP_1 + Aux + v_t + NP_2. All other strings are thereby excluded. The T_{pas} rule would then read as follows:*

$$NP_1 + Aux + V_t + NP_2 \Longrightarrow NP_2 + Aux + (be + \text{-}en) + V_t + by + NP_1$$

Chomsky also argues that a TG grammar is more "revealing" than other grammar theories. Crucial to this argument is his belief that the structuralists' objection to "mixing levels" is both unnecessary and confusing. In fact, it is precisely on the grounds that the various levels of a grammar *are* interdependent that he urges the renunciation of the discovery procedure goal. Moreover, he insists that it is not necessary to solve all the problems on one level before moving on to the next level in the hierarchy. To evaluate a grammar theory properly, one needs to be able to picture the whole system in its entirety, to be able to look both forwards and backwards.

Again, an example (not Chomsky's) may help to illustrate this point. Without the perspective gained from knowing how a sentence will behave syntactically under transformation, we might very well consider the following three sentences constituently identical; i.e., as being derived from equivalent terminal strings of the pattern NP_1 + V_t + NP_2:

S1   John hit the ball

S2   John had the ball

S3   The meat weighed a pound

*The double-shaft arrow notation means "is transformed to."

Yet, the behavior of each sentence under the passive transformation reveals that they are different in an important way:

T1   The ball was hit by John

T2   The ball was had by John

T3   A pound was weighed by the meat

Sentences T2 and T3 are clearly not acceptable English sentences. Thus the verbs *have* and *weigh*, which look like ordinary transitive verbs in the kernel sentences, turn out not to be ordinary at all. (It took a while, incidentally, for TG linguists to make this discovery. The earliest TG grammars listed all of these sentences as the same kind of kernel sentence pattern. As soon as the behavior of verbs like *have, weigh, total, cost,* and so on, was discovered to be unique in at least some sentences, a new verb category had to be devised: the middle or mid-transitive verb.)

Thus we can see that what happens to a sentence at the transformational level can provide insight into the phrase-structure level and can contribute to our understanding of the constituent strcuture of the terminal strings underlying kernel sentences. It is for this reason that Chomsky says a transformational grammar is more revealing than other grammars. Likewise, it is this forward-backward potential provided by the inclusion of a transformational level that prompts Chomsky's claim that a TG grammar is more powerful than other theories.

Chomsky's unique and enduring contribution to linguistics is in demonstrating how grammar rules can be presented in rigorous formulations. He shows that both context-free and context-sensitive rules can be formalized: context-free rules in the phrase-structure part of the grammar (some of which had already been done when he published *Syntactic Structures*); and context-sensitive rules in the transformational part. It is Chomsky's insistence upon this kind of scientific rigor which has most influenced the direction of linguistic research since 1957, for it has since become incumbent on linguists who want their ideas to be seriously considered or who would challenge part or all of Chomsky's TG grammar theory to present their alternative theories in the form of equally well-formulated rules.

Let us then briefly summarize Chomsky's argument— as he himself does in the last chapter of *Syntactic Structures*. Arguing that the most that can be reasonably required of a grammar theory is that it provide an evaluation procedure, he insists that there should be no objection to the "mixing of levels" within the framework of such a theory. Indeed, a grammar theory is made more powerful and more revealing by the provision of a completed picture.

Secondly, Chomsky contends that, at least for the time being, a grammar theory can best be developed as a syntactic rather than a semantic theory. This is not to say that he considers meaning considerations to be unimportant to the understanding of the sentences of a language. From the start, he has acknowledged that the goal of a grammar is to show the relations between sounds and meanings. The syntax is basic only in the sense that this relationship is abstract and thus requires a syntactic component as mediator between sound and meaning.

The task which Chomsky sets for himself and for other linguists is formidable: (1) to write formal rules for all of the sentences in the language, proceeding from the assumption that language is rule-governed (that is, an infinite number of sentences are both generated and understood on the basis of a finite number of rules); and (2) to formulate these rules in such a way that they represent the abstract "facts" of language which every native speaker-listener "knows." In other words, the linguist's task is to provide formulated, objective explanations for the intuitive language behavior of the native speaker. He concludes *Syntactic Structures* with the reminder that the theory presented here is incomplete, and that further elaboration is clearly required.

During the next six or seven years, Chomsky and others did, in fact, elaborate on and considerably refine the early TG model. But even with the publication of *Aspects of the Theory of Syntax* in 1965 (a volume in which Chomsky incorporates revisions suggested by a number of transformational linguists), TG theory was not set for all time. Criticisms, suggestions for further revision, and outright challenges continue to this day. Nevertheless, it seems safe to say that despite the considerable revisions in the early TG model, the fundamental theory has not changed.

Within a short time after the publication of *Syntactic Structures*, a number of pedagogical TG grammars were readied for use in the schools.* The first, and possibly the most famous, of these texts was *English Sentences*, a high school grammar published by Paul Roberts in 1962; followed two years later by his *English Syntax*, an autoinstructional transformational grammar.

Probably the most serious shortcoming of these first TG texts, at least from the point of view of the theoretical linguist, was their practice of considering kernel sentences (Roberts used the term "basic sentences") as synonymous with terminal strings. In defense of Roberts and others, I suggest that this apparent confusion is understandable. Chomsky himself, in *Syntactic Structures*, sometimes treats the two as synonymous.

---

*As I mentioned earlier, nearly all of these early TG texts contained some misunderstandings and/or distortions of Chomsky's theory.

In discussing the value of a transformational level, for example, he states that "understanding a sentence" can be greatly aided by reconstructing it "on each level, including the transformational level where the kernel sentences underlying a given sentence can be thought of, in a sense, as the 'elementary content elements' out of which this sentence is constructed."*

Most pedagogical TG grammars also have cut down on or have eliminated altogether the business of rule-writing. This too is a perfectly understandable practice on the part of some textbook writers, who felt that the inclusion of formal, mathematically structured rules would scare off a good many students and would thus prove self-defeating. The difficulty, of course, is that by avoiding rule-writing in favor of relying on verbal explanations, these books manage to obscure much of the important scientific thrust of Chomsky's work. Serious linguists quite naturally view such a pedagogical approach with dismay, since it is merely old-fashioned school grammar in a new wrapping.

In the chapters which follow, this book will take a middle course. It will keep rule-writing at a minimum; and sometimes in the interest of simplifying an explanation, a sentence will be illustrated with an abbreviated set of rules or with a tree diagram that is less than a full representation. With the background already given, I trust that no serious distortion of TG grammar theory will result from these shortcuts.

PHRASE STRUCTURE   EXERCISE 50

Directions: Using the list of phrase-structure rules on pages 224 and 225, draw branching tree representations to show the derivation of the terminal string underlying each of the following sentences.

1. The boys are running.

2. John has given the boy some books.

3. The men may have been feeling sad.

*Syntactic Structures, pp. 107–108.

22

TG Grammar, Early Form: Kernel Sentences

What are some of the things about language which native speakers, without ever having formal grammar training, simply know? For one thing, they can create their own sentences in order to say whatever they wish to say. This kind of linguistic creativity has always intrigued language scholars. For another thing, they can understand and interpret any grammatical sentence they hear, a remarkable feat when one considers that nearly every sentence spoken is a novel one. Of course, speakers who are not linguistic scholars would find it difficult (if not impossible) to explain how they know what they know about language.

As illustrations of some of the abilities every speaker possesses, consider the following pairs of sentences:

1.a. She made herself a leader.
  b. She made herself a sandwich.

2.a. Jill is working.
  b. Jill is charming.

3.a. Mary called him a brute.
  b. Mary called him a taxi.

Native speakers of English know that even though the two sentences in each pair above are structurally identical, they mean different things. How do they know this?

Transformational-generative grammar explains that these pairs of sentences are alike only on the surface. Chomsky calls sentences which have identical surface structures but mean quite different things examples of "constructional homonymity." Sentences like these cannot possibly be explained, however, if linguists restrict themselves (as the structuralists did) to the observation and analysis of surface structures only. Sentences must be analyzed on all levels if their ambiguities, their meaning similarities, or their meaning differences are to be explained. The addition of a transformational level to a grammar theory enables the grammarian to make such explanations for the first time.

Now examine these sentences. Despite their obvious surface differences, a native speaker has no difficulty in understanding all of the sentences in each set to mean the same thing:

4.a. Jane made that dress.
b. That dress was made by Jane.

5.a. Some ants are in our lunch.
b. In our lunch are some ants.
c. There are some ants in our lunch.

How does a native speaker know that these very different sentence structures mean the same thing? Again, Chomsky points to the explanatory power of a transformational grammar. TG theory explains what every speaker understands: that the sentences in each set are somehow related. A grammar which provides transformation rules can explicitly show that the sentences in each set, whose surface syntaxes are unalike, *are in fact* related: they are all derived from the same terminal string at the phrase-structure level of the grammar.

A third phenomenon which cannot be satisfactorily accounted for by a one-level phrase-structure grammar, but which can be quite easily explained by a transformational grammar, is ambiguity as illustrated by these sentences:

6. He saw the moving trucks.

7. They entered the smoking room.

A transformational grammar enables us to understand that each of these sentences is ambiguous because each can be traced back to two different sets of underlying strings:

8.a. He saw the trucks.
The trucks were moving.
b. He saw the trucks.
One moves things with the trucks.

9.a. They entered the room.
The room was (still) smoking.
b. They entered the room.
One may smoke in the room.

Of course, not all cases of ambiguity can be explained by syntactical analysis. In expressions like "His suit is light" (color? weight?) or "The students were stoned" (persecuted? drunk? drugged?), the ambiguity is a semantic one having to do with lexical reference. Still, an impressive number of linguistic explanations are made possible through transformational syntactical analysis.

Crucial to the theory of TG grammar, then, is an understanding of the notion that underlying every sentence in the language there exists one or more kernel sentences, and that underlying every kernel sentence is a terminal string of the phrase-structure level of the grammar. Sometimes an actual English sentence emerges, after the application of only a few obligatory transformation rules, in a pattern that is almost identical to the form of the underlying terminal string. At other times, a sentence surfaces in a form whose syntax is greatly transformed from that of the original, underlying string or strings.

Thus, Chomsky has argued, there are two fundamental processes involved in language. The first of these, which can be represented at the phrase-structure level of the grammar, is the system (rules) which speakers/hearers follow to derive the simplest sentences (kernel sentences) of their language. The second process, which is represented at the transformational level, is the system (rules) by which speakers convert or transform these basic patterns into different syntactic structures.

The theory of early TG grammar, in consequence, is rooted in the idea that there are a finite number of core or kernel sentence patterns with which all native speakers become familiar. These kernel sentences are the basic elementary sentences of the language. All other sentences are then created, by means of a systematic set of transformation rules, from the terminal strings which underlie the kernel sentences.

Kernel sentences can be defined as those sentences which are derived exclusively from phrase-structure rules plus a small number of obligatory transformation rules. It is from the terminal strings underlying these kernel sentences that all the other sentences of the language are then formed.

Pedagogical grammarians of the early school of TG grammar theory eventually settled on eleven kernel sentence types. It is interesting to note that, with the one or two exceptions discussed below, these kernel sentence patterns are the same as those which traditional grammarians called the elementary sentences of English. For the most part, the behavior of sentences under transformation have offered verification for what had been only an intuitive judgment of the traditionalists: namely, that verb type (intransitive, transitive, linking) is significant.

One exception turned out to be sentences containing the verb *be*. Traditional grammar, you will recall, classified *be* as a linking verb of the same type as verbs like *become, appear, seem,* and *feel,* an analysis which makes rather good sense so long as we observe elementary sentence patterns only. The addition of a transformational level to the grammar, however, demonstrates that sentences containing *be* behave quite differently under transformation than do sentences containing other linking verbs. Moreover, a third kind of elementary complement, the adverbial subjective complement, had been overlooked by earlier grammars. This complement, which can be illustrated by the sentence "The boy is here," is common after forms of *be* but not possible after other linking verbs. Thus, we shall list among our kernel sentences three different patterns containing the verb *be,* in addition to the two patterns for linking verbs like *become* and *seem.*

Similarly, observation of surface structure only had led traditionalists to classify these two sentences as identical types:

The boy fired a gun. $(NP_{subj} + V_t + NP_{do})$

The boy had a gun. $(NP_{subj} + V_t + NP_{do})$

On the transformational level, however, it becomes clear that the two sentences differ significantly. The first sentence accepts the passive transformation, but the second one does not:

A gun was fired by the boy.

A gun was had by the boy.

Thus, as mentioned earlier, some sentences containing the main verb *have* and verbs which behave in the same way as *have* in Sentence 2 above (*cost, weigh, total*) must be classified as separate and distinct from those sentences containing regular transitive verbs.

A kernel sentence can be defined as having the following characteristics:

1. It is a declarative statement.

2. It is always positive (rather than negative).

3. Its main verb is always in the active voice, though it may be of any tense or aspect.

4. It contains no compounds.

5. Its word order is always "normal": subject + verb (+ complements).

6. It is spoken with normal intonation, i.e., in a normal tone of voice, progressing smoothly from beginning to end with no unusual pauses, stresses, or pitch variations.

7. It contains no noun modifiers (other than determiners) in immediate prenoun or postnoun positions.

Here, then, are the eleven basic or kernel sentence patterns:*

Intransitive Verb

Pattern 1. There is only one intransitive kernel sentence pattern. The sentence may consist of only two words, a *noun* (or *pronoun†*) plus a *verb*; or the noun may be preceded by a determiner and the verb may make use of auxiliary words. In addition, this sentence pattern—as is true of all kernel sentence patterns—may or may not include an adverb of place, time, and/or manner as part of the verb phrase.

Birds fly.   *The birds have flown.*
≠ *The boys ran.‡*   *The boys ran swiftly.*

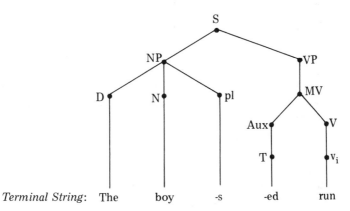

Terminal String: The   boy   -s   -ed   run

Transitive Verb

Pattern 2. Because the transitive verb may be followed by four distinct types of complement, we must classify sentences containing transitive verbs into four different kernel sentence patterns. Pattern 2 consists of NP$_{subj}$ + transitive verb + NP$_{do}$. An important requirement for all kernel sentences in the transitive verb category (Patterns 2, 3, 4, and 5) is that they be capable of accepting the passive transformation.

---

*Some of the early transformational texts followed Paul Roberts in presenting these ten or eleven sentence "patterns." Actually, Chomsky and TG grammarians in general rejected the idea of patterns as pure structuralism, since there were hundreds of "patterns" of kernel sentences. Still, even though such listing of these patterns of kernel sentences is a kind of structuralism in transformational guise, it has proved to some to be a useful teaching concept.

†In all cases, a *pronoun* may be used instead of a *noun* or a *noun phrase*. For the sake of simplicity, however, *NP* will be used hereafter to represent all of these possibilities.

‡Throughout this section, the sentence preceded by the symbol ≠ is the one represented by the branching tree diagram.

John loves Mary.   *John may have loved Mary.*

#*The boy liked the dog.*   *They put out the fire.*

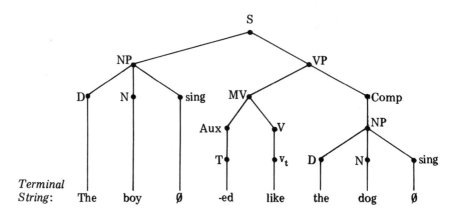

Terminal
String: The   boy   Ø   -ed   like   the   dog   Ø

Pattern 3. Pattern 3 sentences consist of $NP_{subj} + v_t + NP_{io} + NP_{do}$, always *in that order*. Not all transitive verbs suit this particular pattern: for example, "He drove me the car" is not an acceptable sentence. There are quite a few verbs, however, which may be used in Pattern 3 sentences (*give, take, send, tell,* and so on).

She sells John eggs.

The man gave the boy the car.

#*The teacher lent the boy some books.*

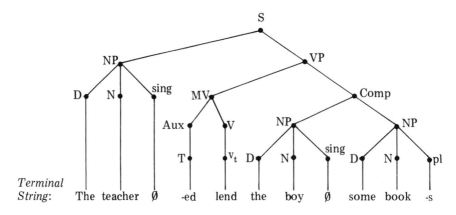

Terminal
String: The teacher Ø   -ed   lend   the   boy   Ø   some   book   -s

Pattern 4. Once again, as with Pattern 3, only particular transitive verbs are suitable for this pattern. Typical of such verbs are *think, consider, name, elect,* and so on. Pattern 4 consists of $NP_{subj} + v_t + NP_{do} + NP_{oc}$:

We elected John president.

They called Jim a coward.

 # The boys think the girls babies.

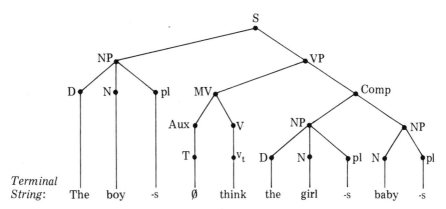

Pattern 5. At first glance, Pattern 5 appears to be similar to Pattern 4, because some transitive verbs like *think, call, consider,* may be used in either pattern. (A verb like *elect* can never be used in a Pattern 5 sentence, however.) Pattern 5 sentences consist of $NP_{subj} + v_t + NP_{do} + Adj_{oc}$:

People think Janet pretty.

We considered her silly.

 # The movie made the boy sad.

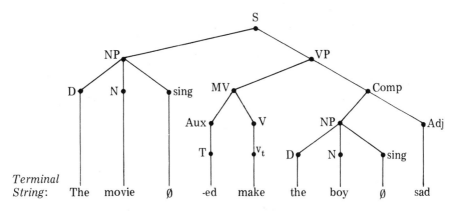

Pattern 6. Kernel sentences of the Pattern 6 type are those which, in their kernel or basic form, look exactly like Pattern 2 sentences. These are the sentences containing a mid-transitive verb—one which cannot accept the passive transformation; and, in fact, the earliest transforma-

tional grammars missed this pattern (just as the traditionalists had before them). Pattern 6 sentences consist of $NP_{subj} + v_{tm} + NP_{do}$:

> *The meat costs a dollar.*
>
> *The car weighed a ton.*
>
> *#The man had several guns.*

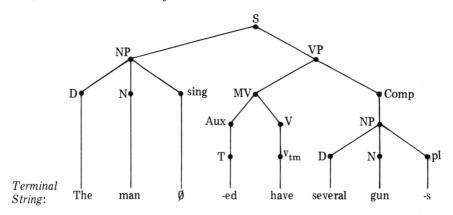

Linking Verb

Pattern 7. The linking verb, you will remember from traditional grammar, is one which is followed by a subjective complement. Pattern 7 sentences are those which contain a linking verb (other than *be*) plus a noun phrase subjective complement, $NP_{subj} + v_l + NP_{sc}$:

> *John remained a friend.*
>
> *#The boy became a leader.*

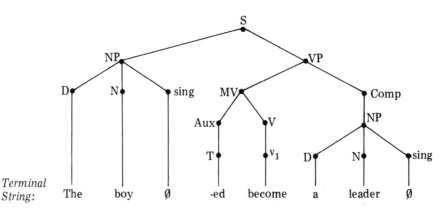

Pattern 8. Pattern 8 kernel sentences consist of a noun phrase subject plus a linking verb (other than *be*) plus an adjective subjective comple-

ment. Verbs typically suited to this pattern are *seem, feel, look, smell, taste, sound,* and so on. The pattern consists of $NP_{subj} + v_1 + Adj_{sc}$:

Roses smell sweet.

The music sounds beautiful.

#The girl seems happy.

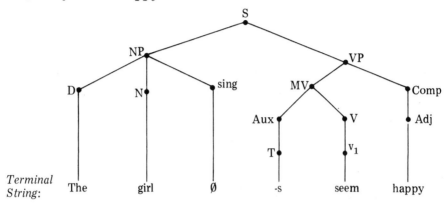

Terminal String:

Linking Verb *BE*

Pattern 9. Because the verb *be* has eight separate forms (*be* [ø₁], *am* [ø₂], *are* [ø₃], *is* [s], *was* [ed₁], *were* [ed₂], *being* [ing], *been* [en]) and therefore behaves differently at both the phrase-structure level and the transformational level, we shall list the three *be*-verb kernel sentences separately as Patterns 9, 10, and 11. Pattern 9 sentences consist of $NP_{subj} + be + NP_{sc}$:

Mr. Brown is the chairman.

The boy is a coward.

#The girls are the winners.

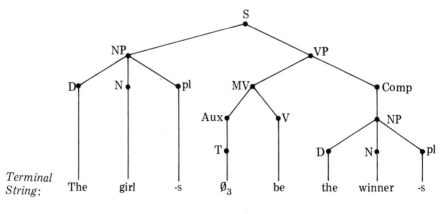

Terminal String:

Pattern 10. Pattern 10 kernel sentences follow the form: $NP_{subj} + be + Adj_{sc}$:

John may have been sad.

Some people are happy.

#*The students are smart.*

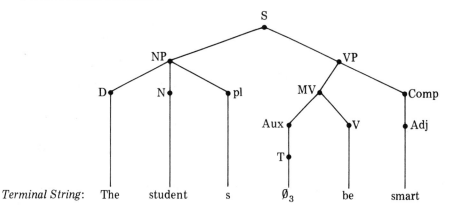

Terminal String: The   student   s $\emptyset_3$ be   smart

Pattern 11. Pattern 11 is a kernel sentence pattern which earlier grammar systems either missed altogether or simply ignored. Why this pattern failed to be mentioned is somewhat puzzling, for not only is it frequently used as a kernel sentence but it is also a pattern underlying a good many quite common transformations. The pattern consists of $NP_{subj} + be + ADV_{sc}$:

The dog is there.

The time is now.

#*The boy is here.*

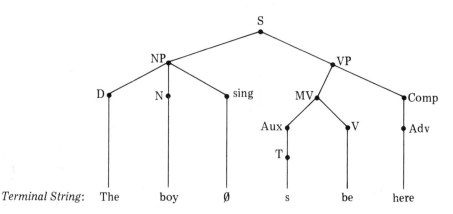

Terminal String: The   boy $\emptyset$ s   be   here

Variations of Kernel Sentences. As we examine more and more actual English sentences, and as we attempt to determine which sentences are kernel and which are nonkernel, we discover we must further enlarge both our PS rules and our M rules in order to account for many sentences at the PS level of the grammar. Thus, the following phenomena must be accounted for:

Pronoun. A noun phrase may be rewritten as determiner plus noun, noun alone, or pronoun:*

$$NP \longrightarrow \begin{Bmatrix} (D)\ N \\ Pro \end{Bmatrix}$$

We are running.

He hit the ball.

Adverbial. A verb phrase may include an adverbial of place, time, and/or manner: VP $\longrightarrow$ MV (+ Comp) (+ Adv)†

$$Adv \longrightarrow \begin{Bmatrix} adv_p \\ adv_t\ \text{(No more than one of each)} \\ adv_m \end{Bmatrix}$$

John walks *rapidly.*

They will go *there now.*

She loves him *blindly.*

Verb + Particle Combination. Verb + particle combinations (also called verb + adverbial combinations) are extremely common to English idiom. Such a combination consists of a verb form, either transitive or intransitive, plus a particle like *in, out, up, down, on, off, over, with.* Here are some examples:

TRANSITIVE	INTRANSITIVE
The thieves *blew up* the bank.	Jeff should *ease up.*
He *called up* a friend.	He *got up* early.
She *handed out* the leaflets.	The tension finally *let up.*
He *signed on* some volunteers.	The plane suddenly *took off.*

*The use of a pronoun is not merely a free option. Whether or not one may use a pronoun depends upon the existence of a previous noun referent which is unambiguous and not too remote.

†Adverbials are likewise not a free option, as had been formerly thought. In fact, this was what explicit formulations forced linguists to reconsider.

Kernel Sentence Patterns

PATTERN NO.	VERB TYPE	COMPLEMENT TYPE	EXAMPLES	PATTERN FORM
1	Intransitive	None	Birds fly. The birds have flown. The boys ran.	$NP_s + v_i$
2	Transitive	NP_{do}	John loves Mary. John may have loved Mary. They put out the fire. The child liked the dog.	$NP_s + v_t + NP_{do}$
3	Transitive	$NP_{io} + NP_{do}$	She sells John eggs. The man gave the boy a car. The teacher lent the boy some books.	$NP_s + v_t + NP_{io} + NP_{do}$
4	Transitive	$NP_{do} + NP_{oc}$	We elected John president. They called Jim a coward. The boys think the girls babies.	$NP_s + v_t + NP_{do} + NP_{oc}$
5	Transitive	$NP_{do} + Adj_{oc}$	People thought Janet pretty. We considered him silly. The movie made the girl sad.	$NP_s + v_t + NP_{do} + Adj_{oc}$
6	Mid-transitive	NP_{do}	The meat costs a dollar. The car weighed a ton. The man had several guns.	$NP_s + v_{tm} + NP_{do}$
7	Linking	NP_{sc}	John remained a friend. The girl became a leader.	$NP_s + v_l + NP_{sc}$

PATTERN NO.	VERB TYPE	COMPLEMENT TYPE	EXAMPLES	PATTERN FORM
8	Linking	Adj_{sc}	Roses smell sweet. The music sounds pretty. The girl seems happy.	$NP_s + v_1 + Adj_{sc}$
9	*be*	NP_{sc}	Mr. Brown is the chairman. The boy is a coward. The girls are the winners.	$NP_s + be + NP_{sc}$
10	*be*	Adj_{sc}	John may have been sad. Some people are happy. The students are smart.	$NP_s + be + Adj_{sc}$
11	*be*	Adv_{sc}	The dog is there. The time is now. The boy is here.	$NP_s + be + Adv_{sc}$

You will notice the following things:

1. Such a combination carries an altogether different meaning from that of the same verb used alone. In fact, in most cases, you can probably think of a synonymous verb—usually one with a prefix: *blow over/pass; call up/telephone; hand out/distribute; give in/succumb; get up/arise; let up/lessen; take off/depart; turn up/arrive;* and so on.

2. The word order is usually verb plus particle. That is, in most cases one would not move the particle to a position in front of the verb: *Off* the airplane *took; Out* they *handed* the leaflets; *Up* he *got* early.

3. An intonation clue can perhaps tell you that the expression is a verb + particle combination rather than a verb followed by a prepositional phrase:*

He *called* up the stairs.   They *easéd* up the hill.
He *called úp* a friend.   The pressure *eased úp.*

She *passed* out the door.   He *signed* on the dotted line.
She *passed oút* the papers.   He *signed ón* some volunteers.

Our PS rules will therefore have to be modified as follows:

$$V \longrightarrow \begin{Bmatrix} v \\ be \end{Bmatrix}$$

$$v \longrightarrow \begin{Bmatrix} v_i \, (+ \text{ part}) \\ v_t \, (+ \text{ part}) \\ V_{tm} \\ v_l \end{Bmatrix}$$

Qualifier. A qualifier may precede any adjective or any adverb of manner. Thus, where the symbol *Adj* appears in the PS rules (it occurs in the rule for rewriting the complement), the symbol *Q* in parentheses may precede it:

$$\text{Comp} \longrightarrow \begin{Bmatrix} \text{NP} \\ \text{NP} + \text{NP} \\ \text{NP} + (\text{Q}) \text{ Adj} \\ (\text{Q}) \text{ Adj} \\ \text{Adv} \end{Bmatrix}$$

---

*As mentioned earlier, controlled tests have now shown that in normal use there is no difference in intonation, either as used by the speaker or as perceived by the hearer.

Likewise, the symbol (Q) may appear in the rule for rewriting the adverb:

$$\text{Adv} \longrightarrow \begin{cases} \text{adv}_p \\ \text{adv}_t \text{ (No more than one of each)} \\ (Q) \text{ adv}_m \end{cases}$$

In addition to these PS rule modifications, we must also enlarge our lexical rules to allow for a much wider choice:

Determiner. We must list enough choices to indicate that words other than the articles *a, an,* and *the* may be used as determiners:

D $\longrightarrow$ {*a, an, the, some, several, any, every,* . . .}

Noun. We must indicate that a noun may be either an inflectional or a derivational word:

N $\longrightarrow$ {*man, boy, girl, chaos, health, wealth, riches,* . . .}

Adjective. Similarly, we must indicate that an adjective may be either an inflected or an uninflected word; or even a phrase:

Adj $\longrightarrow$ {*bad, good, sad, beautiful, in the pink, out of sorts,* . . .}

Adverb. We must provide phrases as well as single words among the various adverbial choices:

adv$_p$ $\longrightarrow$ {*there, here, in the room, at the store,* . . .}

adv$_t$ $\longrightarrow$ {*now, then, often, in the morning, during recess,* . . .}

adv$_m$ $\longrightarrow$ {*quickly, rapidly, in a minute, on the double,* . . .}

Qualifier. And, of course, since we have now added the symbol Q to our rules, we must list lexical choices for the qualifier:

Q $\longrightarrow$ {*quite, very, more*, less*, much*, extremely,* . . .}

As you can see, our phrase-structure rules have now been greatly modified and enlarged. A revised set of PS rules follows.

Modified Phrase Structure Rules (Rules of Formation)†

1. S $\longrightarrow$ NP + VP

2. NP $\longrightarrow$ $\begin{cases} \text{(D) N + num} \\ \text{Pro + num} \end{cases}$

---

*Although words like *more, less,* and *much* may be thought of as inflectional adjectives (*much, more, most; little, less, least*), most grammarians have concluded that when they are used as qualifiers, they may be viewed as uninflected words of the same type as *quite* and *very.*

†Some texts refer to phrase-structure rules as "rules of formation."

3. num $\longrightarrow$ $\begin{Bmatrix} \text{sing} \\ \text{pl} \end{Bmatrix}$

4. sing $\longrightarrow$ ø

5. pl $\longrightarrow$ *s*

6. VP $\longrightarrow$ MV (+ Comp) (+ Adv)

7. MV $\longrightarrow$ Aux + V

8. V $\longrightarrow$ $\begin{Bmatrix} \text{v} \\ be \end{Bmatrix}$

9. v $\longrightarrow$ $\begin{Bmatrix} \text{v}_i \ (+ \ \text{part}) \\ \text{v}_t \ (+ \ \text{part}) \\ \text{v}_{tm} \\ \text{v}_l \end{Bmatrix}$

10. Aux $\longrightarrow$ T (M + ø) (*have* + *en*) (*be* + *ing*)

11. T $\longrightarrow$ $\begin{Bmatrix} \text{past} \\ \text{pres} \end{Bmatrix}$

12. past $\longrightarrow$ *ed*

13. pres $\longrightarrow$ $\begin{Bmatrix} \text{s} \\ \text{ø} \end{Bmatrix}$

14. Comp $\longrightarrow$ $\begin{Bmatrix} \text{NP} \\ \text{NP} + \text{NP} \\ \text{NP} + \text{(Q) Adj} \\ \text{(Q) Adj} \\ \text{Adv} \end{Bmatrix}$

15. Adv $\longrightarrow$ $\begin{Bmatrix} \text{adv}_p \\ \text{adv}_t \\ \text{(Q) adv}_m \end{Bmatrix}$

16. D $\longrightarrow$ {*a, an, the, some, several, any, every,* ...}

17. N $\longrightarrow$ {*man, boy, dog, book, John, chaos, health, riches,* ...}

18. v$_i$ $\longrightarrow$ {*walk, run, fall, fly,* ...}

19. v$_t$ $\longrightarrow$ {*like, take, give, write, consider, make,* ...}

20. v$_{tm}$ $\longrightarrow$ {*have, cost, total, weigh,* ...}

21. v$_l$ $\longrightarrow$ {*seem, appear, feel, remain,* ...}

22. M $\longrightarrow$ {*will, can, must, may, ought to,* ...}

23. part $\longrightarrow$ {*in, out, up, down, on, off, over, with,* ...}

24. Adj $\longrightarrow$ {*bad, good, as, beautiful, in the pink, out of sorts,* ...}

25. adv$_p$ $\longrightarrow$ {*there, here, in the room, at the store,* ...}

26. adv$_t$ $\longrightarrow$ {*now, then, often, in the morning, during recess, . . .*}

27. adv$_m$ $\longrightarrow$ {*quickly, rapidly, in a minute, on the double, . . .*}

28. Q $\longrightarrow$ {*quite, very, more, much, less, extremely, absolutely, . . .*}

KERNEL SENTENCES   EXERCISE 51

Directions: Indicate which of the following sentences may be classified as *kernel sentences*:

1. You shouldn't study so hard.

2. John burned himself on the hot grill.

3. She hit the dog with a broom.

4. When he saw her, Jack gave her the message.

5. Jeremiah is terribly sleepy.

6. Jack gave her the message reluctantly.

7. Which book did the teacher assign?

8. Grimacing, she kicked the dog outside.

9. Some people go too far always.

10. You should study more systematically.

11. Mary climbed up to the summit.

12. Several problems are bothering Jim apparently.

13. Did she give up easily?

14. She quit for obvious reasons.

15. Suddenly Mary forgot her lines and had to be coached.

16. He found out my secret quickly.

17. Several dogs went along on the hunt.

18. I think he had been practicing the speech for a week.

19. Seeing is believing.

20. He must have been practicing the speech constantly.

21. The team has finished the course very quickly.

22. The children quickly discovered the teacher's hiding place.

23. I gave up the struggle too soon.

24. Several dogs went along on the hunt.

25. Some kind of a problem has been bothering Jim today.

AUXILIARY PS RULE OF FORMATION   EXERCISE 52

Directions: English verbs may take the following kinds of auxiliaries:

1. Inflectional forms: *ø, -s, -ed, -ing, -en*
2. Modals: *will, can, may, must, should, could, might, ought to, used to,* and so on
3. Auxiliary verbs: *have, be*

Write out, for each of the verb phrases below, all auxiliaries plus the base form of the verb headword. Underline the headword as in the examples. You may refer to the auxiliary verb formation rule:

$$\text{MV} \longrightarrow \begin{Bmatrix} ø \\ \text{-}s \\ \text{-}ed \end{Bmatrix} (\text{M} + ø)\ (have + en)\ (be + ing) + \begin{Bmatrix} \text{V} \\ be \end{Bmatrix}$$

Examples: say   ø + *say*
        must have done   ø + M + ø + have + en + *do*

1. walk	14. had written
2. found	15. may have caught
3. lives	16. ought to go
4. have decided	17. will write
5. am going	18. ate
6. are asking	19. am doing
7. is taking	20. was found*
8. were giving	21. shall have had
9. has chosen	22. could have been giving
10. were being given	23. had been singing
11. was doing	24. has sung
12. will be taking	25. may have been liking
13. has been done*	

*Note that these examples do not follow the PS rule. They are passive rather than active.

KERNEL SENTENCES   **EXERCISE 53**

>   ***Directions:*** Using the kernel sentence pattern chart as a reference, indicate by pattern number in which of the patterns each of the following structures *may* appear. If a structure may not appear in a kernel sentence, write down a zero (0).

1. Modal

2. Noun Phrase subject

3. Adjective

4. Qualifier preceding Adjective

5. Noun Phrase in predicate

6. *Be* as main verb

7. Prepositional Phrase

8. Intransitive Verb

9. Determiner

10. Pronoun

11. Adverbial of manner

12. Mid-transitive Verb

13. Conjunction

14. Relative

15. Auxiliary Verb

16. Adverbial of place in Complement position

17. Particle

18. Transitive Verb

19. Interrogative

20. Subordinate Clause

23

TG Grammar, Early Form: Transformations

Obligatory Transformations

Phrase-structure rules (PS rules) instruct us to rewrite only one element at a time. Transformation rules (T rules), on the other hand, instruct us to make changes in an entire string of elements, and thus require that we be able to look back beyond the immediately preceding element and forward beyond the element immediately following a given constituent.

We have said that to arrive at even the simplest kernel sentence we must apply a small number of obligatory transformation rules to the terminal strings of the PS grammar. These are the kind of rules which Chomsky referred to as "context sensitive": that is, they are made necessary by the context of a particular string of elements. Although a great many additional obligatory transformations are required after the application of optional transformation rules (which may rearrange constituents or introduce new ones), there are two or three obligatory transformations that are required for converting terminal strings to actual English sentences.

NUMBER TRANSFORMATION (OBLIGATORY). Our PS rules have said that the present tense marker (morpheme) might be either ø or *s*:

$$\text{pres} \longrightarrow \begin{Bmatrix} \text{s} \\ \text{ø} \end{Bmatrix}$$

Yet, the PS rules do not give instructions for the conditions under which one choice should be made over another. We need a context-sensitive rule which is able to account for the existence of an observable linguistic fact:

subject-verb agreement. That is, the verb in the verb phrase must agree in number with its subject (the noun in the NP immediately preceding it). This means that we must be able to look back to the third PS rule to determine whether the subject is singular or plural. We can formulate this instruction with the following transformation rule:

$$\text{pres} \Longrightarrow \begin{cases} \text{s (in context of NP}_{\text{3rd, sing}}) \\ \text{ø (in all other contexts)} \end{cases}$$

Then, when we rewrite the symbol for tense (T), we look at the entire string derived by the PS rules up to this point, determine whether the NP is or is not third person singular, and choose the appropriate tense morpheme accordingly. Observe the following strings to get a rough idea of how this number transformation operates:

The # *boy* + ø # *T* + *like* # the # *dog* + ø $\Longrightarrow$
The # *boy* + ø # *s* + *like* # the # *dog* + ø

The # *boy* + *s* # *T* + *like* # the # *dog* + ø $\Longrightarrow$
The # *boy* + *s* # *ø* + *like* # the # *dog* + ø

AUXILIARY TRANSFORMATION (OBLIGATORY). Even after we have applied the number transformation and have run through all of our PS rules, the terminal string which results is still not an actual sentence. An example of a terminal string which the PS rules and the obligatory number T rule have generated might be the following:

The # man + s # ø + shoot # bear + s

We can convert the constituents *man* + *s* and *bear* + *s* by applying the morphophonemic rules (M rules):

man + s $\Longrightarrow$ *men*

bear + s $\Longrightarrow$ *bears*

so that now we have the string: The # men # ø + shoot # bears. But we still do not have an actual sentence. We need yet another obligatory context-sensitive T rule which will instruct us to reverse the order of the tense morpheme and the verb stem: ø + shoot $\Longrightarrow$ shoot + ø.

If we have chosen to use other auxiliaries in addition to the tense marker (see the phrase-structure Auxiliary Formation Rule), our terminal string will contain a series of morphemes and stems whose order needs to be converted:

ø + M + ø + have + en + be + ing + go

What we need, then, is a rule which will give instructions for transforming the entire string of elements:

$$
\left\{\begin{array}{l} \text{ø} \\ \text{s} \\ \text{ed} \\ \text{ing} \\ \text{en} \end{array}\right\} + \left\{\begin{array}{l} \text{M} \\ \text{have} \\ \text{be} \\ \text{verb} \end{array}\right\} \Longrightarrow \left\{\begin{array}{l} \text{M} \\ \text{have} \\ \text{be} \\ \text{verb} \end{array}\right\} + \left\{\begin{array}{l} \text{ø} \\ \text{s} \\ \text{ed} \\ \text{ing} \\ \text{en} \end{array}\right\}
$$

This rule is called the Auxiliary Transformation Rule, or the Flip-Flop Rule.* It is an obligatory transformation.

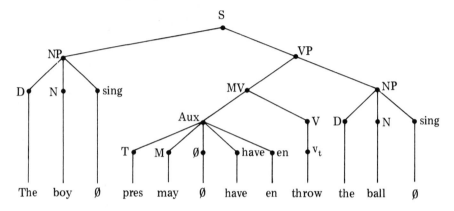

Phrase Marker (Tree Diagram) showing *Deep Structure* derivation after application of all PS rules

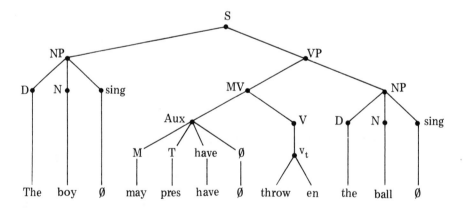

Phrase Marker (Tree Diagram) showing *Surface Structure* derivation after application of the Obligatory Auxiliary Transformation Rule

VERB-PARTICLE SEPARATION TRANSFORMATION (OBLIGATORY). Another context-sensitive rule applies to those strings which contain a transitive verb

---

*Also called "affix hopping"; and called the "flip-flop" rule by Owen Thomas in his *Transformational Grammar and the Teacher of English* (1965).

+ particle, such as *find out, call up, blow up*, and so on. When the direct object of the verb is a noun, it may occur either after the verb + particle combination or between the verb and the particle. Thus both versions of the following sentences are grammatically acceptable:

<table>
<tr><td>We *found out* the answer.</td><td>We *found* the answer *out*.</td></tr>
<tr><td>He *called up* a girl.</td><td>He *called* a girl *up*.</td></tr>
<tr><td>They *blew up* the bank.</td><td>They *blew* the bank *up*.</td></tr>
</table>

The separation of the V_t and the particle in such sentences is therefore an optional transformation (abbreviated as T_{sep}^{op}). When a pronoun is chosen instead of a noun phrase, however, the separation becomes obligatory:

We *found* it *out*.

He *called* her *up*.

They *blew* it *up*.

As a native speaker of English, you know that such sentences as these are unacceptable:

We *found out* it.

He *called up* her.

They *blew up* it.

The obligatory verb + particle separation rule can be formulated thus:

$$NP_s + V_t + part + Pro \Longrightarrow NP_s + V_t + Pro + part$$

As has been noted, there are other obligatory T rules, some of which become necessary only after optional T rules have rearranged elements or introduced new ones.* This book will make no attempt to provide a complete list of transformations, either obligatory or optional ones, but

---

*Here are just a few examples of situations which, because optional Ts have changed their syntactic context, now require new obligatory T rules:

1. In a string like *He # is # the # man # who # I # saw*, we need a rule which tells us that when *who* is a subject, it takes the subjective (null) form, but that when *who* is an object, it takes the object form (*whom*).

2. In a situation where we have two successive sentences like *Mary saw Joan and she said "Hello,"* we need a rule which prohibits the use of a personal pronoun when there is more than one noun antecedent in the previous string. Thus, we need to be able to look back at an entire string in order to avoid pronoun ambiguity (one form of faulty pronoun reference).

3. Consider the sentence *Joan hurt her*, when we want the pronoun to refer to *Joan*. Here we need a rule which tells us that in a sentence where the pronoun object refers to the same person as the subject, the reflexive form, *pronoun + -self*, is required: *Joan hurt herself*.

you should bear in mind that a complete TG grammar would include all possible rules.

Optional Transformations

As we have seen, obligatory transformations are ones which we must perform to produce an actual sentence of even the simplest type. Optional transformations, on the other hand, are ones which we may or may not perform. That is, we will be able to generate a sentence whether or not we decide to apply optional T rules.

Optional transformations, then, have the effect of permitting stylistic variations in sentences. They permit us to join constituents or entire strings (conjunction), to ask questions (interrogation), to change intonation (emphasis), to convert a sentence from active to passive (passivization), or to change a statement from positive to negative (negation), to mention a few of the possibilities.

Once an optional T rule has been applied to a string, the resulting string is no longer a kernel sentence. Rather, we call it a transform, or transformed sentence. Such transformations can range from being only a simple change performed on a single string to being a series of complex changes performed on one or more strings.

Early TG grammarians categorized optional transformations as either *single-base transformations* or *multiple-base transformations*. If, after all transformation rules have been applied, the resulting sentence can be traced back to *only one* kernel sentence, the transformation is called a singulary or *single-base* transformation. If, on the other hand, *two or more* terminal strings underlie the resulting sentence, the sentence is a double-base or *multiple-base* transformation.

24

TG Grammar, Early Form: Single-Base Transformations

A single-base transformation involves only one underlying kernel string. Some of the possible operations in performing a transformation are the following:

1. Changing the intonation pattern

2. Changing the word order pattern

3. Deleting one or more elements from a string

4. Adding one or more elements to a string

5. Performing several of these operations at the same time

A list of single-base transformations follows. Exercises for each of them appear at the end of the chapter.

EMPHASIS TRANSFORMATION (T^{emph}).* The T^{emph} rule can be applied to the terminal string underlying any of the eleven kernel sentences. This transformation most commonly is performed by changing the basic intonation pattern—a procedure which a speaker accomplishes by the simple expedient of altering the normal stress and pitch pattern of the sentence. Such intonation transformations can be represented in writing by mechanical devices like italics (to show that certain words should receive strongest stress) or by a punctuation symbol like the terminal exclamation mark (to show that the entire sentence is to be spoken with greater than usual stress):

---

*This T^{emph} rule is slightly unorthodox. Normally, only the emphasis of the auxiliary is mentioned as an emphasis transformation.

(a) John is going now $\Longrightarrow$ $\left\{\begin{array}{c} \textit{John} \text{ is going now.} \\ \text{or} \\ \text{John } \textit{is} \text{ going now.} \\ \text{or} \\ \text{John is } \textit{going} \text{ now.} \\ \text{or} \\ \text{John is going } \textit{now.} \end{array}\right\}$ (Italics to stress a particular word)

(b) John is going now $\Longrightarrow$ John is going now!

Do-Emphasis Transformation ($\text{T}^{\text{do-emph}}$). A third device may also be used to show emphasis when a simple present or past tense verb is the element to be stressed:

John eats supper fast. $\Longrightarrow$ John does eat supper fast.

John ate supper fast. $\Longrightarrow$ John did eat supper fast.

You eat supper fast. $\Longrightarrow$ You do eat supper fast.

The $\text{T}^{\text{do-emph}}$ rule can be formulated as follows:

$$\text{NP}_\text{s} + \left\{\begin{array}{c} \text{ø} \\ s \\ ed \end{array}\right\} + \text{V} + \text{remainder} \Longrightarrow \text{NP}_\text{s} + \left\{\begin{array}{c} \text{ø} \\ s \\ ed \end{array}\right\} + do + \text{ø} + \text{V} + \text{remainder}$$

Notice what the rule instructs us to do: (1) add the auxiliary *do*; (2) move the tense marker to the auxiliary; (3) change the verb to its null form. (Thus, when *do* is introduced as an auxiliary, it imposes the null form on the verb which follows. In this respect, *do* behaves like a modal auxiliary.)

Word Order Transformation (T^{wo}). Word order in some Pattern 7, 8, 9, 10, and 11 terminal strings may occasionally be rearranged in one of two ways:

1. Reverse the positions of the subject and the subject complement

$$\text{NP}_1 + \left\{\begin{array}{c} \text{V}_1 \\ be \end{array}\right\} + \left\{\begin{array}{c} \text{NP}_2 \\ \text{Adj} \\ \text{adv}_\text{p} \end{array}\right\} \Longrightarrow \left\{\begin{array}{c} \text{NP}_2 \\ \text{Adj} \\ \text{adv}_\text{p} \end{array}\right\} + \left\{\begin{array}{c} \text{V}_1 \\ be \end{array}\right\} + \text{NP}_1$$

2. Put the complement in the initial position, but do not alter the order of the remaining constituents

$$\text{NP}_1 + \left\{\begin{array}{c} \text{V}_1 \\ be \end{array}\right\} + \left\{\begin{array}{c} \text{NP}_2 \\ \text{Adj} \\ \text{adv}_\text{p} \end{array}\right\} \Longrightarrow \left\{\begin{array}{c} \text{NP}_1 \\ \text{Adj} \\ \text{adv}_\text{p} \end{array}\right\} + \text{NP}_1 + \left\{\begin{array}{c} \text{V}_1 \\ be \end{array}\right\}$$

The T^{wo} rule is seldom applied to simple terminal strings, except for some Pattern 11 ones. Most commonly, it applies to strings which have already undergone one or more transformations:

He felt (so) *hungry* (that——) $\Longrightarrow$ (So) *hungry felt he* (that.........)

$\Longrightarrow$ (So) *hungry he felt* (that.........)

He was a comic (and) *he remained a comic* $\Longrightarrow$ *A comic he was* (and) *a comic he remained.*

*My brother is John Henry $\Longrightarrow$ John Henry is my brother.

The man is happy (who......) $\Longrightarrow$ *Happy is the man* (who......)

A Pattern 11 string, however, need not be part of a larger, complex transformation in order to undergo the word order transformation:

$$\text{The dog is here} \begin{cases} \Longrightarrow \text{Here is the dog.} \\ \Longrightarrow \text{Here the dog is.} \end{cases}$$

A second kind of word order transformation can be performed on the terminal string of any of the kernel sentence patterns, so long as an adverbial of place, condition, purpose, time, manner, and so on has been chosen as an option. The "normal" (that is, kernel sentence) position for such an adverbial is that following all other sentence constituents. However, the optional adverbial is probably the most flexible of all parts of speech, in that it can assume a great variety of transformed sentence positions. The most common of these transformed positions—and this T rule applies to any sentence pattern—is as the initial word of a sentence; TG grammarians, like the structuralists, say that in this position the adverbial is a sentence modifier:

NP + VP + Adv $\Longrightarrow$ Adv + NP + VP

Examples might be: John ran swiftly. $\Longrightarrow$ Swiftly John ran.

He lent her the car reluctantly. $\Longrightarrow$ Reluctantly he lent her the car.

However, the adverbial may also usually be moved to a position either immediately before (or sometimes in the case of *be*, immediately after) the main verb; and when the main verb is preceded by one or more auxiliary words, the adverbial may ordinarily occur either immediately before or after any one of these auxiliary words:

---

*The use of the possessive *my* is considered by some early TG grammarians to be a transformation. One might illustrate the word order transformation on a Pattern 9 terminal string, however: *The name is John* $\Longrightarrow$ John is the name.

KERNEL SENTENCE	ADVERBIAL WORD ORDER T
He served the ball *quickly* $\Longrightarrow$	He *quickly* served the ball.
John is happy *surely* $\Longrightarrow$	$\begin{cases} \text{John } surely \text{ is happy.} \\ \text{John is } surely \text{ happy.} \end{cases}$
They must have eaten *quickly* $\Longrightarrow$	$\begin{cases} \text{They } quickly \text{ must have eaten.} \\ \text{They must } quickly \text{ have eaten.} \\ \text{They must have } quickly \text{ eaten.} \end{cases}$

IMPERATIVE TRANSFORMATION ($\mathbf{T}^{imp}$). The imperative transformation, which changes a declarative statement to a command, can be applied to some of the terminal strings of all kernel sentence patterns so long as *you* is the subject (although the nature of some subject-verb combinations makes for awkwardness at best and ungrammaticalness at worst, as in the sentence "You weigh a ton" $\Longrightarrow$ "Weigh a ton").* The imperative transformation is performed by deleting the subject (*you*) and all auxiliary words in the verb phrase, then changing the tense marker for the main verb to the null form (ø). Since *be* has three null forms, however, we shall use the symbol $ø_1$ in our rule to indicate infinitive-null form:

$$\text{You} + \begin{Bmatrix} ø \\ s \\ ed \end{Bmatrix} + \text{aux} + \begin{Bmatrix} V \\ be \end{Bmatrix} + \text{remainder} \Longrightarrow ø_1 + \begin{Bmatrix} V \\ be \end{Bmatrix} + \text{remainder}$$

You should stop crying. $\Longrightarrow$ Stop crying.

You must finish the work. $\Longrightarrow$ Finish the work.

You ought to be a winner. $\Longrightarrow$ Be a winner.

You are inventive. $\Longrightarrow$ Be inventive.

You will be there at noon. $\Longrightarrow$ Be there at noon.

NEGATIVE TRANSFORMATION ($\mathbf{T}^{neg}$). Terminal strings of all kernel sentence patterns may take the negative transformation. The nature of the transformational procedure will vary, though, according to the structural analysis of the main verb phrase. Examine the following sentences to see if you can determine how we should write the rule for T^{neg}:

1.a. The boys must eat lunch $\Longrightarrow$ The boys $\begin{Bmatrix} \text{must not} \\ \text{mustn't} \end{Bmatrix}$ eat lunch.

---

*There is an entire class of verbs you cannot tell someone to do, and an entire class of adjectives you cannot tell someone to be (*short, fat,* and so on) to which the T^{imp} rule does not apply.

b. They may have done the work $\Longrightarrow$ They may not have done the work.

c. I should be reading a book $\Longrightarrow$ I $\begin{Bmatrix} \text{should not} \\ \text{shouldn't} \end{Bmatrix}$ be reading a book.

d. He must have been sad $\Longrightarrow$ He $\begin{Bmatrix} \text{must not} \\ \text{mustn't} \end{Bmatrix}$ have been sad.

2.a. You eat lunch $\Longrightarrow$ You $\begin{Bmatrix} \text{do not} \\ \text{don't} \end{Bmatrix}$ eat lunch.

b. John eats lunch $\Longrightarrow$ John $\begin{Bmatrix} \text{does not} \\ \text{doesn't} \end{Bmatrix}$ eat lunch.

c. John ate lunch $\Longrightarrow$ John $\begin{Bmatrix} \text{did not} \\ \text{didn't} \end{Bmatrix}$ eat lunch.

3.a. I am very sorry $\Longrightarrow$ I am not very sorry.

b. John is a leader $\Longrightarrow$ John $\begin{Bmatrix} \text{is not} \\ \text{isn't} \end{Bmatrix}$ a leader.

c. They are here $\Longrightarrow$ They $\begin{Bmatrix} \text{are not} \\ \text{aren't} \end{Bmatrix}$ here.

Depending upon the structure of the main verb phrase, we have three different situations. Set 1 illustrates a verb phrase consisting of one or more auxiliary words plus the main verb. Strings with this structural analysis can be transformed to negative by the simple addition of *not* (or *n't* in most cases) *after the first auxiliary*:

$$\text{NP}_\text{s} + \begin{Bmatrix} \text{ø} \\ s \\ ed \end{Bmatrix} + \text{Aux}_1 \text{ (Aux)} + \begin{Bmatrix} \text{V} \\ \text{be} \end{Bmatrix} + \text{remainder} \Longrightarrow \text{NP}_\text{s} + \begin{Bmatrix} \text{ø} \\ s \\ ed \end{Bmatrix} +$$
$$\text{Aux}_1 + not + \text{(Aux)}$$
$$+ \begin{Bmatrix} \text{V} \\ be \end{Bmatrix} + \text{remainder}.$$

When the main verb phrase, as in Set 2, consists of only a tense marker plus verb (other than *be*), the transformation rule is written:

$$\text{NP}_\text{s} + \begin{Bmatrix} \text{ø} \\ s \\ ed \end{Bmatrix} + \text{V} + \text{remainder} \Longrightarrow \text{NP}_\text{s} + \begin{Bmatrix} \text{ø} \\ s \\ ed \end{Bmatrix} + do + \text{ø} + not +$$
$$\text{V} + \text{remainder}.$$

As you see, we must supply an auxiliary (*do*), shift the original tense marker to this *do* auxiliary, and use the null ending on the verb which follows.

Strings with *be* as a single word verb, as in Set 3, do not require the addition of *do*. We simply add *not* or *n't* immediately after *be*:

$$NP_s + \begin{Bmatrix} \text{ø} \\ s \\ ed \end{Bmatrix} + be + \text{remainder} \Longrightarrow NP_s + \begin{Bmatrix} \text{ø} \\ s \\ ed \end{Bmatrix} + be + not + \\ \text{remainder.}$$

Yes-No Question Transformation ($T^{q\text{-yes/no}}$). A yes-no question is the kind of question which can be answered by the words *yes* or *no*. All kernel sentence patterns can accept this transformation. If you will use the same sets of kernel sentence strings as we used for the negative transformation, you will discover that once again, depending on the structure of the MV phrase, we need three different yes/no question T rules. When there are auxiliary words, for example, the word order is rearranged as follows:

$$NP + T + Aux_1 (+ Aux_2) (+ Aux_3) + V + \text{remainder} \Longrightarrow$$

$$T + Aux_1 + NP (+ Aux_2) (+ Aux_3) + V + \text{remainder.}$$

Here are some examples:

You may drive the car $\Longrightarrow$ May you drive the car?

She has left a book $\Longrightarrow$ Has she left a book?

He must have been feeling sad $\Longrightarrow$ Must he have been feeling sad?

If the verb consists of one word only (i.e., if it is a simple present or past tense verb other than *be*), the *do* auxiliary word must be provided:

$$NP + T + V + \text{remainder} \Longrightarrow T + do + NP + \text{ø} + V + \text{remainder}$$

Babies like candy $\Longrightarrow$ Do babies like candy?

Mary loves the book $\Longrightarrow$ Does Mary love the book?

The cow kicked the farmer $\Longrightarrow$ Did the cow kick the farmer?

When the single word verb is *be*, however, the auxiliary *do* is not needed: $NP + T + be + \text{remainder} \Longrightarrow T + be + NP + \text{remainder}$

He is late $\Longrightarrow$ Is he late?

She was a teacher $\Longrightarrow$ Was she a teacher?

They are friends $\Longrightarrow$ Are they friends?

There-Expletive Transformation (T^{there}). Examine these sentences to see if you can determine just what conditions must exist before the there-expletive transformation may be applied to a string:

A boy is at the door $\Longrightarrow$ There is a boy at the door.

Someone was looking for him $\Longrightarrow$ There was someone looking for him.

Weeds must have been $\underset{\Longrightarrow}{}$ There must have been growing in the garden   weeds growing in the garden.

Water will soon be $\underset{\Longrightarrow}{}$ There will soon be flooding the street   water flooding the street.

You have probably noticed two things that are common to all of the initial strings: (1) the subject of each string is an indefinite noun (i.e., the noun is not specifically identified as it would be if it were an expression like *John, that man,* and so on); (2) the verb phrase in each initial string contains *be* either as an auxiliary or as the main verb. The problem, however, is that this last condition fails to account for strings like these, which can also be transformed by the there-expletive rule but whose verb phrases do not contain *be*:

Some copies exist somewhere $\Longrightarrow$ There exist some copies somewhere.

A house stood on the lot $\Longrightarrow$ There stood a house on the lot.

Several questions remained $\Longrightarrow$ There remained several questions.

Determining exactly what conditions must prevail in order for the T^{there} rule to be applicable thus becomes a fairly complicated matter. Certainly the subject ought to be an indefinite noun. As for the verb form, it should either contain *be* (as an auxiliary or as the main verb), or it should be a "state of being" verb like *appear, exist, happen, materialize, occur, remain, stand.*

Notice how the there transformation operates. It adds a word, the expletive ("filler word") *there,* in the initial sentence slot. And it moves *be* (or, alternatively, the "state of being" verb) plus all the auxiliary words which precede it to a position immediately following *there* but immediately preceding the NP subject. We can write the rule as follows:

$$NP_s + T \, (+ \, Auxs) + be + \begin{Bmatrix} ing \\ en \end{Bmatrix} (+ \, V) + remainder \Longrightarrow$$

$$There + T \, (+ \, Auxs) + be + NP_s + \begin{Bmatrix} ing \\ en \end{Bmatrix} (+ \, V) + remainder*$$

*The reason for the $\begin{Bmatrix} ing \\ en \end{Bmatrix}$ choice is that the passive transformation might already have been applied to a string, in which case a *be* auxiliary will have been provided, thus making it possible to apply the T^{there} rule: Ice was left in the glass $\Longrightarrow$ There was ice left in the glass.

PASSIVE TRANSFORMATION (T^{pas}). The passive transformation rule can be applied only to strings which contain a transitive verb (Patterns 2, 3, 4, and 5). Note the procedure:

Pattern 2. The boy helps the girl $\Longrightarrow$ The girl is helped by the boy.

Pattern 3. John gave Mary a ring $\Longrightarrow$ $\begin{cases} \text{A ring was given Mary by} \\ \text{John.} \\ \text{Mary was given a ring by} \\ \text{John.} \end{cases}$

Pattern 4. The class should have elected John president $\Longrightarrow$ John should have been elected president by the class.

Pattern 5. The boys think Jane pretty $\Longrightarrow$ Jane is thought pretty by the boys.

Notice that, except for Pattern 3, for which there are two alternatives, we perform the passive transformation as follows: (1) move the second NP (the direct object) to the initial or subject position; (2) follow the new subject with all auxiliaries in the original verb phrase; (3) add the elements *be* + *en* before the transitive verb plus any remaining complement; (4) introduce the word *by*; (5) follow *by* with NP_1 (the original subject). Here is the rule:

NP_1 + T(M + ø) (*have* + *en*) (*be* + *ing*)v_t + NP_2 (+ remainder)

$\Longrightarrow NP_2$ + T(M + ø) (*have* + *en*) (*be* + *ing*) *be* + *en* + v_t (+ remainder) + *by* + NP_1

For Pattern 3 strings, we must add an alternative T^{pas} rule:

NP_1 + T(M + ø) (*have* + *en*) (*be* + *ing*) v_t + NP_2 + NP_3 $\Longrightarrow$

NP_3 + T(M + ø) (*have* + *en*) (*be* + *ing*) *be* + *en* + v_t + NP_2 + *by* + NP_1

Wh QUESTION TRANSFORMATION ($T^{q\text{-}wh}$). The Wh question transformation is one which converts a statement to a question that requires an answer other than *yes* or *no*. Any structure which contains lexical meaning can thus be questioned: a noun, a pronoun, an adjective, an adverbial, (or even a whole sentence). We can illustrate how the wh question transformation operates with the sentence: "Jan will put the cups in the sink quickly after the meal." Here is an abbreviated tree diagram of the sentence:

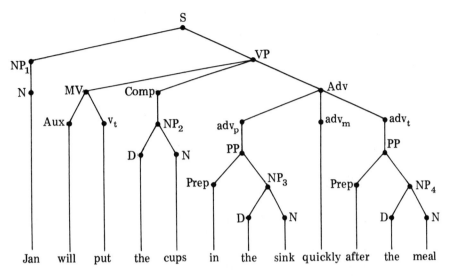

As you will see, it is possible to ask a wh question about almost any node on this tree. (Exceptions are structure words, like auxiliaries and prepositions, and indefinite determiners, like *a*, and *an*; if, however, we were to use a definite determiner, like *this, that, those,* and so on, even that could be questioned.) The procedure works this way: (1) the unknown item of information is questioned by the use of an appropriate interrogative or wh word (*who, what, which, how, when, where*); (2) the interrogative word appears as the first word in the transformed sentence; 3) the remainder of the sentence is transformed by the same process as we used for the $T^{q\text{-}yes/no}$.

STRUCTURE QUESTIONED	Q-WH TRANSFORMATION
NP₁ (*Jan*)	*Who* will put the cups in the sink . . .?
NP₂ (*the cups*)	*What* will Jan put in the sink quickly . . .?
NP₃ (*the sink*)	*In what place* will Jan put the cups . . .? (We have to borrow the structure word to ask this question)
NP₄ (*the meal*)	*After what* will Jan put the cups . . .? (Again, we must borrow the preposition)
advₚ (*in the sink*)	*Where* will Jan put the cups quickly after . . .?
advₘ (*quickly*)	*How* will Jan put the cups in the sink . . .?
advₜ (*after the meal*)	*When* will Jan put the cups quickly in . . .?

STRUCTURE QUESTIONED	Q-WH TRANSFORMATION
MV (*will put*)	*What* will Jan *do with* the cups in the sink . . .? (A bit awkward, but the question can be asked. Note that *do* is used to request information about the verb or the predicate)
VP (*put the cups in the sink quickly after the meal*)	*What* will Jan *do?*
Sentence	*What* will *happen?*

SINGLE-BASE TRASFORMATIONAL RULES   EXERCISE 54

Directions: Give the following information for each of the kernel sentences below: (1) list the kernel sentence patterns restricted to each transformation, making sure also that you mention other restrictions; (2) write out the transformed sentence. Finally generalize or, better yet, formulate a transformation rule which will apply to the sentences in question. (The Answer Key for Ex. 54 is in the form of a Chart which lists these single-base T rules, restrictions on their application, illustrates how the rules operate, and informally sums up the procedure.)

1. T^{emph} (emphasis)
　　a. John is running very fast.

2. T$^{do\text{-}emph}$ (do-emphasis)
　　a. He eats supper.
　　b. You eat supper.
　　c. They ate supper.

3. T^{wo} (word order)
　　a. John is here.
　　b. He ran quickly.
　　c. Tim is the leader.

4. T^{imp} (imperative)
　　a. You close the door.
　　b. You should stop.
　　c. You are quiet.

5. T^{neg} (negative)
　　a. They may leave soon.
　　b. He has been reading.
　　c. He is being silly.
　　d. You hit the ball.
　　e. He hits the ball.
　　f. They ate lunch.
　　g. I am happy.
　　h. John is here.
　　i. We were friends.

6. $T^{q\text{-}yes/no}$ (yes/no question)
    a. You may drive the car.
    b. He has been living abroad.
    c. He is flying to Europe.
    d. Children like candy.
    e. She loves the job.
    f. They ate lunch.
    g. He is late.
    h. They are friends.
    i. She was a student.

7. $T^{there\text{-}expl}$ (there-expletive)
    a. Someone is in the room.
    b. A man is calling you.
    c. A flood occurred.

8. T^{pas} (passive)
    a. John hates soup.
    b. Jim gave Tom a ball.
    c. We named the dog Max.
    d. Jim thinks Jane silly.

9. $T^{q\text{-}wh}$ (wh question)
    a. John found a dog in the park today.

SINGLE-BASE OPTIONAL TRANSFORMATIONS: $T^{do\text{-}emph}$ EXERCISE 55

Directions: Using the $T^{do\text{-}emph}$ rule, transform each of the following sentences from declarative statement to emphatic statement. Make no other changes.

1. Mary sings very well.

2. Barney used to sing for a living.

3. I feel good at the moment.

4. Mary writes quite poorly.

5. John always does well in a crisis.

SINGLE-BASE OPTIONAL TRANSFORMATIONS: T^{neg} EXERCISE 56

Directions: Using the T^{neg} rule, transform each of the following sentences from positive statement to negative statement. Make no other changes.

1. He got the answer very soon.

2. Several men were in the posse.

3. She heads the university.

4. The children like spinach.

5. He will give up the struggle quickly.

SINGLE-BASE OPTIONAL TRANSFORMATIONS: $T^{q\text{-}yes/no}$ EXERCISE 57

Directions: Using the $T^{q\text{-}yes/no}$ rule, transform each of the following sentences from declarative statement to yes/no question. Make no other changes.

1. Sam went out in the rain.
2. Mr. Jack prefers solitude.
3. The paper is here now.
4. She may have been dozing off.
5. John should have left the party early.

SINGLE-BASE OPTIONAL TRANSFORMATIONS: T^{there} EXERCISE 58

Directions: Using the T^{there} rule, transform each of the following sentences to a there-expletive statement. Make no other changes.

1. Some problem is always bothering Tom.
2. Several students will be absent.
3. A crisis always exists in that house.
4. Some books were in the library.
5. Several girls have been crying for hours.

SINGLE-BASE OPTIONAL TRANSFORMATIONS: T^{pas} EXERCISE 59

Directions: Using the T^{pas} rule, transform each of the following sentences from active statement to passive statement. Make no other changes.

1. Sy may carry out the trash.
2. Jerry must do the dishes.
3. Fear gripped the city.
4. The rain has ruined the picnic.
5. Al is finally turning off the water.

6. Fischer should sacrifice the title.

7. Amy has stapled the pages.

8. Jones will put up the cash.

9. Jo ought to write the book.

*10. Several boys have tried out for the part.

SINGLE-BASE OPTIONAL TRANSFORMATIONS: $T^{q\text{-}wh}$ EXERCISE 60

Directions: Using the $T^{q\text{-}wh}$ rule, see how many wh transformations you can derive from the following kernel sentence:

Those boys have been sleeping in class during the lectures.

*Consider the verb in this sentence to be v_t + part + part (*tried out for*)

25

TG Grammar, Early Form: Ordering of Transformation Rule Application

One of the things which Chomsky points out in *Syntactic Structures* is that in many cases where more than one transformation is performed on a single string, we must follow a definite order of rule application. To illustrate this fact, let us take the sentence:

The boy ate lunch

and assume that we wish to perform three different transformations on this string: T negative, T passive, and T q-yes/no. If we should decide to apply the T^{neg} rule first, we derive the transform

The boy didn't eat lunch.

We find, however, that if we now try to apply the T passive rule to this new string, we are faced with a problem. The passive T rule is restricted to only those transitive verb strings whose verb phrases contain three possible auxiliary words: a *modal*, *have*, and/or *be*. We have no instructions for verb phrases containing the auxiliary *do*. Yet, we know that the string "Wasn't lunch eaten by the boy?" is derived from the terminal string "The boy ate lunch," upon which three transformation rules have been applied.

The solution seems to be that we must first apply the T passive rule; then we can apply the negative and the yes/no question transformations:

T^{pas} $\Longrightarrow$ Lunch was eaten by the boy.

T^{neg} $\Longrightarrow$ Lunch wasn't eaten by the boy.

$T^{q\text{-}yes/no}\Longrightarrow$ Wasn't lunch eaten by the boy?

272

Let us look at one more example of rule ordering. See if you can transform the following sentence by the application of T there-expletive and T passive:

Someone turned on a light.

This example enables us to grasp the significance of rule ordering more easily, perhaps, than the first one did. First of all, as the string now stands, it *cannot accept* the there-expletive transformation. We can, however, apply the T^{pas} rule:

Someone turned on a light $\Longrightarrow$ A light was turned on by someone.

Then, once we have converted the string to a passive transform, we find that we *do* have the requisite *be* auxiliary, and we may therefore proceed to apply the $T^{there-expl}$ rule:

A light was turned on by someone $\Longrightarrow$ There was a light turned on by someone.

We can sum up this section by repeating one or two points. First, the single-base transformation may be applied to any string whose structural analysis meets the conditions required by a given T rule. Second, such an initial string may be either the terminal string of a kernel sentence or a transformation. Third, more than one transformation may be applied to a given string. (This will be true for multiple-base transformations as well as for single-base ones.) Last, when two or more T rules are applied to a single string, these rules must sometimes be applied in a given order.

SINGLE-BASE OPTIONAL TRANSFORMATIONS: EXERCISE 61
T RULE ORDERING

Directions: In this exercise, you are to apply more than one T rule to a given string. As in the example below, do only one transformation at a time, *in the required order.* Your last string should be one to which all requested T rules have been applied.

T RULE ORDER   TRANSFORMED SENTENCE

Example: Mary was feeding the dogs $\Longrightarrow T^{neg} + T^{q\text{-}yes/no} + T^{pas}$

T^{pas} $\Longrightarrow$ The dogs were being fed by Mary.

T^{neg} $\Longrightarrow$ The dogs $\begin{Bmatrix} \text{were not} \\ \text{weren't} \end{Bmatrix}$ being fed by Mary.

$T^{q\text{-}yes/on}$ $\Longrightarrow$ Weren't the dogs being fed by Mary?

1. The dog barked too much $\Longrightarrow$ $T^{do\text{-}emph}$ $+$ T^{neg}

2. The officer arrested the driver $\Longrightarrow$ T^{pas} $+$ $T^{q\text{-}yes/no}$

3. The drunk broke a glass $\Longrightarrow$ T^{there} $+$ $T^{q\text{-}yes/no}$ $+$ T^{pas}

4. They called in some cops at midnight $\Longrightarrow$ T^{there} $+$ T^{pas} $+$ $T^{op\text{-}sep}$

SINGLE-BASE OPTIONAL TRANSFORMATIONS   EXERCISE 62

Directions: Determine whether each sentence below is a kernel sentence or a transformation (i.e., *not* kernel). If it is a transformation, indicate which optional T rule or rules have been applied. Then, write out the kernel sentence from whose terminal string the transformation is derived. (In some cases, such as with some passives and with wh transformations, you will have to provide an element for one which has been deleted.)

1. Isn't he angry now?

2. She gave up the struggle very quickly.

3. The book does say that!

4. Now everyone wants peace.

5. Who will drive the swimmers to the meet?

6. Didn't John leave the party at ten?

7. There weren't many revelations made by the victim.

8. In Mississippi there have occurred some floods.

9. Was the food eaten immediately?

10. Where is the professor now?

11. Some people always go too far.

12. Be quiet!

13. Only recently the army crossed over the bridge.

14. Did David really give Betsy the ring?

15. Stop the sniffling immediately!

16. The children didn't want the cake very much.

17. There used to be a ghost in the house.

18. Jerry must have become lost very quickly.

19. Under the table peacefully slept the dog.

20. The letter didn't really say that.

21. I'm not appreciated!

22. Was she angered by the accusation?

23. John didn't tell me the news.

24. Finish the exercise quickly.

25. There have been several incidents reported.

26

TG Grammar, Early Form: Multiple-Base Conjunction Transformations

A multiple-base transformation is one which involves a minimum of two underlying terminal strings (of kernel sentences). Generally speaking, there are two fundamental methods by which we may derive multiple-base sentences: (1) by conjunction, i.e., the compounding of equivalent constituents or equivalent strings; and (2) by embedding one or more subordinated strings into a dominant or main string. Whatever the process, the result is a transform in which two or more terminal strings have in some way been combined.

Conjunction is the grammatical process of joining two or more equivalent structures. The elements joined are said to be *coordinate*; the entire conjunction process is also called *coordination,* and the structure which does the joining is a *coordinator.**

The common coordinators are the single words *and, but, or, nor, for, so, yet,* and *still*; and correlative pairs like *either/or, neither/nor, not only/but also,* and so on.

Chomsky argues in *Syntactic Structures* that earlier grammar theories have been inadequate to explain the process of conjunction. Any left-to-right model (which both the simple Markov model and the phrase-structure, immediate-constituent model are) must depend entirely upon the most recent operation in order to determine the next step in a derivation. With discontinuous elements, however, it is necessary to be able to look back at an earlier string or set of strings. A top-to-bottom grammar theory which includes a transformational component is a better theory because it can do precisely that. It can provide a transformation rule for conjunc-

---

*Traditional grammar calls these connectives *coordinating conjunctions.*

tion which says that if two strings have identical constituents, differing only in that X and Y are different lexical structures of the same minimal type (NP, VP, Adj, . . .), then a third string can be derived by one of two methods: (1) by joining the two strings (with a coordinator between them) to derive a compound string; or (2) by joining the X and Y minimal constituents.

S1: $X_{NP} + VP$ (Tom ate lunch)

S2: $Y_{NP} + VP$ (Bob ate lunch)

$$S3 \Longrightarrow \begin{cases} X + VP + Y + VP \\ \\ X + Y + VP \end{cases} \qquad \begin{cases} \text{(Tom ate lunch and Bob ate} \\ \text{lunch)} \\ \text{(Tom and Bob ate lunch)} \end{cases}$$

When a transformation is performed with the T^{conj} rule, the underlying strings are said to be equally dominant. Here are some more examples:

Coordination of Constituents that Occur in Terminal Strings:

  1. *John* grew angry.

  Jill grew angry.

  $\Longrightarrow$ *John* and *Jill* grew angry.

  2. He *came*.

  He *saw*.

  He *conquered*.

  $\Longrightarrow$ He *came, saw,* and *conquered*.

  3. John worked *swiftly*.

  John worked *happily*.

  $\Longrightarrow$ John worked *swiftly* and *happily*.

  4. The bird flew *from the tree*.

  The bird flew *into the sky*.

  $\Longrightarrow$ The bird flew *from the tree* and *into the sky*.

Coordination of Equivalent Strings

  1. *John was late.*

  Jill grew angry.

  $\Longrightarrow$ *John was late* so *Jill grew angry.*

2. *He came.*

He saw.

He conquered.

$\Longrightarrow$ *He came, he saw,* and *he conquered.*

3. *He pouted.*

He was quite immature.

$\Longrightarrow$ *He pouted,* for *he was quite immature.*

4. *He wanted a sundae.*

She wanted a milkshake.

$\Longrightarrow$ *He wanted a sundae,* but *she wanted a milkshake.*

Correlation of Equivalent Strings or Parts of Strings

5. *Jane will go to college.*

Jane will work.

$\Longrightarrow$ Either *Jane will go to college* or *she will work.*

or

$\Longrightarrow$ *Jane* either *will go to college* or *will work.*

or

$\Longrightarrow$ *Jane will* either *go to college* or *work.*

Note that the constituent which follows the first correlative and that which follows the second correlative are grammatically equivalent.

Besides coordinators and correlators, we may also use two other kinds of connectives in performing the conjunction transformation: the sentence connector (*however, moreover, therefore*) and the comparative conjunction.

COMPARATIVE CONJUNCTION. The comparative conjunction functions to connect two grammatically equivalent structures and to indicate a comparison or contrast between the two. Like correlatives, comparative conjunctions function in pairs. Occasionally, however, one of the members of the pair will be a morpheme (*-er, -est*) rather than a word.

1. Jane is tall.

John is tall.

$\Longrightarrow$ Interim: Jane is *-er* tall *than* John is tall.

$\Longrightarrow$ Jane is tall*er* *than* John [is tall].

Note that the final transform is derived by affix-hopping plus the deletion of the repeating words.

2. Mary is beautiful.

Jane is beautiful.

$\Longrightarrow$ Mary is *more* beautiful *than* Jane [is beautiful].

3. He packed crates poorly.

He lost the job.

$\Longrightarrow$ He packed crates *so* poorly *that* he lost the job.

Note: When strings are compared or contrasted in this way, an obligatory deletion transformation is sometimes required.

There follows a partial list of common comparative conjunctions:

-er . . . than	*more . . . than*	*so . . . that*
-est . . . that	*most . . . that*	*so few . . . that*
too . . . to	*so much . . . that*	*too many . . . to*
enough . . . to	*so many . . . that*	*more than enough . . . to*

Notice also that those comparative conjunctions which require *to* as the second element in the pair are followed by the null form of a verb. Actually, this verb is part of an embedded sentence (its main verb), all other constituents being "understood"—or in the vocabulary of TG grammar, "recoverable," and thus deleted:

1. He made money.

He will retire.

$\Longrightarrow$ He made *enough* money *to* retire.

2. He was sleepy.

He stayed up. ($\Longrightarrow$ by T^{neg} rule to: He did not stay up.)

$\Longrightarrow$ He was *too* sleepy *to* stay up.

CONJUNCTION TRANSFORMATION   EXERCISE 63

Directions: Two or more strings are listed below for each numbered question. Using the specified T^{conj} rule, perform a grammatical conjunction transformation.

T Rule to be Used

1. Coordination, with *and*

He wasted time during the test.
He wasted time after the test.
He wasted time before the test.

2. Coordination, with *and*

He liked to watch TV.
He liked teasing the dog.
He liked tormenting his sister.

3. Correlation of constituents with *both . . . and*

He drove the car well.
He drove the car fast.

4. Correlation of constituents with *both . . . and*, plus coordination with *but*

Jane cannot drive a car.
Jane can cook.
Jane can sew.

5. Correlation with *either . . . or*

Jody will wash her hair tonight.
Jody will go to a movie tonight.

6. Comparison with *morpheme . . . than*

Cindy is good at tennis.
Sue is good at tennis.

27

TG Grammar, Early Form: Multiple-Base Embedding Transformations: Adverbialization

The transformational process of embedding always results in a string which is derived from a minimum of two underlying terminal strings, one of which is dominant. Traditional grammarians do not, of course, speak about transformations, but they do classify sentence types according to the number and kinds of clauses they contain. Some sentences which we will now call embedded transforms are referred to as dependent clauses within complex or compound-complex sentences by traditional grammarians. The traditional complex sentence is a transform which consists of one main clause (the dominant string) plus two or more dependent clauses (the embedded or insert strings). The traditional compound-complex sentence is a double transformation: that is, it results from the application of both the T^{conj} rule (and thus contains two or more dominant strings) and one or more embedding transformation rules (which produce one or more embedded sentences).

Adverbial Clause Transformations

You will remember that in kernel sentences, adverbials of place, manner, time, condition, reason, and so on, can be optionally added to the verb phrase of any pattern. These optional kernel adverbials always modify the verb in the verb phrase of which they are constituents. Their kernel positions do not, therefore, vary greatly. Their semantic or lexical functions, on the other hand, as well as their forms, can vary considerably. They always occur either as uninflected words (-ly adverbs like quickly; uninflected, no-ending words like there, then, often, always) or as adverbial prepositional phrases. We never find an adverbial clause (or any other kind of dependent clause, for that matter) in a kernel sentence.* A dependent clause is, in fact, an embedded sentence, derived from one of a number of complex or embedding transformation rules.

As we examine the various kinds of embedding T rules, we shall, following the practice of most pedagogical grammars, use actual sentences rather than strings of morphemes and words, but with one warning: do keep in mind that this is a shortcut. The transformations are really performed on the constituent structures of underlying strings.

In the adverbial clause transformations illustrated below, the sentences given before the occurrence of the double-shaft transformation arrow ($\Longrightarrow$) are kernel sentences which underlie the transformation which follows the arrow. The first kernel is dominant:

1. He studies at some time. [sometime: adverb of time]

   The deadline is near at that time.

   $\Longrightarrow$ He studies *when the deadline is near.*†

2. He studies $\begin{Bmatrix} \text{because of something.} \\ \text{for some reason.} \end{Bmatrix}$ [adverb of reason]

   He must pass the test.

   $\Longrightarrow$ He studies *because he must pass the test.*

3. He studies at any place. [adverb of place]

   He can find a desk at that place.

   $\Longrightarrow$ Interim: He studies at any place where he can find a desk.

   $\Longrightarrow$ He studies *wherever he can find a desk.*

4. He studies at some time, somewhere, for some reason.

   The deadline is near.

   He wants to pass the test.

   He can find a desk.

   $\Longrightarrow$ *Because he wants to pass the test,* he studies *wherever he can find a desk when the deadline is near.*

---

*Actually—and this idea predates the *Aspects* revision—adverbials of manner may be viewed as double-base. For example, the sentence "John left quickly" can be viewed as derived in the following manner:

   Dominant Sentence: John left in some manner.
   Embedded Sentence: The manner was quick.
   $\Rightarrow$ Interim: John left in a manner which was quick.
   $\Rightarrow$ John left quickly.

†Transformed, embedded sentences are italicized in all examples.

The rules for the adverbial clause transformation require that each embedded sentence first be subordinated, a process which we can easily accomplish simply by putting a subordinator before the sentence. Words like *when, where, wherever, if, because, unless,* are subordinators, and they have the effect of altering a string in such a way that it may no longer stand as a main clause. Rather, it must now function as a sentence constituent—in this case, with an adverbial grammatical function. We can write the adverbial clause transformation rule as follows:

$$S \implies subordinator + S$$

In Example 4, we have performed a word order transformation in addition to the adverbial clause transformation.

Recursiveness. We spoke in an earlier chapter about the recursive property of language: the fact that a transformation rule can be applied over and over again. There is no grammatical limit to the number of times a rule may be repeated, although, of course, there is a practical and stylistic limit. Recursiveness allows us, therefore, to have a derivation which has a transformation within a transformation *ad infinitum.** This phenomenon is referred to in some texts as "nesting." Study these sentences, which illustrate recursiveness:

Dominant: John ought to train the dog for some reason.

Embedded: The dog will frighten people under some conditions.

Embedded: The dog jumps up on people in some circumstances.

Embedded: The dog sees people sometimes.

$\implies$ John ought to train the dog because he will frighten people if he jumps up on them when he sees them.

Dominant: He fed the cat at some time.

Embedded: The cat came home for some reason.

Embedded: The cat was hungry sometimes.

Embedded: The cat had spent the night somewhere.

Embedded: Cats spend nights somewhere.

$\implies$ He fed the cat when it came home because it was hungry after it had spent the night wherever cats spend nights.

In the last example, we have the dominant or main sentence *He fed the cat at some time,* which contains as a replacement for *at some time* the embedded sentence *The cat came home for some reason.* This embedded

---

*Each such recursive element is a duly transformed embedded sentence that iterates indefinitely.

sentence then contains its *own* embedded sentence, *The cat was hungry sometimes*. The second embedded sentence, in turn, contains its own third embedded sentence; and the third contains a fourth. We have here a five-layered nesting or embedding process, and up to this point the final transformation is quite easy to comprehend. Theoretically, the recursive rule repetition could go on indefinitely, but of course at some point the sentence would become unmanageable. Nevertheless, this is what grammarians mean when they make the statement that there is no "longest" English sentence. And so far as language scholars know to this date, the same thing is true of all other natural human languages.

Before we leave these last two transformations, I should mention yet another transformation rule which has been applied to both examples. It is the pronoun replacement transformation, an obligatory T rule which requires that instead of repeating the same noun over and over again, we must replace this repeated noun with the appropriate pronoun. (Of course, this rule no longer holds if there are intervening nouns which could cause ambiguous reference.) Observe how incomprehensible—and indeed ungrammatical—each of the transformations would be if the $T^{pro-replcmt}$ rule were not applied:

John ought to train the dog because the dog will frighten people if the dog jumps up on people when the dog sees people.

He fed the cat when the cat came home because the cat was hungry after the cat had spent the night wherever cats spend nights.

Exercises for all adverbial transformations occur at the end of this chapter.

Adverbial Phrase Transformations

The only kind of adverbial phrase which may occur in a kernel sentence is the prepositional phrase as a verb modifier, its kernel position being somewhere in the predicate, usually at the end of a sentence. All other adverbial phrases result from the application of a T rule, the adverbial phrase transformation, which is a reduction process: a transformation which deletes one or more constituents.

In performing any transformation, remember, we first need to know the preconditions (or as Chomsky put it, the "structural analysis"). In other words, we must know the constituent structure of the string or set of strings to which a given T rule may apply. The preconditions here are these: (1) each of the original kernel strings must have the same noun phrase subject; (2) one of these kernel strings must already have been subordinated and embedded in the other string by means of the $T^{advl-cl}$ rule. Thus, the adverbial phrase transformation rule is one which instructs us to perform a transformation upon a transformation.

the adverbial phrase transformations which follow,
out the system. Take note of which constituents
not a random process), and observe that only those
which are "recoverable." (Traditional grammar rec-
c phenomenon, referring to such deleted constituents
ents.)

tive Voice

t Kernel:	John becomes angry at some time.
ed Kernel:	John thinks about the fight at that time.
$T^{advl\text{-}cl} \implies$	John becomes angry *when he thinks about the fight*.
$T^{pcpl\text{-}ph} \implies$	John becomes angry *when thinking about the fight*.
$T^{pcpl\text{-}ph} \implies$	John becomes angry *thinking about the fight*.

Example B:

Dominant Kernel:	John becomes angry at some time.
Embedded Kernel:	John is thinking about the fight.
T1: $T^{advl\text{-}cl} \implies$	John becomes angry *when he is thinking about the fight*.
T2: $T^{pcpl\text{-}ph} \implies$	John becomes angry *when thinking about the fight*.
T3: $T^{pcpl\text{-}ph} \implies$	John becomes angry *thinking about the fight*.

Example C:

Dominant Kernel:	John became angry at some time.
Embedded Kernel:	John thought about the fight.
T1: $T^{advl\text{-}cl} \implies$	John became angry *when he thought about the fight*.
T2: $T^{pcpl\text{-}ph} \implies$	John became angry *when thinking about the fight*.
T3: $T^{pcpl\text{-}ph} \implies$	John became angry *thinking about the fight*.

Example D:

Dominant Kernel:		John became angry at some time.
Embedded Kernel:		John was thinking about the fight.

T1: $T^{\text{advl-cl}}$ $\implies$ John became angry *when he was thinking about the fight.*

T2: $T^{\text{pcpl-ph}}$ $\implies$ John became angry *when thinking about the fight.*

T3: $T^{\text{pcpl-ph}}$ $\implies$ John became angry *thinking about the fight.*

In Examples A through D, the two alternative participial phrase transformations result in the same derivations, even though the form of the verb differs in each of the four embedded sentences. Notice, however, that in each example, the tense of the verb in the dominant string (*present, past*) is the same as the tense of the verb in the embedded string (simple present, present progressive, simple past, past progressive). Before we come to any final conclusions about the participial phrase T rule, however, we should study some examples in which the time relationship of the two kernel verbs is different. The examples which follow are ones in which the verb in the embedded string is a perfect verb form (i.e., it uses a form of *have* as an auxiliary).

Examples E and F:

Dominant Kernel: John becomes angry at some time.

Embedded Kernel: John $\begin{Bmatrix} \text{has thought} \\ \text{has been thinking} \end{Bmatrix}$ about the fight.

T1: $T^{\text{advl-cl}}$ $\implies$ John becomes angry *after he* $\begin{Bmatrix} \text{has throught} \\ \text{has been thinking} \end{Bmatrix}$ *about the fight.*

T2: T^{wo} $\implies$ *After he* $\begin{Bmatrix} \text{has thought} \\ \text{has been thinking} \end{Bmatrix}$ *about the fight,* John becomes angry.

T3: $T^{\text{pcpl-ph}}$ $\implies$ *After* $\begin{Bmatrix} \text{having thought} \\ \text{thinking} \end{Bmatrix}$ *about the fight,* John becomes angry.

T4: $T^{\text{pcpl-ph}}$ $\implies$ *Having thought about the fight,* John becomes angry.

Examples G and H:

Dominant Kernel:	John became angry at some time.

Embedded Kernel: John $\begin{Bmatrix} had\ thought \\ had\ been\ thinking \end{Bmatrix}$ about the fight.

T1: $T^{advl\text{-}cl} \implies$ John became angry *after he* $\begin{Bmatrix} had\ thought \\ had\ been\ thinking \end{Bmatrix}$ *about the fight.*

T2: $T^{wo} \implies$ *After he* $\begin{Bmatrix} had\ thought \\ had\ been\ thinking \end{Bmatrix}$ *about the fight,* John became angry.

T3: $T^{pcpl\text{-}ph} \implies$ *After* $\begin{Bmatrix} having\ thought \\ thinking \end{Bmatrix}$ *about the fight,* John became angry.

T4: $T^{pcpl\text{-}ph} \implies$ *Having   thought   about   the   fight,* John became angry.

Now, after studying all of the above examples, we can reach these conclusions:

1. The transformation is performed on the adverbial clause.

2. The NP_s is always deleted.

3. The subordinator may or may not be deleted, with these further restrictions:
  a. If the subordinator is deleted, the *have* auxiliary may not also be deleted.
  b. If the subordinator is retained, have *may* (or may not) be deleted.

4. The ending on the first word of the transformed verb phrase must be *-ing*.

5. The *be* auxiliary is always deleted.

The question, then, is how to write the rule for the participial phrase reduction in such a way as to include all of these restrictions. The best solution seems to be two separate T rules: one which will apply to an adverbial clause string which includes *have* among its auxiliaries, and another which will apply to a string without a *have* auxiliary:

$T^{pcpl\text{-}ph}$ *rule for Examples A through D:*

$$\text{subord} + NP_s + \begin{Bmatrix} \text{ø} \\ s \\ ed \end{Bmatrix} (be + ing) \begin{Bmatrix} V \\ be \end{Bmatrix} \implies (\text{subord}) + ing + \begin{Bmatrix} V \\ be \end{Bmatrix}$$
$$+ \text{ remainder}$$

$T^{pcpl\text{-}ph}$ *rule for Examples E through H:*

$$\text{subord} + \text{NP}_s + \begin{Bmatrix} \text{ø} \\ s \\ ed \end{Bmatrix} \text{have} + en \; (be + ing) \begin{Bmatrix} \text{V} \\ be \end{Bmatrix} + \text{remainder}$$

$$\Longrightarrow \begin{Bmatrix} \text{subord} + \begin{Bmatrix} ing \\ ing + have + en \end{Bmatrix} \\ ing + have + en \end{Bmatrix} + \begin{Bmatrix} \text{V} \\ be \end{Bmatrix} + \text{remainder}$$

Participial Phrase, Passive Voice

The same preconditions must exist for the passive as for the active participial phrase transformation, with the addition, of course, that the T^{pas} rule will have had to be applied to the verb phrase in the embedded sentence. With the examples which follow, we shall therefore abbreviate the derivations by giving first the triply transformed string (already transformed by $T^{advl\text{-}cl}$, T^{wo}, and T^{pas}). Below each such string we will list the alternative passive participial phrase transformations.

Verb Forms without the Auxiliary HAVE:

When she is criticized by John, Mary leaves.

When criticized by John, Mary leaves.

Criticized by John, Mary leaves.

When she is being criticized by John, Mary leaves.

When being criticized by John, Mary leaves.

Being criticized by John, Mary leaves.

When she was criticized by John, Mary left.

When criticized by John, Mary left.

Criticized by John, Mary left.

When she was being criticized by John, Mary left.

When being criticized by John, Mary left.

Being criticized by John, Mary left.

Verb Forms with the Auxiliary HAVE:

After she has been criticized by John, Mary leaves.

After having been criticized by John, Mary leaves.

Having been criticized by John, Mary leaves.

Because she had been criticized by John, Mary left.

Because of having been criticized by John, Mary left.

Having been criticized by John, Mary left.

Once again, then, depending upon whether or not *have* appears as an auxiliary, we have two different T rules for the derivation of passive participial phrases:

Without HAVE:

$$\text{subord} + \text{NP}_s + \begin{Bmatrix} ø \\ s \\ ed \end{Bmatrix} (be + ing) + be + en + V_t + \text{remainder}$$

$$\Longrightarrow (\text{subord}) + (ing + be) + en + V_t + \text{remainder}$$

With HAVE:

$$\text{subord} + \text{NP}_s + \begin{Bmatrix} ø \\ s \\ ed \end{Bmatrix} + have + en \ (be + ing) + be + en + V_t +$$

remainder

$$\Longrightarrow (\text{subord}) + \begin{Bmatrix} ing + have + en + be + en + V_t \\ ing + be + en + V_t \end{Bmatrix} + \text{remainder}$$

Absolute Participial Phrase Reduction (Active Voice)

Traditional grammar calls the participial phrase with a retained subject by the name of *absolute phrase*, implying by this label that the construction is self-contained and grammatically independent of the sentence with which it is combined. Transformational grammar, however, enables us to see that the so-called absolute phrase is really a reduction derived from an adverbial wh clause transformation. Thus, like the wh clause which is its immediate source, this phrase is adverbial in function. Specifically, it functions as a sentence adverbial (or sentence modifier).

After the storm stopped, the boys went for a sail.

⇓

The storm having stopped, the boys went for a sail.

Because dinner was ready, Jane called us to the table.

⇓

Dinner being ready, Jane called us to the table.

Absolute Participial Phrase Reduction (Passive Voice)

Because Mary has been awakened, we all must get up.

⇓

Mary having been awakened, we all must get up.

When the book had been found, Mary was very happy.

The book having been found, Mary was very happy.

ADVERBIAL INFINITIVE PHRASE TRANSFORMATION. In addition to being able to derive a participial adverbial phrase from an adverbial wh clause, we can sometimes derive an infinitive phrase from the same transformation. The only requirement is that the wh word be one that indicates *why* or *how*; that is, the subordinator must be a word like *because* or an expression like *in order to*, or *so that*. We won't attempt to write out the T rule for this operation, but if you will examine the examples below, you can see how the rule operates:

Infinitive Phrase Reduction Transformation (Active Voice):

John went home *because he wanted to wash the car.*

John went home *to wash the car.**

He will join the demonstration *so that he can protest the war.*

He will join the demonstration *to protest the war.*

Infinitive Phrase Reduction Transformation (Passive Voice):

She stood up *because she wished to be counted.*

She stood up *to be counted.*

John campaigned hard *because he wanted to be elected.*

John campaigned hard *to be elected.*

WORD-REPLACEMENT ADVERBIAL TRANSFORMATIONS. There was apparently considerable disagreement among the early TG linguists about whether noun phrases might occur as verb modifiers in kernel sentences. The question is whether sentences like these are to be considered kernel sentences or transformations:

The boy went *home.*
He worked at the store *every night.*

---

*Note that the infinitive phrase transformation is derived through a series of reductions: John went home for some reason + The reason was something: [John wash car] + John wanted something.

One school of thought considered NPs like *home* and *every night* to be basic, and therefore they admitted them to kernel strings. Another school—and this is the point of view taken here—took the position that *home* and *every night* are reduction transformations. Thus, a noun phrase may occur in a kernel string only in a basic nominal position (subject, object, subject complement). Expressions like those in the examples above cannot therefore be adverbs, for following the same logic, one may insist that the only possible adverbs (or adverbials) in kernel sentences are uninflected words like *often, always, quickly, surely,* and so on, or a prepositional phrase. Any other structure in a kernel adverbial position (and function) signals that we are dealing with a transformation:

Kernel Sentence: The boy *went to his home.*

Transformation $\Longrightarrow$ The boy went *home.*

Kernel Sentence: He worked at the store *during* $\begin{Bmatrix} each \\ every \end{Bmatrix}$ *night.*

Transformation $\Longrightarrow$ He worked at the store $\begin{Bmatrix} each \\ every \end{Bmatrix}$ *night.*

The transformation, if one accepts this explanation, is one which instructs us to delete the preposition.

SENTENCE MODIFIERS (SENTENCE ADVERBIALS). As we have already seen briefly, the adverb function is the least understood and the most controversial of all "part-of-speech" functions. Linguists cannot altogether agree whether the adverb is a basic or a transformed element. But whether or not agreement can be reached about the derivation of a word like *quickly* in the sentences below, it can be agreed that regardless of whether it occurs in a pre-, mid-, or postverb position, it functions as a verb modifier:

He should *quickly* have won the race.

He should have *quickly* won the race.

He should have won the race *quickly.*

A word like *certainly* or *probably,* on the other hand, is quite different. First of all, such a word can occur in a great many more sentence positions than can the verb modifier:

Probably, he should have won the race.

He *probably* should have won the race.

He should *probably* have won the race.

He should have *probably* won the race.

He should have won the race, *probably.*

Such evidence has led some transformationalists to conclude that a word like *probably* is a *sentence modifier* (rather than a verb modifier). They reason that sentence modifier words like *probably* and *certainly* are derived from adjectives that occur grammatically across BE from their entire sentence:

That he should have won the race *is* probable.

Notice that this is not possible for *quickly*:

That he should have won the race is quick.

ADVERBIAL PHRASES AND CLAUSES. All of the italicized phrases and clauses below are adverbial in function. Those preceded by daggers are sentence modifiers.

EXAMPLES OF MULTIPLE-BASE SENTENCE ADVERBIAL TRANSFORMATIONS
A. Verbal Phrases
  1. Participial Phrase
  Having worked hard, Mary felt good.
      Dominant: Mary felt good (for some reason).
      Embedded: Mary had worked hard.
  2. Infinitive Phrase
  †*To be sure*, he was in some doubt.
      Dominant: He was in some doubt.
      Embedded: One can be sure.
  To find the child, they organized a search party.
      Dominant: They organized a search party (for some reason).
      Embedded: They wanted to find the child.
B. Adverbial Clause
  Although he called me, I refused the invitation.
      Dominant: I refused the invitation (in spite of something).
      Embedded: He called me.
C. Absolute Phrase
  The lights having gone out, I went to bed.
      Dominant: I went to bed (for some reason).
      Embedded: The lights had gone out.
D. Interjected Clause
  †You are, *I suppose*, in a hurry.
      Dominant: You are in a hurry.
      Embedded: I suppose something.
E. Yes/No Question Clause (tagged on at end of sentence)
  †Mary is sad, *isn't she?*
      Dominant: Mary is sad.
      Embedded: Mary is sad.
      (The dominant and the embedded sentences are the same kernel sentence)

ADVERBIAL WH-CLAUSE TRANSFORMATION   EXERCISE 64

Directions: Transform each of the following sets of strings by application of the adverbial $T^{wh\text{-}clause}$ rule. The first string of each pair is to be the dominant clause of your transform.

1. Archibald lost his appointment as prosecutor at some time.
   Archibald defied the boss at that time.

2. Everyone is miserable for some reason.
   Amos is unhappy.

3. Lou is pompous $\begin{cases} \text{sometimes.} \\ \text{at some times.} \end{cases}$
   Lou interviews people $\begin{cases} \text{at some times.} \\ \text{sometimes.} \end{cases}$
   People apply for jobs.

4. The bird will sing in some place at some time.
   Someone uncovers the bird.
   The bird is in the kitchen.

ADVERBIAL PARTICIPIAL PHRASE TRANSFORMATION   EXERCISE 65

Directions: Transform the following sets of strings by application of the adverbial participial phrase transformation rule, deleting the wh word whenever possible. Make the first sentence of each pair the dominant clause in your transform. (Do not transform the word order unless you must.)

1. We became cynical for some reason.
   We listened to the hearings on television.

2. The dog came to the door in some manner.
   The dog was barking frantically.

3. Jake paid the fine for some reason.
   Jake had lost the library book.

4. The family was freezing after some event.
   The furnace broke down.

5. The weather turned bitter after some time.
   The weather had been balmy for a week.

ADVERBIAL INFINITIVE-PHRASE TRANSFORMATION   EXERCISE 66

> *Directions:* Transform the following sets of strings by application
> of the adverbial infinitive phrase transformation rule, deleting the
> wh word whenever possible. The first string of each pair should be the
> dominant clause in your transformation.

1. You must pretend happiness.
   You must keep up your spirits.

2. He joined the marines for a reason.
   He will fight for his country.

3. He put his money under the mattress for a reason.
   He saved his money.

4. Convert this transformation, by the process of reduction, to a dominant clause plus
   an infinitive adverbial phrase:
   The dog came in because he wanted to be fed.

28

TG Grammar, Early Form: Multiple-Base Embedding Transformations: Adjectivalization

In kernel sentences, the only positions which adjectives can occupy are predicate positions: the object complement posisition in Pattern 5, and the subject complement position in Patterns 8 and 10:

Pattern 5: We considered Jane *foolish**

Pattern 8: The girl seems *happy*.

Pattern 10: The students are *smart*.

An adjective never occurs in a noun phrase in kernel sentences. This means that a sentence in which an adjective occurs either immediately before or immediately after a noun or nominal is a transformation.

Adjectivals which immediately follow a noun are called noun complements, and the process which transforms them to this position is called *complementation*.

Relative Clause Transformation (*The Adjectival Clause*)

The relative clause is a wh clause in which one of the kernel nouns is replaced with the appropriate wh word and then the transformed sentence is embedded after the identical noun in a dominant kernel

---

*Later TG grammar explains the sentences with direct object + object complement as transformations. This sentence derives, therefore, from the dominant S: "We considered Jane," and the obligatory embedded S: "Jane is foolish."

sentence. Here are some examples:

1. The boy *who is walking down the street* is John.

Dominant: The boy is John.

Embedded: The boy is walking down the street.

2. This is the house *that Jack built*.

Dominant: This is the house.

Embedded: Jack built the house.

3. The teacher *whom we hated* was fired.

Dominant: Someone fired the teacher.

(This sentence had been transformed by the T^{pas} rule.)

Embedded: We hated the teacher.

4. The child feared the man *whose head was bald*.

Dominant: The child feared the man.

Embedded: The man had a head.

Embedded: The head was bald.

(*The man's head was bald* is considered by some early TG grammarians to be a transformation rather than a kernel.)

5. She visited the house $\begin{Bmatrix} where \\ in\ which \end{Bmatrix}$ *she had grown up*.

Dominant: She visited the house.

Embedded: She had grown up in the house.

6. July is the month $\begin{Bmatrix} when \\ during\ which \end{Bmatrix}$ *we go on vacation*.

Dominant: July is the month.

Embedded: We go on vacation during the month.

7. This is the store $\begin{Bmatrix} where \\ at\ which \end{Bmatrix}$ *I buy meat*.

Dominant: This is the store.

Embedded: I buy meat at the store.

Notice the structural analysis (the preconditions) for transforming a sentence into a relative clause. The sentence which is to become embedded as a noun complement must contain the *same noun* as that which is to be complemented in the dominant sentence.

Recursiveness. As with adverbial clause transformations, nesting may also occur with relative clauses. This nesting phenomenon, you will recall, can result in a transformation within a transformation:

This is the dog <u>who chased the cat</u> <u>who ate the rat</u> <u>that lived in the</u>

                Insert 1   Insert 2   Insert 3

<u>house that Jack built.</u>

        Insert 4

Dominant Sentence: This is the dog.

Embedded Sentence: The dog chased the cat.

Embedded Sentence: The cat ate the rat.

Embedded Sentence: The rat lived in the house.

Embedded Sentence: Jack built the house.

Relative Clause Reduction Transformations

Deleting the Wh word

In Examples 1, 2, and 3 above, it is possible to reduce the relative clause by deleting the wh word:

1. The boy *walking down the street* is John. (deletion of *who* and the auxiliary *is*)

2. This is the house *Jack built.* (deletion of *that*)

3. The teacher *we hated* was fired. (deletion of *whom*)

Remember, the linguistic principle which governs the deletion process is "recoverability." One may omit only those words which are recoverable (i.e., clearly "understood").

Active Participial Phrase as Noun Complement

By deleting the *wh word* plus the *be* auxiliary of relative clauses whose verb forms are T + *be* + *ing* + V, we derive a participial phrase noun complement. The first wh word deletion example above is an illustration. Here are some more examples:

1. Relative clause T: The man *who is washing the car* is Bob.

   Pcpl-Ph Reduction: The man *washing the car* is Bob.

2. Relative clause T: I know the girl *who is singing "Aida."*

   Pcpl-Ph Reduction: I know the girl *singing "Aida."*

$$\text{Wh} + \begin{Bmatrix} \text{\o} \\ s \\ ed \end{Bmatrix} + be + ing + \text{V} + \text{remainder} \Longrightarrow ing + \text{V} + \text{remainder}$$

Passive Participial Phrase as Noun Complement

We can derive a passive participial noun complement phrase by deleting the *wh word* plus the *be* auxiliary from a passive relative clause:

$$\text{Wh} + \begin{Bmatrix} \text{\o} \\ s \\ ed \end{Bmatrix} + be + en + \text{V} + \text{remainder} \Longrightarrow en + \text{V} + \text{remainder}$$

1. The pond, *which was frozen solidly,* was good for skating.

$\Longrightarrow$ The pond, *frozen solidly,* was good for skating.

2. I found a letter *which was written by the child.*

$\Longrightarrow$ I found a letter *written by the child.*

Active Infinitive Phrase as Noun Complement

The infinitive noun complement phrase can be derived from a relative clause with the form $\text{WH} + \begin{Bmatrix} \text{\o} \\ s \\ ed \end{Bmatrix} + \begin{Bmatrix} will + \text{\o} \\ shall + \text{\o} \\ be + to + \text{\o} \end{Bmatrix} + \text{V} +$ remainder. The relative clause is then reduced to the form: $to + \text{\o} + \text{V} + \text{remainder}$:

1. She hired a man *who will drive her to the airport.*

$\Longrightarrow$ She hired a man *to drive her to the airport.*

2. At the door are the men *who are to mow the lawn.*

$\Longrightarrow$ At the door are the men *to mow the lawn.*

Passive Infinitive Phrase as Noun Complement

The passive noun complement infinitive phrase is a reduced form of a passive relative clause whose verb contains the modal *be + to* or some other modal auxiliary. The relative clause is transformed according to this rule:

$$\text{Wh} + \begin{Bmatrix} \text{\o} \\ s \\ ed \end{Bmatrix} + \begin{Bmatrix} be + to + \text{\o} \\ \text{Modal} + \text{\o} \end{Bmatrix} + be + en + \text{V} + \text{remainder}$$

$\Longrightarrow to + be + en + \text{V} + \text{remainder.}$

1. This is a job *which is to be done quickly.*

$\Longrightarrow$ This is a job *to be done quickly.*

2. He is a person *who ought to be admired.*

$\Longrightarrow$ He is a person *to be admired.*

Appositive Noun Phrase as Noun Complement

The last kind of reduced relative clause is the appositive noun phrase. This is a reduction of any relative clause derived from a Pattern 7 or a Pattern 9 kernel sentence, in which a noun phrase functions as a subject complement. We arrive at the appositive noun phrase by deleting the NP_s and the verb:

1. Timothy, *who became the captain,* received many votes.

$\Longrightarrow$ Timothy, *the captain,* received many votes.

2. Mary, *who is my sister,* is very late.

$\Longrightarrow$ Mary, *my sister,* is very late.

Other Relative Clause Transformations

In addition to the relative clause and the various forms of relative clause reductions, we can trace a number of noun modifier tranformations to other kernel sentence sources. The position of a noun modifier in the noun phrase can vary, although as a general rule, a single-word structure tends to occur before the noun which it modifies, and larger structures (phrases and clauses) occur in immediate post noun or post nominal positions.

Structures Which Appear in Other Kernel Sentence Positions

A. *Adjective*
1. Jane is a *pretty* girl.
   Dominant: Jane is a girl.
   Embedded: The girl $\begin{Bmatrix} \text{is} \\ \text{seems} \end{Bmatrix}$ *pretty.*

2. *Almighty* God made the *wondrous* world.
   Dominant: God made the world.
   Embedded: God $\begin{Bmatrix} \text{is} \\ \text{seems} \end{Bmatrix}$ *almighty.*
   Embedded: The world $\begin{Bmatrix} \text{is} \\ \text{seems} \end{Bmatrix}$ *wondrous.*

B. *Noun*
1. A *stone* wall surrounded the house.
   Dominant: A wall surrounded the house.
   Embedded: Someone made the wall with *stone.*
2. He is a *fire* fighter.
   Dominant: He is a fighter.
   Embedded: The fighter fights *fires.*

C. *Pronoun*
  1. Paul is a *he* man.
      Dominant: Paul is a man.
      Embedded: A man is a *he*.
  2. They named her the *It* Girl.
      Dominant: They named her the girl.
      Embedded: The girl had *it*.
          (This example is a bit farfetched, but it does illustrate the transformational creativity possible in language.)

D. *Possessive Noun and Possessive Pronoun*
  1. *John's father's* dog has fleas.
      Dominant: The dog has fleas.
      Embedded: The *father* has a dog.
      Embedded: *John* has a father.
  2. She lost *her* watch.
      Dominant: She lost the watch.
      Embedded: *She* had a watch.

E. *Verb*
  1. We felt sorry for the *weeping* child.
      Dominant: We felt sorry for the child.
      Embedded: The child *was weeping*.
  2. We saw the boys *playing*.
      Dominant: We saw the boys.
      Embedded: The boys *were playing*.
  3. The time *to change* is now.
      Dominant: The time is now.
      Embedded: Something *should change* at some time.
  4. This is a moment *to remember*.
      Dominant: This is a moment.
      Embedded: One *ought to remember* the moment.
  5. The *broken* vase had been pretty.
      Dominant: The vase had been pretty.
      Embedded: Someone *broke* the vase.
          (This derivation is the result of a double transformation: $T^{pas} \Longrightarrow$ The vase was broken by someone.)

F. *Adverb*
  (Transformation of Adverb Subjective Complement: Pattern 11)
  1. I like this boy *here*.
      Dominant: I like this boy.
      Embedded: The boy is *here*.

2. The dog *outside* has been barking for hours.
   Dominant: The dog has been barking for hours.
   Embedded: The dog is *outside*.

G. *Preposition*
   1. This is a *through* street.
      Dominant: This is a street.
      Embedded: The street goes *through* somewhere.
   2. He went up the *down* staircase.
      Dominant: He went up the staircase.
      Embedded: One should go *down* the staircase.

H. *Prepositional Phrase*
   (Pattern 11 use: adverbial prepositional phrase)
   1. The tree *on the patio* is an oak.
      Dominant: The tree is an oak.
      Embedded: The tree is *on the patio*.
   2. Several boys *from the class* are absent.
      Dominant: Several boys are absent.
      Embedded: The boys are *from the class*.

Structures Which Do Not Appear in Kernel Sentences

We have already discussed the relative clause and its reductions, none of which appear in kernel sentences. In addition to these structures, there is one more structure which does not appear in kernel sentences but which may appear in transformations as a noun modifier. I refer to the subordinate clause, a structure which can be identified by its form characteristic: i.e., a subordinator has been added in the initial position. By far the most common function for the subordinate clause transformation is, as you have already seen, adverbial.

ADJECTIVALIZATION TRANSFORMATIONS   EXERCISE 67

Directions: For each of the following sets of strings, make the string preceded by a dagger a dominant clause, and transform the other string according to the adjectivalization rule specified. (Do not perform any further reductions beyond the one asked for.)

T^{adjtl} *Rule to be used*

Rel Clause	**1.** The newcomer is breaking every rule.
	†He is the newcomer.
Rel Clause	**2.** †The street is in this block.
	The robbery took place on this street.

Reduced Rel Clause	**3.** I am crazy about the boy. †The boy is named Jeffrey.
Participial Phrase	**4.** Grandpa is mowing the lawn. †The man is Grandpa.
Inf Phrase (Active)	**5.** †John Horsley is the boy. The boy will do the job.
Inf Phrase (Passive)	**6.** A job must be done. †Where is the job?
Participial Phrase	**7.** †The person changes frequently. A person drives the school bus.

ADJECTIVALIZATION TRANSFORMATIONS   EXERCISE 68

Directions: A variety of T^{adjtl} transformation rules will be needed for the transformations in this exercise. Make the string preceded by a dagger the dominant clause, and convert the other string (or strings) to adjectivals. (Try to construct adjectivals with minimal constituents).

1. The apparition was hideous.
†The apparition disappeared.

2. People should fear corruption.
†Dishonesty is a corruption.

3. †The person is Harry Jones.
Someone should scold Harry Jones.

4. †Those children drive me crazy!
The children are screaming.

5. †The house withstood the attack.
Someone constructed the house with brick.
The wolf made the attack.

6. †The wind frightens the cat.
The wind is outside.
The cat is in the window.

29

TG Grammar, Early Form: Multiple-Base Embedding Transformations: Nominalization

Many linguists make the claim that English is primarily a "nominalizing" language. They argue that by far the most flexible and creative linguistic device available to the speaker of English is the system of rules which enable us to transform nonnominal constituents (and even entire sentences) into nominal ("naming") ones.

Of course, it is true that we may convert any word or word group to a nominal simply by mentioning it in a sentence, but that is not really what these linguists mean by *nominalization*.* What they refer to are the various transformational processes which enable the speaker of English to convert words and word groups to nominals.

We shall examine only a few nominalization transformation rules,† but before we do, let us be certain that we understand the definition of the term *nominal*. A nominal is any grammatical construction which *functions* as a noun or NP. (*Function* involves both position and constituent relation: subject, nominal complement, object.) Since only two kinds of structures may occur as nominals in kernel strings (the *noun phrase* and the *pronoun*), all other nominal structures are transformations.

---

*I am reminded of one of my favorite "commandments"—a statement which I spotted some years ago in a traditional grammar text whose name I have forgotten. In explaining sentences which begin with the expletive *there*, the book (trying to be helpful) stated: "*There* can never be the subject of a sentence."

†For an especially thorough and detailed study of English nominalizations, see Robert B. Lees, *The Grammar of English Nominalizations*, 1963.

The italicized constituents in the following examples illustrate the transformed nominalizations we will study in this chapter:

1. I know *what you told him.*

2. He forgets *where he puts things.*

3. He showed me *how one should make pizza.*

4. He showed me *how to make pizza.*

5. *That he is angry with me* astonishes me.

6. I know *(that) he will call me soon.*

7. *Talking to Ethel* is a strain.

8. I enjoy *sleeping late in the morning.*

9. I dislike *his teasing the dog.*

10. *For Jean to be angry* seems foolish.

11. *To expect an apology* is futile.

12. It surprises me *that you are on time.*

13. It is futile *to expect an answer.*

14. *The poor* will always be with us.

As you can see from these examples, nominal transformations can assume many forms: relative clause, subordinate clause, infinitive phrase, gerund phrase, and so on. We will briefly look at how some of these processes may occur.

CLAUSES AND CLAUSE REDUCTIONS

WH CLAUSE NOMINALIZING TRANSFORMATION. We have already become familiar with some wh clause transformations. We have seen, for example, how a kernel sentence can be converted to a wh question (single-base: $T^{q\text{-}wh}$); and how a sentence can be converted to a wh clause to be used as an adverbial (multiple-base: $T^{advl\ wh\ cl}$). In this section we shall see how wh clauses can be used as nominals ($T^{nom\ wh\ cl}$).

Study the following derivations:

1. *Wh Clauses as Subject Nominals:*

   What he told me shocked me.

   Dominant: *Something* shocked me.

   Embedded: *He told me something.*

2. *Wh Clauses as Object Nominals:*

He forgets *where he puts things.*

   Dominant: He forgets *something.*

   Embedded: *He puts things somewhere.*

He showed me *how one should make pizza.*

   Dominant: He showed me *something.*

   Embedded: *One should make pizza in some manner.*

3. *Wh Clauses as Subject Complement Nominals:*

The problem is *when John should resign.*

   Dominant: The problem is *something.*

   Embedded: *John should resign at some time.*

We already know that to transform a sentence to a wh clause, we initiate the string with the appropriate wh word (*where*, *when*, *how*, *why*, *who*, *what*, and so on). With wh questions, we also re-ordered the words according to the $T^{yes/no}$ question transformation. But in these derivations the question is abstract rather than direct, and thus the remaining words in the kernel sentence keep their usual order. Having converted the sentence which is to be embedded, we simply replace the word *something* in the dominant sentence with the wh clause:

   SOMETHING (in dominant sentence) $\Longrightarrow$ Wh Clause

REDUCTION OF NOMINAL WH CLAUSE TO WH INFINITIVE PHRASE. Some, though not all, nominal wh clauses can be reduced to wh infinitive phrases. The precondition is that the wh clause must make a general rather than a specific statement:

He showed me *how one should make pizza* $\Longrightarrow$

He showed me *how to make pizza.*

He knows *what people should do in an emergency* $\Longrightarrow$

He knows *what to do in an emergency.*

Notice, however, than we cannot reduce the wh clause to a wh phrase when the nominal is not a generalization:

Jane knows *what you told John.*

If we convert this sentence to "Jane knows *what to tell John,*" we have altered the meaning of the wh clause. We can, however, reduce the transformation: *Jane knows what she should tell John* to *Jane knows what to tell John.* The last transformation can then be interpreted to mean either "Jane knows what *she* should tell John" (the subject noun is recoverable) or "Jane knows what *anyone* should tell John" (a generalization). We must therefore write the $T^{nom\ wh\ inf\ ph}$ reduction rule with a qualification or restriction which explains when it may be applied:

Wh + NP + Aux + V + remainder (when clause is a generalization) $\implies$

Wh + *to* + ø + V + remainder

THAT-CLAUSE NOMINALIZING TRANSFORMATION. Study the following that-clause nominalizations:

(*The fact*) *that he is angry with me* astonishes me.

> Dominant: *Something* astonishes me.

> Embedded: *He is angry with me.*

I realize (*the fact*) *that he will call me soon.*

> Dominant: I realize *something.*

> Embedded: *He will call me soon.*

In these examples, the that-clause construction may or may not include the preceding words, *the fact.* (Because of this phenomenon, some TG linguists refer to this kind of clause as a factive clause rather than as a that-clause.)

In some cases, on the other hand, we are *required* to begin the factive clause with the expression, *the fact that.* See if you can determine which qualification determines this result:

The plan was based on *the fact that war was imminent.*

> Dominant: Someone based the plan on *something.* (Notice we must go back two steps, since the dominant sentence both includes an embedded sentence and is passive.)

> Embedded: *War was imminent.*

Al bought Mary a ring before *the fact that she hated him became evident.*

> Dominant: Al bought Mary a ring before *something.*

> Embedded: *Something became evident.*

> Embedded: *She hated him.*

It seems likely from these examples that when a factive clause is embedded in an object-of-preposition position, the words *the fact* cannot be deleted. Before we leave these examples, you should note that the last of them once again illustrates recursiveness.

PHRASES

Gerund Phrase Nominalizing Transformations. The gerund phrase nominalization is probably another form of reduction—in this case, of a factive nominal clause (that-clause). Consider these transformations, for example, which begin with an embedded nominal that-clause:

Example 1: *That one must talk to Ethel* is a strain.

Ger Phrase: *One's talking to Ethel* is a strain.

Ger Phrase: *Talking to Ethel* is a strain.

Dominant: *Something* is a strain.

Embedded: *One must talk to Ethel.*

Example 2: I enjoy (*the fact*) *that I sleep late in the morning.*

Ger Phrase: I enjoy *my sleeping late in the morning.*

Ger Phrase: I enjoy *sleeping late in the morning.*

Dominant: I enjoy *something.*

Embedded: *I sleep late in the morning.*

Whether we explain gerund phrase nominal transformations as that-clause reductions or simply as having direct kernel sentence sources, we can analyze transformations with embedded nominal gerund phrases as deriving from the same ultimate kernel string sources. We would write the transformation rule differently, though, depending on which position we decide to take.

If we wish to explain the gerund phrase derivation as a transformation upon a transformation, we can write the T rule as follows:

(*the fact*) + *that* + N_s + V + remainder $\Longrightarrow$
(N_s + *'s*) + *ing* + V + remainder.

If, as I prefer, we explain the gerund phrase derivation as one which derives directly from a kernel sentence source, the T rule might read:

N_s + V + remainder $\Longrightarrow$ (N_s + *'s*) + *ing* + V + remainder

We must also note that the precondition for the application of this rule, which permits the deletion of N_s + *'s*, is that either the string to be embedded must be a generalization or its subject must be identical to the subject of the dominant string.

INFINITIVE PHRASE NOMINALIZING TRANSFORMATION. One type of infinitive phrase nominalization has already been identified as a wh clause reduction. Now, however, we want to look at the kind of infinitive-phrase-as-nominal which can be derived directly from a kernel sentence source.* The nominal positions where an infinitive phrase may be embedded are illustrated in these examples:

Infinitive Phrase as Subject of V_t, V_1, or BE

$\begin{Bmatrix} To\ wash\ the\ car \\ For\ Mary\ to\ wash\ the\ car \end{Bmatrix}$ annoys John.

> Dominant: *Something* annoys John.

> Embedded: $\begin{Bmatrix} John\ washes\ the\ car. \\ Mary\ washes\ the\ car. \end{Bmatrix}$

$\begin{Bmatrix} To\ finish\ before\ the\ deadline \\ For\ Mary\ to\ finish\ before\ the\ deadline \end{Bmatrix}$ would seem remarkable to me.

> Dominant: *Something* would seem remarkable.

> Embedded: $\begin{Bmatrix} I\ might\ finish\ before\ the\ deadline. \\ Mary\ might\ finish\ before\ the\ deadline. \end{Bmatrix}$

$\begin{Bmatrix} To\ apologize \\ For\ Jean\ to\ apologize \end{Bmatrix}$ is futile.

> Dominant: *Something* is futile.

> Embedded: $\begin{Bmatrix} Someone\ (or\ I)\ should\ apologize. \\ Jean\ should\ apologize \end{Bmatrix}$

Infinitive Phrase as Subject Complement

To expect an apology is *to hope in vain.*
   (subject of *be*)   (subject compl)

> Dominant: *Something*₁ is *something*₂.

> Embedded: *One expects an apology.*

> Embedded: *One hopes in vain.*

---

*Here again, we might consider this derivation to be a that-clause reduction, but I prefer to consider it a direct transformation from a kernel sentence source.

Infinitive Phrase as Direct Object

Here the transformation instructions become complicated, because English contains different types of transitive verbs, some of which behave differently from others when infinitive phrases are embedded as their direct objects. The examples which follow should illustrate these differences:

TYPE I. Verbs of the type *hate, mind, want, intend,* ..

John wants $\begin{Bmatrix} \textit{to go to the movies.} \\ \textit{(for) Mary to go to the movies.} \end{Bmatrix}$

Dominant: John wants *something.*

Embedded: $\begin{Bmatrix} \textit{John goes to the movies.} \\ \textit{Mary goes to the movies.} \end{Bmatrix}$

TYPE II. Verb + Particle of the type *plead for, try for, wait for*

John waited $\begin{Bmatrix} \textit{to go with the group.} \\ \textit{for Mary to go with the group.} \end{Bmatrix}$

Dominant: John waited for *something.*

Embedded: $\begin{Bmatrix} \textit{John will go with the group.} \\ \textit{Mary will go with the group.} \end{Bmatrix}$

(Notice that the particle *for* is deleted in the second transformation.)

TYPE III. Verbs of the type *wave, call, say, signal*

John said (*for someone*) to begin the performance.

Dominant: John said *something.*

Embedded: *Someone should begin the performance.*

The policeman signaled (*for someone*) to turn right.

Dominant: The policeman signaled *something.*

Embedded: *Someone should turn right.*

(There is a conceptual implication with this type of verb, namely that there are two different source subjects.)

All of the examples above set up these preconditions: that an infinitive phrase may occur only as (1) the subject of a linking verb, a transitive verb, or *be*; (2) the subject complement of a linking verb or *be*; or (3) the direct object of a transitive verb. The rule for converting a kernel sentence to a nominal infinitive phrase can then be formulated as follows:

N_s (Aux₁) (Aux₂) + V + remainder $\Longrightarrow$
for + N_s + *to* (Aux₂) + V + remainder.

It will then be necessary to add a subrule which explains that *for* + N_s may be optionally deleted when the verb is of the type: *wave, beckon, say, signal, call,* and so on. For all other verb types, *for* + N_s is deleted when the source nouns are identical, but retained when the source nouns are different.

OTHER NOMINALIZING TRANSFORMATIONS. There are two more nominalizations which we should mention: elliptical constructions (forms of reductions), and derivational transformations.

Elliptical Constructions
Some of these are direct transformations of kernel strings, while others are reductions of transformed strings. In the examples below, however, the dominant and embedded sentences represent the original kernel string sources:

Gerund Nominals

Walking is fun.

    Dominant: *Something* is fun.

    Embedded: *Someone walks.*

He devoted his time to *writing.*

    Dominant: He devoted his time to *something.*

    Embedded: *He writes (something).*

Infinitive Nominals

To give up is wrong.

    Dominant: *Something* is wrong.

    Embedded: *Someone gives up (something).*

He likes *to relax.*

    Dominant: He likes *something.*

    Embedded: *He relaxes.*

Adjective Nominals

The poor will always be with us.

Dominant: $\left\{ \begin{array}{l} \textit{Someone} \\ \textit{Some people} \end{array} \right\}$ will always be with us.

Embedded: *Some people are poor.*

The beautiful are damned.

Dominant: Something damns *some people.*

Embedded: *Some people are beautiful.*

Derivational Transformations

The early TG linguists did not really solve the problem of derivational constructions. In fact, this same problem is still hotly debated among linguists today.* The debate centers on the question of whether certain word classification types are more basic than others: for example, is the word *reduction* a kernel noun, or is it derived from the embedded verb, *reduce?*

The early transformationalists did not solve this problem, but refusing to dismiss the possibility that at least some derivational forms have deeper sources and are thus transformations, they devised a tentative derivational T rule which can be illustrated with the following example:

John's insistence angered the crowd.

Dominant: *Something* angered the crowd.

Embedded: *John insisted on something.*

The reasoning here is that the transformational process takes place in stages:

1. The embedded kernel sentence, *John insisted on something*, is transformed, by application of the $T^{nom \ ger \ ph}$ rule, to *John's insisting on something.*

2. The gerund phrase, *John's insisting on something*, is then transformed, by means of a derivational rule, to *John's insistence.*

Thus, we might write a derivational affix rule ($T^{der \ af}$) as follows:

$$ing + V \Longrightarrow der \ af + V$$

*The current debate, still far from settled, extends to such questions as whether personal pronouns are not really basic (or deep) determiners, and whether all adjectives ("pure" ones like *sad* as well as derivational ones like *beautiful*) are not really deep verbs. For a good discussion of these positions, see Jacobs and Rosenbaum, *English Transformational Grammar*, 1968.

Then, in the morphophonemic rules, we can list a number of nominal derivational affixes:

der af $\Longrightarrow$ *ence, ment, ance, al, tion, th,* . . .

Not only do we native speakers transform "parts of speech" with derivational endings (we can derive verbs, adjectives, and adverbs this way too), but we then proceed to fit the new word from into a syntactical construction which will accept a word of this class:

KERNEL FORM	POSSIBLE INTERIM FORM	TRANSFORMATION
X *insists* on Y	$\begin{cases} \text{the } insisting \text{ of X on Y} \\ \text{X's } insisting \text{ on Y} \end{cases}$	X's *insistence*
X *involves* self with Y	X's *involving* of self with Y	X's *involvement*
X *relies* on Y	X's *relying* on Y	X's *reliance*
X *defies* Y	X's *defying* of Y	X's *defiance*
X *denies* Y	X's *denying* of Y	X's *denial*
X *deduces* Y	X's *deducing* of Y	X's *deduction*
X *heals* Y	X's *healing* of Y	Y's *health*

We cannot be certain that this explanation is correct. But it seems clear that some such process takes place. Transformational linguists contend that linguistic processes of this sort are "built in" to the human brain, and therefore they are not even conscious operations. They have come to believe, for reasons that we will go into in the next chapter, that there are a number of linguistic universals; and it is the search for these universals that has come to absorb scholars of language and other cognitive disciplines in recent years.

THE IT-EXPLETIVE TRANSFORMATION. One of the single-base transformations we mentioned was the there-expletive rule, which added the "filler" word *there* as the first word of the transformed string, and then reordered the words so that the subject followed the verb. Now we shall look at another expletive transformation, one that can be applied only to certain kinds of transformed strings whose subjects have already been nominalized. The examples below illustrate the transform types which will accept the $T^{it\text{-}expl}$ rule:

1. Transforms with that-clause subjects:

That she hated him is evident $\Longrightarrow$ *It* is evident *that she hated him.*

That he was angry astonished me $\Longrightarrow$ *It* astonished me *that he was angry.*

2. Transforms with gerund phrase subjects:

Talking to Ethel is a strain $\Longrightarrow$ *It* is a strain *talking to Ethel.*

But not: *His snoring all night* annoys me $\Longrightarrow$ *It* annoys me *his snoring all night.*

3. Transforms with infinitive phrase subjects:

To win at poker is easy $\Longrightarrow$ *It* is easy *to win at poker.*

To have to wash the car annoys John $\Longrightarrow$ *It* annoys John *to have to wash the car.*

NOMINALIZATION TRANSFORMATIONS   EXERCISE 69

Directions: The string in each set below which is preceded by a dagger should become the dominant clause; the other string or strings are to be nominalized according to the T rule requested.

T^{nom} *rule to be used*

That-clause	**1.** †He thinks something. He must know everything.
Wh Clause ($Advl_{time}$)	**2.** The passenger should get off the bus at some time. †The conductor signaled something.
Wh Clause ($Advl_{reason}$)	**3.** †She knew something. Mabel ought to forget Tom for a reason.
Wh Clause	**4.** †Something was a loud noise. The noise frightened the puppy.
Gerund Phrase	**5.** Someone must practice the piano for an hour a day. †Somthing is a bore.
Infinitive Phrase	**6.** †Something is very difficult. One must make a choice.
Gerund Phrase (with possessive)	**7.** Mike bosses his friends constantly. †I hate something.
Gerund	**8.** †Something is Gordon's biggest problem. Gordon drinks.
Infinitive Phrase	**9.** She would learn Italian in a month. †She hoped something.
That-Clause	**10.** †Something seems strange. Mary will be fifty tomorrow.

TRANSFORMATIONS (REVIEW)   EXERCISE 70

> *Directions:* Examine each of the following sentences, and determine whether each is a kernel sentence or a transform. If it is a transform, write out all underlying kernel sentences, being careful to distinguish between dominant and embedded ones. Do not worry about trying to account for kernel sources of derivational words. Do, however, give sources for compounds.

1. There were some people left behind by the bus.
2. Did she give you a quick answer?
3. That she should have bought the coat is really sad.
4. When the time to vote arrived, the students and the faculty didn't want the responsibility.
5. John's reputation was being destroyed.
6. The awful destruction was caused by a record-breaking storm.
7. John, the little boy playing in the wading pool, doesn't hear his mother calling him.
8. The battered old car in the used car lot was sold to Jim.
9. Jane's constantly being late was an annoying habit to her friends.
10. In my opinion, the play is a direct insult to the intelligence of the viewer.

TRANSFORMATIONS   EXERCISE 71

> *Directions:* Analyze the kernel sentence derivations of these sentences in the same way you did for the previous exercise.

1. Jack prized the book of rules and regulations even though it was old and tattered.
2. The waste paper basket had been filled to overflowing.
3. To yield to cowardice is a terrible personality flaw.
4. John's dad's flea-bitten old bird dog died during the night.
5. The International Certificate of Vaccination is an official statement that you are adequately protected against a disease which could be a threat to America and other countries.
6. On the application form, print your full name, your correct address, and your reason for applying for the job.
7. Did you see the eclipse of the moon, or were you studying instead for a difficult, unfair, mind-bending grammar test?

30

Revisions of *Syntactic Structures* Model

After a slow start, transformational-generative grammar finally took hold. Chomsky and others worked at extending and refining the early theoretical model, and eventually arrived at enough modifications and revisions that the original theory had to be reformulated. In addition to the work on the TG model, Chomsky devoted much time to enlarging and refining the assumptions and the philosophical views which had led him to develop a TG grammar in the first place, and to defending his views to a still-skeptical group of linguists.

One of the most controversial of these assumptions was Chomsky's assertion that the linguist must rely on the linguistic intuitions of native speakers. Most structuralists balked at the word "intuition," and they condemned Chomsky's method as subjective, unscientific, and circular: if the linguist begins a study by consulting the native speakers' intuitions, then constructs a grammar which describes these intuitions, and finally tests the correctness (or truth) of the grammar against the original intuitions, isn't the procedure a circular one? And doesn't such a procedure, so utterly lacking in objectivity, disqualify linguistics as a science? Should one take seriously a method which incorporates such a dangerous lack of objectivity?

Chomsky answered such charges by insisting first of all that it is far more dangerous to view objectivity as an end in itself. If the goal is insight and understanding (the concern of all science), objectivity is used merely as a *tool* for the search. Besides, as with any science, it scarcely makes sense to begin by demanding the very evidence you are looking for. He admitted that there are certainly problems inherent in relying on intuition, but at the moment he knew of no better way to begin. As for

315

reliance on intuition as the ultimate test of his theory, Chomsky answered that if linguistic intuition is what the linguist seeks to explain, there is no better way to test results than to see if they are satisfactory explanations to native speakers.*

Still not convinced, the structuralists retorted that if Chomsky's grammar has as its aim the study of intuition, then its results will not tell us anything we do not already know, since we are all native speakers. They accused Chomsky of describing intuition, not grammar. Chomsky agreed that intuition was indeed precisely what he was describing. His empirical data were the native speaker's linguistic intuitions, for which his grammar was seeking an explanation. What this means, of course, is that his predictions can be quite easily tested: they will always be either obvious or wrong. He emphasized that, quite properly, the study of linguistic intuition *is* the study of language. But he underlined the importance of going *beyond* mere description to explanation. The goal of transformational-generative grammar theory is to gain insight into and understanding of the nature of the language user's intuitive linguistic judgments.

Chomsky pointed out that the study of linguistic intuition poses many problems, however. For example, a speaker's "knowledge" that a given sentence is or is not grammatical is most often a tacit knowledge, below the level of conscious awareness and not therefore immediately available to him. The task of the linguist, as Chomsky saw it, was to provide explanations and to present them in such a way that a language user's linguistic consciousness would be raised to the level of awareness. He was not suggesting, however, that such consciousness-raising would involve teaching the speaker anything new about language; the goal is to find ways of pointing out things that language users have "known" all along, of making them aware of their considerable linguistic intuition.

To illustrate the point that explanations are not always ones to which a competent speaker has ready access, Chomsky discussed the problem of ambiguity. At first impression the speaker-hearer may not, for a number of reasons, recognize a sentence as ambiguous. Or he or she may

---

*These arguments on intuition are taken from remarks made during a series of panel discussions at the *Third Texas Conference on Problems of Linguistic Analysis*, May 9–12, 1958. This was a meeting at which the structuralists Archibald Hill, Robert Stockwell, and Henry Lee Smith, as well as a number of other linguists were, to judge from their opening remarks, determined to discredit Noam Chomsky in public. Instead, Chomsky managed to gain the respect of all of them. In fact, it was his performance at this meeting which caused all but a tiny handful of die-hard structuralists to start seriously studying what Chomsky had had to say in *Syntactic Structures*. This was the great public triumph of transformational-generative grammar (early form).

realize that it can be interpreted in two ways but miss a third or fourth. Consider the following sentence, for example:*

I had a book stolen at the library.

At first glance, most speakers of English will probably recognize that the sentence is ambiguous. Yet, they will very likely not be aware that there are at least *five* ways it can be interpreted—and possibly more:

1. A book of mine was stolen while I was at the library.

2. A book of mine was stolen while it was at the library.

3. I arranged for someone to steal a book while it was at the library.

4. I had in my possession a book which had been previously stolen at the library.

5. I almost completed the stealing of a book at the library (but was caught).

Another interesting fact about language use on which linguists have focused in recent years is that the speaker's linguistic *performance* is different from and seldom fully reflects linguistic *competence*. The actual sentences native speakers utter can tell us very little about their language competence, for in the normal course of daily living it is inevitable that all kinds of distractions (noise, interruptions, emotional state, and so on) are bound to interfere with linguistic performance. In other words, there are limits to performance that have nothing to do with grammatical ability.

It was this realization that led Chomsky, from the beginning, to reject the structuralists' data-collecting approach to language study. By deliberately confining themselves to a description of actual spoken utterances, the structuralists limited themselves to the study of linguistic performance. This was to miss the really important and compelling goal, however, for what linguists should seek to describe and explain is intuitive language competence.

The research of Chomsky and other transformationalists into linguistic competence led them in turn to new inquiries. As soon as one reflects upon the actual "mish-mash" performance (of others) from which a child inevitably learns his language, it becomes all the more astonishing that language acquisition is possible at all. Transformational linguists, like language scholars from Plato to Descartes before them, came to marvel

---

*This example is similar to but not exactly the same as one given by Chomsky when he discusses ambiguity in *Aspects*, p. 21.

at the awesome fact that every normal child is *able* to acquire so undeniably complex an ability as language competence. Moreover, language is acquired so matter of factly and in such a short time by children everywhere (by the age of three or four) that the entire process, so long deceptively taken for granted as a "matter of course," is all the more remarkable.

The complex feat of language acquisition is made triply remarkable by the fact that, as researchers discovered from a number of careful investigations conducted at about this time, language learning has little or no direct relationship to a child's basic intelligence. It was conclusively demonstrated, for example, that a child must be *severely* retarded (with an IQ of less than 50) before language learning becomes an impossibility. Yet, no nonhuman species, not even the most intelligent of the anthropoid apes, has ever managed the task. The ability to learn a language is clearly one which is unique to the human species.

Structural linguists had long contended that language learning can be explained solely as a form of conditioned behavior. By the processes of observation, imitation, and cultural reinforcement, they argued, a child learns the sounds and the syntactical patterns of the language to which it is exposed. It is solely from powers of observation and induction that it is able to learn a language. Proof of their argument, the structuralists insisted, is the obvious fact that a child learns only that particular language to which it has been exposed.

Chomsky, on the other hand, although he was perfectly willing to admit the existence and importance of such environmental influence, contended that exposure alone is simply not enough to explain the remarkable feat of language acquisition. The most he was willing to grant was that the existence of a spoken language in the child's environment might be the necessary catalyst that serves to put the learning process in motion. The task would nevertheless be an impossible one without some kind of preconditions. For one thing, few if any children are subjected to a formal, deliberate language training program. Quite the contrary (and this is Chomsky's famous "input-output" argument), most of the language which a child hears (its primary data) is a random series of ill-formed sentences and semi sentences which are not only often of poor quality but which are necessarily finite and narrow in scope. Yet, despite the nature of the primary data, the child makes some sort of sense out of these data and manages to construct for itself a working grammar of the language in a very short time. And except in minor ways, the nature of the primary data does not determine the outcome. In fact, within any given language community, the results are strikingly uniform.

All of the evidence therefore led Chomsky to conclude that language acquisition cannot be attributed to some kind of inductive process, for the language user can go beyond the evidence supplied by the primary data. What all of this means is that the child itself must bring some additional component to the task, some specific, innate, concept-forming capacity, which enables it to sort out from the available information exactly what is needed and what should be discarded.

Descartes and his disciples, of course, had come to similar conclusions when they insisted that certain linguistic ideas or principles must be present in the human mind at birth. But Chomsky went a giant step further, for he argued that there exist in the mind innate structures which determine, in advance of its acquisition, certain of the specific forms of the acquired knowledge. In other words, a child must possess some kind of inherent linguistic theory that generally limits and specifies the possible form of any human language; it must have, at birth, a predetermined strategy for choosing which information, among the vast amounts of random data to which it is exposed, is important and which should be ignored.

Such conclusions led to a renewed interest in the existence of language universals. If a child who automatically acquires a language knows more than it has learned, and if this is true of all normal human children, regardless of the particular language learned, then certain linguistic universals must exist. It is the task of the linguist to discover, if possible, what these universals are.

A particularly interesting and informative explanation of Chomsky's views on the subject of linguistic universals is contained in a radio interview conducted by Stuart Hampshire.* In this interview, Chomsky defined a linguistic universal as a property or set of properties which are common to all natural languages and which therefore are necessarily present in the physiological properties of the human mind.

To illustrate the kind of thing he considers a language universal, Chomsky gave this example: suppose there is a language in which the system for transforming a simple, declarative sentence into a question is by the simple process of exactly reversing the order of the words. In such a language the statement "John is in the kitchen" would be made into a question simply by saying it backwards: "Kitchen the in is John." Such a system is, on the face of it, logical, easy, and efficient. Yet, this question transformation process is *never* used in a natural language. Instead, the question-making process for most languages is incredibly complex—a process that can be described as neither easy nor obviously logical.

The study of languages reveals, in fact, that certain operations never occur in natural languages, even though they are fairly simple operations in and of themselves. The operations which do occur, on the other hand, are often very complex.

*Reprinted in Mark Lester, *Readings in Applied Transformational Grammar.*

As further evidence that human language is far more than imitation, Chomsky pointed to the same facts about language that had intrigued Descartes and the other seventeenth-century rationalist philosophers: namely, its *creativity* and *appropriateness*. Humans can freely use language as both an *innovative* and *appropriate* vehicle of thought. Except for a few standard clichés, greetings, and the like, most sentences are novel ones which have never before been uttered and will in all probability never be uttered again; yet they are entirely appropriate to the situation and entirely understandable to anyone who hears them.* In other words, language users can say anything they want to say, which is what we mean when we say a child knows more than it has learned.

Thus, it becomes strikingly clear that language competence is an important phenomenon to investigate. Linguists must necessarily begin with a particular language, and furthermore, are probably best qualified to investigate their own native language. Eventually, however, as more and more languages are subjected to TG analysis, a larger pattern should emerge. Early hypotheses concerning universals, which necessarily will be based on single languages, may have to be discarded when they are tested against other particular languages. But sooner or later, Chomsky and his disciples are convinced, we are bound to gain more insight into language-learning theory and the workings of the human mind.

Thus Chomsky found himself drawn once more to the notions of the philosophical rationalists and the older traditional linguists. The ancient philosophical questions about human nature, questions which in recent decades scholars had lost sight of, always have been and still are, according to these linguists, the really important ones. Thus they argued for discarding the near-sighted, narrowly compartmentalized approach to scholarly disciplines embraced by the behaviorists in favor of a more general and far-reaching interdisciplinary approach. Psychologists, anthropologists, political scientists, philosophers, and linguists, all of whom are interested in cognitive processes, should stop walling themselves off from one another, for surely each of these disciplines has important contributions to make to the total picture. Inasmuch as language ability in particular is a uniquely human possession, linguistic study offers one of the brightest promises of leading to really important answers, and the linguist has an especially significant part to play.

---

*At this point, I cannot resist sharing a sentence which was spoken by my then three-year-old daughter only a few minutes after she had gone outside to play in her first snow—an event which had been enthusiastically described by her two older brothers as "something *super* that happens here in Connecticut in the winter."

"I don't like this 'winter'!" she exclaimed, as she came inside mittenless and crying. "It *hurts* when you put your hands on the floor of it!"

Once Noam Chomsky had succeeded in interesting many serious linguistic scholars in his ideas, there was a virtual explosion of research. In fact, from that time until the present day, there has been no let-up in the number and variety of suggested modifications, additions, and revisions of the original TG grammar model. Chomsky was reluctant to make major changes unless the argument for doing so was a valid syntactic one, but he came to admit that there were certain defects in the early model. In 1965 he published *Aspects of the Theory of Syntax*, referred to hereafter as *Aspects*, his first major revision of transformational-generative grammar theory. By writing this book, in which he incorporated those ideas which he had found the most compelling and valid, he lent his own considerable weight to them. The revised version came to be referred to in the literature as either the *Aspects* model or, more commonly, as *Standard Transformational Grammar Theory*.

Chomsky had four principal aims in writing *Aspects*:

1. to clear up misunderstandings and to answer questions that had been raised about TG theory, especially those raised by the structuralists;

2. to point out the weaknesses and defects in the early model, along with the arguments and evidence that had convinced him of the validity of some criticisms;

3. to suggest revisions and modifications which would remedy these defects;

4. to call attention to unresolved problems still in need of investigation.

We have already discussed the first of these. Let us now survey some of the developments which led to the eventual revision of the early TG model.

Among those things which made some linguists unhappy with the early form of transformational grammar was its failure to deal satisfactorily with the problem of meaning and meaning relationships. Many linguists came to feel that meaning is basic to language competence, and that therefore the grammar theory ought somehow to incorporate semantic considerations in the phrase-structure part of the grammar.

Chomsky had argued in *Syntactic Structures* that a grammar is best formulated as a self-contained syntactic theory, without reference to and independent from considerations of semantics. This was not to deny the importance of meaning in language. He simply believed at that time, possibly as a holdover from his training in structural linguistics, that once one discovers the syntactic structure of a language, that knowledge can be put to use in discovering the meaning function of the language.

Robert Lees, writing in 1960, argued that the negative statement should be regarded as the derivation of a kernel string rather than as a transformation. And at about the same time, Edward Klima presented a similar formal argument regarding the interrogative sentence. Both of these sentence types, you will remember, had been included among the single-base optional transformations in the early TG model. But these linguists now contended that, since there is no known language in which the question and the negative statement fail to exist—and even more important, since there is a fundamental meaning difference between the simple declarative statement on the one hand and either a question or a negation on the other—these linguistic facts should be reflected in the basic rules (i.e., the phrase-structure) of the grammar. Their suggestion was to include a "phrase marker" constituent in the terminal string. The presence of a particular phrase marker (NEG, Q) would then signal or trigger the application of the appropriate obligatory transformation. In effect, what they were arguing was that *all optional transformations should be meaning-preserving.*

To understand this reasoning, consider the following five sentences:

1. John always eats lunch.

2. John does not ever eat lunch.

3. John never eats lunch.

4. John always eats no lunch.

5. John does not always eat lunch.

In the early form of TG grammar, all five of these sentences would be analyzed as derivations from the same underlying kernel string, *John + eat + lunch*. The intuition of the English speaker, however, is that there are at least three separate meanings or interpretations of these five sentences. Sentence 1 is a positive statement that John eats lunch at all times. Sentences 2, 3, and 4 are all negative statements that mean roughly the same thing. (And, incidentally, these three sentences come closer to stating the exact negative of Sentence 1 than does Sentence 5, which according to the early optional T^{neg} rule is its negative transformation.) Sentence 5 means that John sometimes eats lunch and sometimes doesn't. It is this kind of problem which caused some transformational linguists to feel that a modification of the early rules was needed.*

*The words "always" and "never," which are what cause the difficulty here, are viewed as members of a class of "preverbs." The problem with these sentences is over the "domain" of the negative.

Chomsky was skeptical at first. But then Jerrold Katz and Paul Postal, in *An Integrated Theory of Linguistic Descriptions* (1964), worked out the outlines of a transformational semantic theory which demonstrated the feasibility of assigning semantic features to particular lexical items, and which also demonstrated that the syntactic structure of a sentence is often influenced by the semantic features associated with a particular lexical choice. They speculated that the device of assigning features might make it possible to simply get rid of the notion of optional generalized transformations altogether, and to account for the generation of compound and complex sentences directly from the PS rules, instead.

Chomsky had accepted the notion that all transformations should be meaning-preserving, but it was not until Katz and Postal's system of assigning distinctive features to lexical items made it possible to build feature characteristics into the base of the grammar that he saw a good way to revise the early model. Now he conceived a revised model with a base component called, for the first time, the *deep structure*. The base component would include syntactical rules, semantic and phonological information represented by feature matrixes of lexical items, and phrase markers (NEG, Q, PAS). All sentences would then be generated directly from the deep structure, or base, by means of various transformation operations, to become actual sentences or *surface structures*.

One can understand the reluctance of Chomsky and the other TG linguists to adopt such a major revision of the theory. The decision to account for meaning in the deep structure would lead to many new problems, a situation which seems to be the story of modern linguistics. Among other things, it would become necessary to devise as simple a means as possible for indicating the feature characteristics of each lexical item. It also meant that the term *transformation* would now have a radically different meaning. No longer optional processes, most transformations would now be obligatory operations by which the abstract information in the deep structure phrase markers would be converted to surface structure sentence form.* Despite these obstacles, however, the idea of making this kind of revision was appealing, for what it would mean is that all the abstract material contained in the deep structure (the base) of the grammar would represent linguistic universals. Only the transformation operations would give instructions for the idiosyncratic forms of particular languages. (Specific lexical items would be language particulars, but their semantic features would be linguistic universals.)

---

*Word order T rules, such as particle shifts, and certain reductions, like the wh reduction, continued to be called optional. Such transformations are "stylistic" ones.

Another advantage of the revised model is that the linguistic property of recursiveness (the ability to repeatedly embed one sentence into another), which the *Syntactic Structures* model had for the most part assigned to the transformation rules, would now be completely accounted for in the base. This would mean, for example, that whenever the constituent NP appears in a deep structure derivation, we would have the option of embedding an S (sentence) after it.

The most serious problem encountered in reformulating the grammar model was that of deciding how to include both semantic and syntactic information in the deep structure rules. Chomsky's solution (in *Aspects*) was to continue to consider the syntax rules primary. Semantic rules would then be merely interpretive. (The same relationship would exist between the post transformational surface structure and the phonological rules.) The difficulty with keeping the two components separate in this way, however, is that linguists cannot agree, even today, on where the line between semantics and syntax should be drawn. Clearly both syntactic features and semantic features are important, but in some cases it isn't clear whether a feature is a syntactic one, a semantic one, or both. Consider, for example, the feature male-female, probably a linguistic universal. There is no question that the concept +*male* or −*male* has semantic meaning. Yet in some cases, such as choice of pronoun, the feature has syntactic significance as well. (We would not say *John hurt herself*.) Or consider the words *who* and *which*: *who* has the semantic feature [+*animate*]; *which* has the feature, [−*animate*]. Yet one of these words (*who*) has the syntactic feature of "case," as well. Various solutions to this problem have been proposed, but a great many linguists are far from satisfied that the issue is settled. In fact, this is one of the "residual problems" Chomsky discussed in the last chapter of *Aspects*.

Other Unresolved Problems

Semantic theory is still in its infancy, and many problems remain unsettled. In *Aspects* Chomsky expressed the belief that in all probability these questions will remain unanswered for some time. It isn't clear, for example, how a grammar can account for the kind of semantic considerations that are beyond the scope of the lexicon; nor is it clear whether certain semantic considerations are universal or are, rather, particular language idiosyncrasies. As an example of the kind of problem he was referring to, Chomsky gave some examples of sentences using the verb *have* + *a*: We can say

The man has an arm.

The ant has a kidney.

but we cannot say

The arm has a man.

The kidney has an ant.

The reason these last two sentences are unacceptable (in English, at least) has nothing to do with their grammatical syntax. Rather, we have here a problem of broad meaning relationships, a problem having to do with more general "field properties" than with semantic features. If this particular use of "have a" can be shown to be a linguistic universal, then linguists must find a way to include field-property information in the base of the grammar. If, on the other hand, it turns out that the problem is merely a particular language peculiarity, it must be provided for in the transformational rules. At the moment, however, no one has discovered how to include such generalized information in the grammar rules in either case.* And there are many other mysteries of semantic and syntactic structures of natural languages that remain unsolved.

Another unresolved problem is that of deciding how to explain the derivational process. For a series like *destroy, destruction, destructive, destructible, destroying, destructionist, destructively*, how should these words be entered in the lexicon? Should each word be entered separately along with its list of features? Or can we determine that one among the series is a more basic word than the others? If so, then only that word might be a lexical entry. A third possibility might be to enter only the base morpheme *struct*, but if the lexicon undertakes to list all roots, prefixes, suffixes, and the like, it would surely become unwieldy.

A further problem is that of idioms. Chances are that most if not all idiomatic expressions are characteristics of particular languages. If that should be so, do we have lexical entries for them? We certainly need to include information about their meaning, but if they are not linguistic universals, many transformationalists would be reluctant to put such information in the base component of the grammar.

In summary, then, a good many thorny problems were solved by the decision to revise the early model; many difficulties remain unresolved and possibly unresolvable.

*Of course many semantic markers do provide just this sort of information.

31

Standard TG Grammar Theory: *Aspects* Model

OVERVIEW OF THE SYSTEM

In *Syntactic Structures* and in other early work with TG grammar theory, Chomsky, like the structuralists, still viewed language study as an independent and autonomous discipline. However, by the time he wrote *Aspects of the Theory of Syntax* some ten years later, he had come to regard linguistics as a branch of cognitive psychology. To be sure, he still thought a grammar theory should contain a syntax as the principal mediating component, but he was no longer willing to ignore the influence of semantics. This, as you will see, was an important and far-reaching change.

Before we examine the revised TG model,* it needs, I think, to be emphasized that a transformational-generative grammar model is *not* to be viewed as the actual process speakers go through to produce the sentences of their language. In the early years this view was a commonly— and mistakenly—held one, possibly because of Chomsky's use of the word "generative." Actually, the term is one borrowed from mathematics and refers not at all to the actual production of a result—of sentences, in the case of a grammar model. In mathematics, a generative model is one which, taken together with a general theory about mathematics, tries to define explicitly and precisely a particular set of mathematical relations using a process model of description. A transfor-

---

*The grammar model presented here is basically the same one that was given in *Aspects*. However, several points which were shortly to supplement the *Aspects* theory have been added.

mational-generative grammar, then, is a theory which attempts to explain what speakers *have in their heads*, not what they do.

The *Aspects* TG grammar model has three major components: a *syntax*, a *semantics*, and a *phonology*. Of these three, the syntax is central. It contains a base component and a transformational component. The base component contains a finite set of phrase-structure rules (both branching rules and subcategorization rules), a lexicon or dictionary (also finite), and some preliminary context-free lexical insertion rules (L rules). The transformational component contains context-sensitive transformational rules of three types: lexical insertion rules, general transformation rules (these are the familiar optional T rules of the *Syntactic Structures* grammar), and two kinds of local transformation rules: affix-incorporation and segment structure T rules. The rules of the base component are said to be context-free, which means that each one of them applies "in ignorance" of any other rules. The transformation rules, on the other hand, are by their very nature context-sensitive: they apply only in certain restricted environments.

The semantic component and the phonological component of the *Aspects* grammar are said to be interpretive. The semantic component operates on the deep structure level; it determines a semantic interpretation of a sentence generated by the rules of the syntactic component. (For example, the semantic component must be consulted for information concerning the inherent semantic features of words: whether a noun, for instance, is common or proper, abstract or concrete, animate or inanimate, and so on—all of which information has syntactic consequences.) In other words, the semantic component takes as "input" the information generated by the base rules of the grammar and assigns a semantic or "meaning" interpretation to the string.

The function of the phonological component is also interpretive. It provides information concerning the pronunciation of constituents. That is, once all transformations have been performed, the phonological component of the grammar finishes the job of converting a deep structure to a surface structure (an actual spoken sentence) by assigning pronunciation features to it.

Although this general explanation is somewhat complicated and difficult to follow, it is important for you to have a preview of what the completed grammar model will look like before we proceed to study the *Aspects* grammar theory in more detail. On the pages immediately following, you will find both an outline and a diagram of the overall grammar.

THE TOTAL GRAMMAR SYSTEM

I. SYNTACTIC COMPONENT

The Base (Context-Free)

A. Phrase-Structure Rules

1. Branching Rules

2. Subcategorization Rules

a. Strict Subcategorization Rules

b. Selectional Rules

B. The Lexicon and Preliminary Lexical Insertion Rules

C. Transformation Rules (Context-Sensitive)

1. Final Lexical Insertion T Rules

2. General T Rules

3. Local T Rules

a. Segment Transformations

b. Other Local Transformations

II. SEMANTIC COMPONENT

Operates on the base component. Influences subcategorization rules and lexicon, and assigns a semantic interpretation to the deep structure generated by the PS rules.

III. PHONOLOGICAL COMPONENT

Contributes phonological feature matrix information to the lexicon. After application of all T rules, provides a phonological interpretation for the surface structure.

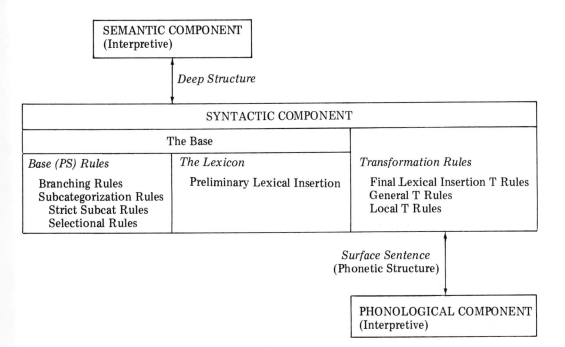

32

Aspects Model:
The Base Component, I

Phrase-Structure Rules

BRANCHING RULES

The generation of a sentence begins with the rewriting or branching rules. You are already familiar with this kind of rule, because we used branching rules in the earlier TG model. A few significant changes have been made in the branching rules of the *Aspects* grammar, however.

One important change is that of including transformation-signaling abstract ("dummy") phrase markers in the PS rules of the grammar. In the first model (*Syntactic Structures* form), a distinction was made between kernel sentences and transformed sentences. For this reason, every constituent in a terminal string of the phrase-structure part of the grammar eventually became realized as a *formative* (a word or word segment) in the actual surface sentence. For reasons discussed above, the rewriting rules of the revised grammar contain, in addition to formative constituents, abstract phrase markers (Q, NEG, PAS, and so on) which will not be realized as actual words or word parts. These phrase markers, which appear only in the deep structure, provide semantic information to the semantic component and trigger a particular transformation process at some point in the generation of a sentence.

In addition to the old "single-base" optional transformations, now signaled by abstract markers, the revised phrase-structure rules have also moved the explanation of the "multiple-base" transformations to the base component of the grammar. Thus, whereas in the early model the universal language property of indefinite recursiveness was wholly accounted for by the optional double-base transformation rules, this property can now be explained by the branching rules of the base component. In other words, the PS rules now provide for the possibility of embedding one sentence within another sentence and the possibility of combining two or more sentences with a conjunction T rule. Furthermore, either one of these operations may occur repeatedly.

These are major changes. What they do is to move *all* transformation *signals* to the PS rules of the base of the grammar, with the result that the base rules are now capable of explaining a much deeper level of abstraction than was permitted by the earlier PS rules. Moreover—and this is the real justification for the change—the base rules are now able to reflect at least two properties of language which transformational linguists recognize as linguistic universals. One of these properties is recursiveness: the possibility, in any natural language, of generating infinitely long sentences. The other is the fact that all known natural languages make use of transformations; or to put it another way, every sentence in every known natural language *is* a transformation. These rule changes mean that we will no longer speak of "optional" transformations—at least not in the same sense as we used that term in the early TG model.* If a given phrase marker occurs in the deep structure, the transformation operation it calls for will be obligatory.

The very abbreviated deep structure tree diagrams on pages 332–334 illustrate some of these rule changes.

Figures T1, T2, and T3 are tree structures which illustrate the revised rewriting rule for Sentence:

$$S \longrightarrow (SM)\ NP\ VP$$

$$SM \longrightarrow (NEG),\ (Q),\ (PAS)$$

The first of these rules says that preceding an entire string there may occur one or more abstract phrase markers or sentence modifiers (SM). The second rule explains that a sentence modifier may be one or more abstract "dummy" symbols like NEG (negative), Q (question), PAS (passive). All such abstract phrase markers will continue to appear in the phrase marker tree until we reach the stage in the sentence generation process for the application of the general T rules. (This procedure will not take place until after all PS rules have been run through and lexical insertion transformations have taken place.)

This revised derivational concept has two advantages: (1) it permits us to see that two sentences like "Janice may like this book" and "Janice may not like this book" are different in meaning at the deep structure

---

*In the *Aspects* grammar, the only transformations which are a matter of choice are word order or "stylistic" ones.

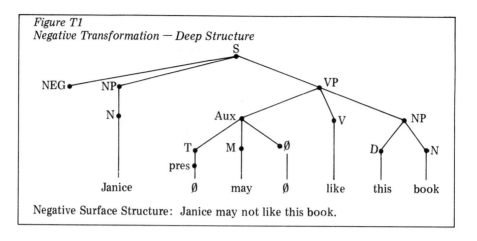

Figure T1
Negative Transformation — Deep Structure

Negative Surface Structure: Janice may not like this book.

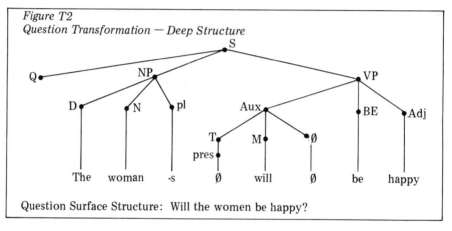

Figure T2
Question Transformation — Deep Structure

Question Surface Structure: Will the women be happy?

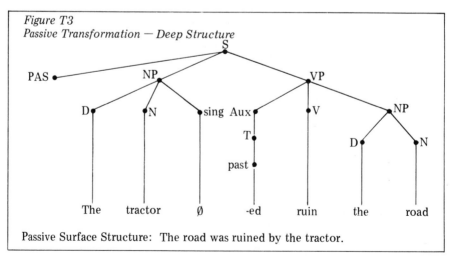

Figure T3
Passive Transformation — Deep Structure

Passive Surface Structure: The road was ruined by the tractor.

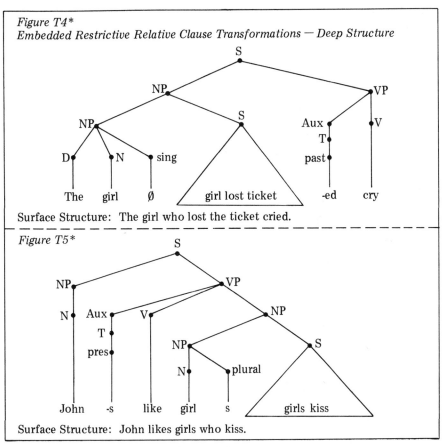

Figure T4*
Embedded Restrictive Relative Clause Transformations — Deep Structure

Surface Structure: The girl who lost the ticket cried.

Figure T5*

Surface Structure: John likes girls who kiss.

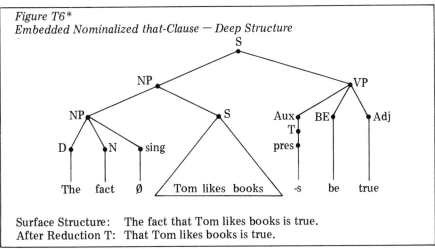

Figure T6*
Embedded Nominalized that-Clause — Deep Structure

Surface Structure: The fact that Tom likes books is true.
After Reduction T: That Tom likes books is true.

*The triangle represents an approximated structure which, itself, can be fully specified in a tree diagram.

333

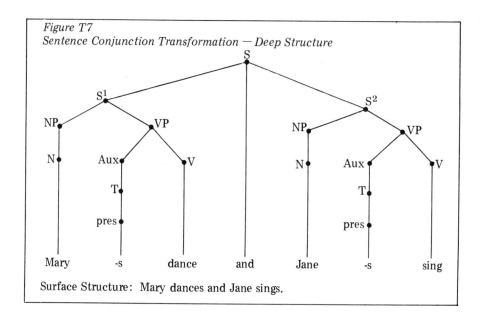

Figure T7
Sentence Conjunction Transformation — Deep Structure

Surface Structure: Mary dances and Jane sings.

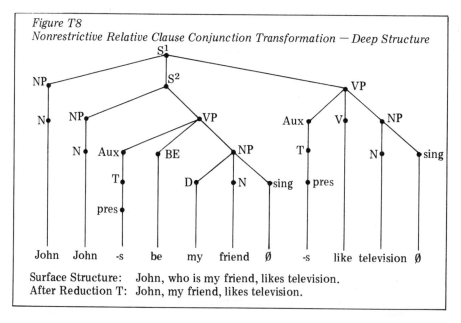

Figure T8
Nonrestrictive Relative Clause Conjunction Transformation — Deep Structure

Surface Structure: John, who is my friend, likes television.
After Reduction T: John, my friend, likes television.

semantic level; (2) it also provides an explanation for the speaker's intuition that the sentences are otherwise syntactically identical.

The tree structures in Figures T4, T5, and T6 illustrate sentence embedding, one of the two sentence combining processes. In each of the three diagrams there are two underlying deep structure sentences, one of which will become embedded, the other of which will dominate by the time the structure surfaces. Notice that these phrase marker trees offer a satisfying explanation for the surface structure fact that one string (the main clause) is felt to be more important than the other (the subordinate clause). In all such derivations, only the main clause will have immediately branched off from the original S node. All embedded sentences, on the other hand, are shown to be immediately dominated by an NP node; i.e., their embedding takes place later in the derivation.

The last two tree diagrams (Figures T7 and T8) illustrate the second sentence-combining process, conjunction. Figure T7 shows the deep structure sources for two equally dominant surface structure main clauses. Notice that each of them branches off from the original S node simultaneously, and thus each clause has a separate but equal existence of its own from its initial inception. Moreover, neither sentence is immediately dominated by an NP node (as in the case of an embedded sentence) but rather by an S node.

Figure T8 illustrates a sentence which will surface with an embedded nonrestrictive relative clause. This kind of sentence, most linguists thought, had simply not been adequately explained by the old rewriting rules, for these early rules had treated restrictive and nonrestricted relative clauses as if they are alike. Yet, although they *are* somewhat alike, the English speaker also knows that there is an important difference both in the meaning and in the pronunciation of the two sentences:

1. The girl who is wearing the red dress was late.
2. Joyce, who is wearing the red dress, was late.

The relative clause in Sentence 1 is felt by the speaker to be a vital and intimate part of the dominant subject noun phrase.* It is essential to have this relative clause modifier if we are to understand which girl the sentence is talking about, and grammarians have recognized this fact by labeling such a relative clause "restrictive." In Sentence 2, on the other hand, the relative clause is not essential. It is not necessary to restrict the subject noun with a modifier which further identifies it, for the proper name *Joyce* is specific identification enough (the assumption being, of course, that there is not more than one Joyce in the context in which

*Sentence 1 is restrictive *only* if *girl* has been previously unidentified in an earlier context.

the sentence is spoken). In other words, the clause "who is wearing the red dress" is not felt to be an intimate part of the dominant sentence. Rather, it is more like a parenthetical element—a kind of "aside" which *adds* a bit of extra information.

Rather than treat the nonrestrictive relative clause as an embedded part of the subject NP, (as makes sense for the essential restrictive modifier), it is explained as a sort of compromised embedded sentence with a separate existence in its own right. It is as if the meaning of Sentence 2 is a reduced version of

> Joyce—and Joyce is wearing the red dress—was late.
>
> or
>
> Joyce (Joyce is wearing the red dress) was late.

Thus the tree diagram shows the nonrestrictive relative clause as branching off immediately from the main S node (as a conjoined sentence does) but *from the same S node* and *at the same time* as its fellow triplet constituents, *NP* and *VP*, do.

SUBCATEGORIZATION PS RULES

When all of the branching PS rules are exhausted, they will yield phrase marker tree structures like these:

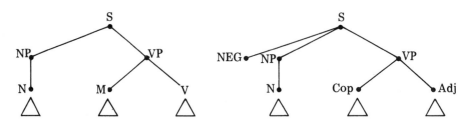

The notation which looks like a triangle represents a constituent which must be replaced with a lexical formative (a word or word segment). We cannot make these lexical insertions at random, however. We must, obviously, replace a noun node with a word that the dictionary says is a noun, a verb node with a verb, and so on. But beyond that, there are grammatical and semantic restrictions concerning what kind of a noun or verb or adjective is required. We must therefore add further specifications to the nodes which are marked with these symbols.

STRICT SUBCATEGORIGATION RULES. Consider the following sets of sequences:

Set A
go should the not he and work
by however book this sad is of

he will lie the book on the table
Set B   the girl seemed the pencil
they hit a sad

John frightened the house
Set C   the milk that he ate admired them
the little boy is pregnant

All of these strings are ungrammatical, for they all violate basic phrase-structure rules. But they are ungrammatical for different reasons. The strings in Set A, native speakers of English would no doubt agree, are the worst of the lot. The explanation for their complete unacceptability is that they violate the most basic of the PS rules: the branching rules. Except for the accident of recognizable English words, these sequences cannot even be called "English." The strings in Set B are better; at least we recognize something of English syntax in them. Yet, we are jolted by the choice of *pencil* after the words "the girl seemed"; by the choice of the verb *lie* (which is an intransitive verb) where a transitive verb is required; by the word *sad* in a position that should be occupied by a noun. These sequences violate the *strict subcategorization PS rules*, which tell us that certain verbs require complements of specific "part-of-speech" categories. Thus, a noun phrase must follow a transitive verb, an adjective must follow a verb like *seem*, and so on.

The early TG grammar model made an effort to handle strict subcategorization problems of this sort by identifying transitive, intransitive, and linking verb types in the branching rules. And indeed, those rules would prevent such mishaps as are illustrated in the strings of Set B. In the revised grammar, it was decided to take syntactic instructions of this type out of the branching rules, however, and to specify verb type instead with a feature-specifying notation. This change makes for more accurate specifications, for it has the added advantage of specifically identifying the particular syntactic (contextual) feature characteristics of each individual lexical verb. The word *seem*, for example, would be identified as a word in the verb category $[+V]$, but in addition we can add the notation that *seem* must be followed by an adjective : $[+\underline{\quad\quad} \text{Adj}]$. A bracketed notation of this kind is called a feature notation. And as you will see when we discuss the ungrammatical sequences of Set C, the grammar model will be a much better and more accurate one if we adopt this new method of listing the distinctive features for all the lexical words of the language. Here, then, are some examples of verbs with their contextual features specified (the blank space represents the place where the item possessing the feature must stand):

eat $[+ \text{V}, +\underline{\quad}\text{NP}]$ (*eat* is a verb; *eat* must be followed by an NP)

walk $[+ \text{V}, +\underline{\quad}\#]$ (*walk* is a verb; *walk* requires no complement)

believe$\left[+ \text{V}, \left\{ \begin{matrix} +\underline{\quad}\text{NP} \\ +\underline{\quad}\text{that-S} \end{matrix} \right\} \right]$ (*believe* is a verb; *believe* must be followed by either an NP or a that-sentence)

Incidentally, by noting contextual verb features in this new way, we are able to simplify the branching rules. It is no longer necessary to rewrite *Verb* and v_t, v_i, or v_l.

SELECTIONAL RULES. The strings in Set C, above, are ungrammatical for a third reason, having to do in this case with semantic impropriety. They violate a second kind of subcategorization PS rule: a rule of lexical *selection* within a given category. One does not *frighten* an inanimate object like a *house*; one does not *eat* milk, one *drinks* it; only a *person* (or perhaps an animal) can *admire* something, but an inanimate object, a situation, an idea cannot; only a *woman*, not a little *boy* (nor even a little girl) can be *pregnant*. We therefore need yet another set of PS rules, selectional rules that will specify the semantic relationship required by certain words of other words in a string. Such relationships, incidentally, may involve words other than the one immediately preceding or immediately following a given lexical item. The predicate adjective *pregnant*, for instance, requires that the noun it modifies be an adult woman.

In order to write selectional PS rules, it will be necessary to consult the lexicon or dictionary of the grammar. Then, armed with the required information about a word's meaning, we can specify its selectional features. It is at this point in the development of a grammar theory which will include feature specifications that the linguist runs into a difficulty, however. It is not always easy to distinguish between those features which are syntactic ones and those which are semantic. Consider, for example, the italicized word in each of the following sentences:

1. Joan is *pregnant*.

2. When Joan arrived, the host gave *her* a drink.

For the first sentence, it is fairly easy to separate the features of *pregnant* that have syntactic grammatical consequences: the string's context calls for an adjective in the post-copula slot;* its semantic content specifies that the adjective must modify a noun with the features [+female] and [+adult]. The line between syntax and semantics is more difficult for the word *her* in Sentence 2, however. The rules of syntax call for a third person pronoun. The personal pronoun must, however, be one with the

---

*A copula is a verb which identifies its predicate with its subject. Semantically speaking, the copula is a "state of being" verb like *be*, *feel*, *seem*, and so on.

inherent semantic feature: [+female]. Third, and now we're back to a syntactical consideration, the pronoun must take the object form [+accusative].

In order to simplify matters, the syntactic and semantic features of words are listed in a single bracketed group arrangement called a *feature matrix*. A complete list of lexical formatives, along with a feature matrix for each, would then be compiled into a lexicon, which must be consulted at the time that we begin to replace dummy symbols with lexical items.

Before we talk about the rules for lexical insertion, therefore, we must discuss the second important base component: the lexicon.

The Lexicon

The base of the grammar consists so far of (1) *branching rules*, context-free rules which act "blindly" to produce any one of a number of strings terminating in category nodes; (2) two types of *subcategorization rules*: *strict subcategory rules*, which define the syntactic requirements to be met by each constituent in a given string; and *selectional rules*, which define the semantic requirements which are required of these constituents. Up to this point, the phrase-structure rules have been able to operate "blindly." They are defined, therefore, as context-free rules.

FEATURE MATRIXES

Before we can continue with a derivation by inserting actual lexical items in place of the dummy symbols, it will be necessary to have a list of lexical words, a definition for each word, and a notation of all the semantic features that are inherent in the word's basic meaning. And as long as we must compile such a list of words, we may as well also consult the phonological component of the grammar in order to record information relating to the pronunciation of the word.

The lexicon, therefore, is a kind of dictionary which lists, by category, all of the lexical words of a particular language. Each word will be accompanied by a "dictionary definition" plus two feature matrixes. One feature matrix will list phonological (pronunciation) features; the second feature matrix will list the semantic and syntactic features inherent in the basic meaning of a word.

Not all such features have been worked out, but the pioneer effort of Katz and Postal ultimately made it feasible to include at least some feature specifications of this sort in the grammar theory.

The distinctive *noun* features now thought to be universally linguistically significant include at least the following semantic properties:

PAIRS OF SEMANTIC FEATURES	SYSTEM OF NOTATION	
Common or Proper (*boy, John*)	[+Common]	[−Common]
Concrete or Abstract (*book, idea*)	[+Concrete]	[−Concrete]
Count or Mass (*book, dirt*)	[+Count]	[−Count]
Animate or Inanimate (*plant, book*)	[+Animate]	[−Animate]
Human or Nonhuman (*man, dog*)	[+Human]	[−Human]
Adult or Nonadult (*man, child*)	[+Adult]	[−Adult]
Masculine or Feminine (*boy, girl*)	[+Masc]	[−Masc]

In addition, a noun may have special inherent features: *water* [+Fluid], *knife* [+Artifact], or *finger* [+Proper Part].

Some of these semantic features are "cross classifications," but others are hierarchically ordered. If, for instance, we were to list the semantic features for the word *man*, we could omit [+Animate] since [+Human] implies animateness.

The typical feature matrix for an *adjective* would include, in addition to the general category feature [+Adj], any other inherent semantic or syntactic distinctive features which a particular lexical adjective automatically imposes on other related words in a string. Thus, the adjective *pregnant* would have to be accompanied by the feature notations [+Animate], [+Adult], [−Masc].

An *adverb* must have a feature matrix specifying such things as [+Manner], [+Time], [+Place], [+Direction], [+Condition], and so on.

A *pronoun*, in addition to the general category specification [+Noun], [+Pro], must specify whether the word is a personal pronoun [+Person], a relative pronoun [+Rel], or a demonstrative pronoun [+Dem].

A personal pronoun must be further characterized as first, second, or third person: [+I], [+II], [+III], respectively; as singular or plural: [±Plural]; and as being in the nominative [+Nom], accusative (objective) [+Accus], or possessive [+Poss] case.

A relative pronoun (*who, which, that*) must include the feature [+Animate] for *who*, [−Animate] for *which*, and nothing for *that*, which can be assumed, in the absence of a specific feature restriction, to be acceptable in either situation. The relative *who*, however, must also carry the specification for case: [+Nom], [+Accus], or [+Poss]. And the relative *which* must carry, in addition to [−Animate], the further feature specification [−Human]. (We can say "the dogs which ate their dinner," but we cannot say "the men which ate their dinner.")

A demonstrative pronoun (*this, these; that, those*) must have not only the feature specification [+Pro], but also [±Plural] and [±Near].

A determiner must have the feature [±Common] (proper nouns are not preceded by a determiner), and if [+Common] the additional specification [±Def] (a common noun can be either definite: *the boy*, or indefinite: *a boy, an apple*). If it is [+Def], then it must be further specified as [±Dem]; and if [+Dem], it must be characterized as [±Plural] and [±Near].

The lexicon, therefore, is similar to but infinitely more detailed than a large dictionary. A complete lexicon of a language will include as many entries as there are words in the language. But beyond that, it will also include as many separate entries as there are different meanings for any one particular word. Here, then, is the one level of the grammar where all three of its major components meet.

It is obvious that the compilation of a reasonably complete lexicon is a massive undertaking. Yet, it is precisely this vast amount and variety of linguistic information that every speaker carries in his head. Chomsky and other transformationalists saw no other explanation of this extraordinary human ability than that every human being already knows the structures of language at birth. Our linguistic capacity must be attributable to more than the biological "predisposition" to learn a language. Information which predetermines and restricts the possible syntax, meanings, and sounds of any language is already "there" in the brain of the newborn baby.*

On the following pages are some sample feature matrixes such as might appear in an English lexicon, and following the feature matrixes you will find a set of PS Rules as they were revised for the *Aspects* grammar model.

LEXICON†

Nouns

Chicago	doctor	dog	Jane	man
+N	+N	+N	+N	+N
−Common	+Common	+Common	−Common	+Common
+Concrete	+Concrete	+Concrete	+Concrete	+Concrete
−Count	+Count	+Count	+Count	+Count
−Animate	+Human	+Animate	+Human	+Human
−Plural	+Adult	−Human	−Masc	+Adult
				+Masc

*Admittedly, some things, such as the particular vocabulary of a given language, must be learned.

†These entries include only semantic-syntactic feature matrixes and are therefore incomplete. Phonological feature matrixes are omitted because of space limitations. The reader should nevertheless be aware that phonology has progressed to the stage where phonological feature matrixes are, in fact, more detailed and accurate than the semantic-syntactic matrixes here included. A short definition would also be included in a complete lexical entry.

milk

$$\begin{bmatrix} +\text{N} \\ +\text{Common} \\ +\text{Concrete} \\ -\text{Count} \\ -\text{Animate} \\ +\text{Fluid} \\ -\text{Plural} \end{bmatrix}$$

slacks

$$\begin{bmatrix} +\text{N} \\ +\text{Common} \\ +\text{Concrete} \\ +\text{Count} \\ -\text{Animate} \\ +\text{Plural} \end{bmatrix}$$

Verbs

admire

$$\begin{bmatrix} +\text{V} \\ +\underline{\quad}\text{NP} \\ +[+\text{Human}] \end{bmatrix}$$

defy

$$\begin{bmatrix} +\text{V} \\ +\underline{\quad}\text{NP} \\ +[+\text{Animate}]\underline{\quad} \\ -\text{Obj Del} \end{bmatrix}$$

expect

$$\begin{bmatrix} +\text{V} \\ +\underline{\quad}[\text{that-S}] \end{bmatrix}$$

frighten

$$\begin{bmatrix} +\text{V} \\ +\underline{\quad}\text{NP} \\ +\underline{\quad}[+\text{Animate}] \\ -\text{Obj Del} \end{bmatrix}$$

Modals

may

$$\begin{bmatrix} +\text{M} \\ +\underline{\quad}\ldots\varnothing \end{bmatrix}$$

will

$$\begin{bmatrix} +\text{M} \\ +\underline{\quad}\ldots\varnothing \end{bmatrix}$$

would

$$\begin{bmatrix} +\text{M} \\ +\underline{\quad}\ldots\varnothing \end{bmatrix}$$

Adjectives

honest

$$\begin{bmatrix} +\text{Adj} \\ [+\text{Human}]\underline{\quad} \end{bmatrix}$$

pregnant

$$\begin{bmatrix} +\text{Adj} \\ [-\text{Masc}]\underline{\quad} \end{bmatrix}$$

Pronouns

he

$$\begin{bmatrix} +\text{N} \\ +\text{Pro} \\ +\text{III} \\ +\text{Masc} \\ -\text{Plural} \\ -\text{Accusative} \end{bmatrix}$$

I

$$\begin{bmatrix} +\text{N} \\ +\text{Pro} \\ +\text{I} \\ -\text{Plural} \\ -\text{Accusative} \end{bmatrix}$$

it

$$\begin{bmatrix} +\text{N} \\ +\text{Pro} \\ +\text{III} \\ -\text{Masc} \\ -\text{Fem} \\ -\text{Plural} \end{bmatrix}$$

we

$$\begin{bmatrix} +\text{N} \\ +\text{Pro} \\ +\text{I} \\ +\text{Plural} \\ -\text{Accusative} \end{bmatrix}$$

Determiners

an

$$
\begin{bmatrix}
+\text{Det} \\
-\text{Pro} \\
-\text{Def} \\
-\text{Plural} \\
+\underline{\quad}[+\text{Common}] \\
+\underline{\quad}[+\text{Vowel}]
\end{bmatrix}
$$

the

$$
\begin{bmatrix}
+\text{Det} \\
-\text{Pro} \\
+\text{Def} \\
-\text{Dem} \\
\pm\text{Plural} \\
+\underline{\quad}[+\text{Common}]
\end{bmatrix}
$$

that

$$
\begin{bmatrix}
+\text{Det} \\
-\text{Pro} \\
+\text{Def} \\
+\text{Dem} \\
-\text{Plural} \\
-\text{Near} \\
+\underline{\quad}[+\text{Common}]
\end{bmatrix}
$$

those

$$
\begin{bmatrix}
+\text{Det} \\
-\text{Pro} \\
+\text{Def} \\
+\text{Dem} \\
+\text{Plural} \\
-\text{Near} \\
+\underline{\quad}[+\text{Common}]
\end{bmatrix}
$$

ASPECTS PHRASE STRUCTURE RULES

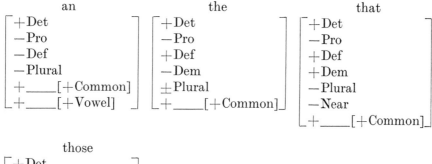

$$
S \longrightarrow
\begin{Bmatrix}
(SM)\ NP + VP \\
NP + (SM)\ S + VP \\
(SM)\ S_1 + and + (SM)\ S_2
\end{Bmatrix}
$$

$$
SM \longrightarrow (NEG)\ (Q)\ (PAS) \ldots
$$

$$
NP \longrightarrow
\begin{Bmatrix}
N \\
NP_1 + and + NP_2 \\
NP + S
\end{Bmatrix}
$$

$$
VP \longrightarrow
\begin{Bmatrix}
\begin{Bmatrix} Cop + Pred \\ V\ (NP)\ (NP) \end{Bmatrix} \\
VP_1 + and + VP_2
\end{Bmatrix}
$$

$$
Aux \longrightarrow T\ (M)\ (Perfect)\ (Progressive)
$$

$$
Pred \longrightarrow
\begin{Bmatrix}
NP \\
Adj \\
Place
\end{Bmatrix}
$$

$$
T \longrightarrow
\begin{Bmatrix}
Past \\
Present
\end{Bmatrix}
$$

$$\text{Lex} \longrightarrow \Delta$$

$$\text{N} \longrightarrow \Delta$$

$$\text{V} \longrightarrow \Delta$$

$$\text{Cop} \longrightarrow \Delta$$

$$\text{Place} \longrightarrow \Delta$$

$$\text{M} \longrightarrow \Delta$$

$$\text{Adj} \longrightarrow \Delta$$

PRELIMINARY LEXICAL INSERTION

Let us suppose that we are in the process of generating the sentence: "Those men who lie must hate the truth." We have run through all of the branching PS rules, and we now have a phrase marker whose bottom line contains nothing but dummy symbols and a few formatives:*

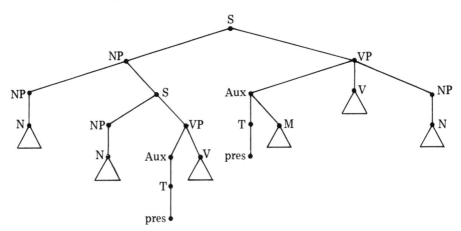

*Linguists have worked out this system since the publication of *Aspects* which omits mention of verb tense endings, determiners, and other such lexical formatives from the tree structure at this stage in the sentence generation process. They contend that verb and noun segments of this sort are syntactically inherent in the lexical word itself, and furthermore, that this approach makes the grammar theory more abstract and more reflective of universal linguistic requirements.

The next step in the derivation will be to replace each of these dummy symbols with a feature matrix. This process requires that we consult the subcategorization rules of the grammar to determine which feature specifications are called for by the constituent structure of this particular string and by the pattern of the branching tree. For although many different surface sentences may result from the tree structure we are dealing with, whatever sentence we derive will have to be one which has one dominant or main clause and one embedded relative or wh clause after the subject noun of the main clause. Moreover, the pattern of the branching indicates that the embedded wh clause has to be a restrictive relative clause, because its source is an embedded S node which branches from an NP node rather than from an S node.

The constituent structure of the string also requires that the verb in the embedded sentence be an intransitive verb (no complement follows it), but that the main clause verb be transitive (an NP follows it). We have no way of knowing, at this time, what the inherent semantic or syntactic properties of the direct object noun must be.

The next step in our derivation, therefore, is to replace each dummy symbol with all of the feature specifications which are required by the subcategorization PS rules. The tree structure below substitutes a complex symbol for each of these dummy symbols:

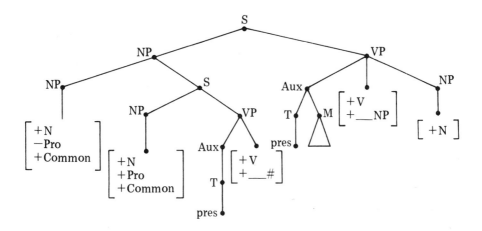

Up to the point preceding this last operation, we needed context-free branching rules only. However, to determine feature specifications, it has now become necessary for us to "look around," so to speak, to discover the contextual restrictions imposed by this particular string. Thus, we are already involved with context-sensitive rules—as we will be from now on. As soon as we have made our first lexical choice, that choice will automatically impose further restrictions on all of the remaining lexical selections. It is for this reason that we must now turn to the transformational rules of the grammar.

LEXICAL ENTRIES   EXERCISE 72

Directions: Fill in semantic-syntactic feature matrixes for the following lexical entries.

1. dirt

2. glove

3. John

4. student

5. truth

6. woman

7. hate

8. lie

9. please

10. think

11. must

12. shall

13. she

14. they

15. you

16. us

17. a

18. this

19. these

33

Aspects Model:
The Base Component, II

Transformation Rules

There are three types of context-sensitive transformation rules: (1) lexical insertion T rules; (2) general T rules; and (3) local T rules. We shall be applying these rules in the order in which they are listed.

FINAL LEXICAL INSERTION T RULES

Before we proceed to insert words from the lexicon, we must decide on the order we will follow. This decision is desirable not because we have any evidence that native speakers actually follow any particular order in choosing words for their sentences. Rather, linguists require ordered rules to achieve the explicitness of operational description which is their goal.

Since every string is bound to contain at least one noun and one verb, one of these two categories seems best as a possible first choice. It is probably for this reason, plus the fact that it is likely for a string to have more noun slots than verb slots, that the prevailing practice has become noun selection first, verb selection next (although there is disagreement on this point).

The process of lexical insertion will involve consulting the lexicon, choosing a noun whose inherent features (as listed in the lexicon) match the subcategorization requirements already listed under the noun node on the tree, and then copying from the lexicon all of the features listed there. These lexical features are added to the features already listed. In the diagram which follows, the features in the upper third of each noun feature matrix are subcategorization features. The ones between the broken lines are features copied from the lexicon. The third set of features are noun segment structure features derived from the segment structure rules and added to every noun feature matrix at the time of lexical insertion.

These are features we will use at a later stage in the derivation, when we apply the local transformation rules.

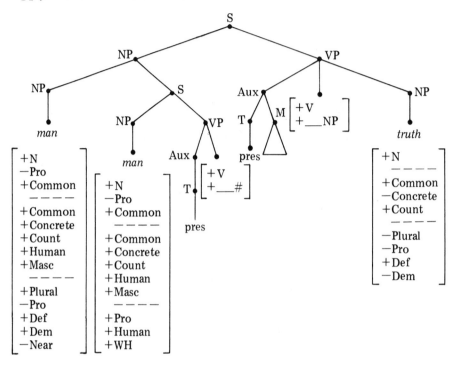

Notice that we may select these particular nouns because none of their lexical features conflict with the feature specifications already inserted on the tree.

Once we have chosen the nouns, we are ready to select the verbs. Again we must turn to the lexicon for verb choices whose lexical features do not conflict with those specified on the tree. And again, we copy the features from the lexicon below the verb features already specified on the tree. We do not add any segment structure rules to these deep structure verbs, however. (This is because the local transformation which adds verb suffixes to insure subject-verb agreement applies only to surface subject-verb relationships. General transformations, which are applied before these local ones, can change the syntactic relationships.) See the first tree diagram on the next page.

Since our string still needs a modal insertion, we consult the lexicon once more and choose the word *must*. We have now made all of the lexical insertions possible at this stage in the derivation. This introduction of lexical items into deep structure trees is called the *first lexical pass*. When we have completed the lexical insertion transformations, the bottom line of our tree looks like this: See the second tree diagram on the next page.

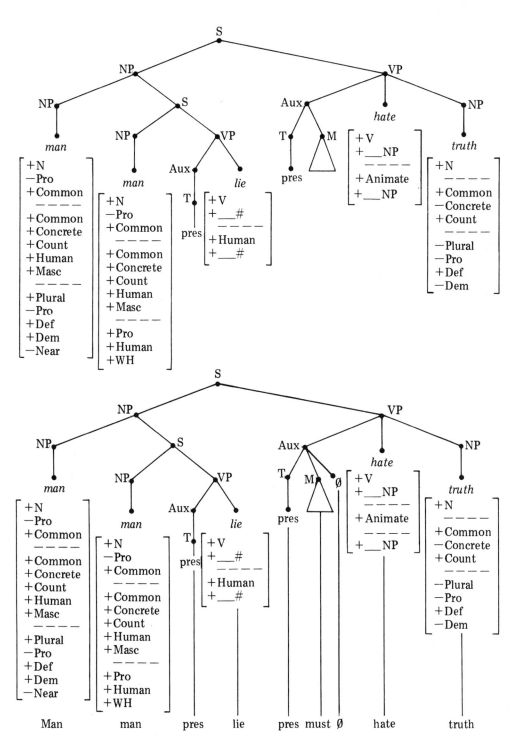

GENERAL TRANSFORMATIONS

The next step in the generation of a sentence is the application of all general transformation rules. The general transformations are the string transformations which we referred to in the early form of TG grammar theory as optional single-base and optional double-base transformations. Both types are now signaled in the phrase marker tree and are therefore obligatory. Single-base or singulary transformations are now signaled by an abstract phrase marker (the SM) which precedes a string from the time when it first branches off from the sentence node. The derivation we have been following through does not happen to have such an SM, but if one or more such phrase markers should occur before a string, now is the time when we would apply the transformation rule called for. As soon as such a transformation is accomplished, the abstract marker is deleted from the tree.

Conjunction and embedding transformations are also signaled in the deep structure, but not by a constituent phrase marker. Rather, as you have seen throughout, transformations apply in any case where their structural indices (left-hand terms) are found in the phrase marker.

Because these general T rules have not changed in the revised grammar model, they will not be repeated here. (You may turn back to the early optional T rules if you need to refresh your memory.) And as was the case in the early model, these general transformations must sometimes apply in a particular order. The system of accounting for complex sentences in the base phrase marker tree now suggests that, in addition to linear ordering (which may be required when two or more transformation rules are applied to a single string), there is also a cyclic ordering which operates for derivations with multiple S embeddings. Consider the following sentence, which contains one dominant sentence (S^1) and two embedded sentences, one of which (S^2) is embedded in S^1, the other of which (S^3) is embedded in S^2.

That Al does not think grammar to be difficult intimidates Sue.

S^1—Dominant Deep Structure: It intimidates Sue.

S^2—Embedded Deep Structure: NEG Al thinks it.

S^3—Embedded Deep Structure: Grammar is difficult.

There is evidence that the transformation rules which account for the embedded sentences must apply in a cyclic order, beginning with the most deeply embedded sentence (S^3), which is the farthest removed from the dominant S^1, proceeding to S^2, and finally to S^1. At any given level where string transformations are required (as is true for S^2), a linear

350

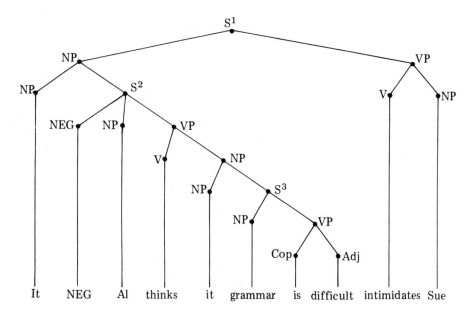

ordering may be also required. The procedure for transformation rule application is outlined below:

Procedure

Cycle 1: Perform any linear transformations called for by abstract phrase marker(s) preceding S^3

Transform S^3 to *that-clause*

Delete "it" from S^2 and subtitute transformed S^3 for the object NP of S^2

Cycle 2: Perform any linear transformations called for by abstract phrase marker(s) preceding S^2

Transform S^2 to *that-clause*

Delete "it" from S^1 and substitute transformed S^2 for the object NP of S^1

Cycle 3: Perform any linear transformations called for by abstract phrase marker(s) preceding S^1

Summary of Ordering for General Transformations

    1. Singulary transformations are (at least partially) linearly ordered.

    2. Embedding transformations are cyclically ordered, on the principle that they apply to the most deeply embedded S first and proceed numerically upward to the dominant S.

LOCAL TRANSFORMATIONS

Local transformation rules are those which apply last, after all of the general T rules have been applied. These transformations differ from general transformations in that they apply only locally to a particular constituent in a string rather than to an entire string. Moreover, they operate on surface structure constituents rather than on deep structures. These segment structure rules are the ones that account for such things as correct case of pronoun, subject-verb agreement, and the like.

Segment Transformations. Consider, for example, the problem of subject-verb agreement in the following string:

Deep Structure: The *husband* **was** washing the dishes.

As you can see, the noun *husband* functions in this sentence as the subject. If however the string is to be transformed by application of the general T^{Pas} rule, the word *dishes* becomes the surface subject, not the deep subject, which determines the form of the verb.

Surface Structure: The *dishes* **were** being washed by the husband.

You can see that subject-verb agreement is a local, surface phenomenon. It is for this reason that transformational linguists came to feel that morphemic structure, dependent as it so often is on the surface relationship of constituents, should be accounted for by transformation rules rather than by the phrase-structure rules.

There were other good reasons for moving certain explanations out of the base component and into the transformational component of the grammar theory. In the early 1960s, transformationalists had become increasingly involved in the search for linguistic universals. While the structuralists, who had confined their grammar descriptions to actual surface utterances, had emphasized the wide differences among human languages, the transformationalists' translinguistic research had led them to the conclusion that human languages are amazingly similar. These similarities are not immediately evident, however, from observation of the surface forms of sentences. Rather, it is in their deep structures that sentences across languages are similar in meaning and form.

Thus, Chomsky and others became convinced that TG grammar theory must be reorganized in such a way that only those constituents which seem to exist in the deep structures of all languages should be accounted for in the base component of the grammar. Surface differences should be handled exclusively by transformation rules.

Consider, for example, constituent categories and their deep structure syntactic and semantic relationships to each other. All of the evidence suggests that there are a limited number of base categories such as the *noun*, the *verb*, and the *sentence* itself. Additionally, many transformationalists hypothesize that there is a limited, universal set of grammatical relations or functions, such as *subject of* and *object of*. (There may be more universal categories and relations than these.) The revisions of the theory, therefore, were primarily designed to reflect, insofar as possible, the existence of these

352

universals. A grammar for a particular language ought to do two things: (1) it should be able, by means of transformation rules, to explain the surface structures peculiar to that language; and (2) it should be developed within the more general framework of a universal grammar theory.

The category, *noun*, (or NP) is apparently a universal. So are such concepts as *common* or *proper*, *count* or *noncount*, *animate* or *inanimate*, *male* or *female*. All of these and other noun features exist as meaning concepts in deep structures. How these meanings and relational fuuctions become translated in the sentences of languages may vary considerably (although many linguists now think there are limits here too).

In English, as in the other Indo-European languages, the noun feature [±Definite], is handled by the determiner system: [+Definite] *the* boy, as opposed to [−Definite], *a* boy. The number feature is accounted for by the use of singular or plural morphemes. Some languages, on the other hand, do not make use of determiners; and some languages do not use separate singular and plural noun forms. Such surface language idiosyncrasies were therefore removed from the rewriting rules of the base component. They are now accounted for in a feature-analysis grammar which lists universal features of nouns in the complex symbols of the deep structure, and which gives instructions for transforming these features in a set of transformation rules specific to a particular language.

These new transformation rules are called segment-structure rules, and they do two things: (1) they create feature segments, which are specified for a given noun at the time of lexical insertion; and (2) they give instructions for the incorporation of these features into the surface structures of the constituents so specified.

Noun Features and Noun Segments

A noun phrase in English may consist of three parts or segments: the noun segment itself, a determiner segment preceding it, and an affix segment following it. At the time of lexical insertion, we put the lexical noun at the NP node, and we list the noun features relevant to its segment structure in the bottom third of the feature matrix. (These features are derived from a set of segment-structure rules.) The phrase marker contains all the information we need, therefore, to apply the local segment structure transformation rules when the time comes. Here are the noun segment-structure rules:

SS1 $N \longrightarrow [\pm \text{Common}]$

SS2 $[+\text{Common}] \longrightarrow [\pm \text{Pro}], [\pm \text{Plural}]$

SS3 $[-\text{Pro}] \longrightarrow [\pm \text{Def}]$

SS4 $[+\text{Def}] \longrightarrow [\pm \text{Dem}]$

SS5 $[+\text{Dem}] \longrightarrow [\pm \text{Near}]$

Rule 1 tells us that a noun will have the feature [+Common] or [—Common]. If it is a proper noun (*Jane, Detroit, England*), we need do nothing more, for proper nouns in English are neither preceded by a determiner nor pluralized. If the noun is [+Common], however, we must indicate whether it is a lexical noun (*dog, book*, and so on) or a pronoun. (The pronoun is considered to be a deep structure noun, with the feature designations [+N], [+Pro].) If it is a surface noun ([—Pro]), we must indicate whether it is [+Definite] or [—Definite]. (Definite noun: *the boy, this book, those pencils;* indefinite noun: *an apple, a boy.*) If it is [+Def], we must know whether or not it has the feature, *demonstrative* ([±Dem]); and if it is [+Dem], we must list the feature [±Near]. For the sentence, "Those men who lie must hate the truth," our fully specified noun nodes look like this:

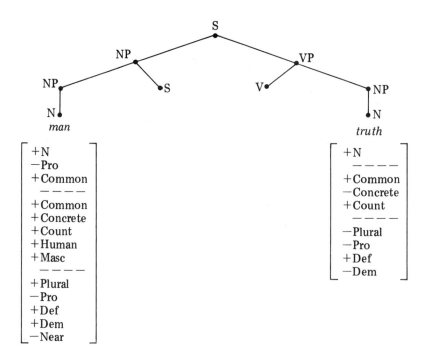

We have two segment structure transformations which particular feature combinations may trigger, the *determiner transformation* (T^{det}) and the *noun suffix transformation* ($T^{n\text{-affix}}$).

Determiner Transformation. The determiner transformation rule provides for the creation of a determiner segment to the left of the dominant (head) noun segment when a noun's feature matrix contains the features [+Common], [—Pro]. Under this newly created determiner-segment node, we copy the same set of relevant segment-structure features as those which appear in the noun's feature matrix:

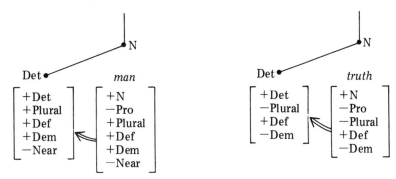

Noun Suffix Transformation. The noun suffix transformation rule provides for the creation of an affix segment to the right of the head noun-segment when the noun carries the feature [+Plural]. (If it has the feature, [−Plural], no new suffix segment is created.)

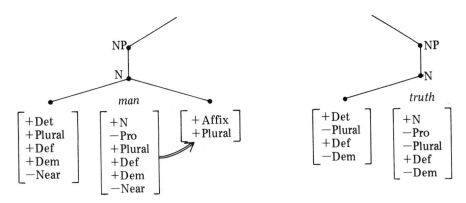

Once all of these segment features have been added to the tree, we must turn once again to the lexicon, which will give us the information we need to make lexical insertions. This second look-up is called the *second lexical pass*.

Verb Features and Verb Segments

Verb-Suffix Transformation. For the grammar rules we have been using (which are very similar to the rules given in *Aspects*), the only feature specification with segment-structure consequences for present tense verbs with noun subjects is the designation [±Plural]. The segment structure rules instruct us to copy this feature from the feature matrix of the surface structure noun subject to insure subject-verb agreement. Thus, if a verb has the feature [+Plural], nothing more need be done. If, however, it has the feature [−Plural], it will be necessary to apply the verb suffix segment transformation. The subject-verb combination, "John runs," would look like this:

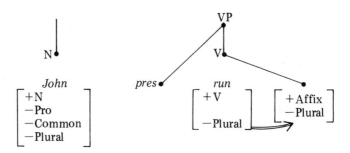

If the subject of a verb is a pronoun instead of a noun, we must specify person (I, II, III,) as well as number. (Nouns are always third person.)

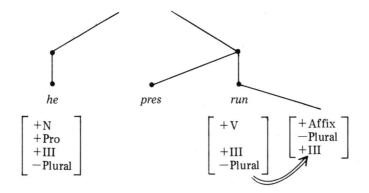

Likewise, if a sentence contains a copula rather than a verb, we must include enough features to enable the grammar to distinguish among the three singular, present tense forms of BE (*am, are, is*) and between the two singular, past tense forms (*was, were*).

Again, as with the noun segments, after all verbal segment transformations have been applied, we turn to the lexicon for a second time (the second lexical pass) and make the final lexical insertions.

Other Strictly Local Transformations. A "strictly local transformation" is a transformation which applies exclusively to a part of a string (a substring). The segment-structure transformations we have just discussed are therefore strictly local: they are transformations which affect only those segments dominated by a single head-segment.

Another local transformation is the contraction transformation, which can convert a substring like *will not* to *won't*. This kind of local transformation is also applied last, after the general transformations have finished determining the final word order of the sentence.

The last step in the derivation of a sentence is to consult the phonological feature matrix for each word in the string (these feature matrixes are recorded, you will remember, in the lexicon), and to apply the phonological transformation rules. These operations will provide a phonological interpretation and thus finish the process of generating a surface structure.

Presumably, to speak only of a phonological component implies that the sentence is being thought of as an utterance rather than as something written. And certainly a grammar theory which is constructed within the general framework of linguistic universals must necessarily make this assumption, for a great many existing natural human languages have no written form.

For languages which have been committed to written forms, a fourth component, which will contain graphemological rules, might be posited. These rules would give instructions for translating the phonological sounds of a language, by means of spelling, punctuation, and the like, to written form.

34

Revisions of the *Aspects* Model

Chomsky's primary contribution in publishing *Aspects* was to gather together the most compelling suggestions for revising the earlier *Syntactic Structures* model and to suggest future directions. And as we have seen, the most far-reaching of the theoretical revisions was the incorporation of distinctive feature matrixes and feature analysis into the grammar theory. The way to accomplish this revision had not yet been worked out, but the possibilities of a feature-analysis grammar seemed encouraging to Chomsky. Thus, while he did not include any segment-structure transformation rules in *Aspects*, he did outline the possibility of proceeding in such a direction.

The segment-structure transformations presented in the last chapter of this book are not, therefore, taken from *Aspects*. Rather, they represent suggestions made by transformational linguists after *Aspects*.

The idea of considering the determiner, the noun itself, and the noun affix as three parts of the entire noun-dominated segment-structure seems to have become widely accepted. Few problems prevent a feature analysis of the noun.

The verb, on the other hand, is much more difficult to explain in a feature-analysis grammar. Even among the transformationalists who agree that it is desirable to move such notions as tense, mood, and aspect out of the phrase-structure (rewriting rules) part of the grammar and to handle them, instead, as verb features which affect segment structure, there is considerable disagreement about how to do this.

The verb analysis presented in the last chapter is only partly successful. *Number*, which affects the syntactical problem of subject-verb agreement, is the only verb feature assigned to segment-structure rules. Yet most native speakers surely have the "feeling" that *tense, mood, aspect* (and perhaps even *voice*) are also inherent verb features.

Various alternative suggestions have been proposed for analyzing the verb in a feature-analysis grammar. The suggestion offered by Jacobs and Rosenbaum is that of revising the rewriting rule for the Sentence (the first of the branching rules) to read S ⟶ NP AUX VP.* (They explain surface sentences such as the imperative "Close the door" and the declarative "John closed the door" as strings which have had an auxiliary deletion transformation rule applied to them.) Thus, they suggest that *Aux* is a base category component of every sentence, a component which carries with it the inherent features [±Modal], and [±Past] (tense). Subject-verb agreement, under this scheme, is explained as a process whereby the relevant features are copied from the noun or pronoun which is the surface subject and are added to the feature matrix of the auxiliary component. If the deep-structure auxiliary carries the feature [+Modal], the string will surface with a modal. If, however, the deep-structure auxiliary carries the feature [−Modal], the modal auxiliary deletion transformation is signaled. This deletion transformation will do two things: (1) it will transfer all of its inherent features, plus the features copied from the noun or pronoun subject, to the next linear verb segment, thus having the effect of conferring [+Auxiliary] status upon that segment; and (2) having thus transferred its feature matrix, it will delete the abstract [−Modal] auxiliary.

The verb, which is a separate base component, is explained as a dominant verb segment containing the inherent features [+Verb], [±Perfect], and [±Progressive] (the last two of which are Aspect features). Thus, when the [+Perfect] feature occurs, it creates a [+Perfect] segment to the left of the verb and a [+Perfect] affix on the verb segment which immediately follows. In a sentence like "John has run," which does not contain a surface modal auxiliary, the auxiliary deletion transformation has the effect of transferring all auxiliary features to the [+Perfect] segment which follows:

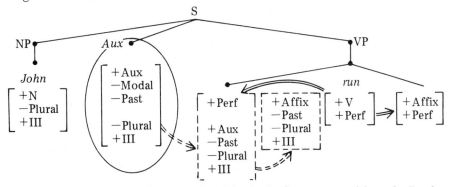

*As evidence for their proposed revision in the Sentence rewriting rule, Jacobs and Rosenbaum cite the effect of the Question transformation and the Negative transformation, in which *do* is used as an auxiliary. See Jacobs and Rosenbaum, *English Transformational Grammar* (1968).

The circled constituent above is the abstract auxiliary component. (We know it is abstract because it carries the feature [−Modal], a feature which will trigger the modal auxiliary deletion transformation.) The dotted lines indicate the results of the auxiliary deletion transformation.

If, on the other hand, we have a surface sentence like "John is running" or "John runs," the auxiliary deletion transformation transfers its feature matrix to the verb segment (the [+Prog] segment or the [+Verb] segment, respectively) which immediately follows:

John is running:

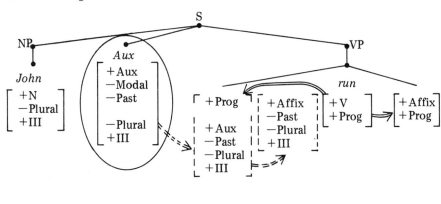

John runs:

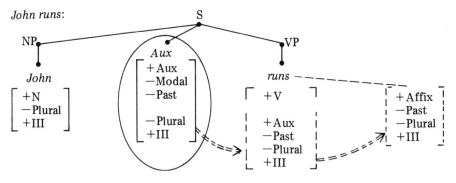

Again, in these two diagrams, the abstract auxiliary component is circled, and the effects of the modal auxiliary deletion transformation are indicated by the dotted lines.

Jacobs and Rosenbaum's method of analyzing the auxiliary and the verb separately is, as they admit, only a tentative solution. Still another school of thought is that the auxiliary is a verb feature, not a base component. Linguists who hold this last view would therefore make no mention at all of the auxiliary in the branching rules. They would rewrite VP as follows: (These rules omit elements irrelevant to this discussion.)

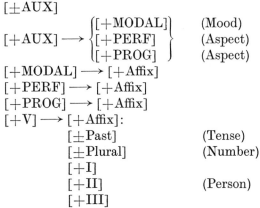

S ⟶ (SM) NP VP

VP ⟶ { V (NP) (NP) / COP PRED }

V ⟶ △

COP ⟶ △

Segment Structure Rules

[±AUX]

[+AUX] ⟶ { [+MODAL] / [+PERF] / [+PROG] }   (Mood) (Aspect) (Aspect)

[+MODAL] ⟶ [+Affix]

[+PERF] ⟶ [+Affix]

[+PROG] ⟶ [+Affix]

[+V] ⟶ [+Affix]:

    [±Past]   (Tense)

    [±Plural]   (Number)

    [+I]

    [+II]   (Person)

    [+III]

English verb forms will then be derived by a series of steps, as follows:

Step 1. All [+AUX] features are listed in a feature matrix below the verb node. The [+V] feature is listed here too.

Step 2. Each [+AUX] feature creates an auxiliary segment to the left of the verb segment, in the order given.

Step 3. The features [+Affix], [±Past] (*tense*, an inherent verb feature), [±Plural] (*number*, an inherent noun feature relevant to agreement) and [+I], [+II], or [+III] (*person*, another noun feature relevant to agreement) are listed in the feature matrix of the first auxiliary segment; or when no auxiliary has been created, in the feature matrix of the verb segment.

Step 4. The features [+Affix] and [+Modal] are listed in the feature matrix of the auxiliary (or verb) segment immediately to the right of the MODAL segment.

Step 5. The features [+Affix] and [+Perf] are listed in the feature matrix of the auxiliary (or verb) segment immediately to the right of the PERFECT segment.

Step 6. The features [+Affix] and [+Prog] are listed in the feature matrix of the verb segment immediately to the right of the PROGRESSIVE segment.

Step 7. The verb suffix transformation rule creates an affix segment to the right of each verb segment.

The diagrams which follow illustrate each of these steps:

Sentence: *John may have been laughing.*

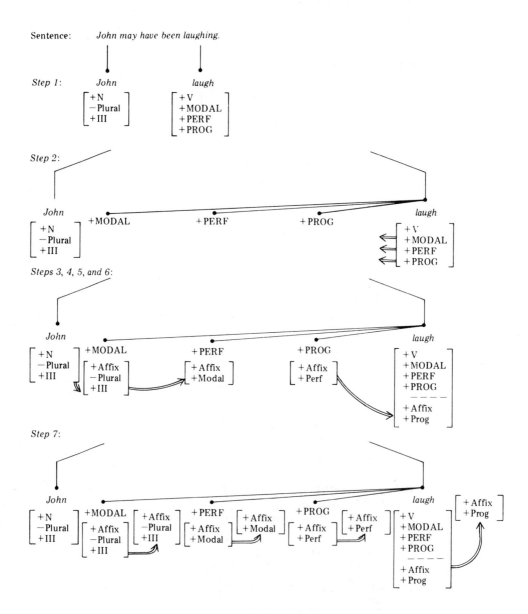

Step 1:

John

$$\begin{bmatrix} +N \\ -\text{Plural} \\ +\text{III} \end{bmatrix}$$

laugh

$$\begin{bmatrix} +V \\ +\text{MODAL} \\ +\text{PERF} \\ +\text{PROG} \end{bmatrix}$$

Step 2:

John

$$\begin{bmatrix} +N \\ -\text{Plural} \\ +\text{III} \end{bmatrix}$$

+MODAL   +PERF   +PROG   laugh

$$\begin{bmatrix} +V \\ +\text{MODAL} \\ +\text{PERF} \\ +\text{PROG} \end{bmatrix}$$

Steps 3, 4, 5, and 6:

John

$$\begin{bmatrix} +N \\ -\text{Plural} \\ +\text{III} \end{bmatrix}$$

+MODAL

$$\begin{bmatrix} +\text{Affix} \\ -\text{Plural} \\ +\text{III} \end{bmatrix}$$

+PERF

$$\begin{bmatrix} +\text{Affix} \\ +\text{Modal} \end{bmatrix}$$

+PROG

$$\begin{bmatrix} +\text{Affix} \\ +\text{Perf} \end{bmatrix}$$

laugh

$$\begin{bmatrix} +V \\ +\text{MODAL} \\ +\text{PERF} \\ +\text{PROG} \\ ----- \\ +\text{Affix} \\ +\text{Prog} \end{bmatrix}$$

Step 7:

John

$$\begin{bmatrix} +N \\ -\text{Plural} \\ +\text{III} \end{bmatrix}$$

+MODAL

$$\begin{bmatrix} +\text{Affix} \\ -\text{Plural} \\ +\text{III} \end{bmatrix}$$

$$\begin{bmatrix} +\text{Affix} \\ -\text{Plural} \\ +\text{III} \end{bmatrix}$$

+PERF

$$\begin{bmatrix} +\text{Affix} \\ +\text{Modal} \end{bmatrix}$$

+PROG

$$\begin{bmatrix} +\text{Affix} \\ +\text{Perf} \end{bmatrix}$$

laugh

$$\begin{bmatrix} +V \\ +\text{MODAL} \\ +\text{PERF} \\ +\text{PROG} \\ ----- \\ +\text{Affix} \\ +\text{Prog} \end{bmatrix}$$

$$\begin{bmatrix} +\text{Affix} \\ +\text{Prog} \end{bmatrix}$$

362

Once all of these operations are completed, the second lexical pass will provide lexical items for each segment.

CHALLENGES TO THE *ASPECTS* GRAMMAR

One of Chomsky's aims in writing *Aspects*, namely that of defending transformational grammar theory against the criticisms of the structuralists, was clearly accomplished. Most linguists have come by now to agree that the concept of transformations is vital to an adequate grammar description and that a grammar theory should and can meet the same formal requirements as other scientific theories are expected to meet. It is also widely agreed today that a grammar theory should seek to explain the roles of phonology, syntax, and semantics in the derivation of sentences, particularly as concerns the contribution of each of these components to the meanings of sentences. Largely convinced that human language acquisition is too remarkable a phenomenon to be attributable only to observation and training, the great majority of linguists today hold the rationalist view that language learning is a psychologically unique and inevitable result of the fact of being human rather than an achievement based on varying degrees of intelligence within the human species. So much evidence has been mustered to support this rationalist point of view that practically none of these things has been seriously challenged since the mid 1960s.*

One current linguistic debate is that being conducted among transformationalists, all of whom are joined in the search for linguistic universals. It is this search, in fact, which led to challenges of Chomsky's syntactic approach even before *Aspects* was published.

George Lakoff leveled the first of these challenges at the *Aspects* theory in his doctoral dissertation, "On the Nature of Syntactic Irregularity."† Lakoff argued then (and argues now) that the categories generated by the phrase-structure *Aspects* rules are surface structure categories, and therefore not the best ones for describing deep structures. In fact, a good many of Chomsky's categories are surface structure classes of *English*; they do not even show up in the surface structures of some other languages.

As one such example, Lakoff first offered the evidence that adjectives and verbs are not realized in some languages as two separate classes of words, and then postulated that adjectives are really verbs in deep structures. In support of this claim, he cited a number of characteristics

---

*See Ronald W. Langacker, *Language and Its Structure* (1968), Chapter Nine.

†Originally completed in 1965 (the same year in which *Aspects* was published), Lakoff's dissertation, with some revisions, has since come out in book form with the title *Irregularity in Syntax* (1970).

that verbs and adjectives share (a fact, incidentally, which had not gone unrecognized by traditionalist scholars):

1. Some verbs and some adjectives can be either *stative* (they indicate "state of being") or *nonstative* (they indicate action or motion, in the sense of "on-goingness"):

STATIVE VERBS

You *know* John.

You *resemble* the dog.

STATIVE ADJECITVES

You are *short*.

You are *dead*.

Furthermore, just as stative verbs may not occur in either imperative sentences or in the progressive aspect, neither may stative adjectives:

STATIVE VERBS

Know John!

Resemble the dog!

You *are knowing* John.

You *are resembling* the dog.

STATIVE ADJECTIVES

Be *short*!

Be *dead*!

You are being *short*.

You are being *dead*.

2. Some verbs are *transitive* (i.e., require a following construction), and the same is true for some adjectives:

TRANSITIVE VERBS

John *pleases* me.

John *fears* the dark.

The book *interests* me.

TRANSITIVE ADJECTIVES

John is *pleasant* to me.

John is *fearful* of the dark.

The book seems *interesting* to me.

3. Some verbs and some adjectives are *intransitive* (i.e., do not take complement constructions):

INTRANSITIVE VERBS

He *died*.

He *thirsts*.

INTRANSITIVE ADJECTIVES

He is *dead*.

He is *thirsty*.

4. The phenomenon of synonymy or paraphrase, the fact that we can often use either a verb or an adjective to "say the same thing," suggests that the two are not so distinct from each other as surface structure would lead us to believe:

PHRASE (WITH VERB)

John *hungers* for attention.

Mary *charms* people.

He *wearied* of studying.

PARAPHRASE (WITH ADJECTIVE)

John is *hungry* for attention.

Mary is *charming* to people.

He is *weary* of studying.

It is important to realize that Lakoff's argument relied heavily on semantic considerations. And what he found led him and others to question the validity of basing a grammar theory on the belief that syntax is primary. His research led him to conclude that Chomsky's *Aspects* grammar theory, a syntactically based description which considered semantics to be interpretive only, was simply wrong. Essentially, Lakoff argued that deep structures are far more likely to be semantic than syntactic categories, and in fact that Chomsky's deep structures are inadequate because they fail to account for many mysteries of meaning. Perhaps what linguists should search for is an even deeper, more abstract linguistic level—a kind of semantic bedrock which dominates the meaning of sentences and which in some way determines the surface syntax of sentences.

There was a branching off from the work of Lakoff and other semantically oriented transformationalists, which soon resulted in two major schools of thought among transformational linguists. The first of these, known variously as the lexicalists, the interpretative semanticists, and most recently as the standard theorists, is composed of scholars like Chomsky, Jerrold Katz, and Ray Jackendoff, with Chomsky more often than not acting as their spokesman. The second school, known now as the generative semanticists, is composed of such equally respected linguists as Lakoff, Paul Postal, John Ross, and James McCawley.

Postal, in fact, was one of those who became interested very early in Lakoff's notions. Shortly after Lakoff had presented his argument concerning the relationship of verbs and adjectives, Postal, in a monograph entitled *On So-Called "Pronouns" in English* (1966), presented a similar proposal concerning definite articles and pronouns. Beginning with the proposition that the presence of a particular form in a surface structure does not necessarily prove it is present in the deep structure, nor, conversely, that a surface form's absence necessarily proves its absence from the deep structure, Postal set out to show that personal pronouns and definite articles originate as deep structure *nouns* (i.e., as NP segments which are features of the dominant N segment), but that pronouns in surface structures are really *articles*. In support of this contention, he cited the following arguments:

1. Articles are not present in the surface structures of many languages.

2. Common nouns in English can be preceded by definite articles, but personal pronouns cannot be so preceded. (We do not say "*the* she" or "*those* they.")

3. Certain dialects of English use personal pronouns as articles, as in the expression "we ones," contracted to "we'uns."

4. Standard English also occasionally uses personal pronouns as articles, as in the expressions "you girls," and "we women."

Although Postal also presented other evidence to support his contention, the details of his argument are too long, complicated, and highly theoretical for us to include in an introductory book.* We need merely note here that he described the following transformation process to explain the phenomenon: First, the noun segment's feature [+Def] creates a new article segment to its left with the features [+Def], [+Art], and [+Pro]. (If the feature designation were [−Pro], presumably the segment would surface as an article rather than as a pronoun.) Second, the noun segment is then deleted (except in certain dialects or for certain limited idiomatic expressions).

Another group of linguists challenged the standard theory of deep and surface subjects and objects, claiming that there is a deeper semantic distinction which explains the functional relation of nouns to verbs, a distinction that is obscured by a syntactically based grammar theory. They postulated that underlying all syntactic structures there is a deep, deep meaning relationship, and that better terms for describing these functions than *subject* or *object* (in the syntactic sense) are terms like *agent, patient* (the semantic object), and *instrument*. They demonstrated these function relations with paradigms like these:

1. The thief broke the window with the wrench.

2. The wrench broke the window.

3. The window broke.

In these sentences (and this is true for a large class of verbs, like *open, close, move, end, run, start, turn,* and so on, when they are used as transitive verbs), there is an **agent** (*thief*) who is the instigator of the action; there is a **patient** or object (*window*) which is the objective of the action; and there is an **instrument** (*wrench*) by means of which the predication is accomplished. Notice that if the agent occurs, it serves as the syntactic subject. If the agent is deleted, the instrument serves as subject. If both the agent and the instrument are deleted, the object itself serves as subject. Evidence of this sort leads to the conclusion that the notions "subject of" and "object of" are just not as simple as purely syntactic descriptions of language would have us believe.

Other problems have also been cited to support the generative semanticists' position that large areas of meaning are left unexplained by the *Aspects* grammar. Consider again the problem of explaining paraphrase (already considered by Lakoff in his argument that verbs and adjectives originate from the same deep structure constituent). Without question, the *Aspects* grammar can explain the synonymy of structures like these:

*If you wish to study the monograph in detail you can find it reprinted in *Modern Studies in English: Readings in Transformational Grammar* (see bibliography).

1. John bought the boat from Jim.

2. The boat was bought from Jim by John.

3. It was from Jim that John bought the boat.

4. It was John who bought the boat from Jim.

5. What John bought from Jim was the boat.

All of the paraphrases above can be accounted for by the hypothesis that each of the five surface structures derive from the same deep structure, and that they have been converted to different surface structures by different transformations.

But how are we to explain synonymous sentences which derive from different deep structures, like these?

1. John bought the boat from Jim.

Jim sold the boat to John.

2. Mary received a gift from Jane.

Jane gave a gift to Mary.

Again, the generative semanticists contend, semantic meaning is the really basic deep structure. What we need to explore are such things as the concepts of "to-ness" and "from-ness" inherent in certain verbs. Why is it that some verbs carry with them the meaning "to" (*give, send, lend, yield*); other verbs carry the meaning "from" (*get, receive, borrow, acquire*); and still others carry both meanings (*carry, move, toss, transfer*)?

In sum, the generative semanticists insist that the deep structure of the *Aspects* model is an artificial level which stands, in reality, somewhere between the surface structure and an extremely deep semantic structure.

Chomsky and the transformational linguists of the standard school disagree. Although they are willing to make some concessions, and Chomsky has recently suggested some further revisions of the *Aspects* model, they still believe that the generative power of language is primarily attributable to its universal syntactic structure. As Chomsky had conceded almost twenty years ago in *Syntactic Structures*, he was even then far from ready to dismiss the importance of semantic considerations. But he thought then that a theory of semantics could not be included in a grammar model until a satisfactory one had been developed. His *Aspects* revision of the early theory made use of the semantic theory which had been recently developed by Fodor, Katz, and others. But as you have seen, the syntactic component was still considered primary, in the sense that it is in the deep structure generated by this component that the basic meaning of surface structures is said to reside.

In recent years, defenders of the standard theory have admitted, perhaps largely as a result of the work of Lakoff, Ross, McCawley, Postal, *et al*, that *all* meaning is *not* accounted for in deep structures. Rather than deciding that a syntactic theory is wrong, however, they have attempted to explain that some meaning is affected by the surface structure. Chomsky, who remains the chief spokesman for this group of linguists, in 1971 suggested a number of revisions of the standard model which grammarians of the standard school think go a long way toward accounting for the influence of surface structures on the meaning of sentences (and which also are meant to defend the *Aspects* grammar against the criticisms of the generative semanticists). These revisions were set out in an article, "Deep Structure, Surface Structure, and Semantic Interpretation," which appeared in a book of readings on philosophy, linguistics, and psychology edited by L. A. Jakobovits and D. D. Steinberg.

In discussing the way in which surface structure can affect meaning, Chomsky analyzes the notions of *focus* and *presupposition*. Sentences like

John lent his car to the girls.

John lent the girls his car.

are basically identical in meaning (as indicated by the fact that they have the same common deep structure), but they are slightly different in *focus*. This difference in focus is easily explained, says Chomsky, by the phonological surface-structure differences in stress. (Chomsky defines focus as determined by the phrase which contains the "intonation center.")

Or consider another set of sentences, the last three of which have had emphatic transformation rules applied to different constituents in the otherwise identical sentence, and all of which have a common deep structure origin:

1. John will study in the library.

2. *John* will study in the library.

3. John will *study* in the library.

4. John will study in the *library*.

Again, as the result of different transformations, the intonation center of each of these four sentences is different and thus the focus of meaning is different. Sentence 1 is an ordinary declaration concerning something that John will do. Sentence 2, however, suggests that *John*, not someone else, is the one who will study in the library. Sentence 3 is an affirmation that John will *study* rather than do something else in the library. And Sentence 4 emphasizes *where* John will study: in the *library*, as opposed to other possible locations.

The difference in focus for sentences of this type can be explained as the result of transformations which, in effect, have changed the topic-comment relationship. The result of shifting the intonation center of a sentence, in other words, is to change the topic of that sentence.

Sentences like

5. This new pattern is easy to make a dress with.

6. A dress is easy to make with this new pattern.

are not identical in meaning because they have different deep structure trees. Again, however, the decision concerning which string to embed and which to make dominant affects focus and therefore changes the topic of the two sentences.

Discussion of focus in Sentences like 1, 2, 3, and 4, above, leads in turn to a consideration of presupposition. Small transformational changes, like those for stress or those for the addition and placement of a single word, affect meaning because they introduce presuppositions. Consider, for example, how the simple addition of the word *even* changes the topic of these sentences because of implied presuppositions:

7. John likes my driving.

8. Even John likes my driving.

9. John even likes my driving.

10. John likes even my driving.

The difficulty is, of course, (as the generative semanticists are quick to point out), that these explanations succeed only partially. They don't explain the synonymy of sentences like those mentioned earlier in which "to" and "for" verbs can be manipulated to produce paraphrases with altogether different deep structures.

The standard theorists, on the other hand, felt that they could incorporate into their grammar model, by means of a few revisions, an explanation for sentences like Lakoff's

11. John pleases me; John is pleasant to me.

12. John fears the dark; John is fearful of the dark.

13. Mary hungers for attention; Mary is hungry for attention.

Recognition of the semantic contribution of certain transformations, coupled with revisions in the lexicon (already suggested in the last chapter of *Aspects*) could account for these and other sentences like them.

The revisions which Chomsky suggested in "Deep Structures, . . ." were therefore as follows:

1. *The Base*: The lexicon should be "enriched" by the addition of stems, prefixes, and suffixes. This enrichment, along with projection rules for word-forming transformations, will greatly add to the explanatory power of the grammar theory. The base, which is composed of categorical branching rules and a revised lexicon, will still generate deep structures.

2. *The Transformational Component:* The transformational component contains transformation rules which relate deep structures to surface structures.

3. *Phonological Component:* Phonological transformation rules relate surface structures to spoken forms.

4. *Semantic Component:* Semantic rules, which are consulted at all levels, relate *both* deep structures and surface structures to semantic, meaning representations.

In spite of these revisions, which have the effect of enlarging the role of the semantic component, linguists of the revised standard transformational school (by now, the "traditionalists" among transformational linguists) are unwilling to deny the primary importance of the syntactical component. They continue to view the semantic and phonological components as largely interpretive, and they continue to believe that basic grammatical relations and meaning are primarily contained in deep structures and therefore determined primarily by the syntactical component of the grammar.

Few would deny that the generative semanticists have raised interesting and important questions. The problem, however, is that no one has been able to give definitive answers. Although few linguists still believe (as Chomsky did when he wrote *Syntactic Structures*) that any one component of a grammar theory is autonomous, the current debate nevertheless centers on the question of primacy: is syntax more important, or is semantics? No one knows. Furthermore, the phonologists, who were shoved out of the picture when Chomsky's theory took hold, have yet to be heard from; and though few are suggesting this possibility at the moment, phonology may yet prove to be an equally important component. Certainly there is mounting evidence that linguistic universals exist in all three of these areas. And chances are that all three play crucial roles in predetermining the structure of any natural human language.

The chief difficulty facing Chomsky's current challengers is that no one has yet developed a well-formulated, reasonably complete, semantic-based model grammar theory. In sum, the generative semanticists have not yet been able to formally prove they are right.

When the generative semanticists claim that their theory is better, the standard theorists are in a position to say "Prove it." Assertions are clearly no longer good enough. What is required is a formal proof. And so far, the generative semanticists can only retort, "You prove that we are wrong."

Thanks to Noam Chomsky, language study has come a long way in the last two decades. Yet it seems that each new "solution" brings with it a host of new questions. At least it can be safely said that in this intellectually exciting field of linguistics there is a great deal of movement. Unfortunately, no one knows at the moment exactly where we are going.

35

The Search
for Linguistic Universals

The notion of linguistic universals developed very early in the history of Western language study and has persisted, in one form or another, ever since. As we have seen, however, the meaning of the term "universal" has varied through the ages. The Ancient Greek scholars debated the universal "rightness" of word meanings, and later, the Greek Stoics speculated that the outer forms of language reveal universal inner truths about human nature. The beliefs of both groups were based solely, however, on their observations of Greek, which they considered to be the only perfect language.

Certain language scholars of the Middle Ages and the Renaissance (Helias, Sanctius, Huarte, Ramus, and others) also hypothesized about language universals, but their speculations were based on comparisons of the European vernacular languages.

Until the seventeenth century, speculations about language universals seem to have been widely scattered and somewhat random. As a result of the philosophical musings of Descartes and his disciples, interest in linguistic universals was at that time renewed and in fact became the consuming fascination of a great many philosophers and language scholars. The debate between the Rationalists and the Empiricists was destined not to die down until it was overshadowed by the work of the nineteenth century historical-comparative linguists.

For nearly two centuries thereafter, empirical language research dominated the linguistic scene, conducted first by the European historical and comparative field workers and later by the American structural linguists. The American structuralists in particular came to question nearly every previous assumption concerning language universals, for in studying the exotic American Indian languages, scholars like Bloomfield and Whorf were impressed by the great diversity they observed among languages. In fact, they concluded that every language was separate and independent, most often bearing little or no resemblance to any other language.

We now know that the very methods of the structuralists' linguistic investigations, unavoidably occasioned by their complete unfamiliarity with the tongues they were deciphering, caused them to concentrate exclusively on the surface forms of Indian languages. The consequent confining of their linguistic descriptions to actual utterances understandably led them to exaggerate surface language differences and to fail to see deeper linguistic similarities. Despite their rejection of the concept of language universality, the structuralists nevertheless contributed a number of useful generalizations about language. They became convinced, for example, that there is no such thing as a "primitive" language, that all languages have equally complex grammars, and that every language is capable of expressing whatever needs to be expressed within a given culture. Moreover, the structuralists insisted that any language is capable of being expanded, by the addition of new vocabulary words for example, to handle any new situation which might arise. They further stated that every language has its own rules of phonology, syntax, and semantics, even though such rules often vary greatly from language to language.

We see, therefore, that regardless of the particular linguistic focus of language scholars throughout the entire history of language study, various hypotheses about the nature of language in general have persisted. It is only in recent years, however, that the work of the transformational-generative linguists has for the first time made it possible to offer scientific, empirical evidence in support of an exlicit theory of linguistic universals.

In *Syntactic Structures*, although Chomsky did not dwell on a discussion of the concept of linguistic universals, he argued that an adequate grammar theory must necessarily be constructed within the framework of a *general* linguistic theory. Indeed, it was precisely Chomsky's insistence that a grammar theory should seek to explain the intuitions of the mature normal native speaker-listener that drew the original fire of the structuralists. They accused Chomsky of being a "mentalist" who simply ignored all of the available scientific evidence—evidence which proved that no claim of language universality could be reasonably made.

In the years since Chomsky's original book, the work of the transformational-generative linguists has made it clear that the really striking observation about languages is how alike they are in their deep structures, despite their superficial differences. The current dispute focuses on the precise nature of linguistic universals, some claiming they are primarily phonological, others claiming that they are chiefly syntactic, and still others arguing that they are semantic.

As Chomsky pointed out in his original book, there are two ways to go about the process of investigating universals. One is to conduct comparative studies of the grammar systems of a great many languages. The second method—and this is the one Chomsky urged—is to conduct in-depth investigations of particular languages, always with the unformulated general goal in mind of explaining the grammar rules of a specific language within the larger framework of a general language theory. Only after a great many detailed generative grammars of particular languages have been analyzed will the linguist be able to determine that corpus of general and specific characteristics which all languages have in common.

In his earliest book, Chomsky argued that syntactic grammar study was an independent, autonomous discipline. But he gradually came to be less certain about this original assumption. In subsequent years, Chomsky and his followers have become interested in the process of language acquisition, and in an explanation for the fact that every language learner inevitably ends up knowing more than could possibly have been learned from the information contained in the primary "input" data. Thus, the whole enterprise of investigating speaker-hearer intuition has had broad philosophical consequences, and has prompted transformational-generative linguists to conclude that mature linguistic competence must be largely attributable to human genetic endowment of a highly specific nature.

GENERAL LINGUISTIC UNIVERSALS

All languages are now known to have sentences, and these sentences are invariably constructed of a sequence of words which are ordered according to a complex system of grammar rules. The sentences of all languages are recursive, and the grammars of all languages exploit redundant grammar signals. All languages have sentences which are transformations of simpler sentences. Moreover, transformation rules universally involve some method of conjoining, or nesting, or both. And T rules are universally performed by means of a limited number of grammatical operations: addition (insertion) rules, reduction or deletion rules, and rearranging or permutation rules.

Because the same grammatical operations occur in all natural human languages, it follows, according to the generative linguists, that certain qualities of mind cannot be ignored. Indeed, it is just such mental properties that must offer explanations for the remarkable sameness of languages, even when they are clearly unrelated either geographically or historically. All language learners must possess a number of innate mental qualities which enable them to learn a language in the first place.

For example, speakers of languages everywhere "know" whether a sentence is put together properly or not, i.e., whether or not a sentence is grammatical. Although speakers cannot necessarily assign label names like *noun* or *verb* to the words of their language, they have some way of distinguishing between word classes, as can be demonstrated by the nature of children's mistakes. An English-speaking child might say, for instance, "John *hitted* me," or "John is *badder* than Jane," but never says anything like "He *spinached* me," or "Jane is *girlest* than me." In other words, a child knows which word classes call for particular inflectional suffixes, and knows these rules before he has learned the irregular forms.

Furthermore, as evidenced by actual linguistic performance, it is clear that all speakers have some means of determining syntactic relationships. For instance, they know the difference between the subject and object of a given verb, for they never interchange such nominals with the subject or object of a verb in another clause.

Speakers also know which elements are modifiers and which nouns or verbs they modify. And given whole sentences, they know that certain structurally dissimilar strings have the same meaning, whereas certain similarly structured strings have different meanings. The fact that mature speakers of all languages have these abilities suggests to the generative linguist that all human beings have similarly "programmed" brains.

Recent studies of language acquisition by children are providing evidence that children everywhere, regardless of language, go through exactly the same language-learning stages. Interestingly, the very kinds of mistakes which children characteristically make at certain stages in the language-learning process indicate that a child's grammar is its own and not that of the mature speaker. Asked to repeat a sentence like "Where can I put this?" a child at a certain stage invariably says "Where I can put this?" Such a sentence is clearly the child's own production, not an imitation of adult speech. It is as if the child cannot help "processing" the utterance according to its own inner system of "rules." Two transformation operations are called for in the sentence he has been asked to repeat (the addition of a question word in the sentence-initial position, and the transposition of "I" and "can"), but at the particular stage of learning where a sentence like "Where I can put this?" occurs, the child is not yet able to perform more than one transformation operation in a single sentence.

At a later stage in the learning process, a child will be able to perform two operations in a single sentence, but not three. That is, if the interviewer says, "Ask me where you can find the book," the child answers correctly, "Where can I find the book?" The addition of a third operation, however, such as a negative transformation, will result in a mistake. That is, when the interviewer says, "Ask me why you can't find the book," the child, who is capable of only two but not three transformation operations, will answer, "Why I can't find the book?"*

Eventually, usually by the age of five or six, children reach a more mature level of competence. At this stage, they "know" the basic grammar rules of their language. Chomsky and other transformationalists have concluded that the only possible answer to such uniformity of learning stages and such uniform results is that certain innate, biologically determined structures and organization principles already reside in the human brain at birth. How else would a language learner be able to sort out from the vast number of syntactic, sound, and meaning signals which actually occur in the sentences of all languages only those few that are significant? How does a language learner arrive at the decision to choose some signals but to reject others? And how explain the obvious fact that all such choosing and rejecting is accomplished at a below-awareness level? Speakers are able to do these things, but they cannot explain how they do them. Nor are they even aware of the enormous complexity of the task.

For very much the same reasons, Descartes and his rationalist disciples arrived at similar conclusions. Humans, they reasoned, must be genetically endowed with language-learning principles or propensities. Chomsky, however, has gone even further, for he believes that the human brain contains something more than capacity; he believes that it contains innate ideas, principles, and actual structures: a fixed, predetermined set of possible sounds, meanings, and syntactic structures that determine and limit the actual form that any natural human language *must* take.

What the generative linguists are interested in, then, is discovering just what is involved in the cognitive process which determines that every language is cut to the same pattern. Generational linguists now believe that all languages are alike in their deep structures, despite the fact that surface sentences do not resemble each other in point by point language comparisons. Many linguists are also coming to believe that even the grammar rules whereby deep structures are transformed to surface manifestations closely follow a restricted number of universal linguistic tendencies.

---

*Detailed results of child language-acquisition studies will not be given here. If you are interested in reading more on this subject, a good general source of information is Dan I. Slobin's monograph, *Psycholinguistics* (Scott, Foresman Basic Psychological Concept Series, 1971).

Linguistic universals seem to be of two broad types: substantive and formal. When the older grammars mentioned universals at all, they generally referred to substantive ones, such as that the sentences of all languages contain nouns and verbs. Formal universals, on the other hand, are much more abstract and deeply general. They include the kind of phenomena implied in statements regarding the specific form which every language *must* take—the restricted set of possible structures and grammar rules which, because they are already "fixed" in the human mind, any natural human language must be limited to. The following list will give you a general idea of the difference between substantive and formal universals:

SUBSTANTIVE UNIVERSALS   FORMAL UNIVERSALS

Syntax

Certain fixed universal syntactic categories, like nouns and verbs, exist in all languages.	The grammar of every language contains transformation rules, probably applicable in a least-to-most-dominant, cyclic, hierarchical order.

Semantics

Certain fixed universal semantic features, like [$\pm$Animate], [$\pm$Human], exist in all languages.	Every language has a lexicon. More specifically, every language has lexical words to represent proper names. The nature of thought predetermines the terms of word representation.

Phonology

Certain fixed universal phonetic features exist in all languages.	The grammar of every language contains phonological rules, probably applicable in a cyclic hierarchical order from least to most dominant.

As the list above might suggest, it is not always easy to draw a sharp line between substantive and formal universals, nor is it easy to distinguish between semantic and syntactic features. There also appear to be both absolute universals and universal tendencies. Those specific forms of grammar rules which occur in all languages are universal absolutes, whereas those structures or rules which are found in many but not all languages are strong universal tendencies.

In the next few pages, as we discuss more specifically some of these universal absolutes and tendencies, we shall follow the usual practice of lumping syntactic and semantic features together.

SYNTACTIC AND SEMANTIC UNIVERSALS

All languages contain sentences, and the simple sentences of all languages contain the following universal semantic concepts:

1. Sentences of all languages can make positive declarative statements.

2. Negative assertions are possible in all languages.

3. The sentences of all languages can pose questions.

4. Certain sentences of all languages can give commands.

All languages make use of transformations of the more elementary sentences, always by means of conjoining, nesting, or both. Furthermore, transformation rules universally perform a limited number of "fixed" operations out of all conceivable possibilities: insertion of additional elements; reduction or deletion of elements; and rearrangement or permutation of elements. Transformation rules are probably also universally applied in a fixed, least-to-most dominant cyclic order.

Certain specific rules of syntax are common to all (or most) languages. For example, it is probably a universal absolute that a syntactic plural exists in one form or another in all languages. Similarly, the existence of a syntactic past tense appears to be an absolute linguistic universal, although again the specific method of indicating pastness varies among languages. Although only one past tense form is present in some languages, there seems to be a strong universal tendency towards different degrees of pastness. Yet another kind of syntactic rule which probably is an absolute is the existence of some form of concord or "agreement" between certain sentence elements.

As for semantic features, not only does every language possesss a lexicon of words, but every language so far studied has been found to contain complex lexical items constructed from simpler ones. This phenomenon is accomplished in one of two ways (or both): by compounding or by the addition of affixes. Among affix types, present information indicates that the infix is the least common, while the suffix is the most prevalent. Compounding, on the other hand, most frequently appears to be binary, singularly in the case of the compounding of only two lexical elements, hierarchically in the case of multiple compounding.

(Thus, *streetcar conductor* consists first of the two elements, *streetcar* and *conductor*; and at the next level down, *streetcar* consists of the elements, *street* and *car*.)

The clauses of complex sentences tend toward the same structural forms. Equally dominant clauses tend to be ones that are compounded or clauses which are in apposition (i.e., a first clause followed by a second, complement clause). Embedded clauses, on the other hand, tend to be of a restricted number of types: relative clauses, adjectival modifier clauses, adverbial modifier clauses, and the like.

The sequential order of elements within a clause differs fairly widely among languages. Yet, there are certain tendencies, the strongest of which seems to favor the occurrence of subject before verb in the simplest sentences of most languages. Many linguists also believe that some form of verb auxiliary or auxiliaries are present in all languages, and further, that the form of auxiliaries is according to one or both of two methods: verb suffix forms and separate verb-related elements.

Languages seem to be about evenly divided as regards the sequential order of a verb and its objects, some being "verb-initial" and others being "verb-final" languages. Interestingly, however, as Ronald W. Langacker points out, the sequential order of verb-final languages seems to be the exact reverse of that in verb-initial languages.* That is, in verb-initial languages, the order is usually Verb + Direct Object + Oblique Object; in verb-final languages, the order is Oblique Object + Direct Object + Verb. Langacker also points out certain other reverse parallels between verb-initial and verb-final languages. In verb-initial languages like Samoan or English, for example, pre-positions seem to dominate over post-positions; conjunctions tend to attach to the second or following element rather than to the preceding one; modifiers— especially complex, larger-than-word ones—tend to follow the nouns they modify; and suffix-addition is used only infrequently as a grammatical device.

In verb-final languages like Japanese or Turkish, however, post-positions seem to dominate over pre-positions, conjunctions tend to attach to the preceding rather than to the following element; modifiers of all kinds, both simple and complex, usually precede the nouns they modify; and suffix-addition is heavily exploited as a grammatical device.

Such observations lead Langacker to conclude that, considering the total range of theoretical possibilities for clause construction, the methods toward which human languages universally tend are highly restrictive.

*See Chapter 9 of Ronald W. Langacker, *Language and Its Structure*, 2nd edition (Harcourt, 1973).

As for specific grammar rules of substitution, deletion, reduction, insertion, and permutation, it appears that certain of these are absolute universals. No language has yet been found, for example, which does not permit the substitution of a pronoun form for a second co-referential noun or noun phrase (a second noun phrase which is identical to an earlier noun phrase within the same clause). Also prevalent, and probably an absolute, is a grammar rule which permits the deletion of a noun or noun phrase when it occurs in a conjoined or embedded clause in the same syntactic position as that of an identical noun phrase in the dominant clause.

Grammar insertion rules across languages also possess strong universal tendencies. It is common to find grammar rules which call for the insertion of a lexically "empty" element in certain transformations (for example, "it" in the transformation, "*It* is raining"; or the insertion of an "empty" element as a subordination marker, such as the use of "that" in a nominal transformation like "*That* he is late is true.")

A grammar rule like the English rule which requires that personal pronouns be marked for case (*I, she, he,* for a subject pronoun; but *me, her,* or *him* for an object pronoun) also tends to occur in many languages. In fact, in many languages nouns are similarly marked for subjective or objective case.

As with reduction, deletion, substitution, and insertion rules, linguists have also discovered universal tendencies among permutation rules. One such rule, which has a strong tendency to occur among verb-initial languages especially, requires that relative pronouns and question words be in clause-initial positions. No exceptions to this last rule have yet been found among verb-initial languages, so that in all probability it represents a kind of universal absolute.

The truly significant thing about the recurrent tendency toward or actual use of certain specific grammar rules in language after language is that out of the entire range of possibilities, only a limited few seem to occur. Moreover, as was mentioned earlier, there is no apparent connection between the occurrence of certain rules and historical relatedness or geographical proximity of languages.

As Chomsky pointed out in his radio interview with Stuart Hampshire, many seemingly rational, simple, efficient grammatical operations never occur, while those which do occur are more often than not complex in the extreme. There exists no natural language, for instance, which makes use of such an obviously conceivable operation as that used in "Pig Latin," whereby every word beginning with a consonant deletes the initial consonant and moves it to the end of the word as the first sound in an "-ay" suffix (*fix* = *ixfay*; *land* = *andlay*). Likewise, no language has a rule which requires a noun to "agree" with any element other than its own modifier, or a verb to "agree" with an element other than its own subject or object.

So unlikely, in fact, are many apparently simple operations, such as the transformation of a declarative statement to a question by some elementary process like exactly reversing the word order or reversing the order of every two words; so unlikely is a rule which requires that the first word of every sentence be a noun with an initial consonant; so unlikely are any number of easily imagined elementary processes, as to suggest that certain operations are linguistic impossibilities. The investigations of linguistic universals to date thus strongly support the conclusion that the human brain is "programmed" to look for certain possibilities and to unconsciously reject other processes as insignificant, even when they show up accidentally.

PHONOLOGICAL UNIVERSALS

Just as all sentences in all languages are composed of strings of words which are put together according to universal concatenation rules, never randomly, so the words of all languages appear to be composed of an extremely limited number of combined sounds. No language has yet been found whose words cannot be subdivided into morphemes, and whose morphemes in turn cannot be further subdivided down to the point of minimal, inherently meaningless sound components or phonemes. Moreover, out of all the possible sounds the human vocal apparatus is capable of producing, only a small number constitute the fixed set of sounds from which the particular phonemes of specific languages are drawn.

As with syntactic and semantic rules, linguists are now able to isolate specific phonological rules which are either linguistic absolutes or universal linguistic tendencies. That is, evidence is accumulating to suggest the existence of a small, fixed number of universal rules of sound combination and organization. Moreover, many linguists now have strong reason to believe that phonological transformation processes are determined by phonological rules that apply in a cyclic sequential order from least to most dominant sounds.

Among the possible phonological universals, the following are some that have been suggested as either phonological absolutes or as strong phonological tendencies:

General, Mostly Substantive Phonological Universals

1. All languages use combinations of minimal, meaningless sounds (phonemes) to form meaningful word components (morphemes), which in turn combine to form the words of languages.

2. All languages make use of both consonant and vowel sounds.

3. All languages seem to make use of three nasal phonemes.

4. All languages make use of "glides" between certain sounds.

5. The phonemes of all languages are chosen from a fixed, restricted list of possible sounds which might conceivably be exploited in human languages.

6. No morpheme in any language has yet been discovered to consist of as many as, say, nine consecutive vowel sounds or nine consecutive consonant sounds.

7. For those languages which are "tone" languages, no morpheme has yet been discovered which consists of more than six "tones"; usually, in fact, a language will exploit only four or five different tones.

More Specific Formal Phonological Universals

There appear to exist certain phonological rules which determine which sounds may occur next to other sounds. For instance:

8. A phonological transformation rule which may be an absolute but which certainly represents a strong universal tendency requires the mutation or the deletion of unstressed vowels. English examples of such a vowel sound mutation principle can be illustrated with such word pairs as *realize/realization*; *senile/senility*; *fancy/fanciful*. The sound deletion principle can be illustrated with the English combinations, *I am/I'm*; *do not/don't*; *was not/wasn't*.

9. Another recurring phonological transformation rule calls for the aspiration of a voiceless consont (like the /p/ of *tap*) when it occurs in a sound-initial position: *pat*.

10. There seems to exist a common phonological rule that requires the insertion of a consonant sound segment between two separate and distinct vowel sounds, as in the English words *a + apple*, which becomes *an apple*.

11. Yet another apparently universal phonological rule calls for the nasalization of a vowel sound when it occurs before a nasal

consonant like /ŋ/. An example is the English word pair: *sin/ sing*.

12. The linguist would never expect to find certain consonant sounds transformed to other consonant sounds, as for example, a /k/ sound changed to /m/ or /l/. On the other hand, it is very common in all languages to find an /s/ or a /t/ sound changed to an /š/ sound: *face/facial*; *part/partial*.

SUMMARY COMMENTS

Work has only just begun in the search for linguistic universals. All linguists understand that their present conclusions must be regarded as tentative, for at any time new evidence may surface which disproves some of their current hypotheses. Nevertheless, enough progress has been made to allow for the conclusion that in all probability, linguistic universals exist as a reality—not only as extremely general, substantive statements concerning phenomena which all languages share in common, but also as more specific statements of formal universal principles that determine the grammar rules of all human languages.

Certainly, the assumption of the existence of such language universals goes a long way toward explaining both human linguistic creativity and the language acquisition process in the first place. From the infinite number of ways the earth might have come into existence, only one was needed. This one means of creation having taken place, evolutionary events followed certain patterns. It is certainly more useful and more interesting to study those patterns than to stand in awe of the fact that one course of events was followed rather than any other. The same applies to the origins and study of language. The evident truth simply cannot be ignored: that of all the myriad conceivable ways that languages could be structured, natural human languages seem to be confined to a limited and apparently fixed number of grammatical processes.

Still, in spite of the distance over which linguists have advanced their knowledge, we are a long way from reaching complete answers. Even if we accept the concept of innate linguistic specifications, there still remain a host of unanswered questions. Exactly what, for example, must language learners discover beyond that which is genetically specified in their own brains? How much of language learning is attributable to external observation and experience with a particular language? Are there precise, predetermined, specific phases through which every child must go before it discovers the grammar rules of its own native language? And to what extent are linguistic abilities and cognition dependent upon other innate psychological restraints? Can we, in fact, separate linguistic cognition from other equally unique human learning abilities?

Clearly, we will not learn all the answers for a very long time. That would require at least the development of an adequate theory of specific universal linguistic structure and a more general theory of human psychological organization, neither of which is currently available. We have learned a great deal, but what we can be reasonably sure of is minuscule compared to that which we still need to know.

Language is difficult to study and in some ways difficult to teach, because in spite of the progress which has been made, we still do not know enough. There seems to be small doubt that linguistic competence is just one part of a much larger psychological phenomenon about which we still have only superficial understanding. It is clear that before we have all or even nearly all the answers, we shall have to know a great deal more about the whole subject of human cognition—a subject about which some of the best modern scholarly minds are in substantial disagreement.

Annotated Bibliography

AARSLEFF, HANS, *The Study of Language in England, 1780–1860.* Princeton, N.J.: Princeton University Press, 1967. A scholarly history.

ALGEO, JOHN, *Problems in the Origins and Development of the English Language,* 2nd ed. New York: Harcourt Brace Jovanovich, Inc., 1972. A history of the English language with accompanying exercises.

ARLOTTO, ANTHONY, *Introduction to Historical Linguistics.* Boston: Houghton Mifflin Company, 1972. A book designed for the nonspecialist on the subject of historical and comparative linguistics.

BACH, EMMON, *Syntactic Theory.* New York: Holt, Rinehart and Winston, Inc., 1974. An up-to-date book on transformational grammar; best suited to the advanced student.

BERRY, THOMAS ELLIOTT, *The Study of Language.* Belmont, Calif.: Dickenson Publishing Company, Inc., 1971. A general book, aimed at the nonspecialist. Fairly current.

BOLINGER, DWIGHT, *Aspects of Language.* New York: Harcourt Brace Jovanovich Inc., 1968. Focuses primarily on structural linguistics for introductory students.

BRENGELMAN, FRED, *The English Language: An Introduction for Teachers.* Englewood Cliffs, N.J.: Prentice-Hall, Inc., 1970. Useful but very brief, and consequently very general.

BROWN, MARSHALL L., AND ELMER G. WHITE, *A Grammar of English Sentences: Parts and Patterns,* Books 1 and 2. Columbus, Ohio: Charles E. Merrill Publishing Company, 1968. A good transformational grammar workbook, but focuses on early form of TG grammar only.

CHISHOLM, WILLIAM S., JR., AND LOUIS T. MILIC, *The English Language: Form and Use.* New York: David McKay Company, Inc., 1974.

CHOMSKY, NOAM, *Aspects of the Theory of Syntax*. Cambridge, Mass.: The M.I.T. Press, 1965. Chomsky's first major revision of TG theory.

————, *Cartesian Linguistics: A Chapter in the History of Rationalist Thought*. New York: Harper and Row, Publishers, 1966. Traces the contributions of Rationalist language scholars.

————, *Language and the Mind*. New York: Harcourt Brace Jovanovich, Inc., 1968. (Enlarged edition, 1972) Includes much on Rationalist underpinnings.

————, *Syntactic Structures*. The Hague: Mouton Publishing Company, 1957. Chomsky's first book, in which he originally introduced TG grammar.

CHOMSKY, NOAM, AND MORRIS HALLE, *The Sound Pattern of English*. New York: Harper and Row, Publishers, 1968. Not a book for the beginner.

EMERY, DONALD W., *Sentence Analysis*. New York: Holt, Rinehart and Winston, Inc., 1961. This is a small paperback book which features traditional sentence diagraming.

EVERETT, EDWIN M., MARIE DUMAS, AND CHARLES WALL, *Correct Writing*. Boston: D. C. Heath and Company, 1948–1969. A workbook in traditional grammar, this freshman college composition text was first published in 1948. Its popularity has evidently been maintained over the years, for in 1954, a slightly enlarged version with new exercises was published as Form A and Form B (the explanations remained basically unchanged); and in 1961, Forms C and D (again with the same explanations, but with different exercises) were published. Finally, in 1964, the same authors rewrote the basic text— with yet another set of exercises— as an auto-instructional text, called Form II. The text is still adopted by many colleges. A second addition has just been published by Eugenia Butler, Mary Ann Hickman, and Lalla Overby—a revision and enlargement of the original.

FRANCIS, W. NELSON, *The English Language, an Introduction*. New York: W. W. Norton and Company, Inc., 1965. A book intended as a background text to be used in freshman writing courses.

FREEMAN, DONALD C., ed., *Linguistics and Literary Style*. New York: Holt, Rinehart and Winston, Inc., 1970. Concentrates on stylistics—specifically, on the analysis of literary styles.

FRIES, CHARLES C., *Linguistics, The Study of Language* (Chapter Two of *Linguistics and Reading*). New York: Holt, Rinehart and Winston, Inc., 1964.

————, *The Structure of English*. New York: Harcourt, Brace and World, Inc., 1952. This book was one of the first important books in structural linguistics.

FROMKIN, VICTORIA, AND ROBERT RODMAN, *An Introduction to Language*. New York: Holt, Rinehart and Winston, Inc., 1974.

GAENG, PAUL A., *Introduction to the Principles of Language*. New York: Harper and Row, Publishers, 1971.

GLEASON, H. A., Jr., *An Introduction to Descriptive Linguistics*, revised edition. New York: Holt, Rinehart and Winston, Inc., 1961. This is a difficult book, but well worth the effort. One of the best on the subject of structural linguistics.

GREENBERG, JOSEPH H., ed., *Universals of Language: Report of a Conference Held at Dobbs Ferry, New York, April 13–15, 1961.* Cambridge, Mass.: The M.I.T. Press, 1963.

GRINDER, JOHN T., AND SUZETTE HADEN ELGIN, *Guide to Transformational Grammar: History, Theory, Practice.* New York: Holt, Rinehart and Winston, Inc., 1973. This text is probably more difficult than the ordinary introductory book on transformational grammar. It incorporates developments in transformational-generative grammar theory from *Syntactic Structures* through *Aspects* and up to current debates, though rather generally.

HERNDON, JEANNE H., *A Survey of Modern Grammars.* New York: Holt, Rinehart and Winston, Inc., 1970. This book describes only the early form of transformational grammar.

HUGHES, JOHN P., *Linguistics and Language Teaching.* New York: Random House, 1968.

JACOBS, RODERICK A., AND PETER S. ROSENBAUM, *English Transformational Grammar.* Waltham, Mass.: Xerox College Publishing, 1968. A very good introductory transformation text which incorporates many post-*Aspects* developments in TG theory.

JESPERSEN, OTTO, *Language, Its Nature, Development and Origin.* New York: Henry Holt and Company, 1933. This book was originally published in 1922, was reprinted in 1923, 1925, 1928, and 1933—which is the edition I consulted. There is little doubt why the book continues to be reprinted, for Otto Jespersen was one of the great scholarly traditionalists whose work is still consulted and respected by linguists today.

KERR, ELIZABETH M., AND RALPH M. ADERMAN, eds., *Aspects of American English*, 2nd ed. New York: Harcourt Brace Jovanovich, Inc., 1971. A general history and survey, not altogether current.

KING, ROBERT D., *Historical Linguistics and Generative Grammar.* Englewood Cliffs, N. J.: Prentice-Hall, Inc., 1969. General survey.

LAIRD, CHARLTON, *The Miracle of Language.* New York: The World Publishing Company, 1953. This book is written for those who are not specialists in linguistics. Despite its apparently obsolete date, the book is one which still will intrigue bright beginners.

LAMBERTS, J. J., *A Short Introduction to English Usage.* New York: McGraw-Hill Book Company, 1972. A general survey.

LANGACKER, RONALD W., *Fundamentals of Linguistic Analysis.* New York: Harcourt Brace Jovanovich, Inc., 1972.

———, *Language and Its Structure: Some Fundamental Linguistic Concepts*, 2nd ed. New York: Harcourt Brace Jovanovich, Inc., 1973. This book has gone through one reprinting and one revision. The author seems to me to be a linguist who is intent on keeping abreast of the newest developments, yet he writes a book which any beginning student will find enjoyable.

LANGENDOEN, D. TERENCE, *Essentials of English Grammar.* New York: Holt, Rinehart and Winston, Inc., 1970.

Language/Rhetoric: the Oregon Curriculum, A Sequential Program in English. New York: Holt, Rinehart and Winston, Inc., 1970. A student of mine, already teaching in a high school, introduced me to this high school series which his school had just adopted. It is, so far as I can judge from Books V and VI, an excellent high school series.

LEE, DONALD W., ed., *English Language Reader.* New York: Dodd, Mead and Company, 1970. Subtitled "Introductory Essays and Exercises," this book was undergoing its sixth printing in 1970. It contains a good collection of essays, which focus primarily on the work of the American structuralists and which also include some traditional grammar background. Very little notice is given to transformational grammar.

LEES, ROBERT B., *The Grammar of English Nominalizations.* The Hague: Mouton Publishers, 1968. Originally published by Indiana University in 1963, this book has gone through numerous reprintings. Lees was one of the early converts to transformational-generative grammar, and this book made other converts. Possibly somewhat difficult for beginners, mostly because of its thoroughness.

LEFEVRE, HELEN E., AND CARL A. LEFEVRE, *Writing by Patterns*, Form B. New York: Alfred A. Knopf, Inc., 1968. A useful workbook. Focuses primarily on early form of TG grammar.

LYONS, JOHN, *Noam Chomsky.* New York: The Viking Press, 1970. Part of the Modern Masters Series edited by Frank Kermode, this paperback is a well written account of Noam Chomsky's contributions to the science of linguistics. The book is written for the nonspecialist. Recommended for beginners.

MARCKWARDT, ALBERT H., reviser, *Modern English: Its Growth and Present Use.* New York: Charles Scribner's Sons, 1969. Originally published in 1909, this book by George Philip Krapp, professor of English at Columbia University, was a pioneer work. Written for the nonspecialist, the book explained the contributions of linguists up to that time and provided an enlightened discussion of then-current usage. Professor Marckwardt, a Princeton University linguist, updated the book in this revision to make it applicable to the present state of English usage.

MAROON, JOHN L., *Writer's Review: A Manual for College Writers.* Glenview, Ill.: Scott, Foresman and Company, 1968. This is a recently published traditional grammar workbook.

MARTIN, CHARLES B., AND CURT M. RULON, *The English Language Yesterday and Today.* Boston: Allyn and Bacon, Inc., 1973. An overall history of grammar systems. Fairly current.

MALMSTROM, JEAN, AND CONSTANCE WEAVER, *Transgrammar: English Structure, Style, and Dialects.* Glenview, Ill.: Scott Foresman and Company, 1973. This recent book reviews in considerable detail the contributions of structural linguistics and transformational grammar to date. It also includes a discussion of applications of TG analysis to the structure of literary style, especially as regards poetry and fiction.

MELLON, JOHN C., *Transformational Sentence-Combining.* Urbana, Ill.: National

Council of Teachers of English, 1969 (NCTE Research Report No. 10). Report of a research project modeled along the lines of the Bateman-Zidonis research, in which Mellon demonstrates that practice in transformational sentence combining increases the maturity of seventh grade writing.

NEWSOME, VERNA L., *Structural Grammar in the Classroom*. Urbana, Ill.: National Council of Teachers of English, 1961. A concise introduction to structural grammar with suggestions for teaching structural patterns. Designed for prospective teachers, this booklet is not a text, but a guide.

PAST, RAY, *Language as a Lively Art*. Dubuque, Iowa: William C. Brown, Publishers, 1970. Written in a jaunty style that students will probably appreciate, this book is thorough, knowledgeable, and linguistically sound. An excellent introductory linguistics text. Does not discuss the most recent linguistic controversies.

PETERS, ROBERT A., *A Linguistic History of English*. Boston: Houghton Mifflin Company, 1968.

POSTMAN, NEIL, AND CHARLES WEINGARTNER, *Linguistics: A Revolution in Teaching*. New York: Dell Publishing Company, Inc., 1966. A small book containing many suggestions for "do-it-yourself" classroom grammar teaching techniques found to be successful in actual classroom situations. Recommended for prospective English teachers.

ROBERTS, PAUL, *English Sentences*. New York: Harcourt, Brace and World, Inc., 1962. Part of a grade-through-high school series, this is an entertainingly written high school text based on some transformational grammar principles, early form.

———, *English Syntax: An Introduction to Transformational Grammar*. New York: Harcourt, Brace and World, Inc., 1964. A self-teaching text in transformational grammar, early form.

———, *Modern Grammar*. New York: Harcourt, Brace and World, Inc., 1968. An abridgement for college use of the Roberts English Series. (See *English Sentences*.)

SALUS, PETER H., *Linguistics*. Indianapolis: The Bobbs-Merrill Company, Inc., 1969. A small monograph, part of the Bobbs-Merrill series in Speech Communication.

SHORES, DAVID L., *Contemporary English: Change and Variation*. Philadelphia: J. B. Lippincott Company, 1972. A thorough and informed discussion of language diversity and variation, designed to provide prospective English teachers with accurate information and to encourage their understanding. Recommended.

SLEDD, JAMES, *A Short Introduction to English Grammar*. Fairlawn, N. J.: Scott, Foresman and Company, 1959. A rather difficult book written as a college-level text in structural grammar.

SLOBIN, DAN I., *Psycholinguistics*. Glenview,, Ill.: Scott, Foresman and Company, 1971. Part of Scott, Foresman's Basic Psychological Concept Series, this small book contains an excellent discussion of recent research in language acquisition by children plus a discussion of linguistic universals. Recommended.

STRONG, WILLIAM, *Sentence Combining*. New York: Random House, 1973. A sentence-composing book designed to increase the writing skills of students who need more writing practice by making them conscious of the transformational processes they already use implicitly in their speech.

Studies in American English: Third Texas Conference on Problems of Linguistic Analysis in English, May 9–12, 1958. Austin: University of Texas, 1962. A transcript of a panel discussion conducted by Archibald Hill. This is the conference at which Noam Chomsky argued so lucidly and so successfully against his structuralist critics. Well worth reading.

THOMAS, OWEN, *Transformational Grammar and the Teacher of English*. New York: Holt, Rinehart and Winston, Inc., 1965. One of the best of the college level transformational grammar texts for the early form of TG grammar. (See next entry.)

THOMAS, OWEN, and EUGENE KINTGEN, *Transformational Grammar and the Teacher of English: Theory and Practice*, 2nd ed. New York: Holt, Rinehart and Winston, Inc., 1974. Despite its having essentially the same title as Thomas's earlier TG grammar text, this book is a completely revised and updated text which focuses primarily on the *Aspects* transformational grammar theory, but which also includes a discussion of post-*Aspects* developments. An excellent book.

WARDHAUGH, RONALD, *Introduction to Linguistics*. New York: McGraw-Hill Book Company, 1972. An introduction to structural linguistics, with special emphasis on phonology and morphology.

Anthologies and Books of Readings

ALLEN, HAROLD B., ed., *Readings in Applied English Linguistics*, 2nd ed. New York: Appleton-Century-Crofts, 1958. Excellent selections, most of which focus on structural linguistics. Recommended.

ANDERSON, WALLACE L., AND NORMAN C. STAGEBERG, eds., *Introductory Readings on Language*, revised. New York: Holt, Rinehart and Winston, Inc., 1966. Very general and not too current.

CLARK, MARDEN J., SOREN F. COX, AND MARSHALL R. CRAIG, eds., *About Language*. New York: Charles Scribner's Sons, 1970. A very good collection of essays covering the nature of language, the power of language, the history of language development, the history of grammar systems, usage, dialects, and so on. In each of these sections the editors include poetry or short fiction which illustrates or satirizes the subject. A good readings book for a freshman composition course.

CLARK, VIRGINIA P., PAUL A. ESCHHOLZ, AND ALFRED F. ROSA, eds., *Language: Introductory Readings*. New York: St. Martin's Press, 1972. Another collection of essays on many aspects of linguistic study. In addition to the usual subjects (language and thought; language and culture; the systems of grammar; words, meanings, and the dictionary; American dialects), the book has a section entitled "Space and the Language of the Body."

FODOR, JERRY A., AND JERROLD J. KATZ, eds., *The Structure of Language:*

Readings in the Philosophy of Language. Englewood Cliffs, N.J.: Prentice-Hall, Inc., 1964. A collection of then-recent papers in the theory of language by linguistic scholars, with the goal in mind of reaching a philosophy of language by means of exploiting the insights of empirical linguists. Not an easy collection for the nonspecialist to read.

Gorrell, Robert M., Charlton Laird, and Ronald E. Freeman, eds., *Modern English Reader*. Englewood Cliffs, N.J.: Prentice-Hall, Inc., 1970. Designed for use in introductory writing courses, the editors preface each section with a discussion of rhetorical principles and follow each section with a list of study guides.

Heffernan, William A., and James P. Degnan, eds., *Language and Literature Reader*. Beverly Hills, Calif.: Glencoe Press, 1968. Another very general reader designed for use in freshman writing courses. Includes many literary applications.

Hogins, J. Burl, and Robert E. Yarber, eds., *Language: An Introductory Reader*. New York: Harper and Row, Publishers, 1969. Another collection of language essays, stories, and so on, for use in freshman composition courses.

Hungerford, Harold, Jay Robinson, and James Sledd, eds., *English Linguistics: An Introductory Reader*. Glenview, Ill.: Scott, Foresman and Company, 1970. A small number of across-the-board selections by linguists from Jespersen to Chomsky. One wishes for a greater number of selections, particularly since the editorial comments are so good.

Jacobs, Roderick A., ed., *Studies in Language: Introductory Readings in Transformational Linguistics*. Lexington, Mass.: Xerox College Publishing, 1973. An excellent little book, more than half of which is written by the author-editor himself. Gives an excellent, concise account of general background and recent developments.

Laird, Charlton, and Robert M. Gorrell, eds., *Reading About Language*. New York: Harcourt Brace Jovanovich, Inc., 1971. A very good reader for linguistically-oriented writing courses.

Lester, Mark, ed., *Readings in Applied Transformational Grammar*. New York: Holt, Rinehart and Winston, Inc., 1970. Contains essays written by leading transformational scholars. Part I is concerned primarily with psycholinguistic questions, Part II with literary and stylistic applications of transformational grammar.

Reibel, David A., and Sanford A. Schane, eds., *Modern Studies in English: Readings in Transformational Grammar*. Englewood Cliffs, N.J.: Prentice-Hall, Inc., 1969. A well-organized collection of articles on English transformational syntax, covering a timespan of ten years (1957–1967). All articles are written by leading transformational linguists.

Salus, Peter H., ed., *On Language: Plato to von Humboldt*. New York: Holt, Rinehart and Winston, Inc., 1969. A small collection of works by early language scholars who were influential in their own time for the most part, but who had since been ignored until Chomsky resurrected an interest in philosophical grammar.

SANDERSON, JAMES L., AND WALTER K. GORDON, eds., *Exposition and the English Language*, Introductory Studies, 2nd ed. Englewood Cliffs, N.J.: Prentice-Hall, Inc., 1969. Geared to a composition teaching approach that focuses on types of exposition (process, classification, argumentation, illustration, comparison/contrast, and so on), this book combines pedagogical writing suggestions with an extensive collection of essays on various aspects of language study. One of the better texts for freshman writing courses. The last section contains a selection of poems and short stories.

Answers to Exercises

PART ONE: TRADITIONAL GRAMMAR

Exercise 1: Parts of Speech (*page 29*)

1. N	**6.** PRO	**11.** CONJ	**16.** PRO	**21.** PREP
2. PRO	**7.** ADV	**12.** ADV	**17.** ADJ	**22.** N
3. PREP	**8.** ADJ	**13.** ADJ	**18.** ADV	**23.** ADJ
4. ADJ	**9.** V	**14.** ADJ	**19.** ADJ	**24.** CONJ
5. PREP	**10.** PREP	**15.** N	**20.** INT	**25.** ADV

Exercise 2: Parts of Speech (*page 30*)

These answers are much more difficult than the ones in Exercise 1. In most of the sentences, words have been used to mean something different from the expected. In fact, the definitions you have been furnished will be of very little help for many of these words. Moreover, there are a number of constructions which cannot be classified at all—for the reason that you have been provided with no category type which might include them.

1. N
2. PRO? ADJ? (A case can be made for either answer.)
3. V (Entire verb = *are leaving*)
4. N? Or, if viewed as an elliptical construction, V.
5. PREP if kneeling is viewed as a noun. CONJ if kneeling is viewed as a verb.
6. CONJ
7. V
8. X (No part-of-speech label given. A lexically "empty" word like this is, however, called an expletive.)
9. PREP (Note that this sentence, which is quite grammatical, ends with a preposition.)

10. ADV (Negative particles like *never, not*, and so on are more closely related to the verb than to any other sentence element.)

11. ADV (This kind of adverb particle actually is so closely related to the verb that it changes the verb's meaning.)

12. Noun Adjunct (Traditional grammars usually call this an adjective, much to the distress of most students, who know it is a noun.)

13. ADJ

14. ADJ (Again, this is a noun form in a position we usually associate with the adjective position. Transformational grammar explains how a noun form can be transformed in this manner, but traditional school grammars generally call possessive nouns and possessive pronouns which precede a noun by the adjective label. See Sentences 2 and 16.)

15. N (A verb form functioning in a noun position.)

16. ADJ (See Sentences 2 and 14 above.)

17. V (The first part of a verb + adverb particle combination. See also Sentences 11, and 23.)

18. INT

19. ADV (This is a conjunctive or connective adverb, perhaps better seen as a sentence modifier than as the verb modifier.)

20. ADV

21. X (Another expletive, like *there* in Sentence 8.)

22. Noun Adjunct (Again, referred to misleadingly as an adjective by most traditional school grammars. See Sentence 12.)

23. ADV (Another verb + adverb particle. See Sentences 11 and 17.)

24. PREP (Note the difference in function between *down* in this sentence and the same word as used in Sentences 11 and 23.)

25. V

26. ADJ

27. N (Note that this is a verb form used in a noun position.)

28. V (The entire verb is *is walking*.)

29. ADJ (In this sentence, a verb form is functioning as an adjective.)

30. Noun Adjunct (Compare with Sentences 12 and 22.)

Exercise 3: Parts of Speech (page 31)

1. The traditional classification system, as given in this book, is not complete. It fails to explain expletives, like *there* in Sentences 8 and 21 of Exercise 2, or like *it* in a sentence like *"It* is snowing." It also fails to explain noun adjuncts, and adverb particles. Thirdly, it does not explain the word *to* in sentences like "He told John *to* go home."

2. The definitions are far from being mutually exclusive. In many cases, such as with possessive nouns and pronouns, one is at a loss whether to call the word an adjective or a noun or pronoun. Or consider the word *working* in the sentence "Working is important in America." *Working* is unquestionably an "action" word in this sentence, yet we are told to consider it a noun. Still another dilemma is posed by the word *Sir*, as used in the sentence "Give it to me, *Sir.*" Since the word is obviously a substitute term of address for a

man who has a proper name, are we to call *sir* a noun or a pronoun? No satisfactory answers to these questions are offered by the definitions provided.

3. No, the principle changes. In fact, at various times three different classification principles are used. Sometimes, as with nouns, pronouns, verbs, and to a lesser extent, adjectives, a word class is determined according to *lexical* or *semantic meaning*. At other times, a class is determined by a word's *position* (prepositions are in prepositional phrase positions; coordinating conjunctions are in positions *between* equivalent constructions; subordinating conjunctions are in pre-clause positions; and so on), or by a word's *function* (adjectives and adverbs modify; prepositions indicate grammatical relationships; interjections interrupt; conjunctions connect), or by a *combination of function and position*. In other words, no consistent classification principle is followed.

Note: It is important to point out that the part-of-speech definitions presented in this book are merely provided as fairly typical of the definitions which most pedagogical grammars provide. Scholarly traditionalists, in their larger and more careful works, did not fail to speak of formal characteristics as well (such things as that nouns have number and can be made possessive, that verbs have a number of inflectional forms), nor did they fail to distinguish very carefully between the form of a word or word group on the one hand and its function (in a given construction) on the other. Fuzzy definitions like those given here nevertheless prevailed (and still, alas, prevail) in our schools.

Exercise 4: Subjects and Verbs (*page 35*)

SUBJECT (Head Noun)	VERB
1. girl	was
2. you (implied)	do touch
3. Who	broke
4. he	had been faced
5. leader	worked
6. reason	was
7. problems	remained
8. Neither	was (An argument could be made here for *attempts* as the subject, except that if that were true, the verb should be *were* in order for it to agree with the subject.)
9. books *and* papers	were found (Notice that the subject is compound.)
10. He	piled *and* left (Compound verb)
11. we	take
12. man	sat (There is some question whether the verb here is *sat* alone or the expression, *sat smoking*. The justification for viewing the verb as *sat* might be

that two sentences have been here combined: (1) the dominant sentence, "The old man sat in front of the cheerful fire," and (2) "The old man was happily smoking a pipe.")

13. she	decided	(Main Clause)
she	would give up	(Subordinate Clause)
14. I	must give	
15. He	made *and* did know	
16. John	has arrived	
17. traps	were	
18. she	could have said	
19. This	is	
20. grin	makes	(Again, one can reasonably question whether the verb might be viewed as *makes suspect* or *makes (to) suspect*. It seems to me that a good argument could be made for any one of these possible answers.)

Exercise 5: Nonheaded Subjects (*page 36*)

The entire subject is given here for the main clause in each of the twenty sentences in this exercise. An X occurs before every subject which is nonheaded.

X	**1.**	Maintaining his excellent game
	2.	She
X	**3.**	What you mean
X	**4.**	Going to eight o'clock classes
	5.	a rusty nail
X	**6.**	To give up now
	7.	Richard
X	**8.**	His always being late
X	**9.**	Teasing her little sister
	10.	That movie you told me about
X	**11.**	What she will do now
X	**12.**	Whoever said that
	13.	the lost test
	14.	Her system of studying
X	**15.**	Playing with matches
X	**16.**	"I don't want to"
	17.	The keys of my typewriter
	18.	He
X	**19.**	*Sentence Analysis*
X	**20.**	That she dislikes you

Note: The subjects of some of these sentences are subordinate or dependent clauses which themselves contain subjects and verbs:

Sentence 3—you/mean
Sentence 10—you/told

Sentence 11—she/will do
Sentence 12—Whoever/said
Sentence 16—I/do want
Sentence 18—he/meant
Sentence 20—she/dislikes

Exercise 6: Verb Types (page 46)

1. I	10. L	19. L
2. L	11. T	20. T
3. T	12. I	21. L
4. L	13. L	22. L
5. I	14. I	23. T
6. T	15. T	24. T
7. I	16. L	24. L
8. T	17. T	
9. L	18. T	

Exercise 7: Verb Types (page 47)

1. T	8. T	15. T
2. I	9. T	16. T
3. T	10. L	17. T
4. T	11. T	18. L
5. L	12. L	19. I
6. L	13. L	20. I
7. I	14. T	

Exercise 8: Complements (page 48)

1. We **elected** *him/the boy most likely to succeed.*	DO/ OC-N
2. My favorite **is** *the history teacher.*	SC-N
3. His account of the trip **was** very *interesting.*	SC-A
4. He **decided** *to quit* because he was sick of studying.	DO
5. He decided to quit because he **was** *sick of studying.*	SC-A
6. The bird **continues** its *singing.*	DO
7. It continues whether or not it **is** *happy.*	SC-A
8. **Send** the *school/a transcript* of your grades.	IO/DO
9. They **gave** *him/* a terrible *schedule*	IO/DO
10. She **called** *him* a big *baby.*	DO/OC-N
11. Her idea **is** *good* enough for me.	SC-A
12. Before I **leave** *you*, wish me luck!	DO
13. Before I leave you, **wish** *me luck*!	IO/DO
14. He **has given** my *idea* much *thought.*	IO/DO
15. We **made** *Alex/responsible* for supplies.	DO/OC-A
16. He **labels** every *attempt* a *failure.*	DO/OC-N
17. Why **is** Martha so *happy?*	SC-A
18. That dress **fits** *her* beautifully.	DO

19. Yes, it really **becomes** *her* too.   DO
20. It **is** very *easy* to please Tom.   SC-A

Exercise 9: *Complements* (*page 49*)

1. I **think** *we are lost*.   DO
2. I think we **are** *lost*.   SC-A
3. I followed the directions *which* he **gave** *me*.   DO/IO
4. **Will** you **give** *me* a *lesson* on the organ?   IO/DO
5. Perhaps you **can teach** *me* the new *steps*.   IO/DO
6. I **cannot guarantee** *to make you a good dancer*.   DO
7. He **made** of himself a *leader*.   DO
8. He **made** *himself* a *leader*.   DO/OC-N
9. She **made** *herself* *beautiful*.   DO/OC-A
10. She **made** *herself* a beautiful *person*.   DO/OC-N
11. She **made** *him* a good *wife*.   IO/DO
12. He **made** *her* a good *wife*.   DO/OC-N
13. She **made** *him* a *sandwich*.   IO/DO
14. **Isn't** language *tricky*?   SC-A
15. She **called** *him*/a *cad*.   DO/OC-N
16. She **called** *him*/a *cab*.   IO/DO
17. She **called** *him*/*wonderful*.   DO/OC-A
18. She **called** *him* on the telephone.   DO
19. **Do** you **see** *why foreigners become confused*?   DO
20. Do you see why foreigners **become** *confused*?   SC-A

Exercise 10: *Active and Passive Verbs + Complements* (*page 52*)

Active Voice	Passive Voice
Intransitive Verb:	
3. The coffee has been boiling furiously for several minutes.	X
Transitive Verb + DO:	
12. The doctor could not feel the child's pulse.	**7.** The child's pulse could not be felt by the doctor.
Transitive Verb + IO + DO:	
6. Tom sent his mother a birthday card.	**4.** A birthday card was sent his mother by Tom.
	11. His mother was sent a birthday card.
Transitive Verb + DO + OC-N:	
10. They will name the baby Junior.	**8.** The baby will be named Junior.
Transitive Verb + DO + OC-A:	
5. The stupid man painted the house red and green.	**2.** The house was painted red and green by the stupid man.

Active Voice	Passive Voice
Linking Verb + SC-N: **9.** That boy over there is my brother. **13.** My brother is that boy over there.	X
Linking Verb + SC-A: **1.** He has been feeling **terrible** this morning.	X

Exercise 11: *Active and Passive Verbs* (*page 52*)

1. was flirting, A
2. was, A
3. should have been told, P
4. is saying, A
5. has been told, P
6. must have been asked, P
7. must have been, A
8. has been done, P
9. was caused, P
10. could have been planned, P
11. seems, A
12. will have been attending, A
13. was known, P
14. could have succeeded, A
15. had been fogged (in), P
16. should be separated, P
17. must have been, A
18. must have been excited, P
19. was considered, P
20. must have been sleeping, A
21. should have been, A
22. was covered, P
23. has been parked, P
24. think, A
    is, A
25. was frowned on, P

Exercise 12: *Some Questions* (*page 62*)

1. Two different principles are used for the classification of verbals. Gerunds and participles are classified according to their grammatical function: a verb form functioning as a noun is a gerund, a very form functioning as an adjective is a participle. Infinitives, on the other hand, are classified not according to function but rather according to form: i.e., one identifies an infinitive by the actual or implied presence of the infinitive marker, "to."
2. Inasmuch as one is unable to classify *walking* and *shouting* in the examples given by means of the classification system provided, it is clear that the system, as presented, is incomplete. The words are -ing (or present participle) forms, but their function in the sentence examples is adverbial.

Exercise 13: *Verbals* (*page 62*)

1. GER
2. V AD
3. GER
4. INF { Unless one views *want to* as an auxiliary.
5. PART
6. PART
7. INF
8. PART } Or perhaps both of these
9. PART } words are passive verbs.
10. GER
11. GER
12. PART
13. PART
14. GER
15. PART

16. PART

17. GER

18. ? } The entire expression, *going skating*, is used as noun subject, but there seems to be a verb-adverb relationship within the phrase.

19. PART

20. GER

21. GER

22. GER

23. V AD

24. PART } Or perhaps both of these

25. PART } words are passive verbs.

Exercise 14: *Infinitives* (*page 63*)

INFINITIVE	N/ADJ/ADV	INFINITIVE	N/ADJ/ADV
1. *to leave*	N	11. *to recover*	ADJ
2. *to help*	ADV	12. *to talk*	N Verb function within
3. *To begin*	N		in vbl phrase)
4. *to care* (Compar)	ADV	13. (*to*) *do**	?
5. *to cry*	N	14. *to say*	ADJ
6. (*to*) *help**	?	15. *to dance*	N
7. *to read*	N	16. (*to*) *go**	?
8. *to relax*	ADJ	17. *to be*	N
9. *to exist*	N	*to be*	N
10. *to forget*	ADV		

Exercise 15: *Verbal Phrases: Function* (*page 69*)

1. *passing the test* = NOM (Appositive); *suited to a genius* = ADJL
2. No verbal phrases
3. *turning off the fan* = NOM (Direct Object)
4. *walking in front* = ADJL
5. *to buy fresh vegetables* = ADVL
6. No verbal phrases
7. *to worry about* = ADJL
8. *being the center of attention* = NOM (Direct Object)
9. *to involve parents in the teaching of students* = ADVL; *the teaching of students* = NOM (Object of Preposition)
10. *carrying the books* = ADJL
11. *carrying the books* = ADVL
12. *carrying books* = NOM (Direct Object)
13. *cheating in college* = NOM (Object of Preposition)
14. *To quit now* = NOM (Subject)
15. *to work hard* = ADJL
16. *smiling like an idiot* = ADVL
17. *to tell his mother about having seen the accident* = ADVL; *having seen the accident* = NOM (Object of Preposition)
18. *to accomplish that year* = ADJL; *winning the trophy* = NOM (Subject Complement)

*Each of these examples (*let help, made do, let go*) actually seem to constitute the entire verb. They are in the nature of verb idioms.

Exercise 16: *Phrases: Form and Function* (*page 70*)

Form	Function		Form	Function
1. PREP P	ADVL	**14.** NP	NOM (DO)
2. VBL P	NOM (APPOS)	**15.** ADJ P	ADJL
3. PREP P	ADJL	**16.** PRED P	VBL
4. VBL P	NOM (SUB)	**17.** VP	VBL
5. VBL P	NOM (SUB)	**18.** ADVL P	ADVL
6. PRED P	VBL	**19.** ABS P	Independent or ADVL sentence modifier
7. VBL P	ADVL		
8. VP	VBL	**20.** VBL P	NOM (DO)
9. PREP P	ADVL	**21.** VBL P	NOM (SUB)
10. NP	NOM (OP)	**22.** VBL P	ADVL
11. PREP P	ADVL	**23.** NP	NOM (OP)
12. PREP P	ADJL	**24.** VBL P	ADJL
13. PREP P	ADJL	**25.** VBL P	NOM (APPOS)

Exercise 17: *Subordinate Clauses: Function* (*page 75*)

1. *which is held every September*	**1.**	ADJL
2. *If I argue with you now*	**2.**	ADVL
that I'm wrong		NOM
3. *as it does when people least expect it*	**3.**	ADVL
when people least suspect it		ADVL
4. *that I couldn't finish it*	**4.**	COMP
5. *who complains about teachers who fail him when he does no work*	**5.**	ADJL
who fail him when he does no work		ADJL
when he does no work		ADVL
6. *he was very sorry*	**6.**	NOM
7. *What she wrote in the letter*	**7.**	NOM
8. *that he isn't very mature*	**8.**	ADJL
9. *as she can be*	**9.**	COMP
10. *if you try to help me*	**10.**	ADVL
that you will criticize my slowness		NOM
11. *how many times they tried to call*	**11.**	NOM
12. *what's up front*	**12.**	NOM
that counts		ADJL
13. *since he came home*	**13.**	ADVL
14. *he worked at last year* (implied wh-word)	**14.**	ADJL

Exercise 18: *Clauses* (*page 77*)

MAIN CLAUSES	SUBORDINATE CLAUSES
1. we/went	storm/stopped
	we/had spotted

Main Clauses	Subordinate Clauses
2. I/do know	I/ponder what/makes I/have done
3. person/asks	motives/are
4. Writing the speech/took	I/had thought it/would (take)
5. Jay/decided	he/wanted who/had
6. He/planned he/was	she/might refuse
7. girls/*stopped* and *had*	
8. aim/is	

Exercise 19: Clauses (*page 78*)

Main Clauses	Subordinate Clauses
1. man/began	he/was
2. authors/start	they/know
3. he/will go	she/apologizes
4. Barking/is	which/needs that/lives
5. how a word functions/determines	word/functions
6. Mr. Brown/attempted	who/had been made
7. veterans/have sent	which/are solicited
8. Works/do need	which/are intended they/are distributed
9. I/think	stopping. . ./can make

Exercise 20: Connectives (*page 83*)

1. CC	**4.** SC	**7.** CC
2. CA	**5.** CC	**8.** CA
3. SC	**6.** PREP	**9.** CC

10. SC	14. CC	18. CA
11. CA	15. SC	19. SC
12. CA	16. CC	20. CA
13. SC	17. CC	

Exercise 21: *Connectives* (*page 84*)

1. SC (of an elliptical clause)
2. PREP
3. PREP
4. SC (of elliptical clause)
5. SC
6. SC (of elliptical clause)
7. SC (of elliptical clause)
8. PREP
9. PREP or SC of elliptical clause
10. SC
11. CC
12. CC
13. PREP
14. SC (of elliptical clause)
15. SC

Exercise 22: *Parts of Speech, Revisited* (*page 84*)

1. *hard* Noun: *Hard* is ordinarily not used as a noun.
   Adj: a *hard* test
   Adv: to try *hard*

2. *he* Noun: *He* is a pronoun. Verb: Don't "*he*" me!
   Pro: *He* is my friend. Part of Compound: a *he-man*

3. *mother* Noun: the *mother* Verb: to *mother* someone
   Part of Compound: a *mother pleaser*
   a *mother's boy*
   Interj: *Mother*! Am I tired!

4. *fast* Noun: a *fast* Adj: a *fast* car
   Verb: to *fast* Adv: to drive *fast*
   fast asleep
   Part of Compound: *religious fast*
   outfast

5. *hell* Noun: Go to *hell*!
   Verb + Particle: to *hell* around
   Part of Compound: a *hell hound*
   to be *hell bent*
   Interj: *Hell*, why didn't you tell me that?

6. *man* Noun: to a *man* Interj: Listen, *man*, I mean it.
   Verb: to *man* a boat *Man*! Is that funny!
   Part of Compound: a *man killer*
   to *man handle*

7. *paper*   Noun: some *paper*   Verb + Particle: to *paper over*
           Verb: to *paper* a room
           Part of Compound: a *paper boy, wall paper, paper thin*

8. *like*   Noun: *likes* and dislikes   Verb: I *like* you.
           Adj: a *like* amount   Prep: She looks *like* me.
           Interj: I'm, *like*, tired, Man!
           Conj: to taste good *like* a cigarette should

9. *well*   Noun: The *well* ran dry.   Verb + Part: for tears to *well up*
           Adj: to feel *well*
           Adv: to drive *well*
           Interj: *Well*, you finally arrived!

10. *pretty*   Noun: *Pretty* is as *pretty* does.   Adj: A *pretty* face
           Verb: to *pretty* oneself   Adv: *pretty* good

PART TWO: STRUCTURAL GRAMMAR

Exercise 23: Nonsense Sentences (*page 107*)

Sentence A:
1. Participle
2. Preposition
3. Noun (plural)
4. Adjective
5. Noun (plural)
6. Adverb (modifies "groved")
7. Verb (past tense)
8. Noun (singular)
9. Conjunction (coord)
10. Adjective (participle)
11. Noun (singular)
12. Verb (past tense)
13. Noun (singular)
14. Verb (past tense)
15. Noun (singular)
16. Adverb (particle; goes with verb, "wabed")

Sentence B:
1. Adjective
2. Noun (plural)
3. Adverb (modifies "garfed")
4. Verb (past)
5. Noun (plural)
6. Conjunction (coord)
7. Adverb (Conj Adv)
8. Preposition
9. Adjective
10. Noun (singular)
11. Noun (singular)
12. Preposition
13. Noun (singular)
14. Verb (past)
15. Adverb (particle)
16. Adverb (modifies "froked out")

Sentence C:
1. Conjunction (subord)
2. Adjective
3. Noun (plural)
4. Adverb (modifies "loofed")
5. Verb (past)
6. Noun (singular)
7. Noun (plural)
8. Noun (demonstrative pronoun)
9. Verb (preceded by auxiliaries, "had" and "been")
10. Noun (plural)
11. Verb (past)
12. Noun (plural)
13. Adverb (particle)
14. Verb (past)
15. Adverb (particle)
16. Preposition
17. Noun (singular)

Exercise 24: *Artificial Language* (*page 108*)

1. na *wobet* (Answer A)
2. Ka *clariea* trafes na platid. (Answer D)
3. Kon roliea *gufiles* na wobetid. (Answer A)
4. ka *clarim* (Answer C)
5. Kon rolima talipes na *ardid*. (Answer B)
6. Kon roliea *sones* na tacketid. (Answer C)

Note: Although this is not a real human language, the same kind of grammar rules and grammar signals are used for this made-up language as are used by many natural human languages. On the basis of the limited evidence given here, we can list the following rules:

1. An article must agree in gender with the noun which follows it: *kon* = masculine, human; *ka* = feminine, human; *na* = neuter, nonhuman.
2. When the subject of a verb is third person, singular, the verb must agree with the subject. (We do not know whether first or second person, singular noun subjects or plural subjects impose an agreement requirement on their verbs.) Agreement is accomplished in this language by means of the *-s* verb suffix.
3. We have no evidence here that there is a plural noun form. We do know, however, that when a noun refers to a human person, the noun is marked to distinguish little or young from big or mature: the diminutive suffix is *-im*; the mature suffix is *-ie*.
4. According to whether a noun is used as a subject or as an object (direct object is all we can be certain of), it is marked with a case suffix: subjective case requires the *-a* suffix; objective case requires the *-id* suffix.
5. From the evidence given here, the language seems to rely on word order as one of its important grammatical markers.
6. Without hearing the language spoken, we can make no determination about the importance or lack of importance of intonation signals.
7. Except for the use of articles, we have no further indication whether or not structure words are significant as grammatical markers.
8. We have no evidence here that derivational suffixes are important language signals. (We do, however, have many indications of the importance of inflectional endings.)

Exercise 25: *Grammatical Signals* (*page 115*)

1. Inflectional subject and verb endings
2. Word Order
3. Intonation
4. Derivational *-ly* ending
5. Word Order
6. Intonation (stress)
7. Word Order
8. Derivational ending
9. Intonation
10. Derivational ending
11. Intonation
12. Presence of structure word, "to"
13. Inflectional endings
14. Word Order
15. Word Order
16. Inflectional ending (*-ing* on verb)
17. Inflectional ending (*-ing* on verb)
18. Word Order
19. Presence of structure word, "a"

20. Intonation
21. Word Order
22. Intonation
23. Presence of structure word,

"with"
24. Word Order
25. Word Order

Note: Word Order is possibly the single most important grammatical signal in English.

Exercise 26: Grammatical Singnals (page 117)

The asterisked answers below are ambiguous for reasons other than "missing signals."

1. It is not clear whether "written" is to function as the main verb with the auxiliary "have," or whether "written invitations" functions as the object of the verb "have." A structure word, like *some* or *the* can clear up the ambiguity:

> They have *some* written invitations. Or   They have written *some* invitations.

2. Again, a structure word can clear up the ambiguity:

> Martha had *several* frosted cakes or Martha had frosted *several* cakes.

*3. The difficulty here concerns the function of the word "French." Does the sentence mean that French people fried something, or that French people were electrocuted? ("Fry" is a slang term meaning to undergo electrocution in an electric chair.) Or are we talking about a particular kind of potato? About the only way to correct the ambiguity of this sentence is to provide more context.

*4. Again, the problem here is not that a signal is missing. Rather, it isn't clear whether the word "thing" is to be interpreted as slang. The best solution is once again to provide more context.

*5. More context is needed for this sentence as well. Does the sentence mean that someone threw stones at the students, or does it mean that they were drunk on liquor or "spaced out" on drugs? More information is needed— and would, of course, be provided in a larger context.

*6. The hearer or reader of this sentence does not know (when it is out of context) how to interpret the expression "for the birds." Depending on the level of usage, the sentence can be either a straightforward declaration that the food is for the birds to eat or a criticism of human food.

7. The problem here is whether the word "frying" is to be interpreted as an adjective (participle) or as a word with a verbal function. There is no way in writing to clear up the ambiguity except to reword the sentence. As a spoken utterance, intonation (pitch, stress, and pace) can probably distinguish between the two possible meanings:

> She hates frýing chicken. (meaning she doesn't like fried chicken)
>
> or
>
> She hates frying chícken. (meaning she dislikes the job of frying chicken).

8. This sentence also represents a writing but not a speaking problem, as do all the rest of the examples. Where one puts the strongest stress makes a difference in meaning:

> the answer called for (meaning the called-for answer, with "needed" as the main verb)

or

> the answer called for needed (necessary) study (with "called for" functioning as the verb and "needed" as an adjective)

9. Where one puts the juncture makes a difference, in this sentence, whether the clause "that he heard" functions as an adjectival modifier of "words," or whether the words "that he heard a trace of a foreign accent" function as the direct object of the verb "sensed."

10. This writing problem, called by some Handbooks a "squinting modifier," concerns whether "precisely" modifies "printed" (the word preceding it) or "to prevent" (the expression following). For the first interpretation, "precisely" receives the strongest stress; for the second, "printing" is stressed more strongly.

Exercise 27: Segmental Phonemes (page 131)

1. /buk/
2. /fatiy/
3. /fawnd/
4. /šayn/
5. /fon/ (or /fown/)
6. /ohrlan/
7. /pruwvd/
8. /midnayt/
9. /šænk/
10. /fædz/
11. /limz/
12. /čopt/
13. /mis/
14. /šuw baks/
15. /diš/
16. /dič/

Exercise 28: Segmental Phonemes: Consonants (page 132)

A. Examples of contrasting pairs showing initial consonant phonemes:

*f*at/*v*at   *t*ot/*d*ot
*s*ue/*z*oo   *c*ut/*g*ut
*p*an/*b*an   *th*istle/*th*is'll

B. Examples of contrasting pairs showing middle consonant phonemes:

sta*p*le/sta*b*le   loo*s*ing/lo*s*ing, la*c*er/la*z*er
plo*tt*er/plo*dd*er   e*th*er/ei*th*er
an*ch*or/an*g*er   me*sh*er/mea*s*ure
kni*f*ed/kni*v*ed   le*ch*er/le*dg*er

C. Examples of contrasting pairs showing final consonant phonemes:

ta*p*/ta*b*   hi*ss*/hi*s*
ca*t*/ca*d*   tee*th*/tee*the*
bu*ck*/bu*g*   et*ch*/ed*ge*
hal*f*/ha*ve*   go*sh*/gara*ge*

(The last example is not a minimal pair, but except for a few words borrowed from French or other languages, English words tend not to end in /ž/.)

Exercise 29: Segmental Phonemes: Vowels (page 132)

p*i*t/p*e*t   *feather/father*
p*i*t/p*a*t   gl*a*ss/gl*o*ss, b*a*t/b*ou*ght
p*i*t/p*u*t, k*i*ck/c*oo*k   *je*st/*ju*st
b*e*t/b*u*t   *je*st/*gi*st
b*a*d/b*u*d   b*oo*k/b*a*lk
b*a*t/b*oa*t

Exercise 30: Suprasegmental Phonemes: Pitch (page 140)

Note: Pitch variations differ among individuals and among dialect areas. The answers given here reflect what I think to be my own normal intonation. Your answers will probably vary somewhat.

1. He's a big sissy.

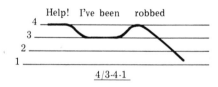

2. You *said* it!

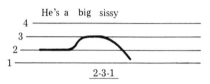

3. Help! I've been robbed!

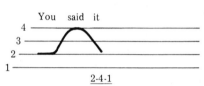

4. Are you hungry?

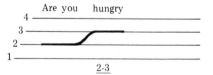

5. Yes, I'm starved.

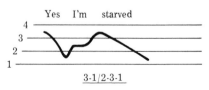

Exercise 31: Suprasegmental Phonemes: Stress (page 141)

1. náturally   **3.** fámily
2. cashiér   **4.** entíre

5. partícipate
6. waítresses
7. fávorite
8. turns óff
9. túrns off
10. fínal
11. finále
12. cóme to

13. come tó
14. cóntent
15. contént
16. carried oút
17. íntimate
18. gráduate
19. tránsplant
20. tránsport

Exercise 32: Suprasegmental Phonemes: Stress (page 141)

1. ábstract / abstráct
2. áddict / addíct
3. cónduct / condúct
4. cónflict / conflíct
5. cóntest / contést
6. éntrance / entránce
7. férment / fermént
8. íntern / intérn
9. mísprint / misprínt
10. próceeds / proceéds

11. próduce / prodúce
12. prógress / progréss
13. réfuse / refúse
14. résearch / reseárch
15. résumè / resúme
16. mád house / mad hoúse
17. sínging teacher / singing teácher
18. Greék pupil / Greek púpil
19. cleáning woman / cleaning wóman
20. móving truck / moving trúck

Exercise 33: Stress (page 142)

1. rán down the road/ran dówn a pedestrian
2. ran úp the dress seam/rán up the stairs
3. rán off the path/ran óff the copies
4. bléw down the street/blew dówn the tree
5. passed oút from hunger/passéd out of the room
6. loóked over the top/looked óver the materials

Exercise 34: Suprasegmentals (page 142)

1. (a) mán|eating tíger
   (b) mán-eating|tíger
2. (a) mínd|provóking expérience
   (b) mínd-provoking|expérience
3. (a) eýebrow|raising doúbt
   (b) eyébrow-raising|doúbt
4. (a) went|to the dãrk róom
   (b) went|to the dárk room
5. (a) come tó
   (b) cóme to
6. (a) wánt|more generous plédges
   (b) want móre|generous pledges
7. (a) caúght thẽm|bõth laúghing & tálking
   (b) caught them bóth|laughing & talking
8. (a) sígned|on the cast
   (b) signed ón|the cast

9. (a) have satisfíed | stúdents

(b) háve | satisfied stúdents

10. (a) we'll take | soón will be óver

(b) we'll take sóon | will be óver

Exercise 35: *Morphemes: Roots* (*page 151*)

The constructions preceded by an X one compounds.

_____ **1.** nomin (nomen)		_____ **11.** cede
_____ **2.** book		X **12.** type/write
X **3.** out/stand		_____ **13.** mar (mare)
X **4.** fire/house		_____ **14.** terr (terra)
_____ **5.** struct		_____ **15.** sex
_____ **6.** morph		_____ **16.** script
X **7.** foot/ball		X **17.** bed/bug
_____ **8.** fix		X **18.** light/bulb
_____ **9.** pain		_____ **19.** fin (fine)
X **10.** hand/maid		_____ **20.** tain

Exercise 36: *Bound Morphemes* (*page 151*)

1, 5, 13, 14, 16?, 19, 20

Exercise 37: *Prefixes* (*page 152*)

1. ambi-	**11.** dis- / re-	**21.** re- / in-
2. bi-	**12.** re- / dis-	**22.** in-
3. demi-	**13.** un- / re-	**23.** un- / de-
4. hyper-	**14.** un- / in-	**24.** trans-
5. retro-	**15.** un- / dis-	**25.** un- / pro-
6. mono-	**16.** anti-	**26.** mis-
7. post-	**17.** pre-	**27.** a-
8. semi-	**18.** sub-	**28.** re- / en-
9. uni-	**19.** pro-	**29.** intro-
10. dis- / en-	**20.** de-	**30.** syn-

TENTATIVE CONCLUSIONS:

1. Examples 11 and 12 suggest that when both *re-* and *dis-* are prefixed to a word, there is no certain, predictable order.

2. Examples 10, 14, 21, and 28 suggest that *en-* and *in-* (when they mean "in" or "into," not when they mean "not") occur immediately before the stem. (As a matter of fact, *en-*, *in-*, *em-*, and *im-* often seem to function as derivational prefixes: i.e., they often have the effect of changing the word class of the word to which they are prefixed.)

3. Prefixes with negative meaning (like *in-*, *un-*, *anti-*, *mis-*) tend to occur before prefixes with other meanings. Examples which suggest that this is true are words like *un*decided, *in*destructible, *un*informed, *mis*represented, *anti*intellectual, *mis*directed, etc.

4. The prefix, *re-*, meaning "again," tends to occur after negative prefixes (un*re*turning, mis*re*directed), but before others (*re*distribute, *re*incarnate, *re*direct, *re*subscribe, *re*introduce).

Exercise 38: Derivational Suffixes (*page 153*)

1. -able (-ible)	Adjective— cap*able*, respons*ible*	
2. -age	Noun— front*age*, ad*age*, dot*age*	
	Verb— band*age*, for*age*	
3. -al	Adjective— pen*al*, ven*al*, fat*al*, fin*al*	
4. -ance (-ence)	Noun— rom*ance*, cred*ence*, pitt*ance*	
	Verb—fin*ance*, rom*ance*	
5. -ate	Noun—mand*ate*, consul*ate*, cogn*ate*	
	Verb— reverber*ate*, initi*ate*, infuri*ate*	
	Adj— affection*ate*, rose*ate*, proflig*ate*	
6. -dom	Noun— king*dom*, fief*dom*	
7. -ee	Noun— employ*ee*, train*ee*	
8. -eme	Noun— morph*eme*, graph*eme*	
9. -esque	Adj— statu*esque*, grot*esque*	
10. -ful	Adj— fanci*ful*, beauti*ful*, care*ful*, fate*ful*	
11. -hood	Noun— knight*hood*, mother*hood*	
12. -ic	Noun (?)— pan*ic*, traff*ic*	
	Adj— terrif*ic*, frant*ic*, polit*ic*	
13. -ify	Verb— de*ify*, glor*ify*, beaut*ify*	
14. -ish	Noun— fin*ish*, varn*ish*	
	Verb— tarn*ish*, furn*ish*, publ*ish*	
	Adj— colt*ish*, child*ish*, prigg*ish*	
15. -ize	Verb— public*ize*, terror*ize*, penal*ize*	
16. -less	Adj— hap*less*, care*less*, hope*less*	
17. ness	Noun— good*ness*, kind*ness*	
18. -ous	Adj— vigor*ous*, por*ous*, marvel*ous*	
19. -th	Noun— heal*th*, fil*th*, tru*th*	
	Verb— archaic third person singular form: do*th*; *-eth* also once so used: prais*eth*, lead*eth*	
20. -ure	Noun— struct*ure*, fiss*ure*, meas*ure*, fract*ure*	
	Verb— meas*ure*, fract*ure*, struct*ure*, vent*ure*	

Exercise 39: Morphemes (*page 154*)

	ROOTS	PREFIXES	DERIVA-TIONAL SUFFIXES	INFLEC-TIONAL SUFFIXES
1. players	play		-er	-s
2. leaflet	leaf		-let	
3. falls	fall			-s
4. signifying	sign		-ify	-ing
5. obnoxiousness	nox	ob-	-ious/-ness	

	Roots	Prefixes	Deriva- tional Suffixes	Inflec- tional Suffixes
6. manliest	man		-ly	-est
7. quickly	quick		-ly	
8. hopefully	hope		-ful/-ly	
9. given	give			-en
10. pacifiers	pac		-ify/-er	-s
11. friendly	friend		-ly	
12. friendlier	friend		-ly	-er
13. misappropriated	propr	mis-/ap-	-iate	-ed
14. golden	gold		-en	
15. stealthy	steal		-th/-y	
16. truthfully	true		-th/-ful/-ly	
17. beheaded	head	be-		-ed
18. unreconstructed	struct	un-/re-/con-		-ed
19. antedated	date	ante-		-ed

Exercise 40: Formal Word Classes (*page 164*)

1. V	**11.** ADV	**21.** ADV	**31.** ADJ
2. PRO	**12.** UW	**22.** N	**32.** V
3. UW	**13.** ADJ	**23.** ADJ	**33.** V
4. N	**14.** N	**24.** V	**34.** N
5. ADJ	**15.** UW	**25.** UW	**35.** N
6. UW	**16.** N	**26.** PRO	**36.** ADJ
7. UW	**17.** V	**27.** ADJ	**37.** UW
8. V	**18.** UW	**28.** V	**38.** V
9. PRO	**19.** V	**29.** UW	**39.** ADV
10. V	**20.** V	**30.** UW	**40.** V

Exercise 41: Verb Forms (*page 165*)

	ø	-s	-ed	-ing	-en
1. love	love	loves	loved	loving	loved
2. earn	earn	earns	earned	earning	earned
3. talk	talk	talks	talked	talking	talked
4. say	say	says	said	saying	said
5. come	come	comes	came	coming	come
6. get	get	gets	got	getting	gotten
7. lie	lie	lies	lay	lying	lain
8. lay	lay	lays	laid	laying	laid
9. see	see	sees	saw	seeing	seen
10. be	be, am, are	is	was, were	being	been

Exercise 42: Syntax: Test Frames (page 168)

1. The test frame is not a good one, for sentences like "Shut up," "Be still," "Come here," etc. are possible. A better solution would be to test for only one slot at a time:

     a) Birds _____.   b) _____ fly.

2. John _____ the ball seems to be a good test frame. It is difficult to devise a test frame for a word like "John," because a pronoun could fill most proper noun slots equally well. For the word "the," this frame seems good: John hit _____ ball. For the word "ball," this is a good frame: John hit the _____-ø.

3. To provide for a determiner plus noun subject, one might use this frame: (The) _____ hit the ball.
   The same device can be used for the object slot: John hit (the) _____.

4. The test frame given is good for none of the patterns, for a great variety of word types can fill the slot: *here*, *sad*, *John*, etc. If testing for an adjective subjective complement, the slot might be preceded with a qualifier (*very*) and/or an adjective suffix might be required: a) The boy was very _____; b) The boy was _____-er. To test for a noun, one might precede the slot with a determiner and/or require a noun suffix: a) The boy was the _____ø.

5. For Pattern #4: The boy thought her very _____.
   Pattern #5: The boy thought her a _____.

6. The test frame suggested is poor, for a word like *here* or *home* will fit the slot. One might precede the slot with a qualifier and require the *-ly* suffix: Birds fly very _____-ly.

Exercise 43: Syntax: Immediate Constitutent Analysis (page 173)

REPLACEMENT CONSTRUCTION(S):

1. *John   he*
2. *drives   may have driven   may have been driving*
3. *driving the car   who drives the car   who is the driver of the car*
4. *the young male driver   the driver   the car driver*
5. *parks   will be parking   has parked   has been parking*
6. *someplace   somewhere   in some place   there*
7. *the white house on top of the hill   something   it*

Exercise 44: Syntax: Immediate Constituent Analysis (page 173)

1. The small boy planted many tulip bulbs in the garden.
   The small boy | planted many tulip bulbs in the garden.
   The | small boy | planted many tulip bulbs | in the garden.
   | small | boy | planted | many tulip bulbs | in | the garden.
   | many | tulip bulbs | | the | garden.
   | tulip | bulbs |

2. *The boy in the garden planted many small tulip bulbs.*
The boy in the garden | planted many small tulip bulbs.
The boy | in the garden | planted | many small tulip bulbs.
The | boy | in | the garden | many | small tulip bulbs.
           | the | garden | | small | tulip bulbs.
                                  | tulip | bulbs.

3. *In the small garden, the boy planted many tulip bulbs.*
In the small garden | the boy planted many tulip bulbs.
In | the small garden | the boy | planted many tulip bulbs.
  | the | small garden | the | boy | planted | many tulip bulbs.
  | small | garden | | many | tulip bulbs.
                                  | tulip | bulbs.

Exercise 45: Syntax: Immediate Constituent Analysis (page 174)

1. on the table
on | the table
  | the | table

2. five very pretty sorority girls
five | very pretty sorority girls
   | very pretty | sorority girls
   | very | pretty | sorority | girls

3. having hit the huge red ball
having hit | the huge red ball
having | hit | the | huge red ball
            | huge | red ball
            | red | ball

4. after the men had left the party
after | the men had left the party
   | the men | had left the party
   | the | men | had left | the party
       | had | left | the | party

5. the young woman who is coming through the door
the young woman | who is coming through the door
the | young woman | who | is coming through the door
  | young | woman | | is coming | through the door
             | is | coming | through | the door
                            | the | door

6. because he should have finished the book
because | he should have finished the book
   | he | should have finished the book
     | should have finished | the book
     | should | have finished | the | book
       | have | finished |

Exercise 46: Syntax: Classifying Larger-Than-Word Constructions by Their Formal Features (page 194)

1. PRED P	**6.** PREP P	**11.** PREP P	**16.** VP	**21.** NP
2. ADV P	**7.** S CL	**12.** PRED P	**17.** PREP P	**22.** ABS P
3. NP	**8.** R CL	**13.** PREP P	**18.** R CL	**23.** S CL
4. REL CL	**9.** NP	**14.** NP	**19.** NP	**24.** NP
5. NP	**10.** PREP P	**15.** ABS P	**20.** PRED P	**25.** PREP P

Exercise 47: Syntax: Classifying by Formal and Syntactical Criteria (page 194)

	I	II		I	II
1.	PRO	NOM	**11.**	VP II	NOM
2.	UW (Modal)	AUX/VBL	**12.**	PRO	DET/ADJTL
3.	V	AUX/VBL	**13.**	UW	COORD
4.	UW	SUBORD	**14.**	UW	QUAL
5.	PREP P	ADVL	**15.**	NP	ADVL
6.	UW (WH)	INTERR/ADVL	**16.**	UW	QUAL
7.	PRO	REL/NOM	**17.**	$\begin{Bmatrix} \text{ADJ P} \\ \text{ADV P} \end{Bmatrix}$?	ADVL
8.	REL CL	ADJL	**18.**	WH CL	NOM
9.	UW	PREP	**19.**	S CL	ADVL
10.	CW	INTENS/NOM	**20.**	PREP P	ADJL

Exercise 48: Form and Syntax (page 204)

1. went *home*; will finish *Monday*

2. *weeping* woman; *broken* vase; time *to go*

3. *Walking* is fun: He hates *singing*; The told him *to sing*

4. *has been* seeing; *do* wish

5. *most* unhappy; *much* better; *less* good

6. goes to work *every morning*

7. John, *the boy in back*, . . .

8. He works *to earn money*. He came into the room *screaming loudly*.

9. *Learning a new skill* is seldom easy. He's good at *hitting homers*.

10. the day *after the storm*; the girl *in the car*

11. drove *toward the town*; tried *with all his might*

12. the girl *who left the room*; the man *whom I saw*

13. He asked me *what I knew about it*.

14. the night *after he lost his job*

15. He ran *until he was out of breath*.

Exercise 49: Form and Syntax (*page 204*)

1. *safety* pin; *ink* well; *tape* measure
2. *John's* hat; *mother's* boy
3. *he*-man; *she*-cat
4. *his* hat; *whose* book
5. boy *whom* I saw
6. *Who* is coming? *What* do you mean?
7. *Whose* coat is this?
8. the girl *whose* book I borrowed
9. *through* street; *through* way
10. *out*look; *out*law; *Out*back
11. *wildly cheering* crowd; the wind *blowing strongly*
12. *That you write music* surprised me.
   He wondered *whether she would arrive early.*
13. *Our work finished*, we relaxed.
14. *in* group; the *in* thing to do.
15. *Pretty* is as *pretty* does. The *beautiful* are damned.

PART THREE: TRANSFORMATIONAL GRAMMAR (EARLY FORM)

Exercise 50: Phrase Structure (*page 234*)

1.

The # boy + s # Ø + be # ing + run

2.

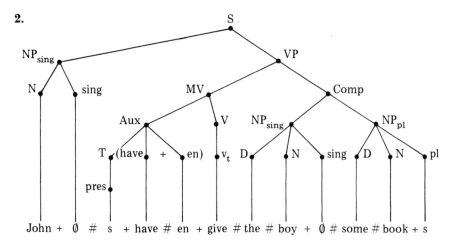

John + Ø # s + have # en + give # the # boy + Ø # some # book + s

3.

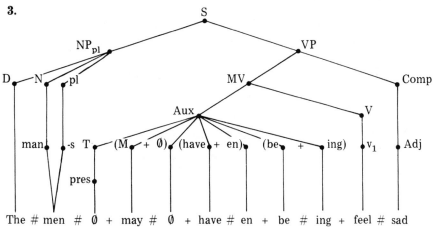

The # men # Ø + may # Ø + have # en + be # ing + feel # sad

Exercise 51: *Kernel Sentences* (*page 251*)

The following are kernel sentences: 3, 5, 6, 9, 10, 11, 12, 16, 17, 20, 21, 23, 24.

Exercise 52: *Auxiliary PS Rule of Formation* (*page 252*)

	AUXILIARIES	VERB
1.	ø	*walk*
2.	*-ed*	*find*
3.	*-s*	*live*
4.	ø + *have* + *-en*	*decide*
5.	ø$_2$ + *be* + *-ing*	*go*

	AUXILIARIES	VERB
6.	$\varnothing_3 + be + \text{-}ing$	*ask*
7.	$\text{-}s + be + ing$	*take*
8.	$\text{-}ed_2 + be + ing$	*give*
9.	$\text{-}s + have + \text{-}en$	*choose*
10.	$\text{-}ed_2 + be + \text{-}ing$	*give*
11.	$\text{-}ed_1 + be + \text{-}ing$	*do*
12.	$\varnothing + M + \varnothing_1 + be + \text{-}ing$	*take*
*13.	$\text{-}s + have + \text{-}en + be + \text{-}en$	*do*
14.	$\text{-}ed + have + \text{-}en$	*write*
15.	$\varnothing + M + \varnothing + have + \text{-}en$	*catch*
16.	$\varnothing + M + \varnothing$	*go*
17.	$\varnothing + M + \varnothing$	*write*
18.	$\text{-}ed$	*eat*
19.	$\varnothing_2 + be + \text{-}ing$	*do*
*20.	$\text{-}ed_1 + be + \text{-}en$	*find*
21.	$\varnothing + M + \varnothing + have + \text{-}en$	*have*
22.	$\varnothing + M + \varnothing + have + \text{-}en + be + \text{-}ing$	*give*
23.	$\text{-}ed + have + \text{-}en + be + \text{-}ing$	*sing*
24.	$\text{-}s + have + \text{-}en$	*sing*
25.	$\varnothing + M + \varnothing + have + \text{-}en + be + \text{-}ing$	*like*

*Remember, the asterisked examples are passive.

Exercise 53: Kernel Sentences (page 253)

1. All
2. All
3. Patterns 5, 8, 10
4. Patterns 5, 8, 10
5. Patterns 2, 3, 4, 5, 6, 7, 9
6. Patterns 9, 10, 11
7. All
8. Pattern 1
9. All
10. All
11. All
12. Pattern 6
13. None
14. None
15. All
16. Pattern 11
17. Patterns 1, 2, 3, 4, 5
18. Patterns 2, 3, 4, 5
19. None
20. None

Exercise 54: Single-Base Transformational Rules (page 268)

T RULE	RESTRICTIONS	KERNEL SENTENCE	TRANSFORMATION	PROCEDURE
T^{emph} (emphasis)	All patterns	John is running very fast.	John is running *very* fast. John is running very fast!	Use italics to show stress. Use exclamation mark.
T$^{do\text{-}emph}$ (do emphasis)	Simple present or past tense verb	He eats supper. You eat supper. They ate supper.	He does eat supper. You do eat supper. They did eat supper.	Use *do* as a verb auxiliary; shift tense marker to *do*, then $\varnothing + v$
T^{wo} (word order)	Strings containing adverbials can always be reordered. Also strings with noun subj complts.	John is here. He ran quickly. Tim is the leader.	Here is John. Quickly he ran. The leader is Tim.	NP + VP + Advl $\Rightarrow$ Advl + NP + VP NP$_1$ + $\begin{Bmatrix} v_1 \\ be \end{Bmatrix}$ + NP$_{2_{sc}}$ $\Rightarrow$ NP$_2$ + $\begin{Bmatrix} v_1 \\ be \end{Bmatrix}$ + NP$_1$
T^{imp} (imperative)	Any string with *you* as subject + a pres tense verb	You close the door. You should stop. You are quiet.	Close the door. Stop. Be quiet	Omit the subject. With *be*, use the $\varnothing_1$ form.
T^{neg} (negative)	All patterns	They may leave soon. He has been reading. He is being silly.	They may not leave soon. He has not been reading. He is not being silly.	Add *not* between 1st aux and rest of verb phrase.

T Rule	Restrictions	Kernel Sentence	Transformation	Procedure
T^{neg} (negative)		You hit the ball. He hits the ball. They ate lunch.	You do not hit the ball. He does not hit the ball. They did not eat lunch.	When verb has no aux, add *do* + *not*. (T + *do* + *not* + ø + verb)
		I am happy. John is here. We were friends.	I am not happy. John is not here. We were not friends.	*Do* not necessary. Simply add *not* after *be*.
$T^{q\text{-}yes/no}$ (yes/no question)	All patterns	You may drive the car. He has been living abroad. He is flying to Europe.	May you drive the car? Has he been living abroad? Is he flying to Europe?	When verb has aux words, rearrange word order to: 1st aux + subject + remainder.
		Children like candy. She loves the job. They ate lunch.	Do children like candy? Does she love the job? Did they eat lunch?	If verb consists of one word only, use *do* as aux.
		He is late. They are friends. She was a student.	Is he late? Are they friends? Was she a student?	*Do* not necessary. Simply reverse order of subj & verb.
T^{there} (there-expletive)	Indefinite subject + *be* as aux or main verb. Exceptions: verbs like *stand, exist, occur*, etc.	Someone is in the room. A man is calling you. A flood occurred.	There is someone in the room. There is a man calling you There occurred a flood.	*There* + all words in VP up to and including *be* + subject + rest of sent.

T^{pas} (passive)	Patterns 2, 3, 4, and 5	John hates soup. Jim gave Tom a ball. We named the dog Max. Jim thinks Jane silly.	Soup is hated by John. Tom was given a ball by Jim; or A ball was given Tom by Jim. The dog was named Max by us. Jane is thought silly by Jim.	(1) Direct object becomes new subject. (2) Add $be + en$ between last aux and main verb. (3) Put by + original subject in slot following verb.
$T^{q\text{-}wh}$ (wh-question)	All patterns. (Wh-question may be asked about any structure with lexical meaning)	John found a dog in the park today.	Who found a dog . . . ? What did John do? What did John find in . . . ? Where did John find a . . . ? When did John find a dog in the park?	(1) Begin transformation with interrogative word. (2) Transform remainder of sent by $T^{q\text{-}yes/no}$ rule.

Note: a second T^{pas} rule is possible for strings consisting of
$NP_s + v_t + NP_{io} + NP_{do}$

Exercise 55: Single-Base Optional Transformations: $T^{\text{do-emph}}$ (page 269)

1. Mary does sing very well.
2. Barney did used to sing for a living.
3. I do feel good.
4. Mary does write quite poorly.
5. John always does do well in a crisis.

Exercise 56: Single-Base Optional Transformations: T^{neg} (page 269)

1. He $\begin{Bmatrix} \text{did not} \\ \text{didn't} \end{Bmatrix}$ get the answer very soon.

2. Several men $\begin{Bmatrix} \text{were not} \\ \text{weren't} \end{Bmatrix}$ in the posse.

3. She $\begin{Bmatrix} \text{does not} \\ \text{doesn't} \end{Bmatrix}$ head the university.

4. The children $\begin{Bmatrix} \text{do not} \\ \text{don't} \end{Bmatrix}$ like spinach.

5. He $\begin{Bmatrix} \text{will not} \\ \text{won't} \end{Bmatrix}$ give up the struggle quickly.

Exercise 57: Single-Base Optional Transformations: $T^{\text{q-yes/no}}$ (page 270)

1. Did Sam go out in the rain?
2. Does Mr. Jack prefer solitude?
3. Is the paper here now?
4. $\begin{Bmatrix} \text{May} \\ \text{Might} \end{Bmatrix}$ she have been dozing off?
5. Should John have left the party early?

Exercise 58: Single-Base Optional Transformations: T^{there} (page 270)

1. There is always some problem bothering Tom.
2. There will be several students absent.
3. There always exists a crisis in that house.
4. There were some books in the library.
5. There have been several girls crying for hours.

Exercise 59: Single-Base Optional Transformations: T^{pas} (page 270)

1. The trash may be carried out by Sy.
2. The dishes must be done by Jerry.
3. The city was gripped $\begin{Bmatrix} \text{by} \\ \text{with} \end{Bmatrix}$ fear.
4. The picnic has been ruined by the rain.
5. The water is finally being turned off by Al.
6. The title should be sacrificed by Fischer.
7. The pages have been stapled by Amy.
8. The cash will be put up by Jones.

9. The book ought to be written by Jo.
10. The part has been tried out for by several boys.

Exercise 60: Single-Base Optional Transformation: $T^{q\text{-}wh}$ (page 271)

Answer	Question
1. Those boys	Who has been sleeping in class during the lectures?
2. Those	Which boys have been sleeping . . .?
3. Sleeping	What have those boys been doing in . . .?
or	
They have been sleeping.	
4. In class	Where have those boys been sleeping during the lectures?
5. Class	In $\begin{Bmatrix} \text{where} \\ \text{what place} \end{Bmatrix}$ have those boys been sleeping during the lectures?
6. Lectures (or the lectures)	During what have those boys been sleeping in class?
7. During the lectures	When have those boys been sleeping in class?
8. Those boys have been sleeping in class during the lectures.	What happened?

Exercise 61: Single-Base Optional Transformations: T Rule Ordering (page 273)

1. T^{neg} $\Rightarrow$ The dog didn't bark too much.
    $T^{do\text{-}emph}$ $\Rightarrow$ The dog *didn't* bark too much.

2. T^{pas} $\Rightarrow$ The driver was arrested by the officer.
    T^{there} $\Rightarrow$ Was the driver arrested by the officer?

3. T^{pas} $\Rightarrow$ A glass was broken by the drunk.
    T^{there} $\Rightarrow$ There was a glass broken by the drunk.
    $T^{q\text{-}yes/no}$ $\Rightarrow$ Was there a glass broken by the drunk?

4. $T^{op\text{-}sep*}$ $\Rightarrow$ They called the cops in at midnight.
    T^{pas} $\Rightarrow$ The cops were called in at midnight.
    T^{there} $\Rightarrow$ There were cops called in at midnight.

*Notice that if the $T^{op\text{-}sep}$ rule has already been applied, it must be "undone" when the T^{pas} rule is applied.

Exercise 62: Single-Base Optional Transformations (page 274)

$T^{q\text{-}yes/no} + T^{neg}$ **1.** Isn't he angry now?
                     He is angry now.

K   **2.** She gave up the struggle very quickly.
$T^{emph} + T^{do(emph)}$ **3.** The book does say that!
                     The book says that.

T^{wo}

$T^{q\text{-}wh}$

$T^{q\text{-}yes/no} + T^{neg}$

$T^{pas} + T^{there}$

$T^{wo} + T^{there}$

$T^{pas} + T^{q\text{-}yes/no}$

$T^{q\text{-}wh}$

K
$T^{imp} + T^{emph}$

T^{wo}

$T^{q\text{-}yes/no}$

$T^{imp} + T^{emph}$

T^{neg}

T^{there}

K
T^{wo}

T^{neg}

$T^{pas} + T^{q\text{-}yes/no} + T^{emph}$

$T^{pas} + T^{q\text{-}yes/no}$

T^{neg}

T^{imp}

$T^{pas} + T^{there}$

4. Now everyone wants peace.
   Everyone wants peace now.
5. Who will drive the swimmers to the meet?
   Someone will drive the swimmers to the meet.
6. Didn't John leave the party at ten?
   John left the party at ten.
7. There weren't many revelations made by the victim.
   The victim made many revelations.
8. In Mississippi there have occurred some floods.
   Some floods have occurred in Mississippi.
9. Was the food eaten immediately?
   Someone ate the food immediately.
10. Where is the professor now?
    The professor is here now.
11. Some people always go too far.
12. Be quiet!
    You should be quiet.
13. Only recently the army crossed over the bridge.
    The army crossed over the bridge only recently.
14. Did David really give Betsy the ring?
    David really gave Betsy the ring.
15. Stop the sniffling immediately!
    You should stop the sniffling immediately.
16. The children didn't want the cake very much.
    The children wanted the cake very much.
17. There used to be a ghost in the house.
    A ghost used to be in the house.
18. Jerry must have become lost very quickly.
19. Under the table peacefully slept the dog.
    The dog slept peacefully under the table.
20. The letter didn't really say that.
    The letter really said that.
21. I'm not appreciated!
    Someone appreciates me.
22. Was she angered by the accusation?
    The accusation angered her.
23. John didn't tell me the news.
    John told me the news.
24. Finish the exercise quickly.
    You should finish the exercise quickly.
25. There have been several incidents reported.
    Someone has reported several incidents.

Exercise 63: *Conjunction Transformation* (*page 280*)

1. ⟹ He wasted time before the test, during the test, and after the test.

or

He wasted time before, during, and after the test.

or

He wasted time before the test, he wasted time during the test, and he wasted time after the test.

2. ⟹ He liked to watch TV, and he liked teasing the dog and tormenting his sister.

3. ⟹ He drove the car both fast and well.

4. ⟹ Jane cannot drive a car, but $\begin{cases} \text{she can cook, and she can sew.} \\ \text{she can cook and sew.} \end{cases}$

or

Jane can cook $\begin{cases} \text{and she can sew,} \\ \text{and sew,} \end{cases}$ but she cannot drive a car.

5. ⟹ Either Jody will wash her hair tonight, or she will go to a movie.

or

Jody either will wash her hair or will go to a movie tonight.

or

Jody will either wash her hair or go to a movie tonight.

6. ⟹ Cindy is $\begin{cases} \text{better} \\ \text{worse} \end{cases}$ $\begin{cases} \text{at tennis than Sue.} \\ \text{than Sue at tennis.} \end{cases}$

Exercise 64: *Adverbial Wh-Clause Transformation* (*page 293*)

*1. ⟹ Arch lost his appointment as prosecutor $\begin{cases} \text{when} \\ \text{after} \end{cases}$ he defied the boss.

*2. ⟹ Everyone is miserable because Amos is unhappy.

*3. ⟹ Lou is pompous when he interviews people after they apply for jobs.

*4. ⟹ The bird will sing if it is in the kitchen when someone uncovers it.

*In all cases, the adverbial clause may also precede the main clause.

Exercise 65: *Adverbial Participial-Phrase Transformation* (*page 293*)

*1. ⟹ We became cynical listening to the hearings on TV.

*2. ⟹ The dog came to the door barking frantically.

*3. ⟹ Jake paid the fine after losing the library book.

or

Having lost the library book, Jake paid the fine.

or

Jake, having lost the library book, paid the fine.

*4. ⟹ The furnace having broken down, the family was freezing.

*5. ⟹ Having been balmy for a week, the weather turned bitter.

or

The weather, having been balmy for a week, turned bitter.

*In all cases, the participial phrase may precede the main clause.

Exercise 66: *Adverbial Infinitive-Phrase Transformation* (*page 294*)

*1. ⇒ You must pretend happiness to keep up your spirits.
*2. ⇒ He joined the marines to fight for his country.
3. ⇒ To save it, he put his money under the mattress.
(If the infinitive phrase follows the word "mattress," an ambiguity will result.)
4. ⇒ The dog came in to be fed.

*The infinitive phrase may precede the main clause in the first two transformations.

Exercise 67: *Adjectivalization Transformations* (*page 301*)

1. ⇒ He is the newcomer who is breaking every rule.
2. ⇒ The street where the robbery took place is in this block.
3. ⇒ The boy I'm crazy about is named Jeffrey.
4. ⇒ The man mowing the lawn is Grandpa.
5. ⇒ John Horsley is the boy to do the job.
6. ⇒ Where is the job to be done?
7. ⇒ The person driving the school bus changes frequently.

Exercise 68: *Adjectivalization Transformations* (*page 302*)

1. ⇒ The hideous apparition disappeared.
2. ⇒ Dishonesty is a corruption to fear.
or
Dishonesty is a fearful corruption.
3. ⇒ The person to scold is Harry Jones.
4. ⇒ Those screaming children drive me crazy!
5. ⇒ The brick house withstood the {attack of the wolf. / wolf's attack.}
6. ⇒ The wind outside frightens the cat in the window.

Exercise 69: *Nominalization Transformations* (*page 313*)

1. ⇒ He thinks that he must know everything.
2. ⇒ The conductor signaled when the passenger should get off the bus.
3. ⇒ She knew why Mary ought to forget Tom.
4. ⇒ What frightened the puppy was a loud noise.
5. ⇒ Practicing the piano for an hour a day is a bore.
6. ⇒ To make a choice is very difficult.
7. ⇒ I hate Mike's bossing his friends constantly.
8. ⇒ Drinking is Gordon's biggest problem.
9. ⇒ She hoped to learn Italian in a month.
10. ⇒ It seems strange that Mary will be fifty tomorrow.
or
That Mary will be fifty tomorrow seems strange.

Exercise 70: Transformations (*Review*) (*page 314*)

   1. Dominant: The bus left some people behind.
   2. Dominant: She gave you an answer.
       Embedded: The answer was quick.
   3. Dominant: Something is really sad.
       Embedded: She has bought the coat.
   4. Dominant: (1) The students wanted the responsibility.
                    (2) The faculty wanted the responsibility.
       Embedded: (1) The time arrived.
                    (2) People vote at some time.
   5. Dominant: $\left\{\begin{array}{l}\text{Something}\\ \text{Someone}\end{array}\right\}$ was destroying a reputation.

       Embedded: John has $\left\{\begin{array}{l}\text{the}\\ \text{this}\end{array}\right\}$ reputation.

   6. Dominant: A storm caused the destruction.
       Embedded: (1) The storm broke the record.
                    (2) The destruction was awful.
   7. Dominant: John hears something.
       Embedded: (1) John is a boy.
                    (2) The boy is little.
                    (3) The boy is playing in the pool.
                    (4) People wade in the pool.
                    (5) John has a mother.
                    (6) The mother is calling John.
   8. Dominant: Someone sold the car to Jim.
       Embedded: (1) Something battered the car.
                    (2) The car is old.
                    (3) The car was in a lot.
                    (4) Someone parked the car in the lot.
                    (5) Someone has used the cars.
   9. Dominant: Something is a habit.
       Embedded: (1) Jane is late constantly.
                    (2) The habit annoys friends.
                    (3) Jane has friends.
   10. Dominant: The play is an insult.
       Embedded: (1) I have an opinion.
                    (2) The insult is direct.
                    (3) The insult is to intelligence.
                    (4) A viewer has intelligence.

Exercise 71: Transformations (*page 314*)

   1. Dominant: Jack prized the book.
       Embedded: (1) The book contains rules.
                    (2) The book contains regulations.

(3) The book is old.

(4) Something tattered the book.

2. Dominant: Someone filled the basket $\begin{Bmatrix} \text{to some state.} \\ \text{in some manner.} \end{Bmatrix}$

Embedded: (1) The basket $\begin{Bmatrix} \text{contains} \\ \text{is for} \end{Bmatrix}$ waste.

(2) The waste is paper.

(3) The basket is flowing over.

3. Dominant: Something is a flaw.

Embedded: (1) One yields to cowardice.

(2) The flaw is terrible.

(3) The flaw concerns personality.

4. Dominant: The dog died during the night.

Embedded: (1) John has a dad.

(2) The dad had a dog.

(3) Fleas bit the dog.

(4) The dog was old.

(5) The dog hunted birds.

5. Dominant: The certificate is a statement.

Embedded: (1) The certificate is international.

(2) The certificate certifies a vaccination.

(3) The statement is official.

(4) Something protects you adequately against disease.

(5) The disease could be a threat.

(6) The threat is to America. (or America faces a threat.)

(7) The threat is to other countries. (or Other countries face a threat.)

6. Dominant: (1) You (should) print a name.

(2) You (should) print an address.

(3) You (should) print a reason.

Embedded: (1) You have a name.

(2) You have an address.

(3) The address should be correct.

(4) You have a reason.

(5) You applied for the job.

7. Dominant: (1) You saw the eclipse.

(2) Tou were studying for a test (instead).

Embedded: (1) The moon $\begin{Bmatrix} \text{had an eclipse.} \\ \text{was in an eclipse.} \end{Bmatrix}$

(2) The test examined grammar.

(3) The test bent the mind.

(4) The test was unfair.

(5) The test was difficult.

(The verbs in 2, 3, 4, and 5 might be in present tense.)

Exercise 72: Lexical Entries (page 346)

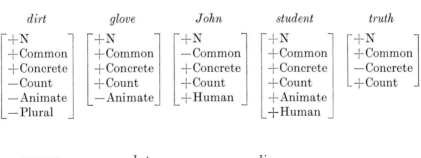

dirt
$$\begin{bmatrix} +\text{N} \\ +\text{Common} \\ +\text{Concrete} \\ -\text{Count} \\ -\text{Animate} \\ -\text{Plural} \end{bmatrix}$$

glove
$$\begin{bmatrix} +\text{N} \\ +\text{Common} \\ +\text{Concrete} \\ +\text{Count} \\ -\text{Animate} \end{bmatrix}$$

John
$$\begin{bmatrix} +\text{N} \\ -\text{Common} \\ +\text{Concrete} \\ +\text{Count} \\ +\text{Human} \end{bmatrix}$$

student
$$\begin{bmatrix} +\text{N} \\ +\text{Common} \\ +\text{Concrete} \\ +\text{Count} \\ +\text{Animate} \\ +\text{Human} \end{bmatrix}$$

truth
$$\begin{bmatrix} +\text{N} \\ +\text{Common} \\ -\text{Concrete} \\ +\text{Count} \end{bmatrix}$$

woman
$$\begin{bmatrix} +\text{N} \\ +\text{Common} \\ +\text{Concrete} \\ +\text{Count} \\ +\text{Human} \\ +\text{Adult} \\ -\text{Masc} \end{bmatrix}$$

hate
$$\begin{bmatrix} +\text{V} \\ +[+\text{Animate}]\underline{\quad} \\ +\underline{\quad}\text{NP} \\ -\text{Obj Del} \end{bmatrix}$$

lie
$$\begin{bmatrix} +\text{V} \\ +[+\text{Human}]\underline{\quad} \\ +\underline{\quad}\# \end{bmatrix}$$

please
$$\begin{bmatrix} +\text{V} \\ +\underline{\quad}\text{NP} \\ +\underline{\quad}[+\text{Animate}] \end{bmatrix}$$

think
$$\begin{bmatrix} +\text{V} \\ +[+\text{Animate}]\underline{\quad} \\ +\underline{\quad}[\text{that-S}] \end{bmatrix}$$

must
$$\begin{bmatrix} +\text{M} \\ +\underline{\quad}\ldots\o \end{bmatrix}$$

shall
$$\begin{bmatrix} +\text{M} \\ +\underline{\quad}\ldots\o \end{bmatrix}$$

she
$$\begin{bmatrix} +\text{N} \\ +\text{Pro} \\ +\text{III} \\ -\text{Masc} \\ -\text{Plural} \\ -\text{Accusative} \end{bmatrix}$$

they
$$\begin{bmatrix} +\text{N} \\ +\text{Pro} \\ +\text{III} \\ +\text{Plural} \end{bmatrix}$$

you
$$\begin{bmatrix} +\text{N} \\ +\text{Pro} \\ +\text{II} \end{bmatrix}$$

us
$$\begin{bmatrix} +\text{N} \\ +\text{Pro} \\ +\text{I} \\ +\text{Plural} \\ +\text{Accusative} \end{bmatrix}$$

a
$$\begin{bmatrix} +\text{Det} \\ -\text{Pro} \\ -\text{Def} \\ -\text{Plural} \\ +\underline{\quad}[+\text{Common}] \\ +\underline{\quad}[+\text{Consonant}] \end{bmatrix}$$

this
$$\begin{bmatrix} +\text{Det} \\ -\text{Pro} \\ +\text{Def} \\ +\text{Dem} \\ -\text{plural} \\ +\text{Near} \\ +\underline{\quad}[+\text{Common}] \end{bmatrix}$$

these
$$\begin{bmatrix} +\text{Det} \\ -\text{Pro} \\ +\text{Def} \\ +\text{Dem} \\ +\text{Plural} \\ +\text{Near} \\ +\underline{\quad}[+\text{Common}] \end{bmatrix}$$

Verb Conjugation Chart

REGULAR/IRREGULAR VERBS—ACTIVE VOICE

Verb Tense		Singular	Plural
Simple Present	1	like/do	like/do
	2	like/do	like/do
	3	likes/does	like/do
Simple Past	1	liked/did	liked/did
	2	liked/did	liked/did
	3	liked/did	liked/did
Simple Future	1	shall like/do	shall like/do
	2	will like/do	will like/do
	3	will like/do	will like/do
Present Progressive	1	am liking/doing	are liking/doing
	2	are liking/doing	are liking/doing
	3	is liking/doing	are liking/doing
Past Progressive	1	was liking/doing	were liking/doing
	2	were liking/doing	were liking/doing
	3	was liking/doing	were liking/doing
Future Progressive	1	shall be liking/doing	shall be liking/doing
	2	will be liking/doing	will be liking/doing
	3	will be liking/doing	will be liking/doing
Present Perfect	1	have liked/done	have liked/done
	2	have liked/done	have liked/done
	3	has liked/done	have liked/done
Past Perfect	1	had liked/done	had liked/done
	2	had liked/done	had liked/done
	3	had liked/done	had liked/done
Future Perfect	1	shall have liked/done	shall have liked/done
	2	will have liked/done	will have liked/done
	3	will have liked/done	will have liked/done
Present Perfect Progressive	1	have been liking/doing	have been liking/doing
	2	have been liking/doing	have been liking/doing
	3	has been liking/doing	have been liking/doing
Past Perfect Progressive	1	had been liking/doint	had been liking/doing
	2	had been liking/doing	had been liking/doing
	3	had been liking/doing	had been liking/doing
Future Perfect Progressive	1	shall have been liking/doing	shall have been liking/doing
	2	Will have been liking/doing	will have been liking/doing
	3	will have been liking/doing	will have been liking/doing

CONJUGATION OF BE, ACTIVE VOICE

Verb Tense		Singular	Plural
Present	1	am	are
	2	are	are
	3	is	are
Past	1	was	were
	2	were	were
	3	was	were
Future	1	shall be	shall be
	2	will be	will be
	3	will be	will be
Present Progessive	1	am being	are being
	2	are being	are being
	3	is being	are being
Past Progessive	1	was being	were being
	2	were being	were being
	3	was being	were being
Future Progessive	1	shall be being	shall be being
	2	will be being	will be being
	3	will be being	will be being
Present Perfect	1	have been	have been
	2	have been	have been
	3	has been	have been
Past Perfect	1	had been	had been
	2	had been	had been
	3	had been	had been
Future Perfect	1	shall have been	shall have been
	2	will have been	will have been
	3	will have been	will have been
Present Perfect Progessive	1	have been being	have been being
	2	have been being	have been being
	3	has been being	have been being
Past Perfect Progessive	1	had been being	had been being
	2	had been being	had been being
	3	had been being	had been being
Future Perfect Progessive	1	shall have been being	shall have been being
	2	will have been being	will have been being
	3	will have been being	will have been being

A Partial List of Prefixes

PREFIXES	MEANINGS	EXAMPLES
a-	at, in, of, on, up, to	afire, afoot
a-, an-	not, without	anemic, asexual
a-, ab-, abs-	away, off, from	abdicate, abstain
ac-, ad-, af-, ag-, al-, an-, ap-, ar-	to, toward	admit, adhere
ambi-	both	ambivalent
ante-, anti-	before, previous	antedate, anticipate
anti-	against	antidote, antihero
be-	about, around	becloud, befuddle
bi-	two, twice	bisect, bilingual
co-, col-, com-, con-, cor-	with, together with	cooperate, "co-op," co-author
contra-, contre-, contro-, counter-	against, opposing	contraband, counteract, contradict
de-	away, from, off, down	depart, destroy
di-	two, twice	dissect, divide
demi-	half	demitasse
dia-	across, by, through	diameter, diagnose
dys-, dis-	ill, bad	dysfunction
em-, en-	among, in	endemic, empathy
epi-	on, over, upon, above	epitaph, epidermis
ex-	from, out of, away, former	extract, exwife
for-	apart, away, off	forswear, forbid
hemi-	half	hemisphere
heter-, hetero-	other, different	heterosexual
homo-	same, alike	homosexual, homogenize

432

PREFIXES	MEANINGS	EXAMPLES
hyper-	excessive, over, beyond	hyperactive
hypo-	under, beneath, below	hypodermic
il-, im-, in-, ir-	in, into, not, on, opposing, within	innate, infiltrate, immerse
inter-	between, among	interact, intersperse
intra-, intro-	within, into	intramural, introduce
mal-	bad	malevolent, malpractice
meta-	change of, over	metaphor, metamorphosis
mis-	not, wrong, badly	misjudge, misconduct
mono-	one	monologue, monogamy
multi-	many, much	multicolor, multiply
non-	not, against	nonsense, nonviolent
ob-, oc, of-, op-,	against	obstruct, oppose
par-, para-	besides, contrary	parallel, parasite
per-	through, completely	persist, percolate
poly-	many	polygamy, polygon
post-	after, following	postmortem, postdate
pre-	before, preceding	precede, preset
pro-	forward, in favor of	progress, pro-war
re-	back, backward, again	refund, return, regret
retro-	back, backward	retrogress, retroactive
semi-	half, partial	semiliterate, semicircle
sub-, suc-, suf-, sug-, sup-, sus-	under, beneath, below	submarine, subconscious, suffuse, succumb
syn-, sym-, syl-, sys-	with, together	synonym, sympathy, syllable, system
tel-, tele-	far	telegram, telescope
trans-	across, beyond	transmit, transitive
ultra-	beyond, excessively	ultramodern, ultraviolet, ultrasonic
un-	not, opposing	unlock, unlikely
uni-	one	uniform, unicorn

A Partial List of Roots

Roots	Meanings	Examples
ac, acr	sharp	acrimony
act, ag	do, drive, impel	actor, agitate, react
alter	other, change	alternate, alter ego
anim	life, mind, soul, consciousness	animate, animus
ann, annu	year	annual
anthrop	man, mankind	anthropoid, anthropology
apt, ept	fit, ability, adjust	aptitude, inept
arch	ancient, chief	archdemon, archrival
arm	arms, weapon	armory, armature
aud, aur	hear	auditory, aural
auto	self	autograph, automobile
bel, bell	war	bellicose, belligerent
ben, bene	good, well	benefit, benevolent
bibl, bibli	book	bibliography, Bible
bio	life	biology
brev	brief, short	brevity, abbreviate
cap, capit	head	capital, decapitate
carn	flesh, meat	incarnate, carnivore
ced, ceed, cess	go, yield	recede, depress, proceed
cent	hundred	centennial
chron	time	chronology
civ	citizen	civil, civilization
cogn	learn, know, be acquainted with	cognitive, recognize, precognition
corp	body	corpus, corpulent, corpse

Roots	Meanings	Examples
cosm	order, world, universe	cosmos, cosmic, microcosm
cred	belief, trust	credence, credibility
crypt	secret, hidden	cryptic, cryptogram
curr, curs	run, course	recur, occur, current
cycl	wheel, circle	bicycle, cyclic
dat	give	dative
dec	ten	decimal, December
dem, demo	people	democracy, demographic
dent	tooth	dental, dentrifice
derm	skin	epidermis, dermatology
dic, dict	speak, say, word	dictate, dictionary
dign	worth	dignity, indignant
dox, dog, doc	belief, teaching	paradox, dogma, indoctrinate
duc, duct	lead	induct, deduct, reduce
dyn	force, power	dynamic, dynamite
ego	self, I	egocentric
fac, fact, fic, fect	do, make	factual, factor, infect
fid	belief, faith, trust	fidelity, infidel
fin	end, limit	finite, final, finish
firm	strong	infirm, reaffirm
flect, flex	twist, turn, bend	reflex, flexible
flor	flower, bloom	floral, florid
flux, fluct, flux	flow	fluctuate, influx
form	form, shape	inform, formal, conform
fort, forte	strong	fortify, fortitude
frag, fract	break	fragment, fracture
gam, gamy	marriage	monogamy, bigamy
geo	earth	geography, geology
grad, gress	go, step	graduate, ingress, regress
gram, graph	write, writing	telegram, telegraph
greg	flock, together	gregarious
gyn	woman	gynocology
helio	the sun	heliograph, heliotrope
hemo, hemor	blood	hemoglobin, hemorrhage
hetero	different	heterosexual
homo	same	homogeneous, homograft
homo	man	Homosapiens
junc, junct	bind, join	conjunction, juncture
leg	law	legal
liter, lettr	letter	literature, literary
loc	place	location
locu, locut, loqu, loque	speech, talk	locution, loquacious dialogue, monologue
luc, lumen, lumin	light	lucid, illuminate, luminous
magn	large	magnify, magnitude

ROOTS	MEANINGS	EXAMPLES
mal	bad	malodorous
mar	sea	marine, submarine
mater, matr	mother	matricide, maternity
mega	large	megaphone
meter, metr	measure	metronome, speedometer
micr	small	microcosm, microscope
mor	death	morgue, morbid, moribund
morph	form, shape	amorphous, morphology
multi	many	multitude, multiply
nav, nave	ship, sail	navy, navigate
neo	new	neophyte, neoteric
nomen, nomin	name	nominate, nomenclature
omni	all	omniscient, omnivorous
pac, pace	peace	pacify, pact
pan	all, entire	panasonic, panorama
part	part, partial	partial
pater, patr	father	paternal, patricide
path	feeling, suffering	psychopath, pathology
ped	child	pediatric
ped	foot	pedal, pedestrian
pel	drive	impel, propel
pend, pens	hang, weigh	pendulous, pendulum
phil	love	philanthropy
phob	fear	phobia, hydrophobia
phon, phone	sound, hear	phonograph, telephone
photo	light	photosynthesis, photograph
pon, pos, pose	put, place	impose, posit
port	carry	portable, portfolio
proto	first	prototype
pseudo	false	pseudonym
psych	mind, soul	psyche, psychology
pyr	fire	pyromania, pyrotechnic
rupt	break	rupture, disrupt
sanct	holy	sanctimonious, sanction
sci	know	science
scrib, script	write	scribble, scripture
secut, sequ	follow	consecutive, sequence
sect, seg	cut	section, segment
sol	alone	solo, solitary
soph	wise	sophisticate, sophomore
spec, spect	look, see	spectate, spectacular
spir, spire	breathe	respire, expire
string, strict	bind, tighten	stricture, strangulate
struct	build	construct, structure
ten, tent, tain	hold	contain, contentment

ROOTS	MEANINGS	EXAMPLES
tend, tens, tent	stretch	tension, tense
ter, terra	earth	terrain, inter
the	god	theism
therm	heat	themometer, thermostat
tors, tort	twist	distort, contortion
tract	draw, pull	tractor, traction
und, undu	wave	undulate
uni	one	universe, unite
urb	city	urban, suburb
vac	empty	evacuate, vacuum
ven, vent	come	venture, convene
ver	true	veracity, verify
vers, vert	turn	subvert, versatile
vid, vis	see	video, visible
vit	life	vital, vitamin
voc	call, voice	vocal, vocation
volv, volu, volut roll,	turn	revolve, evolution
vulg	common	vulgar, vulgate
zo, zoo	animal	zoo, zoology

A Partial List of Derivational Suffixes

Noun Suffixes

-age	marriage, tutelage	-iac	maniac, hypochondriac
-ance, -ence	variance, sentence	-ice	jaundice, notice
-art, -ard	braggart, dullard	-ion	erosion, mansion
-ate, -ite	consulate, socialite	-sim	socialism, conservatism
-ation, -ition	relation, recognition	-ity	unity, conformity
-cy	celibacy, democracy	-ment	fragment, emolument
-dom	kingdom, serfdom	-mony	harmony, matrimony
-ee	grantee, employee	-ness	smallness, weakness
-er, -eer	worker, auctioneer	-or	mentor, professor
-ery	grocery, robbery	-th	truth, wealth
-ess, -esse	lioness	-try	dentistry, sophistry
-et, -ette	duet, silhouette	-ure	venture, tenure
-hood	likelihood	-y	melody, jealousy, beauty

Adjective Suffixes

-able, -ible	manageable, possible	-ful	bountiful, hopeful
-acious, -cious	voracious, salacious	-ic	tragic, frantic
-al	lethal, visual	-ish	lavish, babyish
-an, -ian	American, Armenian	-ive	captive, responsive
-ar	insular, regular	-less	thoughtless, faultless
-ate	affectionate, vulgate	-oid	paranoid, tabloid
-en	golden, rotten	-ous	sensuous, porous
-escent	adolescent, quiescent	-some	lonesome, bothersome
-esque	brusque, picturesque	-y	muddy, fiery, mucky

438

Adverbial Suffixes

-ly   swiftly, sadly, poorly
-ward   backward, onward, outward

Verb Suffixes

-ate   frustrate, initiate, formulate
-en   brighten, darken, fasten
-fy   signify, deify, beautify, magnify
-ize   brutalize, traumatize, penalize, phantasize
-ure   venture, fracture, culture, torture

Derivational Verb Prefixes (an apparently special phenomenon)

en-   enrage, enlarge, envelope, entrance
be-   berate, bespeak, belittle, besmirch
de-   deride, delight, denude
im-   impede, impel, impart
in-   inscribe, intend, ingrain

Index

440